Cultural Heritage and Co
Series III Asia, \
General Editor
George F. McLean

M000087266

Dialogue of Philosophies, Religions and Civilizations in the Era of Globalization

Chinese Philosophical Studies, XXV

Edited by
Zhao Dunhua

Department of Philosophy, Peking University
The Council for Research in Values and Philosophy

Box 261
Cardinal Station
Washington, D.C. 20064

Library of Congress Cataloging-in-Publication

Dialogues of philosophies, religions, and civilizations in the era of globalization
: Chinese philosophical studies, XXV / edited by Zhao Dunhua, George F. McLean.
    p. cm. -- (Cultural heritage and contemporary change. Series III, Asia ; v. 25)
Includes bibliographical references and index.
    1.   Philosophy, Comparative--Congresses. 2.   Philosophy, Modern--20th
century--Congresses. 3. Religions--Congresses. 4. Comparative civilization--Congresses.
I. Dunhua, Zhao. II. McLean, George F. III. Title. IV. Series.

B799.D53 2007   2007006771
109--dc22   CIP

ISBN 978-1-56518-243-1 (pbk.)

Table of Contents

Foreword

Zhao Dunhua

This book is edited from the Proceeding of the Philosophy Session of the 2005 Beijing Forum. Starting in the year of 2004, the annual Beijing Forum has been organized by Peking University and Beijing Municipal Education Commission, with support from the SK Group in Korea. The purpose of the Forum is to strengthen the cultural exchanges and mutual understandings among nations throughout the world, especially between Eastern Asia and the West. For this purpose, the general theme of the Forum was designed as "Harmony of Civilizations and Prosperity for All in Globalization". As this theme suggests interdisciplinary and cross-cultural studies, almost all faculties of humanities and social sciences at Peking University were involved in the Forum, of which philosophy, is, of course, one of major divisions.

Philosophy is the hard core of long living cultures and the deep soul of civilizations in the post Axial Age (namely, the history after the time between 800 BC and 200 BC.). No harmony of civilizations could be achieved without a fruitful dialogue between the imbedded philosophies, and no prosperity for all could be expected without the devoted exchange of spirits and ideas. In our times, globalization has witnessed a standardization of rules for the market and international cooperation in the economic domain; the integration of folk cultures becomes a common style of human life as well. Contrary to optimistic expectations, there have been pessimistic and regressive aspects of globalization: a clash of civilizations, conflict in the international politics, systematic confrontation of beliefs and values, and violent struggles among groups or nations, etc.

For those who reasonably trust globalization to be a progressive force in this crucial time of human history, three things are clear enough. First, those phenomena of counter-globalization are caused by the value and/or belief systems which have lagged far behind the process of worldly modernization. Second, those resistant systems have been supported either by some philosophies (pre-modern or post-modern ones), or by some unchanged traditional religions. Lastly and most importantly, the resistance to globalization by certain philosophies and religions can be softened temporally, or resolved ultimately, only through the dialogue regarding the raison d'être between different philosophies, religions and civilizations.

In the above considerations, the Philosophy Session of the 2005 Beijing Forum focused upon the topic of "Dialogues of Philosophies, Religions and Civilizations in the Era of Globalization," the title of the present book. This title sounds like a "great narrative," but in view of the above I want to emphasize that it fits the purpose and feature of the Beijing Forum. The Forum is not a purely academic conference on topics discussed only in an "ivory tower"; it is also concerned practically with public affairs and worldly history. Since we hope to commit ourselves to mutual understanding among peoples, our voices in dialogue do not float in a world beyond, but can be heard by, and have influence on, the people in the street. As matter of fact, philosophers' discussions around the topic of our Session attracted public attention. Many media, including China Central TV, People's Daily, China Daily, reported on the process of the Sessions and introduced some of its participants and their ideas. The great success of our Sessions proved the active and public role played by philosophers in our society and the constructive function of philosophy in globalization. In order for more persons who are willing to listen to the philosophers' voice to share these fruitful discussions, we have collected, edited and published all papers of the Sessions.

The Philosophy Session was divided into three panels as follows.

I. Dialogue between Eastern and Western Philosophies.
II. Dialogue between Confucianism and Christianity.
III. Dialogue between Islamic and Western Civilizations.

It is worth noting that the three panel divisions do not correlate to philosophy, religion and civilization respectively. Each panel was engaged in cross-cultural studies of philosophy and inter-faith dialogues of religions. Consequently, the comparative approach of philosophy and religious studies was always presented.

The comparative approach has always been perplexing, as noted by Zhuangzi two thousand five hundred years ago. Zhuangzi said then, "Looked at from their differences, liver and gall are as far apart as the states Chu and Yue (two neighbor centuries in the middle and eastern China in that time). Looked at from their sameness, the ten thousand things are all one."[1] The audience of the Forum and readers as well can see the contrast between "seeing from difference" and "seeing from similarity" in presentations and discussions. In each panel there were three or four keynote speakers, followed by comments and discussions. It should not be surprising that most commentators expressed their disagreements with the keynote speeches, since philosophers are arguers by nature. Though it may be held that not all philosophical arguments are meaningful, there should be no question that the philosophical argument on the issue of globalization is of great significance.

The papers of Professors Tang Yijie, Roger Ames and Kelly Clark in the first panel deal with the peculiarity of Chinese philosophy vis-à-vis Western philosophy. Professor Roger Ames especially criticized the universalistic views of philosophy in the West. This standpoint received many critical comments. For example, Professor Chung-ying Cheng was no less worried about how to maintain the uniqueness of Chinese philosophy than how to universalize it in the time of the domination of Western civilization. Many other commentators shared the universalistic view of philosophy in spite of the difference between local or national thoughts.

The debate around the nature of Chinese philosophy occurred not only at the Forum, but has taken place among Chinese philosophers recently, yet in a more or less emotional manner. Dr. Carine Defoort's paper explains the background for the problem of "the legitimacy of Chinese philosophy", which has nowadays aroused a campaign against universalism in Chinese philosophical circles. In the era of globalization, the contrast between Eastern and Western philosophies, and cultures in general, becomes a hot topic for discussion and dispute which often have involved ideology, nationalism and counter-globalization movement. The same scenario is happening in Chinese academic circles. In order for readers to understand the background of the different views above, an introductory paper of mine is presented as an appendix.

Dialogue between philosophies in the first Panel was extended to the domain of science and technology as well. Professor Sasaki Chikara in his paper discussed the contrast between Eastern and Western civilizations from the perspective of mathematics and medicine. He saw a certain blockade of modern European medicine, and expected Chinese medical thought to play an important role in medicine.

In the second panel, speakers compared Confucianism and Christianity from different visions. Professor Tu Wei-ming talked about the anthropocosmic characteristics of Chinese cosmology, and evaluated this Confucian model of Heaven as being more compatible with what we know today about the origin of the universe. Commentators gave rise to different evaluations in the comparison of Confucianism with Christianity. Professor Kelly Clark emphasized a similarity in monotheism between the early Chinese notion of Heaven and the Hebrew belief in God. Professor Tran Van Doan questioned the compatibility between Confucian cosmology and modern science of the origin of cosmos, such as the theory of Big Bang. Professor Li Chenyang asked for a metaphysical (or "theological") understanding, more than simply seeing Heaven as a creative and living process. In a similar manner Dr. Chloë Starr pointed out a fundamental difference between the ontological notion of God in Christianity and a Confucian Heaven limited to our earth or universe.

Professor Vincent Shen's and my papers tried to illustrated similarities between Christianity and Confucianism in the domain of ethics. Professor Vincent Shen interpreted strangification and generosity to the other as the basis for both Confucian virtues and Christian values. For modern values, the two key terms are related to localization and globalization. My paper deals with the Confucian theory of human good and the Christian dogma of original sin, revealing the convergence of the two from logical, theoretical and practical perspectives. The similarity of perspective was also subjected to critical assessments. Professor Daniel Bays considered the dialogue between Confucianism and Christianity as an historical fact; as time passed Confucianism did not survive social changes with the consequence that "there are no more Confucians with whom to dialogue". Other commentators, on the contrary, acknowledged the real importance of the dialogue of the two systems, yet demanded an equality of those taking part. From a theological point of view Dr. Evyn Adams raised the question as to which Christian theory to dialogue with in regard to the dogma of sin. On this issue, Catholic Theology, the Theology of the Church of England, Wesleyan Theology and

Eastern Orthodoxy, Pelagianism and Semi-Pelagianism are all possible counterparts of the Confucian theory of human nature.

In the third panel, the dialogue between Islamism and Christianity attracted attention, due to the urgent need for world peace. The paper written "In the Name of God, the Compassionate, the Merciful" by Professor Seyyed Mohammed Khamenei, interprets the difference of Eastern philosophy, specially, the Islamic philosophies from Western philosophy in terms of a clash of religions. The author is a brother of Sayyed Ali Khamenei, the Leader of the Islamic Republic of Iran. As a major ideologist of Iran, he sees the "deadlock" in dialogue as due to the radical divergence between Islamic and Western philosophies and cultures in general. He is concerned also that globalization has been misused as a policy "to destroy everything which is against western logic". His presentation gave rise to some counter-criticisms. One scholar at the conference "thought that the style of Professor Khamenei -- "advocating his own ideas but refusing to listen to others – was not dialogue in its real sense", but showed an attitude of refusing dialogue.[2] I nevertheless thought that Professor Khamenei did not mean to refuse dialogue; but that he set up a prerequisite which is not at present realistic. In fact, he finally wished to conduct dialogue under the principle of "securing the happiness and prosperity of all humanity in the world".

Professor Marietta Stepanyants analyzed the reason of the current conflicts between Western and Islamic civilization, critically raising the question of whether the two civilizations could possibly enter into dialogue. She proposed a pluralist model of religions in dealing with this problem. Nevertheless, the crucial problem is whether the current conflict between terrorism and anti-terrorism really is a clash of two civilizations, or of two religions? For many it definitely is not. Professor Wang Jianping followed a historical line to illustrate the peaceful co-existence of Islamism and Christianity in the Chinese social context. This may suggest that in the proper circumstances Islamic and Christian civilizations are not in conflict. Professor Mel Stewart enumerated ten points of similarity between Christian and Islamic beliefs to show that there is no conflict between those two religions. Professor David Burrell's paper on Al-Ghazali also provides an example of how Islamic theology since Middle Ages has been compatible with its Christian counterpart.

Professor Gholamreza Aavani asked a question: is this a clash in dialogue or dialogue in clash? Like his colleague, Professor Khamenei, he accused the West of making of modern philosophy an ideology which blocked the way of dialogue and hindered the way to Truth. I shared with the many participants that although Professor Gholamreza Aavani's question hits the right point concerning the relation between Islam and the West after 9.11, a fairer and more moderate solution to the question is given by Professor George McLean. In the concluding paper of this book, he examined both bad and good attitudes toward Islamism in the West. It is only by overcoming the bad faith of pseudo generosity, pseudo stability and pseudo peace that, according to Professor McLean, a good attitude toward dialogue can lead to a renewal of religiously based cultures as diverse yet similar, complementary and convergent in character. This solution for me suggests that dialogue is not a theoretical debate limited within the academic society, but a style of life in the era of globalization, open for all nations and civilizations.

Since globalization has been accompanied by clash and conflict, even violence, the emotional and self-interested opinions for or against in everyday life are unavoidably transformed into the arguments pro or con in the world of ideas. We can see in the papers of the present book, more or less, opposite trends. There is opposition: (1) between universalism or particularism in understandings, (2) between convergent or divergent approaches in dialogue, (3) between cosmopolitism and nationalism in international relations, (4) between neo-liberalism and neo-totalitarianism in domestic affairs, and (5) between conservative pre- or post-modernism and enlightenment modernism in dealing with traditions. When we employ the generalization of –isms to simplify the complexity of arguments, we should be warned against hasty generalization. Philosophers usually do not make an "either-or" choice in the face of oppositions and dichotomies, but adopt a "both-and" solution, yet with one preference. From this preference we generalize the trend of the philosopher's thinking. This mode of assessment can be applied to the authors of this book. Though they preferred one position to the other, no one denied the reasonableness of the opposite position or of a possible change thereto. Because of the philosophers' good will to dialogue and their overall rationality, debates in these Sessions proceeded in an orderly, moderate and smooth manner. Although no written agreement was reached, as in any philosophical debate we all agreed that since no human being is God, no scholarly research is divine revelation and no academic book or essay is Holy Scripture. All are able to err; inerrancy does not belong to us humans. With the truism of error-ability, the spirit of the dialogical civilization is expressed in the following manner:

> Even though I believe that I am right and you are wrong at present;
> Most probably, we are both right, or you are right and I am wrong,
> or we are both wrong;
> So let us continue to dialogue until we become the friends of truth.

With the same spirit, it has been a special delight for me to meet scholars from around the world, from Austria, Canada, Chile, England, France, Germany, India, Italy, Japan, Kanagawa, Korea, Malaysia, New Zealand, Oman, Russia, Spain, Thailand, Turkey, Vietnam. I would like to express my gratitude to all participants, especially to the authors of this book, for their contribution to the mutual understanding and benefit of peoples living in global times. I also thank all assistants of the Forum, and Professor Su Xiangui in particular for their excellent work of communication and reception. Special thanks are due to Professor George F. McLean who found important value in the papers of the Sessions and has been willing to publish them in the series "Cultural Heritage and Contemporary Change" edited by him.

NOTES

1 Book of Zhuangzi, Ch. Five, transl. by P. Kjellberg, in in *Readings in Classical Chinese Philosophy*, ed. by P. J. Ivanhoe and B. W. Van Norden, Seven Bridges, New York, 2001, p.227.

2 Quoted from *Interviews with the Scholars of Beijing Forum*, vol. II, ed. by Li Yansong, et al, published by Secretariat of Beijing Forum.

Introduction

George F. McLean

The first part of the title of this work, "Dialogue of Philosophies, Religions and Civilizations," invites one to look at different levels of these dialogues. For this the words of Mohammad Iqbal on the distinction between philosophy and religion can be helpful.

> The aspiration of religion soars higher than that of philosophy. Philosophy is an intellectual view of things; and as such, does not care to go beyond a concept which can reduce all the rich variety of experience to a system. It sees Reality from a distance as it were. Religion seeks a closer contact with Reality. The one is theory; the other is living experiences, association, intimacy. In order to achieve this intimacy thought must rise higher than itself, and find its fulfillment in an attitude of mind which religion describes as prayer -- one of the last words on the lips of the Prophet of Islam.[1]
>
> … and religious life develops the ambition to come into direct contact with the ultimate reality. It is here that religion becomes a matter of personal assimilation of life and power; and the individual achieves a free personality, not by releasing himself from the fetters of the law, but by discovering the ultimate source of the law within the depths of his own consciousness.[2]

In this view, philosophy is theory and provides a speculative view from a distance as it were, whereas religion is the much more outgoing, engaged and lived experience. Civilization integrates the two along with the actual structures and implementation of social life in all its dimensions: economic, political and social. All of these are grounded in the great religious tradition which shaped that civilization as a whole.

The second part of the title "in an Era of Globalization" adds the important dimensions of space, time and history. Thus while the philosophical, religious and civilizational are perduring factors which may be diversely ordered at different times, the reference to our specific era introduces an historical line particularly important for identifying the work needed in the dialogue on these issues at this specific juncture.

This is not to reduce all to a mere succession. In a more dialectical pattern the synthesis and antithesis remain at work and must never be forgotten lest the new synthesis by hollow and without real meaning. Yet this last part of our title "in the Era of Globalization" raises the issue of authentic novelty. Here, danger lies in attempting to solve the challenges of the present and future using a paradigm that is already past. This assures that our efforts will be ill adapted to the present and in danger of being more destructive than creative.

The reason for this lies in a principle of scientific research, namely, that the question serves as a searchlight rendering knowledge only of that to which it is directed. When the question and the ability to receive answers are tightly conceptualized as in modern rationalism we receive or achieve answers only in these precise but delimiting term. Moreover, if these questions are tied to the past in structure and supposition the responses will not be appropriate for the present. Indeed if they are tied to too limited a sense of reality then inevitably they will not only miss but undermine the deeper life of a civilizations and its meaning.

In this historical perspective the sequence of the parts of this work is both illustrative and of particular significance.

Part I "Dialogue between Eastern and Western Philosophies".

Chapter I, by Tang Yijie, "Constructing 'Chinese Philosophy' in the Sino-European Cultural Exchange," traces the history of the academic 'discipline' of philosophy in China, and then proposes a program for its future. The author notes that Western academic philosophy provoked Chinese scholars to separate-out 'philosophy' from the 'canonical' literature and the non-Confucian Masters, the dual matrix in which Chinese philosophical thinking had been traditionally embedded. Chinese philosophy, the author proposes, emphasizes *jing-jie* (the settling of one's body and life, and inside/ outside, into harmony), and can be helpful not only to the future of China, but to that of the world if reconstituted with an emphasis on its deep harmony of the inner and out life.

Chapter II, by Roger T. Ames, "'Getting rid of God': A Prolegomenon to 'A Dialogue Between Chinese and Western Philosophy in the Era of Globalization'," argues that a Christian sub-text has distorted the historical representation of Chinese philosophy in the West, much as a displaced and often unconscious Christian subtext has mislead Western philosophy (both Cartesian dualism and a clandestine transcendentalism, for example). Ames considers Dewey's pragmatism and Whitehead's process to be the closest analogues to Confucianism, but as the title of his paper alludes he considers Chinese philosophy radically humanist and situational after the manner of his earlier 20th century analogues.

Chapter III, by Kelly James Clark, "The Conception of Divinity in Early Confucianism," holds the contrary position. Rather than Confucianism being reductively humanistic, Clark carefully details the many evidences of a sense of transcendence as a context for its meaning that is at least analogous to the place of the divine in other civilizations. For this he looks not to the later, but to the earlier, Confucians.

This dialogue between a Western reductionism and a more open and subtle Confucianism continues throughout the work till its last paper on Islam. This has great significance in a global age for the response of China to the cultural imperialism of Western modernity and its relations with the great civilizations, all of which are religiously based.

A number of Commentaries on the papers of Roger Ames and Tang Yijie follow:

Commentary 1, by Chung-ying Cheng, "Philosophical Globalization as Reciprocal Valuation and Mutual Integration," critiques these two papers. In characterizing Western philosophy, Cheng tends to be more conciliatory than Ames, cautioning that deep-seated influence and transformation often takes 500 years or more. Cheng finds transcendentalism in some Chinese philosophy and immanentism in some Western philosophy, and in general sees Eastern and Western traditions as more diverse than does Ames. Cheng singles-out Immanuel Kant as a fertile pivot of the East-West exchange, and contrasts this to its nadir, the Rites Controversy of the 17th and 18th centuries. Cheng's remarks tend more to supplement than to critique Tang Yijie's paper. Chinese dialogic philosophy is said to have four stages: understanding Western philosophy, locating parallel issues in Chinese philosophy, discovering differences, and as appropriate justifying these differences.

Commentary 2, by Yu Jiyuan, "Making Sense of Cross-Cultural Dialogue," treats the way authentic dialogue functions. Yu locates in Aristotle two forms of 'dialogue' understood as true 'conversation', viz., "friend-as-mirror" and "saving the phenomena." Yu focuses on the first form, arguing that the current popularity of Whitehead and American pragmatism from the Western side and of traditional Process-oriented thought from the Chinese side allows a dialogical transaction whereby each party can know itself better; the same can be said of the recent renewal of enthusiasm for Virtue-ethics in the West and the Neo-Confucianist Virtue-ethic in China.

Commentary 3 by Jeu-Jenq Yuann, contra Tang Yijie, comes to the defense of Chinese philosophy, arguing that dependence on Western philosophy is no better than dependence on the 'Canon and the Non-Confucianist Masters'. The Western sense of 'clarity', demanding 'understandability' and 'accessibility', reveals ignorance of the unique characteristics of Chinese thinking and a misunderstanding of the specific references of Chinese terms. Yuann agrees with the thrust of Roger Ames's paper, but develops its thesis further, arguing that the Western notion of God has been long transposed so it has become the West's preoccupation with unitary truth, with objective technology/science (and with globalization?). Would the West be willing to give up this masked and displaced (into science and secular politics) notion of God? Yuann thinks the West must confront this subtextual issue, or real dialogue will never occur.

Chapter IV, by Carine Defoort, "Western Unacceptance of Chinese Philosophy: The Legitimacy of an Illegitimate Position," explains the background for the problem of "the legitimacy of Chinese philosophy", which has nowadays aroused a campaign against universalism in Chinese philosophical circles. In the era of globalization, the contrast between Eastern and Western philosophies, and cultures in general, becomes an important issue, which has often touched upon such topics as ideology, nationalism and the counter-globalization movement.

Appendix I, by Zhao Dunhua, "Some Progressive and Problematic Features of the Current Philosophy in China," gives us a detailed account of philosophy in Mainland China since the 'opening' of the 1980s. Marxist philosophy, now liberated from Stalinism, either returns to Marx's own works or dialogues with Western Marxism. Chinese philosophers specializing in traditional Chinese philosophy or in Western philosophy are no longer subservient to Marxism. The official Charter of Philosophical Studies in Chinese Universities allows eight disciplines, including Religious Studies. In relation to global philosophy, Zhao prefers convergence over divergence and universalism over a narrow particularism. He urges both a close cooperation with the international community of philosophers and an attentive critique of 'nationalist' ideology.

Chapter V, by Sasaki Chikara, "Dialogue Between Eastern and Western Mathematics and Medicine," deploys a Kuhnian 'historical philosophy of science' to re-interpret the history of mathematics and medicine. Chikara demonstrates that the itinerary of western mathematics differs in fact from the received version, in that it is even in the Middle Ages and Renaissance a Eurasian not a European discipline. Taking the cue from Leibnitz, who appreciated the experiential quality of the Chinese sciences (as opposed to the abstract and axiomatic character of the European mode), Chikara calls for a comparative and complementary approach to medicine. The West's emphasis on surgery and chemical drugs does not work, for example, in the case of much cancer and liver disease. There must be a "rehabilitation of medical practices" following the "way of traditional Chinese medicine," and the "establishment of Chinese and Western Combined Medicine in the contemporary world, especially East Asia."

Appendix II, by Melville Y. Stewart, "Science and Religion in Complementarity." Professor Sasaki Chikara's paper compared Eastern and Western mathematics and medicine from the standpoint of Kuhn's historical philosophy of science. From the same standpoint, science and religion in the Western world can be also compared and, in fact, have been in dialogue for centuries. Professor M. Stewart's paper can be read as a supplement to Sasaki's paper, as it provides a different model of cross cultural dialogue in the philosophy of science.

It invokes several hermeneutics/historians of science, including Thomas Kuhn and his notion of "interdisciplinary matrix," to argue that science and religion sometimes overlap methodologically. Both scientists and religionists, in the author's view, can hold that truth is a property of propositions, that truth is coherent, and that it corresponds to the way the world is. While allowing for provisional freedom, the author proposes several intriguing overlaps between a modified predestinarianism and a moderate scientific determinism. In China, he has co-edited, with Xing Taotao, *Philosophy of Religion* (Beijing: Peking University Press, 2005).

Part II, "Dialogue between Confucianism and Christianity."

Chapter VI, by Tu Weiming, "An 'Anthropocosmic' Perspective on Creativity," proposes, *contra* Mote and Needham, that "the distinctive feature of Chinese cosmology is not absence of cosmogonist concerns, but faith in the interconnectedness of all modalities of being as the result of the continuous creativity of the cosmic process." Tu sets forth what he names the "anthropomorphic perspective," which recognizes on the one hand that "Heaven, as the result of human conceptualization, interpretation, and imagination, is inescapably anthropological," yet on the other hand, that Heaven "as the generative force that has created all modalities of being, . . . cannot be confined to an anthropocentric picture of the universe."

The following are "Commentaries on Tu Weiming":

Commentary 1, by Kelly James Clark, "Ancient Hebrew and Early Confucian Conceptions of Divinity," agrees with Tu that Mote's thesis is unsubstantiated, and that in fact the ancient Chinese accepted the notion of a creator-god. Clark demonstrates that this belief prevailed in the Shang and Zhou dynasties, and that the history of early Chinese religion is much like that of the ancient Hebrews.,

Commentary 2, by Chenyang Li, "Is the Confucian Concept of 'Heaven' Still Relevant Today?" raises questions in relation to Tu's definition of "Heaven." In what sense is "Heaven" identified with "creativity"? How can it be said that "creativity" is "omnisicient"? How does "Heaven" differ from the Dao?

Commentary 3, by Tran Van Doan, notes that Tu's general assumptions are much like those of the famous but controversial Fritzof Capra, though Capra uses Chinese philosophy to reinterpret modern physics and Tu uses the "Big Bang" of modern physics to reinterpret 'creativity' in Chinese philosophy. Both Tu and Capra may help to explain creativity, but since neither is doing pure physics or pure Chinese philosophy, methodologically speaking neither can achieve momentous "effect in engaging in creative work."

Commentary 4, by Chloë Starr, concentrates on how Tu's "Heaven" relates to the Christian "God," and how Confucianism and Christianity relate to language when referring to Heaven/God. Starr points out that the "doctrine of [the] [I]ncarnation" in Christianity undercuts any "anthropocentric account of creation." Starr's discussion of language and Christianity includes interesting references to Anselm, the Pseudo-Denys, Aquinas, and others.

Commentary 5, by Christopher Hancock, finds that Christian theology addresses many of Tu's concerns. Hancock cites "Alexandrine incarnational theology," as well as the "Cosmic Christ" of Colossians 1 and Ephesians 1. On the other hand, Christianity's insistence on God's "otherness" prevents anthropocentrism. Finally, humanity's creative role is derived from the "work of Christ."

Chapter VII, by Vincent Shen, "Globalization, Christianity and Confucianism: On Strangification and Generosity to the Other," argues that *waitui* ("going outside of oneself to the other"), which is represented in this paper by the neologism "strangification," should be the defining characteristic of globalization. Shen presents three modes of *waitui*: linguistic strangification, pragmatic strangification, and ontological strangification. He demonstrates that Christianity at its best is a religion of generosity and strangification, and lauds the Jesuits of the 16th and 17th centuries in particular for the courage of their inculturation into China. On the Chinese side, Shen explains Confucian *shu* and generosity.

The following are "Commentaries on Vincent Shen":

Commentary 1, by Chenyang Li, entitled "The Element of Equality in the Global Era," accepts "strangification" as a "fundamental principle" of the global age, but argues, *contra* Shen, that "generosity" should not also figure as one of these principles, since generosity moves from a superior to an inferior. Li suggests "reciprocity" instead, since reciprocal relation implies equality.

Commentary 2, by Chloë Starr, suggests that globalization is having negative as well as positive effects, and requires checks and balances. Starr dissents from what appears to be Shen's unrestrained affirmation of the globalizing process. In relation to Shen's treatment of "self-enclosure," Starr points out that in Christianity, sin involves transgression of God-given laws and arguably cannot be limited to self-enclosure.

Chapter VIII, by Zhao Dunhua, "Original Sin, and the Goodness of Human Nature: A Point of Convergence in Chinese and Western Culture," disagrees with the prevailing notion that Christianity's doctrine of Original Sin flatly contradicts the Chinese emphasis on an original "goodness" in human nature. Zhao argues that when these two teachings are examined carefully, it becomes clear that they are logically non-contradictory, theoretically complementary, and in the practical order play similar moral roles. Mainstream Christianity insists humanity was created good, and its "fallenness" corrupts but does not vitiate human behavior. On the Chinese side, the Confucian rationalist Zhu Xi, for example, maintained that the good nature Mencius spoke of was humankind's "heavenly nature," and is to be distinguished from "material nature." Mencius had distinguished carerfully between sensuous instincts and desires on the one hand (the result of people's "fate"), and moral essence (which awaits realization in every human being).

The following are "Commentaries on Tu Weiming, Vincent Shen and Zhao Dunhua":

Commentary 1, by Daniel H. Bays, "From a Historian's Point of View," clarifies that historians tend to eschew "large generalization" and "linguistic creativity" [neologisms, etc.], both of which characterize most of the conference presentations thus far. Bays takes care to trace concrete cases, choosing specific Chinese who have considered themselves "Christian Confucianists" or "Confucian Christians." He reviews cases from the late Ming through to the aftermath of the 1911 Revolution, finding that there is no reason to doubt the sincerity of the Chinese involved, nor the 'philosophical' viability—at least for them—of their life-style.

Commentary 2, by Evyn Adams, "From Theological Points of View," compares Tu's Confucianism and Christianity, pointing out the salient differences (Confucianism's historical alinearity vs. Christianity's historical linearity, etc.). Apropos of Shen's paper, Adams contrasts Christianity's stress on the "salvation" of the other, not just "generosity" towards the other. In relation to Zhao, Adams explains that what can be called the "semi-Pelagianism" of Catholic, Eastern Orthodox, Anglican, and Wesleyan theology fits more closely the Confucian understanding of human nature than does the theology of Lutheranism, Calvinism, and what is called "Reformed Theology."

Part III, "Dialogue between Islamic and Western Civilizations."

Chapter IX, by Seyyed Mohammed Khamenei, "Philosophies' Dialogue in the Globalization Era, and Deadlocks," maintains that Islamic and traditional Chinese philosophy form a whole in that they both recognize spiritual values and the importance of community. Contemporary Western philosophy, on the other hand, is materialistic and fragmented, and partakes of the utilitarian and self-centered goals of the West's political powers. In particular, Khamenei argues that 'globalism' as the West understands it is neo-colonialist in purpose and effect. Invoking the age-old observation, philosophical as well as cosmological in intent, that 'It is in the East that the Sun rises', he hopes this present international Conference on Dialogue, taking place in China, will begin a first step towards real peace and justice in the world.

Chapter X, by Marietta Stepanyants, "Is the Dialogue between Western and Islamic Civilizations Possible?" classifies the obstacles to dialogue, such as the skepticism of Westerners (Richard Rorty in particular is cited) on the one hand and the absolutism of Islamic fundamentalists on the other. Among dialogists themselves there are obstacles too, because of great differences in objectives (Francis Fukyama's capitalist triumphalism is cited as a case in point). Stepanyants seems to favor a synthesis of what she calls the "mystical" and "comparativist" approaches, whereby each religion constitutes a prismatic color radiating from a common transcendent core.

The following are "Commentaries on Marietta Stepanyants":

Commentary 1, by Mel Stewart, "Similarities between Christianity and Islam," limits itself to an expansion of Stepanyant's assertion that the two compared religions are both monotheistic. Stewart notes both religions have authoritative scriptures; affirm the Divine compassion, omnipotence, omniscience, and sovereignty; accept life after death and just rewards in the afterlife; regard God as the source of salvation; warn against the world's corruption; and so on.

Commentary 2, by Miikka Ruokanen, disagrees with its "pluralist" thesis, and argues instead that religions are radically different at their doctrinal core. It is impossible to find a common unifying factor at the core of all religions. Ruokanen maintains it is more reasonable to direct dialogue towards social ethics, since the ethics of various religions are compatible.

Chapter XI, by David Burrell, "Al-Ghazali as Philosophical Theologian," examines the grand contributions of this great Muslim theologian, who emphasizes "the free creation of the universe by one God." Al-Ghazali subjects reason to Faith, but shows how reason is an indispensable tool in "directing our minds" towards better understanding of the Faith. Among the topics Burrell treats is Al-Ghazali's method for sorting out Divine "agency" from human "agency"; and Al-Ghazali's cataloguing of the "stages of trust in divine providence."

The following are "Commentary on Marietta Stepanyants and David Burrell":

Commentary, by William C. Chittick, credits Stepanyants's appreciation of Islamic religiosity, but faults her for ignoring the "voice of Islamic philosophy." Without questioning what "civilization" really means, she blithely accepts a Western definition of civilization, and the two spokesmen of contemporary Muslim philosophy she cites both pose their discussion in terms of a conceptual framework supplied by the West. Chittick praises Burrell's paper, saying it provides a welcome counterpoint to that of Stepanyants. Burrell studies al-Ghazali, who represents the grand tradition of philosophical Islam. The unsettling truth which dialogists must face, argues Chittick, is that Islam challenges the assumptions of modern "dialogue" (which are rooted in European "Enlightenment" thinking). Islam summons humanity, including philosophy, back to the bedrock principle that there is a Transcendent, and human beings and their rights are rooted in this Source.

Chapter XII, by Wang Jianping, "Islam and Christianity in the Social Context of China," examines in detail the coming of both religions to China, comparing the history of their relation to the government as well as to the people. He notes the paradox of the present governmental effort to favor Moslems as minority peoples in the face of popular suspicion in contrast to the rising popularity of Christianity despite a less favorable attitude of the government to Christianity.

Chapter XIII, by Gholamreza Aavani, "Islam and the West: Clash in Dialogue or Dialogue in Clash?" traces the history of exchange between Islamic and Western cultures, a history that has often been dark but which has had its bright moments,--the heavy influence of Muslim philosophers, in Spain, North Africa, and the Italian peninsula, on Europe during the heyday of Islamic philosophy, and the occasional collaborations between scholars of the two traditions. Aavani argues that Islam and Christianity share much in common, and should form a solid front against modernism, which is to be identified with secular humanism, subjectivism, reductionism, scientism, profanation of man and nature, and neo-slavery/neo-colonialism.

Chapter XIV, by George F. McLean, "Islam as Perceived from the West--Secular and Religious Views," reports on the bad news and the good from the West in relation to the dialogue. The disheartening news is that the West by and large continues its cultural blindness to authentic Islamic values. This misunderstanding is worsened by a secularizing democracy and the latter's preference of individual rights over the community good. "Neo-conservative" ideology further worsens the impasse by seeing peace as coming only from power harshly applied. The heartening news is from the

Continental philosophical tradition developed in the direction of "existence and creative freedom," values which can cultivate openness to the "other." As for philosophy in the 21st century, McLean says, "We await then the development of appropriate philosophical and theological tools to enable us to proceed in full fidelity to an ever richer appreciation of our faiths and of their interrelation."

McLean sees the "new horizon" as characterized by the following recognitions: (1) that each culture is unique and hence diverse; (2) that there are analogous similarities in the very diversity between cultures; (3) that cultures are therefore complementarity; and (4) that they can also be convergent. He goes further to propose a new philosophical paradigm for a global age in which, while human discovery proceeds from the many to the one, understanding proceeds from the religious "One" and the global whole to the particulars. Thus, each person and people possesses a dignity which cannot be compromised for the utilitarian goals of economics or politics and each is intrinsically, rather than only extrinsically, related each to all others.

It is then not sufficient to rest with an incommensurability of civilizations and their paradigms, for we are engaged across the continents. Ready or not life today is inescapably linked together by developments in economics, politics and communication. No longer can any civilization or its sense of meaning and purpose escape the impact of the other. This brings to the fore the importance of hermeneutics and of the ability to interpret and interact with other cultures and civilizations. As in reading a text, one cannot but begin from one's own horizon or outlook, but this must be broadened until one is able to take account of all that one encounters in this global age.

This generates the option of many papers for a pragmatic, process approach to Chinese thought; indeed they illustrate these elements well. But this should not be redolent of Dewey's description of the modern as a decisive break with antiquity. The danger in this echoes Tang Yijie's initial concern, namely that Chinese philosophy will come to restrict the Chinese spirit, rather than allowing its riches to be continually mined so as to evolve creatively through its encounter with other civilizations in these global times. As Piaget points out the earlier stages of development are not put aside, but further unfolded and implemented. Hence for Heidegger and Gadamer the primitive is not a crudity to be escaped, but foundational insights indispensable for a truly human life.

In this light the approach of Vincent Shen may prove especially helpful in its manner of probing for the basic commitments of Chinese culture. He listens for echoes of the original and basic insights with a view to appreciating more fully their present implications for new ways in which life can be promoted in our times.

But once again, how is one to allow for this across truly unique and conceptually incommensurable cultures? The distinctive beauty, for instance, of Indian or Chinese music cannot be transformed into Western notation or played in its scales, yet an openness to the proper genius and deep resonances of other civilizations is needed in order for peoples be able to mine their own heritage and live with one another in these global times. This must be done not in terms of critical and exclusivist conceptual analysis, but on the aesthetic level where truth and justice, goodness and ethics continually unite and synthesize in terms of beauty and harmony, compassion and reconciliation. This could even "save" Chinese thought from "philosophy" in the sense of Tang Yijie, while contributing to the dialogues in which philosophy can become newly adequate for global times.

In this light the task ahead begins to emerge as the restrictions upon freedom imposed by reduction to exclusively clear and distinct, universal and necessary ideas has now become an ever more evident flaw in the encounter of civilizations.

Some would respond by a post modernity built upon a return to pragmatism, hoping thereby to be open to all by lurching from clarity to a mere tolerance of others based on the all too human ability to err. However, as each civilization is grounded in a great religion, human history suggests a more balanced and positive route in which all can delve deeply into the mystery of their own self and find themselves to be truly one in solidarity with others. This points to the wisdom of the *Vedanta Sutras* based in "that from which, in which and into which all is." If so, then truly open dialogues of philosophers, religions and civilizations in this era of globalization point beyond a negative mutual tolerance of fallibility to positive liberation in the ineffable.

Overall, the work is the eminently true to its theme: "Dialogues of Philosophies, Religions and Civilizations in an Era of Globalization".

Toward a Dialogical Civilization:
Identity, Difference and Harmony
Dialogue between Tu Weiming and Gianni Vattimo

Tu Weiming

I am truly delighted to engage with Professor Vattimo in this joint venture. I first met Professor Vattimo in Seoul at the UNESCO symposium on the dialogue among civilizations two years ago. Then this June, through the good offices of Roger Ames, I moderated a dialogue between Vattimo and the American philosopher Richard Rorty at the East-West Philosopher's Conference in Hawaii. Professor Vattimo and I are invited to speak in Japan on the occasion of the centenary of the founding of Tohoko University this coming spring and I cherish the hope that our dialogue will continue for years to come.

Professor Vattimo's book, *The End of Modernity*, is available in Chinese. His reflections on Nietzsche, Heidegger, post-modernism and ontology of actuality, which, if I understand him correctly, defines a mode of thinking that transcends quantitative analysis and liberates the human mind by philosophizing on the sciences of the spirit, reminds us of the conflict and tension of possible dialogue between natural science and the sciences of the spirit in the 20th Century. This is profoundly meaningful and all of these have been sources of inspiration for my own philosophical reflection. Those of us who take the humanities seriously, as not only modes of scholarship, but also as a way of life, appreciate Vattimo's tremendously powerful and persuasive voice as a pre-eminent European thinker, and also as a public intellectual.

Of course, real dialogue will take place later. At present we would like to address some of our common concerns and aspirations. I would like to begin by sharing my still evolving thought on the enlightenment mentality. I believe that the time is right for us scholars in humanities to underscore that, in addition to economic capital, we should learn to accumulate social capital. In addition to technical competence we should learn to acquire cultural competence in traditional Chinese literature, history and philosophy.

In addition to cognitive intelligence, we should cultivate also ethical intelligence. In short we should be able to appreciate that in the 21st Century, a leader ought to be enriched by spiritual values, and sensitive to religion and identity. By identity I mean all the primordial factors which shape each one of us into a concrete human being, such as gender, language, place, age and religion. Indeed the time is right to try to transcend anthropocentrism and scientism. This is not the scientific rationality, but the out-dated ideology focused exclusively on the tangible and the quantifiable without reference to human values and spiritual ideas that cannot be quantified or identified as tangible entities.

One of the major challenges to China's spiritual and cultural identity is to embrace the market economy without turning the whole country into a market society. It would be disastrous if academic institutions, mass media, city organizations and even families were eventually to be totally marketized. On the 7th of November I had the privilege of delivering a speech at UNESCO in Paris; the topic is "Beyond the Enlightenment Mentality and the Anthropocosmic Perspective." I would offer that abstract as an opening statement in the present dialogue.

The Enlightenment can be perceived either as a cultural movement which originated in the West in the 18th Century, and whose ideal is yet to be realized for the human community (Professor Habermas' work is related to this), or as a mentality characteristic of the modernistic motto sounding throughout the world, especially in cultural China. My focus is this Enlightenment mentality, rather than the cultural movement of the past or an ideal yet to be realized. I would argue that the Enlightenment mentality is perhaps the most powerful ideology in world history. Both socialism and capitalism grew out of it so that the market economy, democratic politics and civil society have advanced economies. As these transform into knowledge societies, the dominance of science, especially information and communication technologies, will be ever more pronounced.

Max Weber perfected the view that modern society will be controlled by experts and managers since the rise of technocracy in the military, government, multinational corporations, social institutions and even non-governmental organizations seems inevitable. Furthermore, the underlying values, such as liberty, nationality and human rights, law and dignity, independence, and the autonomy of the individual, are widely recognized throughout the world as universalizable, if not totally universal, values. The rhetoric of the enlightenment mentality suggesting that there is only one option for the future of the human community is apparently true. However, the enlightenment mentality is also seriously flawed or limited. Rooted in anthropocentrism, dictated by scientism or an instrumental rationality, and driven by an aggressive individualism, it is a form of secularism or secular humanism which suffers from inattention to religion and destructiveness as regards nature.

Looking toward the future, without a fundamental restructuring of its world view the Enlightenment can hardly provide guidance for human survival, let alone for human flourishing. A comprehensive critique of the enlightenment, especially the pervasive mind set it has engendered in China since the May 4th Cultural Movement of 1919, is in order. The insights already accumulated by the feminists, environmentalists, post-modernists, communitarianists, and religionists are intent upon offering a humanistic vision, both as a sympathetic understanding of the contemporary significance of natural reason and as a judicious assessment of the blind spots of the Enlightenment's de-natured and de-spirited mentality. It is vitally important to note that in the cultural tradition of the modern Chinese intellectual, the Enlightenment mentality is so much engrained that traditional culture has been relegated to the background as merely a distant echo heard especially in "the habits of the heart" of the Chinese intellectual.

Since the struggle to develop a full-fledged market economy, a publicly accountable democratic political order and a vibrant civil society are far from being complete, the political and cultural elite in China is committed to the enlightenment project, to become modern, to become global. But it is hardly ready to go beyond the enlightenment mentality; indeed in its developmental strategy it takes the traditional western model as its point of departure for the logic and goals of developing society. It is too much of a luxury to go back to the feudal legacy for inspiration. Yet ironically the spirit of the time demands that for the survival and flourishing of the human community, it is imperative for intellectuals, including Chinese intellectuals, to go beyond the limited and impoverished enlightenment mentality.

In the historical and comparative civilizational perspective, the surest and soundest way to accomplish this challenging enterprise is to use all spiritual resources available to the human community in order to formulate a broadly defined humanistic vision which can transcend anthropocentrism, scientism and aggressive individualism. But this must be done without losing sight of the liberating ideas and practices of the Enlightenment as a movement, as an idea yet to be realized and as a mind set. The interest in the so-called Axial Age civilizations signifies a spiritual turn in philosophy.

The epistemological and linguistic turns have been successful in making the academic discipline of philosophy in the English speaking world a truly respectable professional discipline. However, my concern is with the marginal position of analytical concerns. Professional academic philosophers comfortably and sometimes elegantly confine themselves to the cocoons of technical competence. Not surprisingly this style of philosophizing does not have much relevance to issues defining the human condition. As a result, very few philosophers became public intellectuals, and for those who have out of an aspiration to perform public service their voice is often overwhelmed by the cultural commentators, social critics and political economists. The time is right for a fundamental philosophical reorientation; Asian and comparative philosophy can play a significant role in this critical moment.

Historically, none of the Axial Age civilizations in Asia, Hinduism, Buddhism, Confucianism, and Daoism made a clear distinction between philosophy and religion. Virtually all philosophical contemplation is embedded in spiritual insights and their cultivation. Indeed without spiritual disciplines, sophisticated intellectual reflection is impossible.

The interplay between philosophy and religion, or more precisely the confluence of this interested analysis and understanding is the defining characteristic of the Asian modes of thinking. Actually as philosophically seasoned historians, such as the French academician Pierre Rado, have convincingly demonstrated, for the Greeks philosophy was a way of life, exemplified by spiritual exercisers. This is also how the Harvard professor Hillary Putnam approached the four major Jewish thinkers, Maimonides, Rosenweig, Buber and Levinas. It seems obvious that the revival and flourishing of philosophy as a discipline in the humanities in liberal arts education is in part predicated upon its renewed attention to spiritual traditions all over the world.

I would include additional traditions as well. Philosophers, in close collaboration or friendly competition, with colleagues in many other disciplines in history and in religion can be highly productive in developing new ways of philosophizing in the 21st century. Needless to say, this is also the wholesome practice of turning to the core and source of the philosophical enterprise for the philosophical enterprise is self-managed. The anthropo-cosmic perspective offered by Confucian humanism is historically significant for it addresses the ideal of a universal ethic in the context of cultural diversity. I shall simply listed several items in a sort of short hand.

As a comprehensive and integrated humanistic vision, Confucian humanism encompasses nature and religion in its humanism. It assumes that a concrete living person is the center of relationships. As the center, the dignity, independence and autonomy of the individual are essential features of the person. For relationships, sociality is indispensable for personal identity. The Confucian idea of the person is rooted in body, home, community, world and cosmos; yet it seeks to transcend egoism, nepotism, racism, narrowly defined culturalism and anthropocentrism. Confucius regards the secular world as sacred by overcoming the exclusive dichotomies of body/mind, spirit/matter, creator/creature and sacred/profane.

The Confucian way of life embodies self, community, nature and heaven in an ethic of care and responsibility which is the Confucian idea of humanity, or *ren*. Humanity, as the core value in Confucianism, embodies heaven, earth and myriad things in its sensitivity and consciousness. This is what Cheng Yi and Wang Yangming and others talked about – 仁者以天地万物为一体.

Finally although culture diversity is taken for granted, the Confucian quest for harmony without uniformity (和而不同) is predicated on the belief that the great unity (大同) through the education of global citizenship is not only desirable but realizable.

Gianni Vattimo

Professor Tu Weiming and I discovered that we agree on many points. From an European point of view I could simply accept all that he just said.

I am especially happy to speak here in Beijing, because I belong to a generation of Europeans who 20, 30, and 40 years ago considered China as a possible model of future civilization. I shared for a while the attitude of many young Europeans who revered Chairman Mao as a prophet of a new, really free society. I know that this is not solely a mythology today, and perhaps for Chinese people that period was difficult to cross. But I see also that whether the China of today threatens or promises depends on this people becoming the great new beneficent power in the next hundred years. This China is more liberal than earlier, and it takes advantage of modernization. But today China is the result of the progress, transformations and changes of over 50 years.

That is why I appreciate so deeply this opportunity to speak in this Great Hall of the People. I want to say that Europe and probably the whole world view the China of today with expectations analogous to those which we had in the 1960 and 1970's. We do not expect China to become simply another strong industrial power competing with the United Sates for imperialistic domination of the world. We expect rather that because of its tradition, China will be a new form of eudemonic power with the ability to emerge in the international context. This possibility depends on the new conditions of our civilization: the internet, communication, mass media and so on. In this new situation we can no longer think of the eudemonia of traditional types, especially those depending on military force, mechanical means of action, nature and so on. Much of the new civilization will be a civilization of communication, though some will call it a clash of civilizations. It will be very well if we are simply in a conflict or struggle among civilizations and cultures, rather then between physical and military powers.

The new form of eudemonia in the future world, we hope, will be a subtle conflict of ways of life – in German: "Weltanschauung" or world view – rather like the struggle between representative and an abstract paintings in art galleries: no one struggles against another because he is a representative painter and the other an abstract painter. This is not a matter of competition but of way of life. I live like this, and you live like that. The danger for the future, as we learn from the past, is an obsolete culture which believes that truth belongs to it and that God is with us. Nazism rose on this belief. Post-modernism is against this belief: it is the discovery that there is no truth, but only, fortunately and happily, different interpretations of the world. This means that no one has the right to impose his own truth upon other people; so white civilization is no better than the yellow one.

This attitude toward the world as a conflict of interpretations is nevertheless a conflict, a struggle between different views of life and world. But it is exactly a conflict only of interpretations. The truth will be reached not when somebody is a God, but when different peoples' interpretation of the world agree with one another. So the truth is not the beginning but the end; it is created through social dialogue. I would say this is the task or the endeavor of the future that a possible eudemonic country like China promises to take up.

There is also a very old tradition of wisdom in China which Westerners probably would do well to learn, share and understand. In this new situation exactly because of the up-surge of the communication society, it will be more and more important to persuade people and not to oblige them, to subject them, or imperialistically to oblige them to share a position. Now even the terrorists do not miss the power of the media in building a consensus. A bomb does not destroy the Western capitalistic order, yet it becomes news which draws people to recognize that their power is not untouchable. Thus this very cruel and unacceptable attitude of the world of terrorism is related to our society of communication. If one must counter the extreme reality of terrorism and heal real people we must develop the other aspects: communicative participation, discussion and possibly consensus. In this situation clearly the humanistic sciences – not the hard sciences, but the humanistic philosophers, artists, religious people and so on – acquire a greater importance. These are prophets without weapons whom we welcome. They preach the truth without imposing it with physical and military power.

In this new situation, even the philosophers can help. In Italian we used to say that psycho-analysis was the last step before going to a place for Christian miracles. Philosophers were more or less like psycho-analysts; if you did not have any other recourse, go to a philosopher. But in the new communication society, philosophers now become more important. I speak not of any increase in my salary, but of the possibility of the humanistic becoming more important in our society. I think that China, having a different tradition, not only Confucianism, but also the more recent tradition of Maoism, can become open to new possibilities. We always bet on a new agent, and I am betting on Latin America for many reasons. But I start to bet also on China and hope not to lose my bet. I hope that the new China, the new world, bets also on its philosophers once again.

Tu: I appreciate Professor Vattimo's reference to 1968; at that time many brilliant minds in the West simply identified themselves with Maoism and the Cultural Revolution. The new vision developing in Europe and the United States, especially in the area of humanities about the promises of China, is precisely Vattimo's notion about 'weak thinking' (*pensiero debole*). 'Weak thinking' is a form of reflection which liberates the human mind from simply quantitative analysis. It is related to my colleague, Joseph Nye's notion about 'soft power'. That is reassuring as it sees one's values and ideas being appreciated by others voluntarily and with full commitment. This is a helpful extension of the notion of influence.

So in the age of communication and technology one cannot hide behind the military for it is not simply a time of economic power or political pressure. It is the persuasiveness of the meaning of life, of values, of the sense of shared aspirations, shared visions for the future. These powers generated in art, in literature, in philosophy etc. will be as important as the values and ideas generated by the hard sciences. In this sense perhaps in the 21st century, among all the dialogues among civilizations, there should be also a dialogue regarding dialogue between science and religion.

So there is one question I want to pose to professor Vattimo. As a post-modernist you make very clear that you do not have to pick and choose; you call for openness, for multiplicity, for all kinds of beings rather than great forces. If I interpret this correctly, we also turn to our own cultural roots such as Catholicism or Christianity. This is not only the post-modernist secularist, but the post-modern religionist, very different from Richard Rorty. Rorty really believes that religion is no longer significant and that cultural identity will eventually evaporate. What we have is hybridity, which means that all cultural traditions mix together without differentiation. (Before he visited China, he said maybe only one language will count in the future. After he visited China, he considered that perhaps two languages would count.) That position is very different from yours. So I wonder if you would be willing to share a bit of your personal intellectual and spiritual journey: why are you a Christian and at the same time also a post-modern?

Vattimo: Yes, I am a post-modernist exactly because I am a Christian and in many senses. Why, because Christianity, which we experience very strongly in Europe, especially in Italy, Spain and France, is basically that Jesus came to reorient thinking, namely, that it is more important to love one's fellow man than to persuade him or to oblige him to a truth. There is a dictum, probably of Aristotle that, 'I am a friend of Plato, but first of all of the truth.' Now during the past centuries, in the form of what Plato said, the truth has come to be applied rather to one's fellow men.

So it is not strange that the post-modernist is a Christian because, as a matter of fact, Christianity has liberated humankind from the power of objective truth. Imagine, all the formations of religions – not only the Christian religion, but also Buddhism, Hinduism and so on – if measured by a purely referential idea of language, what would they give; they would not give anything. What does it mean objectively to be a Christian or to be a Buddhist, or to be a Confusion? It is like when you say I love you: what does it mean objectively? Do you measure your position of the past hours on what I objectively saw of you? It is absurd that the intention of love not to be based on that.

If we still keep truth to scientistic terms, we will never get beyond that. It is not a dialogue. Scientists, of course, cooperate, but mathematics is not specifically a human language for it does not involve any personal attitude or affection. So in many senses, as professor Tu Weiming reminded us, I am a disciple of Martin Heidegger, who caused a great scandal among scientists by saying that science does not think. Why? Because as Kant said science knows phenomena, but what is essential to life is to think of what makes possible the knowledge of phenomena. God, freedom, the co-existence of man and nature cannot at all be known positively through experiments and mathematical science. All these have to be developed in the contemporary world if we don't want to give all power to the experts. If everything is a matter of scientific knowledge then there is no discussion or democracy, not even love because when I say I love you, what objectively does that mean?

Tu: I will conclude with one brief comment. We share one rather important mythological concern. Normally for scholarship it is important to be objective and disinterested, but I would note that both of us are personally committed. We made a clear distinction between being personal and being private or subjective. If we are personally committed to somebody's ideas we are still publicly accountable for they can be argued and debated.

Liberty has importance to be sure, but it has to be supplemented by the importance of justice – not just liberty alone, but liberty with justice, with a sense of righteousness. The importance of rationality is self-evident, but it has to be supplemented by the idea of sympathy, empathy and compassion. This is not just instrumental rationality alone but due process of law and a sense of civility; human rights and human responsibility, the dignity of the individual and the sense of cultural and group solidarity. It is in this sense that Confucian humanism with its emphasis on justice, sympathy, civility, responsibility and communal solidarity can engage in a fruitful dialogue with liberal traditions which emphasize liberty, rationality, due process of law, human rights and dignity of the individual

Translated by Qi Li

Part I

Dialogue between
Eastern and Western Philosophies

Chapter 1

Constructing "Chinese Philosophy" in the Sino-Euro Cultural Exchange

Tang Yijie

There was not such a word as "philosophy", or *Zhe-xue,* in the ancient Chinese, and many western philosophers did not think that there was "philosophy" in China at all. For example, Hegel thought there were only "opinions" in China, and that "no philosophic knowledge can be found here."[1] The word *Zhe-xue* was coined by a Japanese scholar Nishiamane (1829-1897), who borrowed the two Chinese characters *Zhe* and *Xue* to indicate the Philosophy originated in Ancient Greece and Rome. This new term was introduced into China by a Chinese scholar, Huang Zunxian (黃遵憲, 1848-1905), and was accepted by Chinese academia. Although this term *Zhe-xue* was accepted, it is still a problem whether there is the equivalent of the Western Philosophy in China. In 2004 there was a discussion precisely on the "validity of Chinese philosophy" in Mainland China.

Western philosophy was imported into China at the end of 19th century. Its earliest and most influential introducer, Yan Fu (嚴複), had translated a great deal of western philosophical works, especially those on Darwin's evolutionism. Afterwards, Kant, Descartes, Schopenhauer, Nietzsche, and so forth, were all introduced into China in succession, which provided a point of reference to the problem of "whether there is Philosophy in China". Some Chinese scholars found out that, although there was such independent discipline as "Philosophy" in Chinese history, there were nonetheless ample "philosophical thoughts" and "philosophical problems" in ancient Chinese canons, such as the *Book of History* (《尚書》), the *Book of Changes* (《周易》), Confucian *Analects* (《論語》), Lao-tzu (《老子》), and Zhuang-tzu (《莊子》). They are akin to those in western philosophy, sometimes with very valuable differences. However, we have to admit that, before the importation of western philosophy, Philosophy was not separated from Canon studies (經學) and non-Confucian Masters studies (子學) as an independent discipline. From the first half of the 20th century on, the doctrines of western philosophy flowed into China, including Marxism, Pragmatism, Realism, Analytical Philosophy, Ancient Greek Philosophy, 19th century German Philosophy, etc., influencing the Chinese academia. With such a point of reference of the western philosophy, the Chinese scholars tried to seek "Chinese philosophy" by combing the voluminous bibliographies of canons and their exegeses, the works of Confucius, Lao-tzu and Zhuang-tzu. Naturally, in the beginning there were only studies on certain individual figures or problems. But by the early 20th century, "Chinese philosophy" had been established, initiated by studying its own history. Several kinds of histories were published in succession to justify the existence of a proper Chinese philosophy ever since pre-Qin, such as *History of Chinese Philosophy* (《中國哲學史》, 1916), *Outline of Chinese Philosophy* (《中國哲學史大綱》) of Hu Shi (胡適) (originally titled as *History of Pre-Qin Sophism* 《先秦名學史》, written between 1915-1917, published in 1922), *A History of Chinese Philosophy* (《中國哲學史》) of Feng Youlan (馮友蘭) (the first volume was published in 1931, and the two volumes were published together in 1934). This was a demonstration that the Chinese scholars consciously began to study "Philosophy" as a discipline independent from the studies of Canons and of non-Confucian Masters; however, almost all these works on philosophical history followed the western model.

From 1930s on, Chinese philosophers had employed traditional Chinese intellectual resources to construct several important modern types of "Chinese philosophy" on the basis of the absorptions and adaptations of western philosophy. First, Xiong Shili (熊十力) and Zhang Dongsun (張東蓀), and then Feng Youlan and Jin Yuelin (金岳霖). After 1949, however, this trend of constructing a modern "Chinese philosophy", as well as further study of western philosophy, was interrupted. It was not until in the 1980s that western philosophy began to flow once again into China, when the policies of opening and reform were put into practice. Existentialism, Western Marxism, Phenomenology, Structuralism, Hermeneutics Post-Modernism, Semiology, etc., all these doctrines were introduced, broadening not only the horizon of Chinese philosophers, but also the referential system for the poly-perspective study of Chinese philosophy.

From the brief retrospection above on the history of the importation of western philosophy into China, we could draw several conclusions as follows for further discussion.

"CHINESE PHILOSOPHY" HAS BECOME AN INDEPENDENT DISCIPLINE DUE TO THE IMPORTATION OF WESTERN PHILOSOPHY

As mentioned above, the word *Zhexue*, or philosophy, did not exist in China, which means that "Philosophy" had not been an independent discipline, but was constructed by Chinese scholars with certain "philosophical thoughts" and "problems" implied in traditional studies of Canons and non-Confucian Masters, according to the framework of western philosophy. Therefore, the so-called "Chinese philosophy", for a long time, was such a discipline compounded, in the main, by certain materials of "philosophical thoughts" or "problems" found in Chinese resources, and then constructed in reference to the model of western philosophy. Taking the *History of Chinese Philosophy* for example, we could see that its structure, terminologies and conceptions were mainly borrowed from the West, such as Idealism and Materialism, Ontology and Cosmology, Monism and Dualism (or Pluralism), or empirical and transcendental, phenomenon and essence, universals and particulars, thought and existence, etc. All of them were borrowed from the

West, and were employed to explain certain notions in Chinese thought, such as Dao (道), Tian (天), or Xin (心), etc.. The original Chinese philosophical thoughts, problems, terminologies, conceptions and propositions were baptized by western philosophy, and were made much clearer. Undoubtedly, this was the first necessary step towards the creation of a "Chinese philosophy"; otherwise, "Chinese philosophy" could not have been separated from the traditional studies of Canons and non-Confucian Masters as an independent discipline.

Modern "Chinese philosophy" emerging in the 1930s and 40s was created by Chinese philosophers' "continuing", instead of "following", traditional discourse of Chinese philosophy. That is to say, on the basis of the absorptions and adaptations of western philosophy, Chinese philosophers required that Chinese philosophy be transformed from the "traditional" to the "modern". Thus, the so-called continued "Chinese philosophy" was conditioned with reference to western philosophy. In other words, they tried to "converge the Chinese and the West", and improve "Chinese scholarship" with "western scholarship". There are two representative examples: the first is the Neo Weishi Lun (唯識, *vijñapti-mātratā*) Doctrine of Xiong Shili, the other is the Neo-Confucianism (新理學) of Feng Youlan.[2]

Xiong Shili completed only the part of "Doctrine of the Jing" (境論) in his *Neo Weishi Lun* (《新唯識論》). The so-called 境論 corresponds to western ontology, though Xiong Shili's ontology has a distinctive Chinese feature. He originally planned to write the part of 量論, or epistemology in the sense of western philosophy. Although this part was not written, we could well envisage, from his other works, the basic structure of the epistemology he was to construct. To him, traditional Chinese philosophy put more emphasis on "Ti-ren" (體認), or the experience and cognition of heart, rather than "Si-bian" (思辨), or the analysis and speculation of reason. Thus, western epistemology is necessary for the substantiation of traditional Chinese philosophy. Therefore, he wished to create an epistemology encompassing the cognition of heart, and the speculation of reason.

In his Neo-Confucianism, Feng Youlan declared clearly that his philosophy was not to follow, but to continue the Neo-Confucianism of the Song and Ming dynasties. To continue is in fact to introduce into Chinese philosophy the Universals and Particulars of Plato and the thoughts of Neo-Realism, to divide the world into the realm of Truth (真際, or 理, or 太極), and the realm of Reality (實際). Things in the realm of Reality become what they are by reason of why they are. Feng Youlan's distinction of the realm of Truth and that of Reality, which on the one hand continued the doctrine of "理一分殊" (the Many sharing the One), and on the other hand transplanted into Chinese philosophy the western notions of Universals and Particulars. Another Neo-Confucian work of Feng Youlan was entitled 新知言, discussing philosophical methodologies and the main epistemological problems. According to Feng, western philosophy excels in analysis (the positive method of metaphysics), while traditional Chinese philosophy in intuition (the negative method of metaphysics), and his method of Neo-Confucianism is a combination of both.

Both Xiong Shili and Feng Youlan tried to discuss "Chinese philosophy" in continuity with the native tradition, but both did so under the condition of absorbing and adapting western philosophy. This trend in the 1930s and 40s of creating a modern Chinese philosophy on the basis of converging Chinese and western philosophies, was regretfully interrupted by exterior factors.

From above we can see that it is impossible either to compile traditional Chinese philosophy (the history of Chinese philosophy) or to construct a modern Chinese philosophy without the western counterpart, and both were initiated with the importation of western philosophy. We could therefore say that the establishment of "Chinese philosophy" was indebted to the West.

SOME BASIC PROBLEMS IN CONSTRUCTING "CHINESE PHILOSOPHY" IN REFERENCE TO THE WESTERN MODEL

As human beings, we inevitably share certain general features in different civilizations and cultures; since we belong to different nations (or countries, or regions), the national civilization or culture would possess certain particular traits because of geographic, historical or even accidental factors. Western philosophy, born in western socio-cultural environment, naturally has its own character; similarly, if a Chinese philosophy is constructed, it would necessarily be conditioned by its society and culture, and consequently possess certain particularities. Thus, Chinese philosophy constructed in reference to western model would unavoidably be problematic. In my opinion, there are at least the following two basic problems.

(1) The properties of Chinese philosophy should be of special significance to the "Philosophy". In my opinion, from ancient Greeks on, especially from Descartes on, Western philosophy has focused more on the systematic construction of philosophic knowledge; while in the Chinese tradition, our sages put more emphasis on the pursuit of a jing-jie (境界, a philosophical realm of virtues or latencies to be realized) of life. A quotation of Confucius may embody this feature: "Better to like it than merely know it; better to take delight in it than merely like it." The ultimate pursuit of life is not to achieve knowledge (or skills), but to seek a place where one can "settle one's body and life" (安身立命), i.e., a *jing-jie* where body and mind, the exterior and the interior, are in harmony. This was pursued also by Sung and Ming Confucian philosophers as "where Confucius and Yan Hui took delight". The Taoist philosopher Zhuang-zi pursued all the more a *jing-jie* of Free Roaming (逍遙遊. [3]) above the ego and the mundane world, which was called by him the selfless (無我) realm. Zen Buddhism in China makes a point of seeing Tao in daily life, as naturally as "Clouds are in heaven and water in vase." A Zen Buddhist poem manifested this *jing-jie* of submission to nature:

> In spring we enjoy the flowers, in autumn the moon;
> In summer there's cool breeze, in winter white snow.
> Bear no trivial chores in mind,
> And you are in the best time of this world.

Such a philosophy characterized by its pursuit of *jing-jie,* like Chinese Confucianism, Taoism and Buddhism, must be quite rare in the West! Although it is distinctively different from western philosophy, there is no gainsaying its value for human society.

Another characteristic of traditional Chinese thought different from the West might be that, for a long time, it was guided by the principle of "the unity of heaven and man", and "the myriad of things are in one", and "the unity of body and mind, the exterior and the interior". All of this is obviously different from the "principle of subjectivity" and the dichotomy of "subject-object" relationship long central to western philosophical history. And if this "principle of subjectivity" and the dualistic thought pattern are applied to "Chinese philosophy" as a regulative framework, surely the intrinsic characters of the latter could not be sufficiently manifested. The Chinese pattern of thinking as "the unity of heaven and man", "the unity of the interior and the exterior" (i.e. the unity of the subject and the object; "unity" here means "adjacency instead of detachment"), is quite similar to contemporary western philosophical doctrines (such as Phenomenology) in continental Europe, which makes a point of intersubjectivity, the syncretism of the human being and the world. Therefore, if this feature in traditional Chinese thinking is made evident, it would benefit both the development of Chinese philosophy and that of western philosophy.

(2). There are ample notions in traditional Chinese thoughts, such as *Tian, Dao, Xin, Xing* (性), *You* (有), *Wu* (無), *Qi* (氣), etc., with special connotations of many aspects and layers, so it is difficult to find corresponding notions in western philosophy. For example, *Tian,* which has at least three meanings: (a) the supreme and dominating Heaven (with the sense of a personal god); (b) the natural heaven (with the sense of nature); (c) the heaven of Truths and Principles (義理) (with the sense of morality and transcendence). The same philosopher might employ the concept of *Tian* to comprise all these three meanings. Another example is *Qi,* which comprises also at least three meanings: (a) a material entity; (b) the spirit (or state of mind) (such as "the boundless and surging *Qi*" of Mencius, the "essential *Qi*" in Guan-zi); (c) the Supreme (such as "the Trinity of Gods transformed from the one *Qi*" in Taoism). It is difficult to find the counterparts of all these notions in the West, and thus, strictly speaking, some of them can not be translated, and perhaps it would be better to use transliterations. However, the indiscriminate applications of western conceptions have already reduced their amplitude and particularity.

If Chinese philosophy could break out of the framework of western philosophy, and cease the improper applications of western conceptions, it would, I think, undoubtedly make special contributions to universal philosophy.

HOW SHOULD THE CHINESE PHILOSOPHY BE DEVELOPED IN THE FUTURE?

In my opinion, Chinese philosophy still needs serious absorption and systematic digestion of western philosophy, especially paying attention to its new trends. This is closely related to the demands of this epoch of globalization. In order to make significant contributions to world philosophy, we should perhaps make a point of two crucial approaches.

From the history of Chinese culture in absorbing and syncretizing Indian Buddhism two pieces of experiences could be drawn in dealing with the relationships between Chinese and western philosophies. First, in the Sui and Tang dynasties (from the sixth to the eighth century A.D.), several sinicized Buddhist schools came into being, which developed Indian Buddhism by absorbing indigenous Confucian and Taoist cultures. Today, in studying the various doctrines of Western philosophy, if we introduce Chinese thoughts in order to amplify their contents and make them more universal we should not only follow, but also continue Western philosophy, and make new contributions to "Philosophy" per se. This trend is just now emerging. Many scholars are trying to construct, for example, Chinese Hermeneutics, Chinese Phenomenology, Chinese Semiology, etc. "Chinese philosophy" should be not only "the philosophy of the Chinese", but also a philosophy influencing the course of world philosophy. Of course, we could also continue the tradition as did modern Chinese philosophy in the 1930s and 40s, that is to say, not only continue the philosophy of Confucius, Mencius, Zhu Xi and Wang Yangming, but also that of Xiong Shili and Feng Youlan. Just because it has well absorbed and adapted the western philosophy, this modern Chinese philosophy was formed as such. Now, if it wants to exert a significant influence on the world Philosophy, it must take up the standpoint of its proper tradition, and appropriately absorb and adapt contemporary western philosophy so as to influence the global philosophical circles, and let Chinese philosophy possess global significance.

Secondly, in China, when we translated Indian Buddhist terminologies, several important notions were transliterated, such as Prajna, Nirvana; after some time, these transliterations became proper Chinese notions. Everyone is used to them and understands them. Thus Dharma-exponent Xuanzang (玄奘) in the Tang dynasty established five principles of "no translation" in translating Buddhist canons, i.e. transliterating instead of translating the meaning, and using notes to explain these transliterations. Therefore, in my opinion, certain special notions in Chinese philosophy should not be adapted to western terminologies at all, but be transliterated with annotations, in order to keep the pregnant particularity of Chinese philosophy. Only when this is kept, could Chinese philosophy make special contributions to world Philosophy.

In contemporary Sino-Euro cultural exchanges, if equal dialogues could be made on both sides, undoubtedly we could help world philosophy to achieve significant developments in the 21st century. Last but not least, I would like to quote the German philosopher, Gadamer, who left us in 2002, that the "understanding" should be expanded to "general dialogue".[4] Only when the "understanding" is elevated to "general dialogue," can the relationships between the subject and the object be transformed from inequality to equality, and only then can dialogues be realized and completed successfully. We must do our best for this cause.

NOTES

1 G. W. Friedrich Hegel. *Lectures on the History of Philosophy.* E.S. Haldane (*trans.*) (London: Thoemmes Press. 1999), p. 98.

2 Actually should be translated as Neo-Neo-Confucianism, in order to distinguish it from Sung and Ming Neo-Confucianism. –Translator's note.

3 This title of a chapter in *Zhuang-tzu* is translated by A. C. Graham as "Going rambling without a destination". –Translator's note.

4 See H-.G. Gadamer, *Truth and Method* (New York: Continuum, 1995).

Chapter 2

"Getting Rid of God:"
A Prolegomenon to Dialogue between
Chinese and Western Philosophy in
an Era of Globalization

Roger T. Ames

TAKING STOCK IN THE WESTERN ACADEMY:
WHERE ARE WE?

Where are we in the "dialogue" between Chinese and Western philosophy? I would simply note that the canons of Chinese philosophy in most
American bookstores—indeed, university bookstores as well—are never to be
found in the designated philosophy section. In fact, if the Chinese philosophical classics are available at all, they are usually to be found somewhere between the bibles and the New Age, and if given any specific designation, they
are usually described as some variant of "Asian Religions." Why is this?

Such exclusion reflects the self-understanding of professional philosophy today. The curricula in most of the philosophy departments in the
best Western universities remain innocent of any whiff of "Eastern wisdom."
If Chinese philosophy is taught at all—and it usually isn't—it is to be found
in Religious Studies or Asian Studies departments. In spite of the most earnest interest of a few good people in this potentially productive conversation
between these rich and very different philosophical traditions, we would have
to admit that, at least from the perspective of the Western academy at large,
the dialogue has yet to begin.

Until recently, most professional Western philosophers have been
notoriously uninterested in any claims on the part of proponents of Chinese
thought that there is much of philosophical significance in the texts of ancient China. Indeed, it can be fairly claimed that geographical rather than
philosophical criteria continue to be invoked to exclude entire philosophical
traditions from consideration. As a consequence, profoundly "philosophical"
texts—the Yijing, the Analects of Confucius, the Daodejing, the Zhuangzi,
the Zhongyong—are not being treated as such within the hallways of professional philosophy.

But why are trained philosophers, in the absence of any real interest
on their part, even necessary in the introduction of Chinese philosophy into
the Western academy? While one of the requisites of a successful translation
of a classical Chinese philosophical text into Western languages is philological expertise in Chinese language and culture, it is equally true that such a

translation requires an understanding of the Western philosophical discourse serving as the target language of the translation.

To report on the past several centuries, in the absence of the contribution of trained philosophers, the Chinese texts have been translated and interpreted initially by missionaries, and more recently by sinologists. Indeed, to date much of the early Chinese corpus has only incidentally and tangentially been engaged by trained philosophers. This assertion is meant neither to impugn the usually good intentions of the missionaries nor to pretend that there is any substitute for the sophisticated philological, historical, literary, and cultural sensibilities that we associate with good sinology.

In fact, if there is an indictment to be made, it is to be directed against professional philosophy in our higher seats of learning that, in its practices as well as its own self-understanding, continues to insist that philosophy is exclusively an Anglo-European enterprise. And the translations of the Chinese canons on offer from non-philosophers do not help to persuade the profession that they are ignoring good philosophy. Indeed, the lack of interest and the philosophically naïve translations create a vicious circle.

The gu that is not a gu (觚不觚, 觚哉, 觚哉)

So at this juncture, Chinese philosophy, like the pervasive fortune cookie, is "Chinese" in name only. That is, Chinese philosophy has been made familiar to Western readers by first "Christianizing" it, and then more recently, by "orientalizing" it and locating it within a poetical-mystical-occult worldview as a boundary on our logical-rational-enlightened self-understanding. It has become a commonplace to acknowledge that, in the process of Western humanists attempting to make sense of the classical Chinese philosophical literature, many unannounced Western assumptions have been inadvertently insinuated into the understanding of these texts, and have colored the vocabulary through which this understanding has been articulated. To the extent that Chinese philosophy has become the subject of Western philosophical interest at all, it has usually been analyzed within the framework of categories and philosophical problems not its own.

Over the last several centuries, the vocabulary established for the translation of classical Chinese texts into Western languages has been freighted by an often unconscious Christian framework, and the effects of this "Christianization" of Chinese texts are still very much with us. There are numerous examples of grossly inappropriate language having become the standard equivalents in the Chinese/English dictionaries that we use to perpetuate our understanding of Chinese culture: "the Way (dao道)," "Heaven (tian天)," "benevolence (ren仁)," "rites (li禮)," "virtue (de德)," "righteousness (yi義)," "principle (li 理),"and so on. Is being someone's son or daughter a "rite"? When (if ever) and in what context would a native English speaker ever utter the word "righteousness?" Can a Western student read the capitalized "Heaven" as anything other than a metonym for the familiar notion of a transcendent

God? Does "principle" or L. *principium* used to translate the Greek *arche* from *archon*—"the beginning, the ultimate underlying substance, the ultimate undemonstrable principle"—that locates li squarely within classical Greek "One-behind-the-many" metaphysical thinking have anything to do with Chinese natural cosmology?

Given the marginalization of indigenous philosophical traditions, philosophy as a discipline has an unfulfilled responsibility to our academy. An essential occupation of philosophers is to identify and describe the generic traits of the human experience in order to locate the problems of the day within the broadest possible context, and then to recommend solutions that we can endorse, and to which we can offer our allegiance. And these defining generic characteristics are significantly different as we move from one cultural and epochal site to another. Indeed, given the complexity of our modern world, philosophers as producers of knowledge have the responsibility to seek out and to understand the uncommon assumptions that distinguish cultures as a preventative against cultural reductionism and the misconceptions that such ethnocentrism entails. Thus it is that the absence of philosophers in the interpretation of Chinese philosophy has come at a real cost to everyone in the Western academy who is interested in knowing the world better.

MAINSTREAM PHILOSOPHY IN CHINA

Lest the honesty of this observation offend only Western missionaries, sinologists, and those Anglo-European philosophers whose only crime is to have been sincerely interested in their own traditions of thought, there is broader complicity in this charge, for the persisting situation is more complex.

That "philosophy" as a professional discipline defines itself largely as Anglo-European is a claim that is as true in Beijing, Tokyo, Seoul, Delhi, Nairobi, and Boston, as it is in Cambridge, Frankfort, and Paris. Philosophers who go about their business within the academies outside of Europe have, through a protracted process of self-colonization, become complicit in excluding the philosophical narratives of their own cultures from being recognized as "real philosophy."

For many reasons—certainly economic and political factors among them—non-Western scholars themselves have not only acquiesced in the exclusive claim of Anglo-European philosophy to have a monopoly on philosophy, but have worked assiduously to make Anglo-European philosophy the mainstream curriculum in the best of their own home institutions. Indigenous traditions of philosophy—Chinese, Japanese, Korean, South Asian, African, and yes, American too—have been marginalized by Japanese, Korean, South Asian, African, and American philosophers themselves, while the heirs to British Empiricism and Continental Rationalism have continued to wage their battles on foreign soil. That is, if indigenous Asian and American philosophies have been ignored by Western philosophers, they have also been significantly marginalized within their own home cultures.

William James was almost right when he began his 1901-2 Gifford lectures at Edinburgh by confessing that "To us Americans, the experience of receiving instruction from the living voice, as well as from the books of European scholars, is very familiar. . . It seems the natural thing for us to listen whilst the Europeans talk." The only caveat offered here is that James would have reported on the situation that much more accurately, if he had included the Asian and African philosophers along with the Americans as the seemingly "natural" audience for European philosophy.[1]

"CHINESE PHILOSOPHY" AND "PHILOSOPHY IN CHINA"

When, in looking for a conversation between traditions, we turn from the Western academy to China, the situation is again complex. Although mainstream philosophy in China continues to be Anglo-European philosophy, the dialogue between Chinese and Western philosophy that has yet to occur in our Western corridors has had a minor yet culturally significant life. In order to locate this dialogue, we must distinguish clearly between "philosophy in China" on the one hand, and "Chinese philosophy" on the other.

In some academic quarters the important distinction between "philosophy in China" and "the history of Chinese philosophy" has been respected by using the foreign term coined in late 19th century Japan by Nishi Amane—"philosophy (Ch. Zhexue哲學, Jap. tetsugaku)"—to refer to Western philosophy as it is taught in China, and the vernacular term, "thought (sixiang思想)," to refer to the history of Chinese philosophy as the exegetical explication of the Chinese canons of philosophy that continues to be integral to the curricula of departments of both philosophy and literature in China.

But again, this "history" of Chinese philosophy is not "philosophy" in the sense of creative philosophizing. In fact, to discuss 20th century "Chinese philosophy" in China we will need to distinguish yet again between the commentarial history of Chinese philosophy and Chinese philosophy itself. It is here at last that some important dialogue between Chinese and Western philosophy has occurred. Whereas the Western philosophy curriculum as presented in the Chinese academy has largely been able to ignore its own indigenous traditions, and the commentarial history of Chinese "thought" has often been taught, especially in literature departments, without a perceived need to reference Western philosophy, there has been over time a small but significant cadre of Chinese philosophers who have been shaped in their thinking and writing about their own tradition through a conscious appropriation of the Western canons—particularly German idealism and Marxist philosophy.

It is this subset of original "comparative" philosophers who in the 20th century have been using Western philosophy as a resource to philosophize about the Chinese tradition that have some claim on the term "Chinese philosophy." This third category of hybridist Chinese philosophers have recently come to be called "New Confucianists (xinruxuejia新儒學家)," a term coined in the mid-1980's to describe a philosophical "movement" that began in the early 20th century and that continues today. The common element in the early life of this otherwise diverse group of philosophers was to try to produce a Western-informed brand of Chinese philosophy that could be used as a tourniquet to stop the hemorrhaging of a long-suffering cultural tradition.

In fact, we can parse the influence of German philosophy on Chinese philosophy in twentieth century China as it moves from Kant through Hegel to the phenomenology of Husserl and most recently, to Heidegger. The marked transition has been from an appeal to German philosophy as a standard by which traditional Chinese philosophy can be justified and legitimized, to German philosophy as a resource available to enrich indigenous sensibilities. Said another way, in contemporary China, Heidegger's critique of traditional Western ontology is being used increasingly to open a space for further reflecting upon and developing the processual sensibilities of traditional Chinese philosophy that began in the classical world as early as the Yijing, or Book of Changes.

As a programmatic aside, while Heidegger in contemporary philosophy is certainly an important critique of the "metaphysical" or "theo-ontological" thinking that is anathema to Chinese natural cosmology, American philosophy too offers an alternative, decidedly positive, vocabulary that takes as its target foundationalist philosophy. American pragmatism further resonates with the traditional Chinese philosophical narrative in respecting the processual nature of experience, and thus can serve as a resource for creative philosophizing. It is only very recently that American philosophy has found a voice in the Chinese conversation.

DEFINING OUR TERMS: WHAT IS CHINESE PHILOSOPHY (ZHEXUE 哲學)?

One obstacle to the possibility of dialogue with the Western academy is that Chinese philosophy does not parse comfortably into the standard Western philosophical categories: metaphysics, epistemology, ethics, and so on. Indeed, in a culture where there is a presumed continuity between knowing and a productive doing (知行合一), epistemology very quickly spills over into ethics and social and political philosophy.

Nor can Chinese philosophy be accommodated wholesale according to the formal disciplines and areas of cultural interest that have come to define the Western academy: philosophy, religion, psychology, and so on. In the case of religion, for example, the well-intended attempt of some recent interpreters to rescue Chinese philosophy from the overlay of a Judeo-Christian worldview fails utterly if, in the process, this rehabilitation secularizes Chinese philosophy by robbing it of its important religious import. After all, there are many ways of being religious.

Although the familiar categories and disciplines of the Western academy could otherwise be qualified and reshaped in sufficient degree to permit their application to the Chinese tradition, any heavy-handed application of the existing taxonomies will, on balance, be a source of more loss than gain. Indeed, the technical vocabularies that define these disciplines would be a persistent and compounding source of equivocation. Of course, the important exception to any decision to abandon such formal categories is the discipline of "philosophy" itself because "philosophy" as opposed to "thought" or "culture" is an evaluative term. Indeed, philosophy is a qualitative claim that speaks to the depth and quality of Chinese thinking with respect to the most important issues that confront us as human beings.

What then is Chinese "philosophy?" The distinguished French sinologist Marcel Granet observes rather starkly that "Chinese wisdom has no need of the idea of God."[2] This characterization of classical Chinese philosophy has had many iterations albeit in different formulations, by many of our most prominent comparative philosophers both Chinese and Western alike. Indeed, our best interpreters of classical Chinese philosophy are explicit in rejecting the idea that Chinese cosmology begins from some independent, transcendent principle and entails the metaphysical reality/appearance distinction and the plethora of dualistic categories that are corollary to such a worldview.[3]

Instead, Chinese philosophy—Confucianism and Daoism too—takes personal cultivation in the relationships that constitute one as a person as its starting point, and as its ultimate source of meaning and value. Stated cosmologically, Tang Junyi considers the cultivation of a holographic, interdependent , and productive relationship between "particular" and "totality" as the distinguishing feature and most crucial contribution of Chinese philosophy broadly. As the underlying spirit of Chinese culture Tang Junyi endorses:

中國文化之根本精神即［將部分與全體交融互攝］之精
神；自認識上言之，即不自全體中劃出部分之精神　（
此自中國人之宇宙觀中最可見之）；自情意上言之，
即努力以部分實現全體之精神　（此自中國人之人生態
度中可見之）。

... the spirit of symbiosis and the mutuality of the particular
and the totality. From the perspective of understanding this
means an unwillingness to isolate the particular from the totality (this is most evident in the cosmology of the Chinese
people), and from the perspective of ties of feeling and affection, it means the commitment of the particular to do its
best to realize the totality (this is most evident in the attitude
of the Chinese people toward daily life).[4]

In interpreting Chinese cosmology, I have followed Tang Junyi and have argued for a radial focus-field model of emergent order in contrast to the single-ordered, One-behind-the-many model more familiar in classical Greek metaphysical thinking.

In the Analects 14.35, Confucius insists that order starts here and goes there: "I study what is near at hand and aspire to what is lofty 下學而上達." The Great Learning (Daxue大學), a second of the seminal canons of Confucian philosophy, establishes the priority of cultivating this focus-field, radial sensibility. The central message of this canonical document is that personal, familial, social, political, and cosmic cultivation is ultimately coterminous and mutually entailing, but must always begin from the personal project of self-cultivation. Each person is a unique window on their own family, community, polity, and so on, and through a process of growth and self-cultivation, they are able bring the resolution of their relationships into clearer and more meaningful focus. That is, cultivating one's own person grows and adds meaning to the cosmos, and in turn, this increasingly meaningful cosmos provides a fertile context for the project of one's self-cultivation.

> The way of achieving greatness through learning lies in demonstrating real character, in cherishing the common people, and making a commitment to doing what is best. Such a course of learning can only be set once one has made this commitment. Only in having set such a course is one able to find equilibrium, only in having found equilibrium is one able to become self-assured, only in having become self-assured is one able to be deliberate in what one does, and only in being deliberate in what one does is one able to get what one is after. There is the important and incidental in things and a beginning and an end in what we do. It is in realizing what should have priority that one gets near to the proper way. . . .
>
> From the emperor down to the common folk, everything is rooted in personal cultivation. There can be no healthy branches when the root is rotten, and it would never do for priorities to be reversed between what should be invested with importance and what should be treated more lightly.

The Great Learning asserts here that it is only by committing oneself to a regimen of personal cultivation that one can achieve the comprehensive intellectual and moral understanding that will ultimately change the world. It is in this singularly important respect that we must get our priorities right.

DEFINING OUR TERMS: "KNOWING GOD" AS THE OBSTACLE TO DIALOGUE

In the Daodejing's critique on Confucianism, we find statements such as "In studying, there is a daily increase, while in learning way-making, there is a daily decrease. 為學者日益，聞道者日損 (ch. 48)" and "Cut off sagacity and get rid of wisdom and the benefit to the common people will be a hundredfold. 絕聖棄知， 民利百倍 (ch. 19)." The Daodejing's point here is that there is a kind of "knowledge" that can be a real obstacle to acquiring wisdom.

While there has been some mutual accommodation between Chinese and Western philosophy among the small yet distinguished group of the Chinese New Confucianists, this same phenomenon has yet to take place within the Western academy. I want to argue that "God" can be used as a synecdoche for the kind of "knowledge" has been the obstacle to the wisdom that might emerge from a real dialogue between these traditions.

Indeed, we can play with an ambiguity between the Chinese and English terms that constitute the title of our panel—"dialogue," "philosophy," and "globalization"—to identify an old and persistent understanding of the business of philosophy anathema to the conversation between cultures that many of us would advocate. There is an equivocation that attends these key terms that, once resolved, might perhaps provide a way forward in a conversation in professional philosophy that has been a long time coming.

In the early days of the Western philosophical narrative, "dialogue" as a form of conversation comes to be understood rather explicitly as "talking through" an issue with the purpose of arriving at truth through the dialectical exchange of logical arguments. For Plato, dialectic is a rational, synoptic ascent in search of "unhypothetized principle (*eidos*)," while for Aristotle, dialectic entails an analytical descent in the process of taxonomic categorization. I would suggest that it is this understanding of "dialogue"—reason in pursuit of the *logos* or the *on* of things respectively—that has allowed philosophy as a professional discipline with its univocal method of "rational argument" and its impatience with any other putative approaches to acquiring knowledge, to become a monologue in its relationship to alternative philosophical traditions. Philosophy understood in such terms can speak, but it cannot listen. A dialogical understanding of philosophy that in its very definition assumes such a monopoly on knowledge might not be open to conversation.

The Chinese translation of "dialogue" as duihua 對話 suggests "conversation:" a "fitting responsiveness" between correspondents. Dui is "to be a counterpart (pei 配)," "to answer (da 答)" in the sense of "having listened to what deserves to be heard, to then reply (聽言則對)" (Book of Songs 詩 ch. 257). Duihua is further normative: it is to make a response that is "suitable and appropriate (dang 當)"—what ought to be said in reply. In such a conversation, there is the pursuit of mutual accord through listening and then speaking. Indeed, in English I would suggest that "conversation" is better term than "dialogue," since "converse" means "to associate with" and "exchange ideas" not held in common.

Another equivocation is resolvable if we think though the term "philosophy" or *philosophia*, that, when first used by Pythagoras, has a strong religious and ethical associations. While *sophia* for Plato is to be identified with true knowledge (*episteme*), it still is associated with *phonesis* or practical wisdom because for him knowledge has practical consequences: knowledge is virtue. For Aristotle on the other hand, who has jettisoned almost all of the religious and ethical import, *sophia* as the highest intellectual virtue that has as its object "being" or *on*, that is eternal, unchanging, and entirely separate from mutable things, is to be distinguished from *phronesis*. Practical wisdom has given way to demonstrable, theoretical truth. Although Aristotle is superseded by philosophers such as the Stoics who would reinstate the practical in *sophia*, the preeminence of a universal knowledge that is accessible though a pure, impersonal reason has become firmly entrenched.

Philo as a fraternal kind of love—being good "friends" with *sophia*—is challenged by Plato's "*eros-sophia*"—becoming a true, penetrating "lover" of *sophia*, while for Aristotle, *philo* has become the "science" of *sophia* (Meta 980a-983a). Religiously and morally inspired love of wisdom has surrendered to the inquiry of cold, univocal science in search of theoretical knowledge. A sanitized, rational understanding of philosophy that takes as its object scientific knowledge attained through logical argument rather than empirical methods, is again not open to conversation.

The translation of "philosophy" into Chinese as zhexue 哲學 harks back to the Pythagorean origins of the term, where zhe 哲 is defined in the Shuowen lexicon as "wisdom (zhi 知/智)" achieved through effective communication (kou 口 as "mouth" and yue 曰 as "to speak"), and xue 學 is the cultivation of one's character—a project that has both moral and a religious consequences. Zheren 哲人 like "sages (shengren聖人)" are deemed wise by virtue of their achieved virtuosic relationality that has made them the embodiment of the flourishing community—they are the thriving communities that they lead. In fact, we could play with the term "philosophy" as it applies to the Chinese tradition, arguing that it reinstates the religious and the moral to become closer to "the wisdom of loving" rather than "the love of wisdom."

"Globalization" like "dialogue" and "philosophy" can suggest two very different meanings. The dominant sense of globalization is that associated at the ideological level with the dissemination of a rational and moral consensus born of the European Enlightenment and, at the practical level, with rights-based democratic institutions, free enterprise capitalism, and rational technologies. In this sense, globalization is a synonym for monolithic modernization—which is itself thought to be synonymous with Westernization.

And globalization construed as a "one-size-fits-all" Westernization is, of course, a distinctly modern dynamic. As long as Western values monopolize the process of globalization, there will be a continuation of the expansionist, colonizing, missionizing impulses associated with the purveyance of liberal democracy, autonomous individuality, and rational technologies.

But there are important signs that this modernist form of globalization is transmogrifying. At least in principle, there is no reason to understand globalization as either European expansion or American sprawl. For beyond the provincial, decidedly Western, sense of globalization as homogenization, there is a competing meaning that recognizes the potential contributions of non-Western cultures. This second sense that we might tease out of quanqiuhua全球化 or "inclusive globalizing" might alternatively refer to the mutual accessibility of cultural sensibilities.

Inclusive globalizing as the mutual accessibility of cultural sensibilities is radically decentered. The shift in world attention away from Europe and toward Asia; the dynamics associated with the complex relations of the Islamic and Christian worlds; the steady, if lumbering, emergence of Africa—all of these trends have provided practical illustrations of the irrelevance of a single narrative to account for past, present, or future events.

The mutual accessibility of all cultures guaranteed in principle by this second sense of inclusive globalizing carries with it the implication that, in the absence of a general consensus, the plurality of cultures and traditions must inevitably lead to local and ad hoc modes of negotiation. In place of the quest for a rational and moral consensus, there will be an increasing need for negotiation among alternative habits and sensibilities. In its most productive sense, global philosophy neither recognizes nor condones claims to any single controlling perspective or master narrative. There can be no consensual model of discourse. Rather, we are urged by our global context to acknowledge a vast and rich variety of discourses. We are thus drawn to the significance of local phenomena.

The term "global," while suggesting comprehensiveness, may in fact accentuate the fundamentally local character of objects and events. The model for understanding this second sense of inclusive globalizing cannot be a consensual or universalist one that seeks common values or institutions across the globe. Rather, the model must be one that allows for the viability of local phenomena as focal in the sense that, while their objective presence may be altogether local, their influence is always potentially global in scope.

Under such conditions, there can be no avoidance of the primary facts of otherness and difference. The articulation of these differences leads inevitably away from universalist concerns and toward the articulation of productive intellectual contrasts. Differences heretofore were placed in the background of discussions, and family resemblances were held to be most crucial. Our post-cultural/multi-cultural age reverses the polarities—and difference now is thought to reign. In its most positive forms, difference is an emblem of tolerance, accommodation, and respect.

The interpretation of inclusive globalizing 全球化 as pan-accessibility and the foregrounding of the local or focal characteristics of forms of life supports a strategy that allows us to sidestep ideologies predicting a coming clash of civilizations. Such predictions are predicated upon understandings of globalization as involving either competing universalist claims, or the resistance of an insular culture against such claims. The conflict of "Western" and Islamic ideologies is an example of the former. The "China as Chinatown of the world" response to the threat of wholesale Westernization during the Maoist era exemplifies the latter. A stress upon local sites of cultural engagement promotes a retail rather than a wholesale approach to cultural politics.

In sum, cultural politics is proceeding along two divergent paths. The first is the most recognizable in terms of processes of modernization associated with the extension of rationalized politics, economics, and technologies—all wrapped in the rational and moral consensus of the Western Enlightenment. The second form of inclusive globalizing involves the recognition of the mutual accessibility of cultural forms and processes leading to ad hoc and local sites of negotiation aimed at the resolution of particular problems.

The obstacle to productive discussion among philosophical traditions is referenced in the title of this panel: a dialogical way of thinking about conversation as leading to some univocal truth, an exclusive, scientific way of thinking about philosophy as having the discovery of certain knowledge as its object and its occupation, and a colonizing, imperialistic way of thinking about the ineluctable forces of globalization.

While the charge of caricaturing the Western philosophical sensibility can be fairly leveled against this synoptic reading of its narrative, if we rehearse the present concrete situation in world philosophy, we have to allow that Anglo-European philosophy has a monopoly on the professional discipline. And that the only way that a conversation can take place is for professional philosophy to abandon its dialogical pretence. The good news is that there is a revolution within the post-Darwinian Western academy that in the fullness of time might create room for this philosophical conversation.

THE GOOD NEWS: THE INTERNAL CRITIQUE

How is the situation changing in the Western academy? Many of the more philosophically-inclined sinologists who have been involved in the translation of classical Chinese texts are beginning to acknowledge that a fuller inventory of semantic matrices might be necessary for the translation of these philosophical texts, and are struggling to get beyond the default, "commonsensical" vocabularies of their native cultural sensibility. As a matter of fact, the recent recovery of new versions of existing philosophical texts and the further discovery of many others that have been long lost, has occasioned the retranslation of many of the classics, and has provided both a pretext and an opportunity for philosophers to step up and rethink our standard renderings of the philosophical vocabulary. Most importantly, it has presented us with the challenge of trying, with imagination, to take these texts on their own terms by locating and interpreting them within their own worldview. And these Chinese texts understood on their own terms constitute a real alternative to God and the dialogical thinking that would discover Him.

But we do not need to invoke Chinese philosophy to problematize these persisting universalist assumptions within the Western tradition that are anathema to the Chinese corpus. Indeed the revolution currently taking place within the Western philosophical community itself provides an opening and an invitation to take Chinese philosophy more seriously. An internal critique continues to be waged within professional Western philosophy under the many banners of process philosophy, hermeneutics, post-modernism, neo-pragmatism, neo-Marxism, deconstructionism, feminist philosophy, and so on, that takes as a shared target what Robert Solomon has called "the transcendental pretense"—idealism, objectivism, logocentrism, essentialism, the master narrative, "the myth of the given" —the familiar reductionistic "isms" that have emerged as putatively novel choices as philosophers switch horses on the merry-go-round of systematic philosophy.

In place of a Cartesian philosophical language that privileges the function of clear and distinct ideas in our quest for an objective certainty, vocabularies of process, change, and indeed productive vagueness have increasingly come into vogue. These recent developments in Anglo-European philosophy itself have begun to foreground interpretative vocabularies more relevant to the articulation of Chinese culture.

Within the context of the Western philosophical narrative, the recent emergence of process philosophy that we associate with philosophers such as Alfred North Whitehead, Henri Bergson, and more recently, with the revival of the classical American pragmatism of Charles Saunders Peirce, William James, and John Dewey, is a sustained reappraisal of substance ontology and the dualistic world view that is entailed by it. Indeed, emerging both from within the Anglo-European philosophical ranks and as an indictment from without, process philosophy has declared itself a serious intervention in the Western philosophical narrative. It sees itself as new direction in philosophical thinking determined to inoculate our corpus of cultural self-understanding against what it takes to have been a long-term chronic illness.

In the wake of Darwin's own great cultural revolution,[5] Alfred North Whitehead accuses our most hallowed precursors of what he calls "the fallacy of misplaced concreteness," an error in reasoning that is committed when the formally abstracted is taken to be what is real and concrete.[6] Whitehead rehearses the history of this "fatal virus" that has inhibited our understanding of the intrinsic, constitutive, and productive nature of relatedness. He accuses Epicurus, Plato, and Aristotle as being "unaware of the perils of abstraction" that render knowledge closed and complete. According to Whitehead, "the history of thought" he associates with these great men

. . . is a tragic mixture of vibrant disclosure and of deadening closure. The sense of penetration is lost in the certainty of completed knowledge. This dogmatism is the antichrist of learning. In the full concrete connection of things, the characters of the things connected enter into the character of the connectivity which joins them.[7]

What Whitehead means here by "the sense of penetration" that is compromised by assumptions about certain knowledge is creativity itself: the creative advance made possible by productive relations. Stated more fully, what is at risk is the spontaneous emergence of novel significance in those increasingly meaningful relationships among things in a continuing present.

Whitehead uses "friendship" as a concrete example of a relationship that is constituted by the unique character of the two persons involved, where the continuity of a real meaningful friendship is a matter of vibrant disclosure in which two persons "appreciate" each other in the most "concrete" sense of this term. Importantly, the realization of this vital relationship is not at the expense of their personal uniqueness and integrity, but indeed a consequence of it. Integrity certainly refers to the persistent particularity of each friend, but it also means the "becoming one together" that is at once the substance of a real relationship and a source of novel cosmic significance. The cosmos grows more meaningful with the deepening of their special friendship. Indeed, not only are the two persons and their relationship equally real, but further, if there is anything that is less than concrete in describing this relationship, it is the abstracting of them from the relationship and treating them as though they are discrete individuals.

This understanding of relationality as intrinsic, constitutive, and productive is what Whitehead means by "aesthetic order." Any aesthetic achievement aspires to the fullest disclosure of the many particular details in the totality of the achieved effect—in the case of our two friends, the "connectivity" of the friendship itself. Whitehead criticizes the classical Greek aesthetic sensibility harshly for losing sight of the balance that must be sustained between the particular details and the achieved harmony.

> The enjoyment of Greek art is always haunted by a longing for the details to exhibit some rugged independence apart from the oppressive harmony. In the greatest examples of any form of art, a miraculous balance is achieved. The whole displays its component parts, each with its own value enhanced; and the parts lead up to a whole, which is beyond themselves, yet not destructive of themselves.[8]

When applied to the human experience, personal disclosure in our family and communal relationships is what makes the family and community meaningful, or said more dynamically, is what makes these personal relationships always situated cases of "meaning making." Indeed, we quite literally "make" our friends in our novel relationships, just as they in turn make us. Any understanding of harmony that emphasizes conformity at the expense of disclosing the unique lives of the particular participants in the evolving process precludes the possibility of the spontaneous emergence of novelty as a creative advance. Strict conformity is quite literally, life-threatening. As Whitehead observes,

> Our lives are passed in the experience of disclosure. As we lose this sense of disclosure, we are shedding that mode of functioning which is the soul. We are descending to mere conformity with the average of the past. Complete conformity means the loss of life. There remains the barren existence of inorganic nature.[9]

The point that Whitehead is making here is that productive harmony can only emerge out of the real, shared experience of unique, living persons. As such, harmony will always be collateral rather than unilateral, correlative rather than univocal, a case of disclosure rather than closure. Harmony is primarily concrete and local, and only then abstracted. What this means, in fact, is that the only kind of creativity is a situated co-creativity.

What Whitehead has called "the fallacy of misplaced concreteness" is really a denunciation of the conventional notion of "God"—the taking of the most abstract as what is real and concrete. This same target was in fact identified and criticized earlier by John Dewey who regarded an uncritical commitment to transcendentalism—Whitehead's abstract harmony—in any of its various forms to be one bit of faulty reasoning that has been so persistently exercised by the philosophical elite that he dubbed this particular deformation profesionelle "the philosophical fallacy." This fallacy has arisen because as a tradition we have become habituated in looking for knowledge in "some transcendent and supernal region." Indeed, it was this abstracting transcendentalism that motivated Dewey's critique of both idealism and realism. As Dewey describes this error:

> There are, indeed, but two alternative courses. We must either find the appropriate objects and organs of knowledge in the mutual interactions of changing things, or else, we must seek them in some transcendent and supernal region. The human mind, deliberately as it were, exhausted the logic of the changeless, the final and the transcendent, before it essayed adventure on the pathless wastes of generation and transformation.[10]

Of course Dewey here in equating the Western philosophical narrative with "the human mind," is making a generalization that overlooks and excludes the kind of process thinking that we will claim has been a signature of Chinese cosmology from ancient times, a cosmology that was never committed to "the logic of the changeless." But Dewey's important assertion is that at least for the Western narrative, "the most pervasive fallacy of philosophical thinking" has been the error of ignoring the historical, developmental, and contextualizing aspects of experience—the processual nature of experience itself. Instead of taking the unchanging "idea" of the oak tree and the "idea" of the chicken to be the true object of knowledge, wisdom should teach us that most acorns in fact become squirrels, and most eggs, omelets.

The methodological problem as Dewey saw it is "the abstracting of some one element from the organism which gives it meaning, and setting it up as absolute" and then proceeding to revere this one element "as the cause and ground of all reality and knowledge."[11] Simply put, the philosophical fallacy is committed whenever the outcome of a process is presumed to be antecedent to that process. Such a problem arises in most of the many variations on the "One-behind-the-many" systematic metaphysics. In any event, what Dewey long ago termed the philosophical fallacy has indeed become the philosophical issue of our day.

COMING TO THE CONVERSATION WITH A QUESTION

One comes to a conversation best with a question. Classical Chinese cosmology, like Whitehead and Dewey, subscribes to the mantra, "the only kind of creativity is situated co-creativity." And, in the wake of Whitehead and Dewey, a sustained reflection on the fact that there is no transcendentalism in the classical Chinese assumptions about cosmic order may pay us important philosophical dividends. The pervasive Chinese assumption about the always emergent nature of order might at this particular historical moment provide us with a salutary intervention in the Western philosophical narrative. That is, in this classical Chinese worldview there is an alternative nuanced and sophisticated processual way of thinking about cosmology that can join the ongoing internal critique of transcendentalism that is taking place within the still Eurocentric discipline of philosophy itself. Simply put, with the present surge of interest in Whitehead and particularly the American pragmatists, this newly emerging Western version of process philosophy as it matures within our own philosophical culture can, with profit, draw both substance and critique from a Chinese tradition that has been committed to various forms of process philosophy since the beginning of its recorded history.

A main problematic in a Cartesian dualistic worldview is one of closure articulated in the vocabulary of salvation, reconciliation, and the quest for certainty guaranteed by the attainment of objective truth. A main problematic in the correlative cosmology we associate with process philosophy in its many varieties, by contrast, is one of self-cultivation and disclosure.

The aspiration of such self-cultivation is a virtuosic sagacity, a productive harmony, and the continuing creative extension of an evolving cultural pattern of becoming consummately human (dao) that ultimately derived from the uniqueness of each person. There is a productive tension to be found in the synergy between a naturalistic determinism in which one is shaped by the world, and in one's own cultivated responsiveness through which one in turn shapes the world. Novelty emerges in the tension between the force of environing natural, social, and cultural conditions, and one's own creative contribution to one's context.

One of the most interesting ramifications of the increasing popularity of process language, from the perspective of our present project, is that the stimulation offered by the need to better understand Asian sensibilities, is in fact recursive. While process vocabularies are leading to increasingly productive interpretations of the classical Chinese world, these process interpretations of Chinese texts in turn provide us with new lenses through which to see our own Western sensibilities. Previously ignored or misconstrued elements within our own cultural self-understanding are beginning to receive new and decidedly more coherent interpretations.[12]

The happy conclusion that may be anticipated from these recent developments is that an era in which philosophy and philosophical thought have been considered essentially Western monopolies is drawing to a close. Further, while Western philosophy—primarily British and German philosophy—has constituted the mainstream curriculum for the discipline of world philosophy in the twentieth century, the revolution that is taking place within the Western academy itself presages a time when the process sensibilities pervasive in the long Chinese philosophical narrative will become increasingly relevant in finding our way forward.

NOTES

1 William James, The Varieties of Religious Experience. Cambridge, Mass: Harvard University Press, 1985, p. 11.

2 Marcel Granet, La pensee chinoise. Paris: Editions Albin Michel, 1934, p. 478.

3 See Tang Junyi, Complete Works Vol 11, Taipei: Xuesheng shuju, 1988, pp. 100-03, Xiong Shili, Mingxinpian 《明心篇》, Taibei: Xuesheng shuju, 1977, pp. 180-91; Zhang Dongsun, Zhishi yu wenhua: Zhang Dongsun wenhua lunzhu jiyao 《知識與文化：張東蓀文化論著輯要》. Edited by Zhang Yaonan 張耀南. Beijing: Zhongguo guangbo dianshi chubanshe, 1995, pp. 271-72; Angus C. Graham, Disputers of the Tao. Chicago: Open Court, 1989, p. 22; Joseph Needham, Science and Civilisation Vol. II, Cambridge: Cambridge University Press, 1956 p.290; Nathan Sivin, The Social Self in Zen and American Pragmatism. Albany: State University of New York Press, 1995, p.3; Chad Hansen, A Daoist Theory of Chinese Thought. Oxford: Oxford University Press, 1992, p.215; Norman J. Girardot, Myth and Mean-

ing in Early Taoism: The Theme of Chaos (Hun-tun). Berkeley: University of California Press, 1983, p.64.

4 Tang Junyi, *Complete Works* Vol 11, p. 8. This proposition is an expression of the *yinyang* 陰陽correlativity ubiquitous in Chinese cosmology that, in one of its most abstract iterations, entails the "continuity between reforming and functioning (*tiyong heyi*" 體用合一)."

5 Daniel Dennett, *Darwin's Dangerous Idea: Evolution and the Meanings of Life*. New York: Simon and Shuster, 1995, pp.21-2. This is categorical in his evaluation of the power of Darwin's idea, not only for the discipline of philosophy, but both constructively and deconstructively, for Western culture in its broadest possible terms:

> Let me lay my cards on the table. If I were to give an award for the single bet idea anyone has ever had, I'd give it to Darwin, ahead of Newton and Einstein and everyone else. In a single stroke, the idea of evolution by natural selection unifies the realm of life, meaning, and purpose with the realm of space and time, cause and effect, mechanism and physical law. But it is not just a wonderful scientific idea. It is a dangerous idea. . . There are many more magnificent ideas that are also jeopardized it seems, by Darwin's idea, and they, too, may need protection.

6 A. N. Whitehead, *Process and Reality: An Essay in Cosmology*. Donald Sherbourne corrected edition. New York: Free Press, 1979, p.10.

7 A. N. Whitehead, *Modes of Thought*. New York: Macmillan, 1938, p.58.

8 Ibid., p.62.

9 Ibid.

10 John Dewey, *The Essential Dewey*. Volume 1. Edited by Larry Hickman and Thomas Alexander. Bloomington, IN: Indiana University Press, 1998, p.41.

11 John Dewey, *Early Works, 1892-98.* 5 vols. Edited by Jo Ann Boydston. Carbondale, Ill.:Southern Illinois University, 1969-72, vol 1, p.162. For the history, the development, and the context of "*the* philosophical fallacy," see J. E. Tiles, *Dewey.* The Arguments of the Philosophers series. London: Routledge, 1988, pp.19-24.

12 For example, elements of mainstream American pragmatism heretofore understood by some in substantialist and analytic terms, are presently receiving important new interpretations by appeal to process vocabularies enlivened and articulated through classical Chinese texts. The recent work of Joe Grange, *Nature: An Environmental Cosmology*. Albany: State University of New York Press, 1997; *The City: An Urban Cosmology*. Albany: State University of New York Press, 1999; Steve Odin (1996), Robert Neville, *Creativity and God: A Challenge to Process Theology*. Albany: State University of New York Press, 1995; Tom Kasulis, *Intimacy or Integrity: Philosophy*

and Cultural Difference. Honolulu: University of Hawai'i Press, 1997; and Warren Frisina, *The Unity of Knowledge and Action: Toward a Nonrepresentational Theory of Knowledge*. Albany: State University of New York Press, 2000.

Chapter 3

The Conception of Divinity in Early Confucianism

Kelly James Clark

It has become commonplace among philosophers who specialize in Chinese philosophy to deny that Confucius was a theist. Hall and Ames, for example, deny that Confucius had any notion of transcendence at all: "Perhaps the most far-reaching of the uncommon assumptions underlying a coherent explication of the thinking of Confucius is that which precludes the existence of any transcendent being or principle. This is the presumption of radical immanence."[1] They endorse the widely held idea that Heaven (Tian) is a departure from Shangdi, the perhaps personal deity countenanced by previous generations, and that Tian evolved into a naturalistic/moral force by the time of Confucius. They contend that while Tian may have been religiously significant, there is no evidence that Tian was considered a personal deity.[2] I shall argue that the transcendent is operative and important for Confucius and that the concept of Tian is not naturalistic and contains more than a "residue" of anthropomorphism. The claim that "there is no written basis for determining whether or not ... *t'ien* was held to be a personal deity" is simply false given the abundance of ancient bronze inscriptions, oracle bones and texts.

THE PRE-CONFUCIAN GOD

Confucius identified himself and his thought with the earliest period of the ancient Zhou tradition (roughly 1050-250 BCE) and with portions of the Shang (roughly 1600-1050 BCE) which exemplified Heavenly justice and was led by just rulers: "The Master said: 'The Zhou gazes down upon the two dynasties that preceded it. How brilliant in culture it is. I follow the Zhou'" (*Analects* 3.14).[3] He conceived of his mission as one of passing on the Zhou model: "I transmit rather than innovate. I trust in and love the ancient ways" (*Analects* 7.1). On another occasion he laments that he is losing his dream of the ideal society: "How seriously I have declined! It has been so long since I last dreamt of meeting the Duke of Zhou" (*Analects* 7.5). What did Confucius admire as he gazed upon the Shang and the Zhou?

During the Shang and Zhou dynasties, Chinese theology countenanced among a plethora of lesser deities, a high God who exercised providence. The Shang affirmed a high God (帝 Di or 上帝 Shangdi) who reigned supreme over a host of lesser Powers and spiritual beings, including ancestors. The hierarchy of these spiritual beings is modeled in accordance with a secular political bureaucracy. The name or title of the Being at the top of this hierarchy was *Di* or *Shangdi*.[4] The adjective Shang (highest, above or supreme) indicates that Di is the Celestial Supreme Ruler. In accordance with the oracle bone records, Di is a being from above who can "'send down' (降

jiang) disasters and approval on men below" (Keightley 1999: 252). In addition, Di directly orders (令 *ling*) rain, thunder, wind and the lesser deities. According to Keightley, the word "orders" here shows that heavenly Di parallels the supreme authority of the earthly King, since in earthly matters only the king could issue such orders. The nature of Shangdi's punishments and rewards indicates that Shangdi's will and authority are moral. It is precisely this conception of divinity that was used by the early Zhou kings to justify their actions to topple the Shang dynasty.

The Zhou dynasty, which arose through the conquest of the decadent and unjust Shang, more typically uses the term Tian (天 heaven) in reference to the divine. Most historians have given up the widely held belief that Tian is a departure from the anthropomorphic deity, Shangdi and Di.[5] The fashionable claim that Tian is an impersonal, natural force is no longer tenable. In the *Shangshu*, portions of which are authenticated ancient governmental documents datable to the early Zhou period, references to Shangdi and Di repeatedly appear, often in the same context as Tian and, moreover, Tian is often a synonym for Shangdi and Di.[6] The *Shangshu* treats Tian as a transcendent, anthropomorphic, providential deity who cares about human welfare as did Shangdi. In "The Great Announcement (*Da Gao*)" we find the earliest reference to the foundational Zhou doctrine of the mandate of heaven (天命 *Tian ming*) (Shaughnessy 1999: 314). By divine reappointment, divine favor was transferred from the Shang to the virtuous and wise founders of the Zhou-- Kings Wen and Wu. The mandate of heaven provided a legitimation of the overthrow of the Shang and the moral establishment of the Zhou. In this seminal document, the mandate of heaven is also the charge of God (*Di*). Tianming is Shangdi ming.[7] There is no contrast between Tian and Shangdi here. Even if the term Di were nowhere to be found in this document, Tian functions in precisely the personal and providential way of Di. The words 'Shangdi' and 'Tian' both connote the supreme political ruler of the universe, to whom subordinate earthly kings owe reverence and obedience. Tianming indicates a sacred relationship between Heaven and his people; the earthly kings, as Heaven's emissaries, exercise their benevolent rule on the people who are Heaven's own possession or direct subjects. The concept of deity then, both in the Shang and Zhou dynasties, is of a personal and political God. Heaven is the moral foundation of human society and Heaven's mandate backed by Heaven's providence ensures that it will find its place on earth.

Confucius aligned himself with the golden ancient traditions of the Shang and Zhou in which peace and harmony permeated the land. And he emulated the majestic rulers—the Kings Wen and Wu and the Duke of Zhou—who served as moral paradigms of wisdom, virtue and benevolence.[8] For Confucius the ideal was real: the heavenly principle was perfectly exemplified in these wise and benevolent dynastic rulers and in the just and harmonious societies that they created and administered.[9] The Zhou affirmed a transcendent, non-human source of morality—Tian or Shangdi—to which humans individually and corporately are subject.[10] Although there is a creative element of individual style in Confucius' thought; it is always within carefully circumscribed boundaries fixed not by human desire or preference, but by the mandate of heaven.

THE TRANSCENDENT IN CONFUCIUS

Given the Zhou background and Confucius' self-confession as a transmitter, we have prima facie reason to believe that Confucius, in the fourteen or so times he uses the term "Tian" in a non-idiomatic fashion, aligns his beliefs with those of the Zhou—holding that Tian is an anthropomorphic Heavenly Supreme Emperor and an independent, authoritative moral source.

One of the most famous passages in the *Analects* unites Confucius' moral journey with the decrees of Heaven (*Tianming*): "At fifteen, I set my mind upon learning; at thirty, I took my place in society; at forty, I became free of doubts; at fifty, I understood Heaven's Mandate; at sixty, my ear was attuned; and at seventy, I could follow my heart's desires without overstepping the bounds of propriety" (*Analects* 2.4). Although he did not understand the decrees of Heaven until age fifty, learning, the foundation of moral development, is aimed at, among other things, understanding and according with the decrees of Heaven. The next step involves one's heart's desires being in accord with what is right, that is with the decrees of heaven. One's outer actions are matched by one's inner spirit of reverence, sympathy and respect. Or, better, one is inwardly moved spontaneously to act in accord with the decrees of Heaven.[11]

Confucius attributed his own virtue to Heaven: "The Master said: 'It is Heaven itself that has endowed me with virtue. What have I to fear from the likes of Huan Tui?'" (*Analects* 7.23). Huan Tui, a minister in the state of Song, had attempted to take Confucius' life but Confucius claims he has nothing to fear with Heaven on his side. This passage makes little sense if Tian is interpreted as an extension of the human community (as do Hall and Ames) or a natural force: his appeal to Tian is a confession of his dependence on divine assistance for his moral improvement and to persevere through life's tribulations. Confucius accepted his virtue and the inner strength it gave him as a gift; he has the inner moral strength to overcome the world through Heaven's special activity.

Yet Confucius thought it possible to incur Heaven's disapproval. Consider his comment to Zilu after a meeting with Nanzi, a woman with a bad reputation: "The Master had an audience with Nanzi, and Zilu was not pleased. The Master swore an oath, saying, 'If I have done anything wrong, may Heaven punish me! May Heaven punish me!'" (*Analects* 6.28). This passage is consonant with Confucius' general view that Heaven exercises a kind of moral providence: "The Master was surrounded in Kuang. He said, 'Now that King Wen is gone, is not culture now invested here in me? If Heaven intended this culture to perish, it would not have given it to those of us who live after King Wen's death. Since Heaven did not intend that this culture should perish, what can the people of Kuang do to me?'" (*Analects* 9.5). Here we find Confucius' confidence in the Mandate of Heaven. And Heaven is portrayed as widely knowing, even of our inner thoughts and motives (humans cannot deceive Heaven [*Analects* 9.12]).

Finally, Confucius endorses the cosmogonic grounding of goodness in Heaven: "The Master said: 'How great was Yao as a ruler! So majestic! It is Heaven that is great, and it was Yao who modeled himself upon it. So vast! Among the common people there were none who were able to find words to describe him. How majestic in his accomplishments, and glorious in cultural splendor!'" (*Analects* 8.19). Although the great Yao is a human moral model, his goodness is derivative; ultimately only Heaven is great. The ultimate moral source is heaven alone, through the modeling of which one may accomplish great things.[12] It is difficult to avoid the conclusion that Tian is god-like in a way that invites comparison to the Western sense.

In spite of the abundant evidence for the anthropomorphic and divine status of Tian, some modern scholars continue to deny that Confucius was a theist. Van Norden writes: "Most of the questions we might raise about Tian or other aspects of Confucius' cosmology have no answers, because, based on the *Analects*, there is no evidence that Confucius had *detailed* theoretical views about cosmology" (Van Norden: 22). But not having *detailed* theoretical views about cosmology is not tantamount to having no cosmological views at all. Confucius does express, apparently clearly, that Heaven is anthropomorphic, distinct from human beings, the moral model of people, providential, etc. And Louden, who argues that Tian is clearly not naturalistic, nonetheless contends that "Confucius…is thus religious but not theistic" (Louden: 79). His evidence, in an otherwise carefully argued essay, is tucked away in a footnote:

> It is true that in several of the passages cited above Tian is said to have intentions (9:5, perhaps 3:24); and in others to possess understanding (14:35. 9:12). These uses of language seem to me to be metaphorical. However, even if one thinks they are not, they do not add up to anything close to the 'God-as-personal-being' that most mainstream believers within the major Western traditions regard as being essential to their faith (Louden: 91).

But on what grounds are these uses of language judged to be metaphorical? Louden doesn't say. There are no internal clues in the *Analects* for making this judgment. And the external clues suggest that they are not metaphorical. The question Louden raised is "Are the reference to Tian in the *Analects* theistic, that is, personal?" If we take the references mentioned previously as non-metaphorical--and I see no reason not to--and as in line with the tradition to which Confucius adheres, we ought to see Tian in the *Analects* as personal; that is, Tian has the attributes of persons (will, intentions, beliefs) and Tian is morally good, caring, etc. The properties ascribed to Tian are surely fewer than those ascribed to the high gods of the Western tradition, but they are not in conflict with them; indeed these properties, and several others that Confucius holds, are proper subsets of the essential properties ascribed to Western deities.

The *locus classicus* for denying that Confucius is not a theist concerns a remark of his disciple Zigong. "Zigong said: 'The Master's cultural brilliance is something that is readily heard about, whereas one does not get to hear the Master expounding upon the subjects of human nature or the Way of Heaven'" (*Analects* 5.13).[13] It is clear that on *certain* occasions to *some* people, Confucius did not speak of Heaven, spirits, etc.[14] He does not, of course, deny the existence of Heaven in these passages, so an argument that Confucius is not a theist based on these passages would be an argument from silence. And it would be a poor argument indeed given that he does speak substantively of heaven in many other passages. What are we to make of Confucius' not speaking of Heaven to Zigong? Are we to take this as evidence of Confucius' agnosticism about heaven? First, it should be noted that the passage also says that Confucius did not speak to Zigong about human nature. But Confucius spoke often, sometimes directly but mostly indirectly, about human nature. Granted Confucius does not have detailed theoretical views about human nature, it is nonetheless clear that he has some.[15] And few scholars contend that he is agnostic about human nature. So Confucius' remark to Zigong should not be taken to imply agnosticism about Heaven any more than it should be taken to imply agnosticism about human nature. Second, perhaps the audience is Zigong alone, not everyone as the anti-theists interpret the passage. That is, perhaps the Master did not express his detailed theoretical views about Heaven and human nature to Zigong (and so was a source of frustration to Zigong).

Why might the Master not speak of Heaven and human nature to Zigong (and perhaps to others)? I suggest that Zigong and many others in Confucius' audience were not morally or spiritually ready for the higher sort of knowledge of which Heaven and human nature consisted.[16] In the passage immediately preceding Zigong's statement, we read: "Zigong said: 'What I do not wish others to do unto me, I also wish not to do unto others.' The Master said, 'Ah, Zigong! That is something quite beyond you'" (*Analects* 5.12). Given the centrality of reciprocity to Confucius' moral system (*Analects* 4.15), Zigong must be viewed as morally deficient or even defective. Sympathetic understanding is a point Zigong has not yet reached, so he is not ready to hear about heaven and human nature; Zigong may have been a clever bureaucrat (6.8) but he lacked the sympathetic understanding so essential to the Confucian moral life.[17]

In several passages of the *Analects*, it is clear that discussion of higher matters requires the prior attainment of moral and spiritual sensitivities and understanding. "The Master said: 'You can discuss the loftiest matters with those who are above average, but not with those who are below average'" (*Analects* 6.21). Since Zigong is not yet better than average, it is not surprising that Confucius would refuse to discuss superior matters with him. In another passage we read: "The Master said: 'I will not open the door for a mind that is not already striving to understand, nor will I provide words to a tongue that is not already struggling to speak. If I hold up one corner of a problem, and the student cannot come back to me with the other three, I will not attempt to instruct him again.'" (*Analects* 7.8). For Confucius, knowledge was not distributed willy-nilly to whomever asked but was dispensed slowly depending on the receptive conditions of the listener: to those who can already supply the other three corners.

Zigong is consistently portrayed as someone not yet ready to learn of the higher things. Of those who are not ready to learn the higher things, Confucius says that he can at best control their behavior, not affect their beliefs: "The common people can be made to follow the Way, but they cannot be made to understand it" (*Analects* 8.9).[18] In not speaking thusly to Zigong, Confucius was following his own advice not to waste words on people of little understanding: "If someone is open to what you have to say, but you do not speak to them, this is letting the person go to waste; if, however, someone is not open to what you have to say, but you speak to them anyway, this is letting our words go to waste. The wise person does not let people go to waste, but he does not waste his words" (*Analects* 15.8). So reticent was Confucius to speak that a legend seems to have arisen that he never spoke about anything at all (*Analects* 14.13)!

It should be noted that the Master's not speaking of something to someone should not be taken as evidence against belief in that thing. For example, although it says, "The Master did not speak of prodigies, force, disorders, or spirits," it does not follow that the Master does not believe in spirits. The interpretive issue here is complicated by two facts (a) first, the Master did speak about spirits (although not a lot and not to everyone) and (b) the Master was self-consciously identified with a tradition that did affirm the existence of spirits. With respect to (a), consider a passage in which Confucius does speak of spirits. Confucius said "Working to ensure social harmony among the common people, respecting the ghosts and spirits while keeping them at a distance—this might be called wisdom" (*Analects* 6.22). With respect to (b), although "keeps them at a distance" is sometimes interpreted to mean that Confucius keeps the idea of spirits at an intellectual distance (on the border of unbelief), a more plausible interpretation, following Dawson, suggests that Confucius believed in spirits and that proper sacrifice to them would keep them from adversely meddling in human affairs (Dawson: 90).[19] This, again, would be a natural expression of Confucius' Zhou commitments.[20] Moreover, it should be noted that the *Analects* several times report the claim that Confucius seldom or never spoke of things he did in fact speak about, sometimes a great deal. For example, in 9.1 we read: "The Master seldom spoke of profit and fate and humaneness" (Dawson: 31).[21] But the Master denigrated profit, bemoaned fate and spoke of humaneness more than any single topic.[22] All of this supports the claim that Confucius did not speak of heaven to Zigong simpliciter on this occasion, probably for moral reasons.[23] But it does not follow that Confucius did not speak of heaven because of his own skepticism or agnosticism about the spirits, any more than his seldom speaking of humaneness entails his agnosticism about humaneness. Finally, the passages mentioned in this paragraph claim that the Master does not speak about ghosts and spirits (鬼神 *guishen*), not Heaven. So even if the Master did not speak of spirits and ghosts (probably in reference to spiritualized ancestors) and is thereby agnostic about them, he surely did speak on many occasions of Heaven.

The Master's not speaking may provide an interpretive clue to much of Confucius' thought. In *Analects* 17.19, we read that Confucius aspired to not speaking, like Heaven.:

The Master sighed: "Would that I did not have to speak!"

Zigong said, "If the Master did not speak, then how would we little ones receive guidance from you?"

The Master replied, "What does Heaven ever say? Yet the four seasons are put in motion by it, and the myriad creatures receive their life from it. What does ever Heaven say?"

Heaven does not speak, but through Heaven the entire cosmos is created and ordered.[24] Heaven is silent, but is the moral order of the universe. The way of Heaven may be discovered not by listening to a revelation but only by looking. One can see the heavenly order and the way of heaven: heaven which does not speak but which orders the world. We can learn of Heaven's principle by seeing not by hearing. By studying all under Heaven, we can discern Heaven's ways; and Confucius sought to model himself on silent Heaven.[25]

The Wittgensteinian distinction between saying and showing may be useful here. The early Wittgenstein believed that only factual sentences say anything about the world; if something cannot be captured in factual language, it is without sense. Ironically, in order to communicate this theory of language and logic, Wittgenstein had to rely on non-factual language, that is language which according to his own theory is without sense. He conceded this performance failure at the end of the *Tractatus* but contended that the language of the *Tractatus*, like the language of logic, while not sensibly *saying* anything can *show* us something about the world.[26] This distinction between saying and showing would, if successful, permit Wittgenstein to show us something about the world that transcends the limits of language (see Wittgenstein 4.113-4.1212). Although the *Tractatus* enshrines factual language, Wittgenstein told Ludwig von Flicker that the book's point is an ethical one (although moral values cannot be expressed in factual language). According to Wittgenstein, the most important things—ethics, the meaning of life, God—lie beyond the limits of human language (see Wittgenstein 6.41-6.522). Wittgenstein does not deny that values or God exist, he simply denies that humans can say anything about them; but, like logic, they can show something about them. He concludes his comments on ethics, God, and the significance of the universe with the following: "There are, indeed, things that cannot be put into words. They *make themselves manifest*. They are what is mystical" (Wittgenstein 6.522). This mystical interpretation of the *Tractatus* foils the pretensions of the positivist who sought to co-opt Wittgenstein's "argument," and also makes sense of Wittgenstein's declared intentions and corpus which includes showings about religion and ethics. Showing rather than saying, I suggest, is not unlike Confucius' strategy. The terse language, the reluctance to speak about some topics at length, the aspiration to silence and the continual offering of models (both good and bad) indicate that Confucius wished not to say but to show us something about the self and its place in society and the cosmos. Those who would demand that Confucius say more about certain topics before they would affirm that he believed them fail to recognize how much Confucius is showing and how little he is saying (about virtually everything). Heaven does not speak but makes itself manifest.

POST-CONFUCIAN SOURCES

Hall and Ames, however, reject this interpretation of the *Analects*. They claim:

> The portrait of *t'ien* that emerges from an analysis of relevant passages in the *Analects* is one that clearly has some anthropomorphic characteristics. But it does not follow that, because of this, *t'ien* is equitable with the Western conception of the deity. On the contrary, any comparison that this similarity might encourage is blunted when measured against their profound differences. These differences center first on the contrast between the transcendence of the Western deity and *t'ien* as unqualifiedly immanent. A further important consideration in this disparity is the fact that the Confucian conception of 'person,' entailed by the seemingly shared characterization as 'anthropomorphic,' is in fact significantly different" (Hall and Ames: 206).

Hall and Ames' questionable methodological strategy in their immanental reading is to view Confucius through the lens of Dong Shongshu.[27] Dong's much later syncretic philosophy (300 years after Confucius) is a metaphysically charged synthesis of Confucianism, *I Ching* ying-yang cosmology, and portions of the naturalistic Taoism. But Hall and Ames use Dong unapologetically:

> Let us face a probable methodological criticism head-on. As an example, some sinologist is sure to ask how we can use a concept as it is defined by the text of Tung Chung-shu's *Ch'un-ch'iu fan-lu* to elucidate its usage in the *Analects*. It would be equally irresponsible to say that the Confucian Tung Chung-shu (ca. 179-104 B.C.) is irrelevant as a resource for understanding classical Confucian vocabulary as it would be to accept his definition of these concepts uncritically. The problem, then, is to try to discover in Tung Chung-shu's presentation and elaboration of Confucian vocabulary

that which is consistent with the *Analects* and that which deviates from it. This problem echoes a similar concern to distinguish a "process" reading of Confucius from a reading of Confucius where a process vocabulary is merely the most appropriate resource available to us to make Confucius clear to a Western reader. We are not presenting a Han dynasty interpretation of Confucius, but rather, are attempting to use Tung chung-shu's commentary critically where it sheds light on the idea being expressed in our record of Confucius (Hall and Ames: 42-43).

They concede: "There is in this approach certainly a playfulness, but it also acknowledges the profoundly organic nature of the Chinese language" (Hall and Ames: 43). "A certain playfulness" indeed, but how does that help us explicate Confucius' understanding of Tian?

Let me suggest a more plausible strategy for using post-Confucius sources to help us understand Confucius on transcendence (although the primary interpretive clue will always be the culture with which he aligned himself and that culture affirmed an anthropomorphic deity). Hall and Ames and many others contend that Tian became increasingly naturalistic after the golden age of the Zhou and that it is this, more naturalistic, view of Tian that Confucius embraced. However, there is ample evidence, for example, in post-Confucius portions of the *Shangshu* that the notion of Tian as a personal deity persisted until and even after the time of Confucius; these post-Confucius texts surely provide, because of their temporal proximity to the time of Confucius and their self-conscious attempts to faithfully replicate Confucian doctrines, better markers of Confucius' views than the thought of the much later and revisionary Dong.[28] Many post-Confucius portions of the *Shangshu* treat Shangdi and Tian as synonymous and understand Tian anthropomorphically (and there are none that don't). For example, in "The Successful Completion of War," the "will of God" and "the determinate counsel of Heaven" are identical; in addition, human beings are spoken of as "the creatures of Heaven" (Legge 1935: Part V.Bk.III.P.6-7, 312-313). In "The Charge to the Viscount of Wei" "Great Heaven" and "God" are used interchangeably to refer to the source of divine favor (the divine mandate), and concern for God's people (Legge 1935: Part V.Bk.VIII.P.2-3, 378-379). Heaven and God are used interchangeably throughout "Prince Shih," and Heaven is portrayed as loyal only to the wise and virtuous, not to a dynasty; Tang is commended for "making his virtue like that of great Heaven" (Legge 1935: Part V.Bk.XVI.P.1-7, 474-477). Etc., etc. On these matters, we have to make our best judgment about which sources best inform or represent the views of Confucius. I suggest that the post-Confucius portions of the *Shangshu* are clearly more faithful to Confucius' understanding of Tian than the consideably later syncretic philosophy of Dong.[29]

The *Zuozhuan*, from the Warring States period (481-221 B.C.), also supports a personal and transcendent understanding of Tian.[30] The *Zuozhuan*, considered a Confucian classic and part of the canon, was often attached to the *Analects* as a key to understanding it. In it, the author (often alleged to be Confucius) ascribes love, concern and creator of the people to Tian: "Heaven gave birth to the people and set up rulers to superintend and shepherd them and see to it that they do not lose their nature as human beings....Heaven's love for the people is very great. Would it then allow one man to preside over them in an arrogant and willful manner, indulging his excesses and casting aside the nature Heaven and Earth allotted to them? Surely it would not" (de Bary and Bloom: 184-185). The transcendent, anthropomorphic and personal nature of Tian is unquestioned here.

Another piece of post-Confucius evidence, among many more, that bears discussion is the *Doctrine of the Mean* 16. The *Doctrine of the Mean*, often attributed to Confucius' grandson, seeks to ground Confucius' views on human nature and human virtue (all under Heaven) within a deeply metaphysical view of reality (Heaven and Heaven's Dao). DM 16, as translated by Hall and Ames, is as follows:

> The Master said, "The efficacy (德 *de*) of the gods and spirits is profound. Looking, we do not see them; listening, we do not hear them. And yet they inform events (物 *wu*) to the extent that nothing can be without them. Because of them, the people of the world fast, purify themselves, and put on their finest clothes in carrying out the sacrifices to them. It is as though the air above our heads is suffused with them, and as though they are all around." The *Book of Songs* says:
>> The descent of the gods
>> cannot be fathomed—
>> How much less can it be ignored.
> Such is the way that the inchoate becomes manifest and creativity is irrepressible. (96)

This passage clearly countenances belief in gods and affirms their power over All Under Heaven: the gods cannot be ignored.[31] Yet Hall and Ames, determined not to countenance any serious reference to the supernatural in ancient China, reject the authenticity of this passage: they argue that 16 would interrupt an argument that moves from 15 to 17 and that 16's "overt appeal to the efficacy of gods and spirits without reference to the moral responsibility of the human community would not sit well with Confucius as portrayed in the *Analects*" (144). But, as we have seen, this sort of reference to the gods and spirits is part and parcel of the worldview that informs the *Analects*. Hall and Ames cannot use the *Analects* as evidence against the authenticity of *DM* 16 without thereby arguing in a circle. One begins to think that non-theistic readings of Confucius are based more on ideology than on the textual evidence. *DM* 19, which identifies Heaven with Shangdi, claims that the efficacy of ritual propriety and etiquette (*li*), by which one taps into the power of the Supreme Efficacy in Heaven, is the vital power that rulers need to subdue their empire: "They used the Winter and Summer festival to make offerings to the Lord-on-High (Shangdi), and used the rituals on the ancestral temple to make offerings to the ancestors. He who could completely disclose the meaning of the Winter and Summer sacrifices, and the great Imperial sacrifice, could govern the country as easily as if he were pointing to the palm of his hand." In short, the post-Confucian texts temporally and cognitively closest to Confucius support a theistic interpretation of Confucius' thought.

CONCLUSION

Perhaps the historically most influential reason for reconsidering the theistic roots of ancient China has been the quest by missionaries to find common ground between their Christian beliefs and the apparently non-theistic Chinese. Matteo Ricci's (1552-1610) *The True Meaning of the Lord of Heaven* was the first in a great line of comparisons between Tian and Yahweh. Early missionaries to China, primarily Jesuits, sought some intellectual and spiritual common ground on which to appeal to the Chinese people (see Mungello and Gernet). Jesuit views on the relationship between Christianity and ancient Chinese religion fell along a broad continuum: some rejected any similarities at all while others believed that every Christian doctrine was contained, sometimes in a hidden form, in the ancient Chinese writings (see Gernet: 26). Ricci fell somewhere in the middle believing that the ancient writings countenanced, at least inchoately, a single, supreme Creator, a soul/body distinction, and an afterlife. Ricci's primary support for Shangdi as creator did not come from the Confucian books, but rather from inferences based on Aristotle's four causes. Although the Confucian *Classics* do not mention heaven or hell, Ricci claimed that these teachings were lost in the Burning of the Books in 213 BC! In the 19th Century the great Sinologist Legge would use similar methods for similar purposes (see Legge 1865 and 1880).

Gernet, rejecting the missionary strategy, would deny that the ancient Chinese were theists at all: "The classical formulae, 'respect' and 'fear Heaven', really meant something quite different from the sense given them by Ricci and by many other missionaries after him who were led on by the mirage of a 'natural religion' or the idea of an ancient transmission of the message of the Bible to the Chinese. These formulae did not refer to a single, all-powerful God, the creator of heaven and earth, but instead evoked the ideas of submission to destiny, a religious respect for rituals, and serious and sincere conduct" (Gernet: 193). Gernet accuses the missionaries of importing Greek concepts onto foreign conceptual soil. While this may be true of the Platonic soul/body distinction, it is not true of the spiritual/earthly realms. The oracle bones and the *Shangshu* clearly maintain belief in spirits and deities that are non-material. Contra Gernet and the widely held conviction that heaven and humanity are one, the spiritual realm is occasionally in conflict with, not one with, the earthly realm.[32] Gernet and many other sinologists have an unfortunate tendency to refer to "the Chinese" as though there were a single Chinese mind on these matters. He says that "the Chinese" held a Daoist, non-transcendent, yin-yang cosmology as developed in the *Yijing* (Gernet: 204). But "the Chinese" is as much a myth of Gernet's own making as some of the Jesuit myths about the similarities between Confucianism and Christianity. Simply put, Chinese thinkers are as diverse as their Western counterparts; indeed Confucius' philosophy was just one among countless many (in the so-called Era of One Hundred Schools). It is one such prominent school that finds clear expression in the *Shangshu,* the oracle bones, pottery shards and the *Odes* and, I have argued, in the *Analects,* includes belief in a transcendent, personal deity.

NOTES

1 While denying the existence of a transcendent being or principle, they nonetheless concede that Tian is treated anthropomorphically in the *Analects*: "In the *Analects, t'ien* is unquestionably anthropomorphic. There is, however, a gradual yet clearly discernible depersonalization of *t'ien* from its identification with the anthropomorphic deity, *shang-ti,* in the early Chou to its delineation as natural regularity and order in several philosophers of the late Chou. Although an important contribution of Confucius was his emphasis on man's responsibility for himself and for his circumstances, there is no doubt that his conception of *t'ien* retains a residue of anthropomorphism evident in *t'ien's* capacity for conscious intervention in human affairs" (Hall and Ames: 205-206).

2 They write: "*T'ien* seems to have had some religious significance for the Chou people who conquered the Shang at the end of the second millennium B.C. Given that the Chou was a federation of militant, semi-nomadic border tribes prior to their conquest of the Shang, there is no written basis for determining whether or not, or to what extent, *t'ien* was held to be a personal deity. The fact that *t'ien* also means "sky" might suggest that in this pre-historic period it was seen as a non-personal, unifying force of considerable dimensions at some distance from the human world.

"A further reason to believe that *t'ien* was perceived as a non-personal force is the fact that somewhere in this period the notion developed that the sum of existence is a unity of *t'ien,* earth, and human being, each force having its peculiar characteristics, and each existing correlative to the other two. It is important to recognize that there is no final beginning or end in this process; rather, it has the identifiable rhythm, immanent order and cadence of a cycle" (Hall and Ames: 202-203).

3 All *Analects* quotations are from Slingerland 2003 unless otherwise noted.

4 There have been several attempts to translate this title adequately into English. For example, Japanese sinologists Michio and Kenichi argue that since the primitive Chinese characters were a sort of hieroglyph, Di might resemble a corporate group of spirits, for the oracle bone graph of Di might refer to the character Di ('tightly tied').

5 See, for example, Schwartz: ch. 2; Ching: 116-118; and Puett: 38-79.

6 The *Shujing,* traditionally conceived, is a collection of official documents from three ancient Chinese dynasties: Xia, Shang, and Zhou. Many scholars from antiquity to the present, however, have been highly critical of the authenticity of the documents. Although the traditional Chinese belief is that all of the Zhou documents in the *Shujing* are genuine and reliable, most contemporary scholars disagree; Edward Shaughnessy argues that: "Among the chapters of the *Shangshu* generally regarded as dating to the Western Zhou, I believe that the following can be used with considerable confidence: the five *gao* (Pronouncement) chapters (that is, "Da Gao," "Kang Gao," "Jiu Gao," "Shao Gao," and "Luo Gao"), two of which ("Da Gao" and "Jiu Gao") probably records the speeches of King Wu's son and successor, King Cheng (r. 1042/35-1006 B.C.), two speeches of Zhou Gong...and one...a speech by Shao Gong Shi, Zhou Gong's half brother..." (Shaughnessy 1999: 294). Virtually all contemporary scholars believe that the alleged Xia and Shang documents are forgeries from the Han or Jin dynasties. The original texts are presumed lost (perhaps due to the burning of books by the Emperor Qin). We don't dispute that others of the *Shangshu* may be authentic. See also Shaughnessy 1993 and Nylan.

7 Yan Shigu, a commentator from the Tang dynasty, affirmed the notion *Shangdi ming* is equivalent to *Tianming* (see Bodde: 309).

8 There is widespread disagreement about the *ippsissima verba* of Confucius. Traditionally scholars held that every word of *The Analects* derived from the mouth of Confucius (although written down later by his disciples). This view is scarcely held by contemporary scholars. Taeko and Taeko, at the other extreme, contend that very little of *The Analects* comes from Confucius. Although their views have been disputed (see Slingerland 2000), it seems clear that Confucius is only distantly related to various parts of the *Analects.* Nonetheless, I shall prescind from this debate and consider the "canonical" Confucius as found in the entire *Analects.*

9 Chinese tradition found the repository of wisdom in the pre-Confucian books (the *History,* the *Poetry,* the *Spring and Autumn Annals,* the *Rites* and the *I Ching*) so thorough and authoritative that the 'Confucian' books (the *Analects,* the *Mencius,* the *Doctrine of the Mean* and the *Great Learning*) were not added to the canon until the time of the Song Neoconfucians.

10 I summarize here the argument of Clark forthcoming.

11 The kind of sustained effort and concentration that Confucian moral education takes suggests that the natural tendency of humans runs counter to the attainment of the highest moral states. Confucius seems to indicate that the natural tendency of human beings is not toward virtue (he says, for example, that he has never met a sage or a good man [*Analects* 7.26]). Confucius is a rigorist about the intense concentration in study and relentless ritual practices that move us in the direction of sageliness. Unfortunately Confucianism would come to be associated with empty ritual which pays little heed to the humaneness, sympathy and respect that, for Confucius, ritual action seeks

both to engender and embody. Given the difficulty of inner transformation it is not surprising that people in power would encourage legalism.

12 Eno concurs: "As a prescriptive force, T'ien plays two major roles in the *Analects*. First, it provides a ground for the Ruist notion of transcendent wisdom, and legitimizes the Ruist claim that traditional ritual forms provide the path to attaining it. Second, it legitimizes Ruist political idealism and the rejection of practical politics" (Eno: 82).

13 For a discussion of the history of interpretations of this enigmatic passage, see Ivanhoe.

14 Consider Zhu Xi on Confucius' selective distribution of information to his disciples: "What Zengzi heard from the Master was not necessarily heard together with Yanzi. What Yanzi heard from the Master was not necessarily heard together with Zigong. Now, however, what each of them heard is combined in the book, the *Analects*. Are not students of later times fortunate?" (as quoted in Makeham: 187).

15 Confucius' views on cosmological matters and human nature may needs be inferred from views he clearly states. On this I am in agreement with Hall and Ames: "Confucius' reticence about speculating on what he perceived to be problems beyond the purview of immediate concerns should not be interpreted to mean that his efforts to organize human experience with consistency and coherence are free of cosmological presuppositions. Although Confucius did not discuss speculative questions, there are tacit intuitions that underlie and serve as ground for his articulated philosophy. We may safely assume that the implicit cosmological vision of Confucius was equally tacit among his chief disciples" (Hall and Ames: 198-199).

16 Eno interprets this passage in such a manner that it has no theistic connotations whatsoever: "If we look for the meaning of the passage in the balanced contrast between the two phrases, it appears to say something such as: 'Don't ask about theories of T'ien or man's nature; you will find all there is to know about these matters in the Master's program of self-stylization.' In other words, T'ien's existence 'out there' does not matter; it gives us no clues as to what we are meant to be. For us, T'ien is manifest in and prescribes those behavioral forms that Confucius laid down as the basis for Ruist practice. If this interpretation is correct, then *A*:5.13 reassigns the considerable rhetorical force of the word '*t'ien*' from images of the heavens or of spirits to the everyday practice of ritual forms" (Eno: 85). This is a big "if" and not a very natural reading of the text.

17 For further evidence that Zigong lacks virtue and understanding, see *Analects* 3.17, 5.4, 5.9, 11.18 and 14.29; see also Slingerland's commentary on 5.4 (Slingerland 2003: 40).

18 Curiously, Confucius does speak to Zigong about heaven and in a deeply anthropomorphic, almost confessional, manner:

    The Master said: 'Alas! No one understands me.'

    Zigong replied, 'How can you say that no one understands you, Master?"

    "I am not bitter toward Heaven, nor do I blame others. I study what is below in order to comprehend what is above. If there is anyone who could understand me, perhaps it is Heaven." (*Analects* 14.35).

19 Hall and Ames write: "Concerning the unknown realm of gods and spirits, Confucius maintained an attitude of respectful detachment" (Hall and Ames: 196).

20 Much later ritual practice would include the subjection of spirits to Shangdi. In "Statutes of the Ming Dynasty (1368-1642) addressed " To the heavenly spirits, "the spirits of the Cloud-master, the Rain-master, the lord of the Winds, and the Thunder-master," we read, "It is your office, O Spirits, to superintend the clouds and the rain, and to raise and send abroad the winds, as ministers assisting Shang Ti. All the people enjoying the benefits of your service." The spirits act from "Heaven-conferred powers, and nurturing influences" (from Legge 1880: 18-19).

21 Slingerland's recent translation is quite different: "The Master openly expressed his views on profit, the Heavenly Mandate, and Goodness." For his well-argued justification of this translation see Slingerland: 86.

22 Confucius discussed and sometimes bemoaned fate or destiny, which are granted by heaven: "Anxiously, Sima Nu remarked, 'Everyone has brothers, I alone have none.' Zixia replied, 'I have heard it said, "Life and death are governed by fate, wealth and honor are determined by Heaven." A gentleman is respectful and free of errors. He is reverent and ritually proper in his dealings with others. In this way, everyone in the Four Seas is his brother. How could a gentleman be concerned about not having brothers?'" (*Analects* 12.5). And when Yan Hui died, he lamented, "Oh! Heaven has bereft me! Heaven has bereft me!" (*Analects* 11.9). I shall not venture into the tricky notion of Confucius' views on fate here.

23 In de Bary and Bloom we find the following comment: "There has been much discussion about why, in [9.1], Confucius is said to have spoken "little" about topics on which there are many recorded pronouncements. This is especially true in the case of humaneness, which is discussed at many points in the *Analects*. While there is no fully convincing answer to this, one possibility is that in many instances when Confucius discusses humaneness, he seems to have been responding to questions from disciples, and then guardedly, preferring to leave the question and its answer open-ended. For him humaneness knew no limit and could not be explicitly defined" (de Bary and Bloom: 52).

24 With violence to this prima facie reading of this passage, Hall and Ames assert: "In this context, *t'ien* is not a preexisting creative principle which gives birth to and nurtures a world independent of itself. *T'ien* is rather a general designation for the phenomenal world as it emerges of its own accord. *T'ien* is wholly immanent, having no existence independent of the calculus of phenomena that constitute it. There is as much validity in asserting that phenomena "create" *t'ien* as in saying that *t'ien* creates phenomena; the relationship between *t'ien* and phenomena, therefore, is one of interdependence" (Hall and Ames: 207).

25 It would be curious indeed if Confucius sought to model himself

on Heaven, as he does here, but Heaven be the human community, ritual activity, or some naturalistic force. Eno agrees that Tian is the cosmic moral model: "There is a parallel between the action of the Sage, which is a function of his totalistic understanding, and the action of T'ien. T'ien itself—whether pictured as Nature or god—seems almost to be a cosmic version of the Ruist Sage" (Eno: 86). I argue that it's more than "seems almost."

26 He writes: "My propositions serve as elucidations in the following way: anyone who understands me eventually recognizes them as nonsensical, when he has used them—as steps—to climb up beyond them. (He must, so to speak, throw away the ladder after he has climbed up it.) He must transcend these propositions, and then he will see the world aright" (Wittgenstein 6.54).

27 Dong's life is dated from ca. 179-104 B.C., more than 350 years after the birth of Confucius.

28

29 To see the extent to which Dong Shongshu was a Confucian revisionary, see de Bary and Bloom: 292-310 and Fung 1953: ch. II.

30 Consider the following comment on the dating and intellectual location of the *Zuozhuan*: "Although not strictly a philosophical work, the *Zuo zhuan* was completed in the Warring States period, and many of its explicit judgments and extended speeches clearly express the ideas of the Warring States 'Confucians.' Even some of the historical anecdotes reflect, if not actually derive from, the pedagogy of the Confucian schools" (Lewis: 591).

31 Compare the opening lines of DM 16 with a portion of DM 1: 莫见乎隐，莫显乎微 *mo xian hu yin, mo xian hu wei.* Mueller translates this as "There is nothing more visible than what is hidden and nothing more manifest than what is subtle" (Mueller). Hall and Ames translate this passage as "There is nothing more present than what is immanent, and nothing more manifest than what is inchoate." The form of this passage is a typical repetitive parallelism frequently used in Chinese literature: it uses several apparently different and parallel words to emphasize the meaning, but the meanings of those parallel words are often synonymous. Thus, *xian* (见) is parallel and virtually synonymous with *xian* (显), and *yin* (隐) is parallel and close to *wei* (微). Although *yin* and *wei* can indicate something arcane, both words can be used to denote something still concealed or amorphous. Translating *yin* and *wei* as imminent and inchoate does not violate the context or the intended meaning of the author, but it might be more ideal, I think, if revised like this: "nothing is more present than what is still concealed, nothing more manifest than what is inchoate. "Revised this way, Hall and Ames' translation might be better than Mueller's, since here *yin* and *wei* denote something embryonic.

32 "The Christian faith relates to a personal and transcendent God of pure spirit and it sets up an opposition between the earth below, where man plays out his eternal destiny, and a Beyond, which is totally incommensurate with it. In contrast, the Heaven of the Chinese is a concept in which secular and religious aspects merge" (Gernet: 193).

BIBLIOGRAPHY

Bodde, Derk. 1981. *Essays on Chinese Civilization*. Princeton: Princeton University Press.

Brooks, E. Bruce and Brooks A. Taeko. 1998. *The Original Analects: Sayings of Confucius and His Successors*. New York: Columbia University Press.

Clark, Kelly James. 2005. "The Gods of Abraham, Isaiah, and Confucius." *Dao: A Journal of Comparative Philosophy*, Vol. V, No. 1, Winter 2005, 109-136.

Dawson, Raymond, trans. 1993. *Confucius: The Analects*. Oxford and New York: Oxford University Press.

De Bary, Theodore and Bloom, Irene. *Sources of Chinese Tradition*, vol. 1, second edition. New York: Columbia University Press, 1999.

Eno, Robert. 1990. "Was There a High God Ti in Shang Religion?" *Early China* 15: 1-26.

Fung Yu-lan. 1952. *A History of Chinese Philosophy*, vol. I. Derk Bodde, trans. Princeton, New Jersey: Princeton University Press.

_____. 1953. *A History of Chinese Philosophy*, vol. II. Derk Bodde, trans. Princeton, New Jersey: Princeton University Press.

Gernet, Jacques. 1985. China and the Christian Impact. Trans. by Janet Lloyd. Cambridge: Cambridge University Press.

Graham, A. C. 1989. *Disputers of the Tao*. La Salle, Illinois: Open Court Publishers.

Hall, David and Ames, Roger. 1987. *Thinking Through Confucius*. Albany, NY: State University of New York Press.

Ivanhoe, Philip. "Whose Confucius? Which *Analects*?" In Van Norden.

Legge, James. 1935. Oxford, Clarendon press

_____. 1880. *Religions of China*. London: Hodder and Stoughton.

Lewis, Mark Edward. "Warring States Political History" in *The Cambridge History of Ancient China*, Edward Shaughnessy and Michaele Lowe, eds. New York: Cambridge University Press, 587-650.

Louden, Robert. 2002. "'What Does Heaven Say?': Christian Wolff and Western Interpretations of Confucian Ethics." In Van Norden.

Makeham, John. 2003. *Transmitters and Creators*. Cambridge, Massachusetts and London: Harvard University Asia Center.

Mueller, Charles, translator. 2003. *The Doctrine of the Mean*.www. hm.tyg.jp/~acmuller/contao/docofmean.htm

Mungello, David. 1974. Curious Land: Jesuit Accommodation and the Origins of Sinology. Stuttgart: Franz Steiner Verlag Wiesbaden.

Shaughnessy, Edward. 1999. "Western Zhou History" in *The Cambridge History of Ancient China*, Edward Shaughnessy and Michaele Lowe, eds. New York: Cambridge University Press, 292-351.

Slingerland, Edward, trans. 2003. *Confucius Analects*. Indianapolis, Indiana: Hackett Publishing Company.

Van Norden, Bryan, ed. 2002. Confucius and the Analects. New York: Oxford University Press.

Wittgenstein, Ludwig. 1922. *Tractatus Logico-Philosophicus*. D. F. Pears and B. F. McGuinness, translators. London: Routledge and Kegan Paul.

Commentary 1

Philosophical Globalization as Reciprocal Valuation and Mutual Integration: Comments on the Papers of Tang Yijie and Roger Ames

Cheng Chungying

TRANSFORMATION ON EQUAL ACCESS AND MUTUAL ENRICHMENT

Roger Ames's presentation gives a realistic picture of the Philosophy Departments in the USA today. He complained about the egocentricity of the Western philosophers. It is a legitimate complaint. But the present scenario also betrays a fundamental fact that people live and think by their philosophical tradition and it is pretty difficult to ask them to change their core visions of life, their paradigms of thinking or commitment of their faith, which would subsist largely 'in the back of' their minds. Besides, some people may not have enough interest or motivation. As Gadamer has observed, philosophers may have their prejudice as part of their tradition and need to open their minds to a space of the indeterminate even before they could have serious dialogue with a stranger. However, I do see useful and gradual change in philosophical trends in USA or in the West over the last thirty years. Yet we must be reminded that sweeping changes will have to wait for five hundred years or more. It is not only the change of the philosophical interest that counts. It is the change of the international atmosphere, the change of cultural attitude, the change of the outlook on life or for that matter, the change of the way in which we evaluate others and the way in which we approach others for a worthy goal or toward a common good.

I recall that when I started to teach philosophy in the middle of the 60's at the University of Hawaii, I had to teach two parallel courses: Classical Chinese philosophy and contemporary analytical philosophy. At that time Hawaii could afford to teach Chinese philosophy because we have local students from Asian or Chinese ancestry. For graduate courses and seminars the concentration is still more on contemporary philosophy subjects. At large, the philosophical circle at that time in USA knew nothing about Chinese philosophy: They knew only Chinese thought or what Benjamin Schwartz calls the "Intellectual History of China". More than one time, people asked me whether I also taught "Chinese thought" apart from American philosophy and analytical philosophy. I replied: "I also teach Chinese philosophy which is not just 'Chinese thought' but also 'Chinese thinking'." To me, philosophy is always thinking rather than thought, process rather than product, activity rather than state of being. It is in actual thinking about ultimate issues and ultimate problems that philosophy emerges and becomes the hallmark of a high intellectual culture. But philosophers in US or Europe tend not to see Chinese philosophical tradition as equal and equivalent to that of the West. Therefore they fail to take Confucianism, Neo-Confucianism, Daoism or Chan Buddhism and other schools of Chinese philosophy as containing the essence of philosophy, namely the essence of philosophizing as argumentation and analytical exposition of objective truth. Instead, they tend to see the ancient texts of these schools of philosophy as exotic cultural products to be studied for curiosity by sinologists.

It has to take a lot of effort with many colleagues, including especially Roger Ames in the Department of Philosophy at University of Hawaii at Manoa in the last two to three decades, to change the situation to the extent that common people and students could come to appreciate Chinese philosophy as an important theoretical alternative to the Western philosophy, not just a practical alternative to the Western religion. It takes further efforts and exchanges to create conditions for holding a dialogue between Chinese philosophy and Western philosophy on an equal basis. This has no doubt benefited both Chinese and Western philosophers so that the interaction between these two great traditions has continued to be a source of inspiration for a enriched philosophical globalization of the world. My founding of the *Journal of Chinese Philosophy* in 1973 and consequently the International society for Chinese philosophy in 1975 were strictly motivated by this spirit of equal access and mutual enrichment, the same spirit which started the East-West philosophical mutual learning campaign as early as the 30's at University of Hawaii.

These efforts in the last 30 years were not wasted and we begin to see a lot of changes. People now come to recognize Chinese philosophy as a philosophy at AAS, APA or AAR in US. Scholars in Europe have also come to take Chinese philosophy as philosophy in many academic meetings. I was surprised to see how many European scholars have embraced both Daoism and Chan Buddhism and have developed a deep ecological consciousness that enhanced the Green Movement.

In light of these facts, I have less complaint than Roger Ames and just wish to use this occasion to ask us how to make Chinese Philosophy even more accessible and even more enriching to the Western philosophical tradition and by doing so to make itself more enriched and more creatively significantly and more significantly creative. Nobody should harbor the unrealistic ambition or design for changing a philosophical tradition by imposing or introducing an exotic one. Take the example of introduction of Buddhism from India in China. It took more than five hundred years to reach its height of influence. At that time it seemed that China could be transformed into a Buddhist country. But that did not happen. Instead Buddhism acted as a stimulus to excite the native tradition of Confucianism and Daoism toward a new development, the net result of which is Neo-Confucianism that in its own terms absorbs the best of Buddhism and Daoism. Neo-Confucianism has become a great theoretical challenge and a great educational force influencing Chinese society in the last one thousand years up to now.

The above fact suggests that for the great traditions of philosophy which are deeply rooted in their respective cultural soils their interaction would not convert one to the other, but instead will lead to a new vista of understanding and reflection which will prompt a new phase of development for each interacting tradition. Therefore, the effective interaction between Chinese philosophy and Western philosophy must create impact on either side and will form a common and mutual understanding which would be open to rational discourse, reflective interpretation and useful integration so that human flourishing as a cultural and a philosophical phenomenon would be reinvigorated and sustained. I hold the principle of equal access and mutual enrichment as the basis for effective dialogue whose purpose is self- transformation in light of transformation of the others.[1] It is in this spirit that Chinese-Western philosophical dialogue will be both meaningful and stimulating.

VALIDATION OF THE CHINESE PHILOSOPHICAL TRADITION

For this reason, to question the validity of Chinese philosophy is either silly (*yu*) or ignorant (*bi*) or both. With regard to the intellectual tradition of China ask whether fundamental questions have been confronted or discussed, whether different views existed and debates and disputes on those views developed, and whether important theories and ideas have evolved in proportion to new experiences of life and in responses to new changes of environments, be it political or social. If the answers to all these questions are positive, to deny validity to Chinese philosophical thinking on fundamental problems is simply a gross mistake and a failure to understand what philosophy really means. Philosophy means love of wisdom which leads to pursuit and achievement of wisdom. Yet wisdom is not just a matter of transcendent and objective truth but a matter of presenting truth as one has deeply experienced, and a 'thinking-through' in light of living problems of humanity.

Evidently, an important item of wisdom is the recognition that there are different wisdoms among different great traditions of philosophizing. We can mention at least four such traditions, namely the Ancient Greek, the Modern European, the Chinese (both Ancient and Modern) and the Indian. They have shared certain concerns and even certain viewpoints and yet they have different ways of approach and different emphasis in their content. They may also have different forms of discoursing and presentation. Specifically, there is no denial that in the Greek tradition abstraction from experience and logical definition of terms and rational organization of arguments are consciously and conscientiously entertained and developed or elaborated in dealing with fundamental problems which are either ontological, ethical or axiological, or both. In other traditions such an approach was not singled out or given dominance nor made an independent discipline and an independent profession. Yet in the classical intellectual tradition of China there is no doubt the *zi*-discourse (*zixue*) tradition that developed before a distinction between *jing*-discourse and *zi*-discourse were made.[2] The *zi*-discourse tradition in which different philosophical schools prospered and competed is no doubt an exercise of philosophical thinking which contains a strong consciousness of correct use of language and a strong effort to define terms and to present argument. In many ways these are hardly distinguishable in intent and concern and even in form or content from early Greek schools. As a matter of fact, they tended to be even more systematic and more argumentative than any early Greek natural philosophers. It is even interesting to note that as in the case of the Greek philosophers many Chinese philosophers in the classical periods may have to earn their living by collecting tuition from students. This may prove that even in the Chinese tradition philosophizing had been an independent educational discipline, a discipline of arguing for reforms of government and a discipline of interpreting the ancient learning for present-day use (now called "*guwei jinyong*").

A good example of this is the Confucian interpretation of the Yijing texts in the later period of Confucius's life.[3] The efforts to understand the meaning of *yi (yi zhi yi)*, to discern moral principles from patterns and forms of change and to conceive the origin and process of change are no doubt profoundly philosophical thinking which lead to insights into reality, creativity, human destiny and human nature. Other examples abound as we can see in the writings of Mozi, Daodejing, Zhuangzi, Mencius, Xunzi, Gongsun Longzi and even Hanfeizi.

It must be noted that philosophical wisdom may take different forms due to differences of human experiences and human understanding in different life contexts. There is no way to require that all philosophical contents must be the same. But there is indeed a possibility that philosophy could be argued and presented in a clear form based on logical analysis and clarification of meaning in the use of language. Because if we wish to understand truth, reality, knowledge and values we could ask ourselves whether we can communicate these in a form which is easy to be understood in reference to experience. Hence the Greek specification of philosophy tends to rely on logical or rational forms resulting from generalization from experience in communication. Perhaps the concern with rational forms that gives rise to formal logic and that is highly characteristic of the Greek philosophizing arose precisely because there was more need for political debate and communication in the public places in the polity of Athens. Since then it carried a great weight for later development of Western philosophy. But in the case of Chinese philosophy, I have not encountered any mention of debate in public places. A debate or a dispute in philosophy was primarily communicated in conversations between a master and disciples such as we see in the case of Confucian Analects or in dialogues between a visiting scholar and a ruler as we see in the case of Mencius.

KANT AS A KEY POINT INTERLINKING
GREEK PHILOSOPHY AND CHINESE PHILOSOPHY

It may be remarked that logical form and analytical presentation reached their height of sophistication in the philosophizing of Kant where all basic views in ontology, theology, epistemology, psychology, ethics and religion are subject to analytical and dialectical critique and many theses are rejected for not being able to pass the logical tests of consistency and coherence. Famously, Kant rejected theological metaphysics and considered God as merely an unproved hypothesis for the need of moral psychology. He makes amply clear that unless we have experience of the objective that occasions our categorization no pure rational thinking independent of experience could make any real epistemic and epistemological sense. In this sense he is the first positivist and also the first pragmatist in the theory of knowledge. Apart from holding that knowledge comes from experience and theory in union, we are justified in making moral and aesthetical judgments based on our reflective experiences of self and the world. This amounts to claiming that pure reason could have a practical use if it relates itself to morality and aesthetical experiences of taste. This is where his pragmatism lies: Unless we can logically show the objective validity of knowledge, our knowledge of ourselves must bear on our moral nature and moral action and other practical experiential concerns. It is interesting to note that classical Confucianism to a great extent takes the position of Kant and that there exists a great resonance between Kantian philosophy and the Classical Confucian philosophy, particularly in the field of morality and aesthetics. I have managed to show that this may not be merely a theoretical coincidence.[4]

In the field of epistemology Kant benefits from the Aristotelian theory of categories and modern scientific theories such as physics of Newton that he takes to be a paragon of knowledge. With this understanding one might also suggest that there is no problem for developing science in Confucianism, as science is a matter of experiential research and rational organization. As there is no contradiction in the theoretical and practical uses of reason in Kant, there need not be any contradiction between science and morality and for that mater between science and religion in the Confucian framework. It is to be pointed out that in actuality the overall Kantian theoretical framework of thinking is Confucian or Neo-Confucian as one can seen from historical connections as well as from a deep mutual theoretical interpretation. Regarding the former I shall not elaborate here. Regarding the latter I merely wish to point out that for both Kant and Confucius the autonomy of the human self and the harmony among the faculties of man are basic tenets of the philosophy of the human person.[5] It is also noteworthy that in arguing for the autonomy of the human self Kant has provided a basis for the dignity of human individuals and the privacy of religious faith that could be protected by law as a measure of reason. In this sense Kant has articulated explicitly theses on human rights and human freedom of religious beliefs that may be said to be implicit and inherent in the Confucian view of the human person. In an implicit way Kant has provided an explicit statement of issues for the Confucian notion of humanity. Conversely, the primordial unity and inner harmony of human nature in the Confucian philosophy of man provide a foundation for Kant to state the human condition analytically and to suggest ways of reconciliation and integration of human faculties.

The importance of recognizing Kant's relation to Confucianism is that it has the consequence of overcoming the egocentricity of European and American philosophers. The present day European and American philosophers are too much engrossed with their specialties to the exclusion of recognizing or understanding humanity in holistic unity that is capable of engaging many forms of interaction and mutual learning. They may also fail to recognize the richness of humanity as embodied in differences of cultural and philosophical traditions. They tend to lose their openness and curiosity as a result of technologization of philosophical thinking. This is indeed a problem that needs to be overcome. But this is not to say that we shall become the same in our philosophical outlook. No, this is not the goal for mutual understanding and dialogue. Philosophizing by nature is ramifying and rhizomatous. In seeking unity it produces plurality. Hence it is an activity that is both unifying and multiplying. The purpose of philosophy is for relating and for refreshing and reaching a conceptual whole of differences and differences in a conceptual whole. The Confucian statement catches it all: "he er bu tong" (Harmonized and yet remain different). I also like to add: "butong er he" (Differentiated and yet remain harmonious). In fact, we must first recognize differences and then affirm that we are all rooted in one source and are united in one harmony, a harmony that allows productivity and continuous growth.

Kantian philosophy is most interesting for me because I see in it a pivotal point of turning for later day Western philosophy, which deviates from Kant due to other forces of influences, notably Christian theology and modern science and technology. But Kant is nevertheless the link between the early and the later developments of philosophy in the West. What has not been made known is that he is also the link between the East (the Chinese) and the West (the Greek and the Hebrew) and points to a complementary paradigm of philosophizing, whole and part, analysis and synthesis, form and content, experience and theory, observation and reflection, self and the world, morality and ontology, science and aesthetics, morality and religion.

GLOBALIZATION OF PHILOSOPHY AND FIVE PREREQUISITES FOR PHILOSOPHICAL DIALOGUE

Philosophy will still move on and will continue to evolve. Separate and independent practices of philosophy in the great traditions of philosophizing are needed for maintaining unity and harmony among sciences and for providing refreshing renewal of moral forms or li in human society. It is even needed for the realization of the human person as an evolving process toward self-transcendence and self-integration. Each tradition could learn something about the form and content of philosophizing from the other. In a globalized world, the globalization of philosophy (appeal to philosophy as ultimate form of mutual understanding in the whole world) is an inevitable task and it requires a correct acknowledgement of the genuine need in human existence as well as a genuine need for inter-tradition interaction. Once we recognize these needs and look squarely into the philosophical task, we shall be able to do dialogue and communication and also to benefit from these activities.

Once we recognize globalization as an inevitable process for human development, we must also become aware of the roots for such development. This means going back to philosophical thinking on fundamental issues before we can have the new understanding of the human world needed for constructing a new order of human society, human economy and human polity. This means that we have to go back to fundamental issues and recognize their relevance for this new organization of a new order. It means also that we shall focus on our openness and sources of creative thinking and be ready to rethink many matters of life and world. It is only under such conditions that we are ready for dialogues, which are processes of mutual learning and mutual appreciation. Philosophy itself is a process in which we come to learn these values of others and to integrate them into a differentiated whole once their values are recognized. This may be the most difficult part, but it is the most creative part of dialogical communication.

Let me recapitulate five pre-conditions or pre-requisites for philosophical thinking and philosophical dialogue in the light of the interdependence of self-understanding and mutual understanding: [6]

1) Self-awakening to the wisdom of life and to knowing oneself. This would mean that one recognizes essential elements of values in the formation of one's own cultural identity and potentiality for growth

2) Recognition of both the creative potentiality for growth and the problems of one's growth which pose a limitation; understanding the need and readiness to open to others and the world in developing the creative potentiality of self-growth by learning.

3) Recognition of others as sharing the same concern and interest in opening oneself and in learning and seeking communication.

4) Dialoguing on the basis of equal and mutual respect: This is equality of human dignity implying respect for the moral nature of man and his potential to reach for self-realization as well as for substantiating care for others and the whole of humanity.

5) Developing our valuation of others and making efforts to reorganize oneself by integrating truth and values from others in an open space of understanding and interpretation.

With these five dimensions of self-growth and self-development in view we are able to see why dialogue becomes necessary. This is because dialoguing is a process of action and form of action, as well as a process of interaction between two intellectual beings. Hence it is a process toward self-transformation and transformation of the whole world.

RITES CONTROVERSY AS A CASE OF DIALOGICAL FAILURE

In connection with my argument for the relevance for Kant, I share

Roger Ames' concern with the problem of how the theology of Christianity has played a role in transmitting Chinese philosophy and in interpreting Chinese philosophy. Yet these are clearly two separate issues: In the 17th century the Jesuits did great work in bridging the China and the West. But by 1721 the bridging collapsed to the great loss of both sides. Perhaps China lost more than the West because the West accelerated its development at that time. In terms of benefits we must also say that the West benefited more than did China from the West.

I regard the Rites Controversy (1716-1721) as the worst mistake two communicating parties could ever commit. A case analysis will show how political and religious intrigue, bigotry and prejudice tied to power and self-interest destroyed genuine philosophical dialogue. It shows how the leading Christian Catholics at the time formed a closure of minds without considering fairness in treating others. It forfeited all the five propositions of the above and led the Church into a deadlock. It is interesting to compare the Christian proselytizing and conversion with the Buddhist way of conversion in earlier centuries when China was exposed to the visiting Buddhists from central Asia. In those periods not only were efforts made to mutually understand and mutually interpret, the ways of conversion were non-exclusive if not all comprehensively open. In fact, the Buddhists promoted the doctrine of *upaya* or *fangpian*, which means expediency and convenience.[7] It is apparent that *upaya* would also include respecting the tradition of others and exercising no force in the form of an artificially made either-or choice in a given situation of confrontation.

With such an understanding of the core reason for the Rites Controversy, we must warn ourselves that major and minor mistakes and conflicts could take place like the Rites Controversy even in today's world. In fact Huntington has spoken of civilizational clashes that are built on the principle of exclusion and adversarial opposition. Then the question is whether we could establish a principle of inclusion to avoid the trap and tragedy of irreconcilable differences and exclusive domination on faith, truth or good. We not only cannot but should not dominate and monopolize these ultimate values as in a free market. In matters of faith and truth, although we have no market thereof, there also need be no domination and monopolization because it is against the principle of growth and self-realization in individuals. This of course does not mean that we should not learn and compete with each other in developing more attractive systems, nor that we cannot learn from each other. This is the application of the principle of "comprehensive integration" that I have discussed in an earlier paper and this principle applies to religions as it applies to philosophies as I see it.[8]

WE NEED NOT "GET RID OF GOD"

In this regard, I wish to state a crucial difference with Roger Ames. Roger Ames sees Christianity as representing a philosophy of absolute transcendence and Confucianism as representing a philosophy of absolute immanence.[9] I am not sure that all forms of Christian faith must be absolutely transcendent, nor do I believe that Confucian is absolutely immanentist. There is no doubt a transcendent God in Calvinist Christianity and there is mandate of heaven and ultimate *li* in the nature and heart-mind of an individual person in so far as the Confucian and Neo-Confucian metaphysics is concerned. Yet I still suggest that we have to take each case individually. On an individual basis, the absolute transcendence of God is not a necessary feature of all forms of Christianity nor should we understand Confucianism to be devoid of a sense of genuine transcendence. It is possible that we could have transcendence in immanence and immanence in transcendence, which for Confucianism means the unity of *tian* and *ren* (unity of heaven and man). We have seen the relation between *tian* and *ren* as dynamic and creative.

We may see that it is the human being who becomes aware of a transcendent heaven or the *ti* (ruler) who is said to create human being. But on the other hand, could we also say that it is the human person who has invented the idea of God so that God can be said to create man? It is not clear whether it is the Jewish people who eventually invented the idea of God in Christianity or a Greek apostle of Christ who rationalized God into an object of transcendent theology. Hence we cannot conceive of God in absolutely transcendent terms, namely as a wholly and total otherness which would even go beyond our conceiving. As a matter of fact, to conceive God as a transcendent or absolute transcendent entity could very well be a result of a way of theologizing the object of worship. In modern times, the God-notion has undergone quite a change. Not only do we have a God like in Spinoza's substance theory or Leibniz 's Monadology in which God is inactive and yet is full consciousness of reality. This philosophical conception of truth and God continues to the present. We may have a God of Kierkegard's theology in which God transcends human knowledge and yet remains humanly concerned. We may also have Whitehead's process philosophy in which God is basically immanent and yet could be partially transcendent. In light of all these vicissitudes, I wish to mention that God has gone through many phases and identities, just like the differentiation of *taiji* in the Neo-Confucian systems. This said, my point is that it is not necessary to get rid of God, because it is not necessary to make God a fixed permanent entity in order to get rid of it. In so far as God is believable for a community in which both morality and science thrive, it could have a different content and a different basis or support from experience and hence not be absolutely transcendent.

Once we see the transformation of God or the name of God, we need not to get rid of God even though God is a symbol of absolute authority and its name has been abused in many human transactions in the world. God could identify with *tian* or with the *dao* or the nature (*xing*) or heart-mind (*xin*), depending on the underlying contexts and purposes or referential frameworks, as for example we have seen in the writings of Leibniz. We need not kill God, nor drive it away. From the Chinese point of view we can pacify him, harmonize him and transform him and let it stand for philosophical reality such as moral power and onto-cosmological order. For Chinese philosophy, which

Granet marks as wisdom having no need of the idea of God,[10] my response is that God in Chinese philosophy has been already harmonized with humanity and becomes part of humanity in so far as the nature of man is recognized to have a potential of creativity which could generate life and values for unlimited time through a process of development and with a underlying unity that sustains ceaseless creativity.

That God could be harmonized or transformed requires a dialogical process that we must recognize and implement. In this process, of course, an appropriate Western philosophical framework is necessarily a consideration. Apart from Kant, I agree that Dewey could be a good choice. But I wish also to point out that Dewey has naturalized all human activities into the fold of experience. But paradoxically this also would lead to allowing the experience of the transcendent to be valid and therefore could lead to a radical pragmatism like William James. Dewey notwithstanding, we must also confront the fact or a natural tendency to externalize for need of objective knowledge, and, like externalization, to transcendentalize for needs of life and emotion. Here again we must take the separation of science and religious faith seriously. Either one routs out God completely, or one has to accept God on a self-contained ground for becoming one in a human person or in a human community.

As to the question of Chinese onto-cosmology I have discussed this issue in many contexts. In a recent paper I speak of five meanings of *yi* in connection with elaboration of the three meanings of *yi* in Zheng Xuan (127-200). [11] The question is whether *taiji* and also *wuji* have a transcendent aspect as well as a generative aspect. This leads again to the meaning of transcendence. I have no interest in identifying *taiji* as God. On the other hand, I can see God as a personalized *taiji*. If so, God cannot be absolutely transcendent and would have to remain as a principle of *wuji* or *wu* indeterminacy. Again, in a recent paper of mine, titled "Toward integrative pluralism: from the point of view of the Yijing and Whitehead and John Cobb", [12] I have shown how mutual interpretation between Whitehead, John Cobb and the Yijing may have the effect of transforming God into the Dao and humanity at large in a process of creative development. Ames's predilection for taking the process interpretation of philosophy in the spirit of Chinese philosophy is no doubt an optimistic note. But action and theory could be two separate things. Without unifying them in a discourse on philosophical globalization in the Chinese spirit of harmonization, it could become an act of irony if America or the West plays the role of God in its action.

IDENTIFICATION AND CONSTRUCTION OF CHINESE PHILOSOPHY IN TANG YIJIE

In light of what I have said about the key views of Roger Ames, I wish to offer some brief comments on Professor Tang Yijie's lucid and suggestive paper. The question on the validity of Chinese philosophy as I mentioned above is actually a problem of the identity of Chinese philosophy. Given some explicit standards for philosophical thinking, it becomes simply a matter of performative action to say that some issues, some forms of discourse or some positions are philosophical and some others are not. Another criterion would be that an identified position in Chinese tradition could be significantly or meaningfully compared with a recognized position in the Western philosophy. Of course in order to do the identification or the comparison one must be able to interpret a traditional position from a philosophical perspective and be able to construe it as a philosophical position as well. I see that there is no reason why such an interpretation, such an identification and such a comparison cannot be made. Language and ideas are made to be interpretive and at the same time to perform the function of an interpreter so that their inherent and emergent meanings could be communicated and shared by others. A philosophical discourse or issue is such that it can be always so interpreted and communicated. One must see that for a major part of the 20th century Chinese philosophy is a matter of interpreting some basic Chinese paradigm of thinking in the light of or by way of Western philosophical understanding. [13] In this way we see how classical Confucianism and neo-Confucianism have been made more philosophically appealing and at the same time how Western philosophical views thus become better understood because it has become re-interpreted in the context of Chinese philosophy.

Tang Yijie claims that Chinese philosophy in the modern sense is constructed against a background of Western philosophy and I agree with this claim. In my study of the Contemporary and 20th Century Chinese philosophy most of Chinese philosophy has been constructed or developed from understanding the Western tradition. But I wish to also add that in doing so Western philosophy becomes also reconstructed, even though unknown to the Western circle. Philosophical globalization is thus a process for encouraging this enterprise of mutual interpretation and sharing its fruits for a more creative development of philosophy and human culture.

It is a matter of addressing the problem of interpretation of the West that the Chinese philosophy wishes to assert its own position and to assert its own right to make philosophical claims. Here without further elaboration I wish simply to list five steps or dimensions in which contemporary Chinese philosophy has taken on in a process of self-construction:

1) A pre-understanding of the Western philosophy and its problems;

2.) A critical investigation of Chinese philosophical texts and locating the issues which have been previously raised by Western philosophy;

3) An exploration or a discovery of the differences of Chinese philosophy in comparison with Western philosophy;

4) An explanation and justification of the differences so that Chinese philosophy can stand on its own; followed by the conclusion that the native Chinese philosophical issues and positions can undergo revival precisely because of the challenges posed by their critics.

NOTES

1 I stated this principle as early as 1985 when I promoted the formation of the International East-West University.

2 It is in fact Feng Youlan who makes this distinction between *zixue* and *jingxue* in his well-known book *History of Chinese Philosophy* (Zhongguo Zhexue Shi) in its earlier version, but he proves misleading in regarding Chinese philosophy as merely a matter of *jingxue* after the Han. Nevertheless, Feng has written his *History of Chinese Philosophy* which seems to abandon such a radical position.

3 As we find in the Mawangdui Silk Manuscripts on the Yijing of 1973.

4 I believed that Kant was influenced by Confucianism in 18th Century Europe through writings of Leibniz, Christian Wolf and Rousseau. Relevant materials will be cited to support this view.

5 A side point: It is curious that Mou Zongsan has not been able to recognize this and thus falls into the self-defeating argument and explanation of the *kanxian of liangzhi* for development of science.

6 Confer Fred R. Dallmayr's paper "Dialogue among civilizations, A hermeneutical perspective", in *Philosophie, Gesellschaft und Bildung in Zeiten der Globalizierung*, edited by Hermann-Josef Scheidgen, Norbert Bintersteiner and Yoshiro Nakamura (Amsterdam: Rodopi Press, 1994), 67-84.

7 The practice of upaya for achieving Buddhahood is specifically explored in the Fahua Jing (Lotus Sutra) in the Tiantai School of Chinese Buddhism.

8 See my paper "Chinese Culture and Comprehensive Integration of Values", presented in 1998 International Conference on Chinese Culture and Its Modern Significance, at the University of Stockholm, Stockholm, Sweden, 1998. For the time being, available in Conference Proceedings only.

9 I note that he did not use the terms absolute transcendence and absolute immanence. But for him genuine transcendence is absolute transcendence that implies a total break and independence of influence.

10 See Ames's reference in his paper to Marcel Granet, 1934, 478.

11 To be presented in a forthcoming International Conference on Yijing and Forms of Life in Tainan, Taiwan.

12 See my article in the book entitled *Deep Pluralism*, edited by David Griffin, published in 2005.

13 See my two chapters *Afterwords* in the book *Contemporary Chinese Philosophy*, edited by Chung-ying Cheng and Nick Bunnin, Oxford and Melden: Blackwell Publishing, 2002, 347-404.

Making Sense of Cross-Cultural Dialogue: Comments on the Papers of Tang Yijie and Roger Ames

Yu Jiyuan

Professor Roger Ames and Professor Tang set a solid stage for our discussion. Together their papers cover almost all the major issues that we face today in doing China-West dialogue in philosophy and they provide numerous insights for us to think and talk about. Inspired by Roger's fascinating play with an ambiguity between the Chinese and English terms that constitute the title of our panel ("dialogue," "philosophy," and "globalization"), my comments will focus on the meaning and methodology of cross-cultural philosophical dialogue.

The term "dialogue" is associated with Socrates' characteristic philosophical practice: having a conversation with someone to cross-examine (*elegchein*) him. This is what philosophy is for Socrates when he uses the term "philosophize" (*philosophein*).[1] After Socrates' death, a number of his followers in the fourth century of ancient Athens chose to remember him by writing philosophical dialogues in which Socrates is always the main speaker, and thus developed a distinct and lively literary genre, called by Aristotle, *Sokratikoi logoi* ("Socratic discourse" or "conversations with Socrates").[2] Plato emerges as the best writer of *Socratikoi logoi*.

It has been a matter of dispute whether the Socratic dialogical way (usually called "elenchus," from the verb "*elegchien*") displays a unified pattern in Plato's dialogues. However, elenchus is clearly different from the sense of "dialogue' in the title of our panel. When Socrates conducts a conversation, he questions the interlocutor and monopolizes the process. Although he claims that he seeks to clarify his own puzzles as well,[3] most dialogues end by reducing the interlocutor into perplexities and refuting him. Although Socrates claims that he knows nothing, he introduces a number of beliefs which he uses to refute his opponents and which he claims that no one can deny without falling into contradiction.[4] In his life-long practice of dialogue, Socrates finds that the set of moral beliefs which he has accepted as true can resist refutation.

If we apply Socratic form of dialogue to cross-cultural dialogue, the result would be what Roger considers the first or dominant sense of globalization, which means "either European expansion or American sprawl." What we are interested in here, however, is the Chinese type of conversation which Roger defines as "the pursuit of mutual accord through listening and then speaking" and his second sense of globalization which "refers to the mutual accessibility of cultural sensibilities."

In judging the current situation of this type of dialogue, Roger points out that "we would have to admit that, at least from the perspective of the Western academy at large, the dialogue has yet to begin." I think this assessment is essentially accurate. At this stage, "comparative philosophy" is generally associated with non-Western philosophy, and, to a great extent, even sounds like a different name for the latter. In studying Chinese philosophy, many scholars are looking for its similarity with Western philosophy, and many others search for its difference from Western philosophy: either way, a comparison with Western philosophy seems to be indispensable. Moreover, western philosophy is usually treated as some established framework or tool of analysis to be applied rather than as a subject matter that is itself subject to investigation. The focus of discussion has always been on the non-Western side. In contrast, scholars who work on the mainstream Western philosophy seldom refer to non-Western philosophy, and usually do not take East-West comparative philosophy as a seriously academic undertaking. We have lots of work to do to convince them.

I would like to learn more from the Chinese intellectual source about how to conduct the Chinese type of conversation. Here, I try to introduce and appropriate two ideas of Aristotle to make sense of this type of cross-cultural dialogue. The first is the "friend-as-mirror" thesis, and the second is the method of "saving the phenomena."

Aristotle uses the metaphor of a mirror to explain what real friendship is:

> [W]hen we wish to see our own face, we do so by looking into the mirror, in the same way when we wish to know ourselves we can obtain that knowledge by looking at our friend. For the friend is, as we assert, a second self. If, then, it is pleasant to know oneself, and it is not possible to know this without having some one else for a friend, the self-sufficing man will require friendship in order to know himself.[5]

A friend is a second self, and can be used as a mirror. Such a mirror is essential for one to know oneself better, and the self-knowledge obtained from a real friend is needed for one's happiness. The methodological implication of this "friend-as-mirror" thesis for cross-cultural philosophical dialogue is that Western philosophy and Chinese philosophy can be viewed as mirrors for each other. To conduct a dialogue between them is to take them as mirrors. We can thus reflect upon the traditional roots of each side, examine their otherwise unexamined presuppositions, uncover hidden assumptions, and generate alternative perspectives to determine why each side emphasizes and argues in the way it does. Furthermore, by promoting mutual understanding, dialogue will also help philosophy transcend cultural boundaries and reach genuine insights that are not culturally bound.

"Saving the phenomena" is Aristotle's characteristic philosophical methodology. In *Nicomachean Ethics* vii.1, he presents us with an outline of this method:

> We must, as in all other cases, set the phenomena [*phainom-
> ena*] before us and, after first discussing the difficulties
> [*aporiai*], go on to prove, if possible, the truth of all the rep-
> utable opinions [*endoxa*] about these affections or, failing
> this, of the greater number and the most authoritative; for if
> we both resolve the difficulties and leave the reputable opin-
> ions undisturbed, we shall have proved the case sufficiently.
> (1145b1-7)

The term phenomena, literally meaning "things that are present or are evident," derives from the verb *phainesthai*, and means "to appear." It can be translated as "appearances." However, in Aristotle, it means mainly "what people commonly say" (*ta legomena*), i.e., "common belief," rather than em-pirical appearance. Phenomena also include views that are not so commonly accepted but are held by a small number of wise people, or even by a single wise person. In this sense it is used interchangeably with *endoxa* ("reputable opinions"). According to the quoted passage, Aristotle's method of "saving the phenomena" consists of the following procedures: (1) collecting and es-tablishing the phenomena; (2) discussing and analyzing the conflicts of these phenomena and the difficulties to which they give rise, and (3) saving the truth contained in all reputable opinions. This is meant to solve conflicts be-tween phenomena by showing that each phenomenon is neither completely wrong nor completely right. It identifies each phenomenon's limit and adjusts "what is said" by all sides of a debate. As Aristotle describes it:

> We must, then, find a method that will best explain the views
> held on these topics, and also put an end to difficulties and
> contradictions. And this will happen if the contrary views
> are seen to be held with some show of reason; such a view
> will be most in harmony with the phenomena; and both the
> contradictory statements will in the end stand, if what is said
> is true in one sense but untrue in another.[6]

The method of "saving the phenomena" can be extended to compara-tive philosophy to the effect that to compare entails saving the phenomena from different cultures. If we extend this method to cross-cultural dialogue, we can proceed as follows: (1) take issues and theories from different philo-sophical traditions as comparable phenomena, (2) examine points of congru-ence and contrast that arise from bringing these cross-cultural phenomena together, and (3) save the truth present in these phenomena.

The mirror and the "saving the phenomena" methods are consistent and complementary. The mirror method requires first of all bringing together different traditions, i.e., establishing comparable cross-culture phenomena, and then examining and revealing the differences and similarities between the two. This is precisely the requirement of the second step of the "Saving the phenomena" method. It is through mirroring that we know the strengths and weaknesses of each ethical system, and are thus able to identify the truth that needs to be saved, the truth which leads to fruitful dialogues. This leads to the third step of the "saving the phenomena" method.

Both methodologies require us to treat both sides in the dialogue equally and to develop an interpretation that benefits both sides. In doing comparison, we should not use Western concept and theory as a ready-to-use framework. Indeed, there is hardly any concept and theory that is not subject to controversy. Consider Aristotle's *Nicomachean Ethics*, for example. There are numerous ongoing disputes not only about the contents of particular views presented in it, but even about the structure of Aristotle's theory of eudaimonia and about whether the Nicomachean Ethics is a unified and consistent work.[7] Most contemporary discussions of virtue ethics go back to Aristotle, but it is far from being the case that they share the same understanding. Rather, as one influential virtue ethicist puts it: "Any virtue ethics which is 'Aristotelian' as described inevitably aims to stick to the author's interpretation of Aristotle, and interpretations of Aristotle, on many of the relevant issues, vary."[8] I think if comparative philosophy can demonstrate that it is able to contribute a better understanding of the Western side, Western scholars would be interested in joining the dialogue.

Comparative philosophy conceived in this way is not to determine, between the parties being compared, which side is the winner. It is indeed un-Aristotelian to think that truth can only be in one tradition or one philosophical system. For Aristotle, the search for truth is not the business of one person or one group of people, but needs to be a collective human endeavor:

> The investigation of truth is in one way hard, and in another easy. An indication of this is found in the fact that no one is able to attain the truth adequately, while, on the other hand, no one fails entirely, but every one says something true about the nature of things, and while individually they contribute little or nothing to the truth, by the union of all a considerable amount is amassed. Therefore, since the truth seems to be like the proverbial door, which no one can fail to hit, in this way it is easy, but in fact that we can have a whole and not the particular part we aim at shows the difficulty of it. (Metaphysics 993a28-993b7)

One major goal of comparative philosophy is to synthesize ideas from different traditions and develop creative thought. When Roger Ames claims that the present surge of interest in Whitehead and particularly the American pragmatists can "draw both substance and critique from a Chinese tradition that has been committed to various forms of process philosophy since the beginning of its recorded history," I take it that he is treating Western and

Chinese process theories as comparative phenomena and attempts to save the truth from both.

I would like to mention another area where we can treat Western and Chinese philosophies as mirrors for each other and save their respective truth. That area is virtue ethics. The contemporary revival of Aristotelian virtue ethics was initiated with Elizabeth Anscombe's "Modern Moral Philosophy," published in 1958. In her paper, Anscombe pointed out that "anyone who has read Aristotle's Ethics and has also read modern moral philosophy must have been struck by the great contrasts between them."[9] Anscombe claimed that all major modern moral philosophers were wrong and that we should stop doing moral philosophy until we have an adequate philosophical psychology. Ethics should be grounded in the notion of virtue, and we must get a better grip on terms like "intention," "wanting," "pleasure," and "action" in order to explain what type of thing a virtue is and how it relates to the virtuous actions. The revival of virtue ethics has significantly changed the landscape of contemporary ethics and has established virtue ethics as one of the most important ethical approaches today.

In the same year of 1958, a group of Confucian scholars published "A Manifesto for a Re-Appraisal of Sinology and Reconstruction of Chinese Culture."[10] This was intended to show the contemporary philosophical significance of Confucian ethics by contrasting it to modern Western moral philosophy:

> In Western ethical studies, discussion of morality is usually devoted to consideration of the regulations of human behavior, or the social or religious values of moral codes. Few writers have particularly stressed this thorough transformation of man's natural life by moral practices so that his attitudes and manners manifest his inner virtues and enrich and illuminate this life. On the other hand, it is precisely what traditional Confucianism has greatly emphasized.[11]

This document became the landmark in the development of "New Confucianism," or what Professor Tu Wei-ming calls "The Third Epoch of Confucian Humanism."[12]

The revival of Aristotelian ethics is mainly an academic phenomenon, while the revival of Confucianism appears to have broad cultural and sociological dimensions. Nevertheless, they share the same target of criticism, that is, Enlightenment values and modern Western morality, and their philosophical orientation is the same, that is, a virtue approach to ethics.

The major differences between Aristotle's ethical thinking and modern moral philosophy are usually said to be the following. First, whereas modern ethics focuses on moral acts, Aristotle's ethics concerns the goodness of the agent's whole life. Second, whereas modern ethics considers the task of ethics to formulate rules and principles to govern moral acts, Aristotle's ethics centers on the character and virtue that a person must have in order to live happily or to flourish. The value of an action can only be judged in relation to the character of the agent.

It is not difficult to see that these two features of Aristotle's ethics also characterize Confucius' ethics. First, the concern of Confucius is to find the human dao, i.e. the way to become a good person and to lead a good life. Second, to become a good person, one must cultivate de, that is, a dispositional character (indeed, de has been generally translated as "virtue" in English translations). Confucius calls this dispositional character ren. Ren has been generally translated as "benevolence" or "humanity," but is also widely referred to as "virtue," "complete virtue," or "cardinal virtue." For instance, James Legge (1815-97), who laid down the foundation of the Western translation of Chinese classics, translated *junzi* (the Confucian concept of the good man, that is, the man equipped with *ren*) as "a man of complete virtue."[13] It is in elaborating how one person can become a good person by cultivating *ren* that Confucius reflects and discusses issues such as human nature and its fulfillment, the doctrine of the mean, the role of social custom and traditions, self-cultivation and moral education, love, family, virtue politics, moral emotion and reasoning, and so on. These are also the central themes in Aristotle's theory of virtue. To a great extent, Aristotle's ethics is taken as the paradigmatic model in contemporary virtue ethics precisely because these important ethical concerns have been left out or at least marginalized in dominant modern moral theories.

So far, the revival of Confucianism and the revival of virtue ethics have not crossed paths. Although both movements are searching for an alternative to modern morality, Western virtue ethicists think that the alternative is Aristotle and they rarely pay attention to Confucius. In contrast, for new Confucians, the alternative is Confucius and they seldom refer to Aristotle. It would be safe to say that the movement of "New Confucianism" has not made much impact in the revival of virtue ethics in the West. The good news, however, is that a number of Confucian scholars in the West have applied the conceptual and theoretical issues raised in virtue ethics to the interpretation of Confucianism. These scholars might not be "new Confucians", but this approach is apparently consistent with the spirit of "New Confucianism."

I think we should conduct more effective dialogues in this area. Virtue has been one of the major focuses of Chinese philosophy. As Professor Tang points out, "in Chinese tradition, our sages put more emphasis on the pursuits of a *jing-jie* (a philosophical realm of virtues or latencies to be realized) of life." (p.7) To explore this rich resource should make Chinese philosophy contribute greatly to the movement of the revival of virtue ethics in the West. It can also construe Confucianism as an alternative system of virtue ethics, and can, in Professor Tang's words, "not only follow but also continue Western philosophy, and make new contributions to 'Philosophy' per se." (p.10)

NOTES

1 Plato, *Apology*, 29c.

2 Aristotle, *Poetics*, 1447b11 and *Rhetoric*, 1417a20.

3 Plato, *Gorgias* 515b, *Protagoras* 348c, *Charmides* 166c-d.

4 Plato, *Gorgias*, 508c-509a.

5 Aristotle, *Magna Moralia*, 1213a20-26. Elsewhere, Aristotle adds "neighbor" in a passage that expresses a similar idea. "If we can contemplate our neighbors better than ourselves and their actions better than our own, and if the actions of virtuous men who are their friends are pleasant to good men (since these have both the attributes that are naturally pleasant)—if this be so, the blessed man will need friends of this sort." (*Nicomachean Ethics*, ix.9, 1169b33-1170a2)

6 Aristotle, *Eudemian Ethics*, vii.2, 1235b13-17.

7 Anthony Kenny expresses the following pessimism about the possibility of a unitary reading of Aristotle's *NE*: "No explanation succeeds in the three goals which most commentators have set themselves: (1) to give an interpretation of book 1 and book 10 which does justice to the texts severally; (2) to make the two books consistent with each other; (3) to make the resulting interpretation one which can be found morally acceptable by contemporary philosophy." *Aristotle on the Perfect Life* (Oxford: Clarendon Press, 1992), 93.

8 R. Hursthouse, *On Virtue Ethics* (Oxford: Oxford University Press, 1999) 9.

9 G. E. M. Anscombe, "Modern Moral Philosophy," in *Virtue Ethics*, eds. Roger Crisp and Michael Slote (Oxford: Oxford University press, 1997), 26. The paper was originally published in *Philosophy*, 33(1958).

10 Signed by Carsun Chang, Tang Chun-I, Mou Tsung-San, and Xu Fukuan, simultaneously published in January, 1958, in *Review of Democracy* (Hong Kong) and *Rebirth* (Taiwan). Its English version is included as an appendix in C. Chang's *Development of New-Confucian Thought* [New York: Bookman Associates, 1962, vol.II].

11 "Manifesto," in Chang, *Development of New-Confucian Thought*, II: 466.

12 Tu Wei-ming, "The Third Epoch of Confucian Humanism," in his *Way, Learning, and Politics* (Albany: State University of New York Press, 1993) 141-59.

13 James Legge, *Confucian Analects, The Great Learning and The Doctrine of the Mean* (1893; reprint New York: Dover Publications, 1971), 137.

Comments on the Papers of
Tang Yijie and Roger Ames

Yuann Jeujenq

NOTES ON PROFESSOR TANG YIJIE

Professor Tang stresses a point in the beginning of this concisely formulated paper concerning the 'origin' of Chinese philosophy: a surrogate of Western philosophy. He says rather explicitly that Chinese philosophy did not even exist until incorporated into a 'new formulation' established on the importation of Western philosophy. The word 'formulation' used here contains a specific meaning. Throughout their long history, Chinese undoubtedly have their "philosophical thoughts and philosophical problems", but they are not yet to be called 'philosophy'. Why not? The reason proposed by the author is this. The property of Chinese philosophy, which existed long before its formulation, was to be an inseparable part of the 'studies of Canons and of non-Confucian Masters'. In other words, Chinese philosophy was not an 'independent discipline' until about a hundred years ago. Chinese philosophy causes its birth by cutting itself from the traditional link and replacing the link with the ideas 'borrowed from' Western philosophy. Ironically, the replacement hence makes Chinese philosophy 'clear'. The author says: "The original Chinese philosophical thoughts, problems, terminologies, conceptions and propositions were baptized by Western philosophy, and were made much clearer". (p.5) With this quote, would it then mean that Chinese philosophy lacks clarity by its own nature unless it is accompanied by its Western partner? The answer cannot be a simple 'yes or no' as it goes deeper than this.

According to the paper, the idea 'clarity' here refers to at least two sorts of meaning: to be understandable and to be accessible. Chinese philosophy has to be understandable to its own people by being detached from its dependence upon the tradition of canonical studies. Without this 'detachment', there is no way to make itself explicitly clear in terms of philosophical thinking. Or, Chinese philosophy would not be accessible to the Western people if it remains entirely within the closure of the traditional studies. With the employment of terms, concepts, structures and even elements of ontology from Western philosophy, Chinese philosophy acquires its needed legitimacy and turns itself towards becoming a subject accessible to philosophers everywhere. To some extent, we can say that the formulation of Chinese philosophy proceeded from dependence upon traditional studies to dependence upon Western philosophy. In either way, the subject is unfortunately not to be independent. What appears to be worse than this is the statement that either the compilation of Chinese philosophical heritage or the construction of a modern Chinese philosophy is impossible until Western philosophy is imported into China in the first place. The 'unfortunate fate' of Chinese philosophy, though ineluctable, is regrettable and problematic for the author.

The problems of 'the dependence of Chinese philosophy on its Western counterpart' consist in the following two aspects: the ignorance of the unique characteristics of Chinese thinking and the misunderstanding of the specific reference of Chinese terms. The two examples concerning the unique characteristics are "the non-systematic way of thinking" and "the rejection of the dichotomization of subject and object". The significance of these examples does not limit itself within the extent of being rarely developed in the philosophical tradition of the West. They are also taken into account in the recent development of Continental European philosophy as a source of internal critique of Western philosophy. The author firmly holds the conviction that Chinese philosophy could contribute to World philosophy if the opportunity is given.

The other problem concerns the "losing" of "its pregnancy and particularity" in the indebtedness of Chinese philosophy to its Western counterpart. The solutions suggested by the author are: sinicization and transliteration, two unusual terms, I have to admit. Sinicization appears to be an ongoing work taking place on all fronts of Chinese philosophy by incorporating everything local to the philosophical framework, whereas the idea of transliteration is a suggestion that Chinese philosophy should get rid of all possibilities of misconceiving its terms. As the author holds the idea of 'intranslatability' up to some point, he considers the best way to translate notions of Chinese philosophy (such as *tian*, *Dao*, *Xin*, *Xing*, etc.) within the principle of 'no translation' is transliteration but adding further annotations. An ideal example in his mind is the practice of the time when Indian Buddhism was introduced into China (during Sui and Tang dynasties). With these solutions proposed here, the author maintains that Chinese philosophy will be better situated to benefit not only World philosophy in general and itself in particular.

I personally am very much impressed by Professor Tang's subtle analysis and valuable suggestions. However, one thing remains to me puzzling. If Chinese philosophy, being unavoidably involved in all these problems since its birth, is as a matter of fact an enterprise less than satisfactory for being dependent on Western philosophy, then what should be the judgment on its development so far? Is there an adequate evaluation possible for the efforts done by all Chinese philosophers up to now? I must try to give a positive answer for this question by stressing the importance of the 'localization' of Chinese philosophy'. As the author also emphasizes that 'the construction of any philosophy would necessarily be conditioned by its society and culture', the part of Chinese philosophy we have till now is by no means an exception; it is equally what we can draw from the conditions of society and culture. Once we realize that in the last hundred years or so, the Chinese society and culture went through a tremendous impact from Western society and culture, we would not be surprised by the development of a Chinese philosophy which incorporates many ideas of the West into this development. With this, I can only say all possibilities are open to be judged on the basis of a dynamic way of thinking, rather than on the foundation of an inalterable essence. There is, of course, no such 'essence' available to us as all judgments are done by the people involved depending upon the constant change of the external environment. It is a fact that Chinese philosophy is destined to be deeply involved with its Western counterpart. The 'involvement' depicts nothing but a piece of historical fact. However, in its own context, the further development of Chinese philosophy must be destined to be 'Chinese' regardless of whether the original notions were borrowed from somewhere else.

NOTES ON PROFESSOR ROGER AMES

Among the distinguished features of the relation to Chinese philosophy drawn from reading Professor Ames' paper, two of them are distinct to my mind: frankness and sympathy. His frankness refers to the fact that dialogue of any form would not start unless the involved partners stand on equal footing. Therefore, "the dialogue between Chinese and Western philosophy has yet to occur in our Western corridors". And he also demonstrates his sympathy towards the Chinese side by stressing the anticipated "mutual enrichment" of Chinese and Western philosophy one fine day. His conclusion goes as follows: "While Western philosophy has constituted the mainstream curriculum for the discipline of world philosophy in the twentieth century, the revolution that is taking place within the Western academy itself presages a time when the process sensibilities pervasive in the long Chinese philosophical narrative will become increasingly relevant in finding our way forward". Why is to be frank and sympathetic essential to our concern here, namely, to the dialogue?

The reasons are these. First, there is, in the "Western corridor", still a question concerning "the legitimacy of Chinese philosophy". Is the thing we endorse as "Chinese philosophy" truly qualified to be "philosophy", rather than a sort of Asian religion, a form of Eastern Wisdom, or a mode of Ancient thought? Why should Chinese insist on considering their heritages of traditional thought a kind of "philosophy", a term which ironically does not even exist in their language? What would happen if 'philosophy' exclusively refers to that tradition of Anglo-European philosophy which is currently the "mainstream philosophy" even in China? Why is it so important to acquire a proper definition of Chinese philosophy? To all these questions, the answers are more complex than what we might think at first sight. Apparently, their answer falls at the point where philosophy, as a tradition descended from the Hellenistic era, has its regional reference which has nothing to do with China. However, this understanding of philosophy is too narrow to be correct. Being a discipline taking into account all issues concerning the human species, philosophy has to be broadened in order to include all ideas available for its significance as deeper thought. Hence, the author says clearly that "philosophy is a qualitative claim that speaks to the depth and quality of Chinese thinking with respect to the most important issues that confront us as human beings".

From this statement, we see the author's intention to accept the utility of Chinese wisdom for the fortification of philosophy, but unfortunately his stand remains in the minority in the Western academy concerning the legitimacy of Chinese philosophy.

The paper says frankly that, while philosophy is defined everywhere around the world as "Anglo-European", Chinese philosophy is excluded from "the designated philosophy section". This may be an obvious fact to most of the Westerners, but the Chinese side thinks differently. They think that there are divergent cultures in the world and each has its philosophical heritage. If the academics of this part of the world can do research on that of the Anglo-European one, the academics of the other world certainly can do so on the Chinese. The ideal appears to be fair, but the expected reciprocity never exists!

The introduction of Chinese thought to the Westerners by the missionaries and the sinologists, despite their immortal efforts, caused misunderstandings. The misunderstandings went through a sequence which manifests itself by undermining the significance of Chinese philosophy. The translation of Chinese texts and the study on Chinese thought have been first Christianized, then philosophized, and eventually marginalized. Undoubtedly, the consequence is undesirable as the status of Chinese philosophy in the mind of trained philosophers is haunted by linguistic and conceptual gaps which appear to be results of cultural incommensurability. Referring to Chinese and European philosophy, the dichotomization of two world views is determined well before it is admitted.

Whose loss is this "dichotomization" if Western academics hold firm the idea of Hegel that there are only opinions rather than true knowledge in Chinese philosophy? This paper demonstrates its sympathy towards Chinese philosophy as it is certainly not to the advantage of anybody if an exclusive attitude is endorsed. The Chinese form of wisdom might appear different from their own, but the Western philosophers have no reason to prevent themselves from "the wisdom of loving" and instead to adhere tightly to "the love of wisdom". This certainty explains why even without equal footing, there are a small number of Western philosophers who would take into full account the value of Chinese philosophy for its contribution to "world philosophy". They remain a minority at home for sure, but the situation is likely to change soon, not because of the willingness to change their attitude, but because of the "revival" of process philosophy proposed, among the many, by A. N. Whitehead and American pragmatists. I do not want to hide the author's optimism concerning the likely change from his point of view, but he does show a good sign concerning the predicament of Western philosophy: "the conventional notion of God."

It is "conventional" for being less concerned with a specific religion than with a general epistemic position: the monolithic "one-behind-the-many model" of knowledge. Regardless of its practical function throughout centuries in the West, it is portrayed in this paper as an obstacle to productive discussions among philosophical traditions. It reifies what could move on their more tolerant track to a track which is not only more 'universal' but also more 'rigid': the ideas of conversation, philosophy and globalization. For these ideas, there are always two-fold ways capturing their meaning. The idea of conversation could be, on its more tolerant track, the pursuit of mutual accord through listening and then speaking philosophy, its association with practical wisdom and globalization, and its mutual accessibility of cultural sensibilities. Yet, with the "conventional notion of God", these ideas in reality stand on a more rigid track as follows: A dialogical way of thinking about conversation as leading to the univocal truth, an exclusive, scientific way of thinking about philosophy as having the discovery of certain knowledge as its object and its occupation, and a colonizing, imperialistic way of thinking about the ineluctable forces of globalization. Is this a deadlock between two incommensurable world views which confront all ideas? It appears so until the author informs us of a piece of good news.

The good news refers to an internal critique of Western philosophy in general and the reinstatement of process philosophy in particular. The above-mentioned idea of God, repudiated by Whitehead as the fallacy of misplaced concreteness, needs to achieve a productive harmony which "can only emerge out of the real experience of unique persons" (p. 31). Having said this, the author immediately draws our attention to the likely contribution of Chinese philosophy in this regard. What he follows is Tang Junyi's idea that "the commitment of the particular to do its best to realize the totality (p. 20) is a perfect exemplar of 'process sensibilities'. It is so simply because these 'possibilities' constitute a tradition pervasive since the beginning of the development of Chinese philosophy'. I accept that this is a sympathetic, and more precisely, an optimistic stand concerning the future of Chinese philosophy. However, the optimistic stand does not thus urge me to deem that the dialogue would start its course soon. The reason is not difficult to detect and it can be reformulated to the following question: Would it be easy to get rid of the notion of God in a tradition which is proud of its distinguished achievements of science and technology, achievements contributed rather ironically by the very notion? Nobody can give a straight answer to this hypothetical question, yet we are keen to say that until the issues of science and technology have been addressed in the first place, I can only see the paper's substantial frankness and its idealistic sympathy. Indeed, as the author says, the dialogue has yet to occur.

Chapter 4

Western Unacceptance of "Chinese Philosophy": The Legitimacy of an Illegitimate Position

Carine Defoort

The particular topic here is communication between Chinese and Western philosophy. Professor Tang Yijie argues that Chinese philosophy became an independent discipline only due to the importing of Western philosophy. That was indeed an exciting event in Chinese history: scholars such as Hu Shi and Feng Youlan saw the creation of Chinese philosophy as a new way of looking at their own culture as well as a bridge for cultural communication with colleagues in the West. Feng Youlan was all the more disappointed that Western philosophers never took their Chinese counterpart seriously. On the last page of the last volume of his *New History of Chinese Philosophy*, written a few weeks before his death in November 1990, Feng concluded that Western philosophers had not even started considering ancient Chinese thought worth their attention: "Chinese traditional philosophy has always been regarded as a part of sinological studies and is considered as having no relation with philosophy."[1] Indeed, various eminent European philosophers, such as Kant, Hegel, Husserl, Heidegger, and more recently Jacques Derrida on his visit to Shanghai in 2001, have proclaimed that ancient Chinese thought is not really philosophy, but only thought.

This Western rejection is to some extent due to the cultural chauvinism and arrogance of scholars less generous towards Chinese culture than Professors Tang Yijie and Roger Ames. Therefore it would have been all the more interesting to invite some of them to hear what they have to say for themselves. But strangely, we are exclusively meeting here with scholars who do believe in the legitimacy and value of Chinese philosophy. Although I am one of them, I nevertheless want to take up the defense of those who are absent, by arguing that at least part of the reluctance to accept Chinese philosophy cannot be simply rejected as mere chauvinism. Put differently, this is a plea for the inevitability of some degree of chauvinism on the Chinese as well as the Western side. Since this chauvinism has prevented the acceptance of Chinese philosophy for about one century, it deserves our attention, rather than mere rejection.

In order to analyze and, to some extend, defend the legitimacy of this illegitimate position, I want to use Whitehead's image of 'friendship' quoted by Roger Ames as an analogy of fruitful communication between people and cultures. Ames uses this analogy in order to promote a harmonious and concrete interaction, a 'vibrant disclosure' as an alternative to the abstract philosophical approach. I want to argue that all friendship, including mine with Roger, also accepts and respects 'closure': there are topics that we avoid, interests that we do not share, concerns that we fail to catch on to, often without being able to give good reasons for our attitude. And yet, we respectfully remain friends.

A second inspiration of my approach is Wittgenstein's idea of 'family resemblances'. Many Chinese scholars have argued that in the debate concerning the legitimacy of Chinese philosophy, we should not search in vain for a definition of philosophy, but rather trace its 'family resemblances'. While they refer to this idea in a negative sense, namely in order to desist from the search for a common essence dwelling behind all the manifestations of philosophy, I would like to take the analogy a step further to highlight something positive. The members of a family may not all share a common essence, but there is something else that binds them: a family name. In contrast to a generic noun, whose meaning may be the object of debate, the average family name is something arbitrary and largely devoid of meaning. It has no abstract essence and cannot be defined. The failure of the cultural communication concerning philosophy also lies, I believe, in the fact that this term to some (even though minor) extent functions like a family name.

The history of philosophy in the West could then also be read as the chronicle of a large family or clan. Descendents are usually born through studying philosophy, lecturing and publishing in it. Now and then a bastard is spawned, from literature, linguistics, history or anthropology, whose right to the family name is unclear or disputed. As in many families, adoption can incite protest, particularly when many foreign authors come to claim the name. This happened in the early 20th century when Feng Youlan proclaimed the ancient Chinese masters 'philosophers'. Some family members simply do not want an outsider to adopt their name, even though they do not quite know why they are themselves deserving of that name. Their protest cannot be adequately founded because there are no defendable criteria or intrinsic reasons to deny this name to others. But the absence of a crystal-clear criterion of what exactly philosophy is only makes the question that much more sensitive.

Therefore, however intimate a proper name, it also remains "ex-timate".[2] Its "unhomeliness" is, according to Rudi Visker, due to a lack of control: one does not choose it, nor can one determine what it means, what privileges or duties are attached to it. The emptiness of the family name thus maintains uncertainty not only concerning the question of who has rights to it, but also concerning the responsibilities it imposes. "The name, as it were, always leaves its job half done, it suggests that there is something proper to its bearer, but there is never 'enough' of the name to know in what that something consists, and yet always 'too much' to simply ignore what it thus singled out." One must hold the name high, but what are its demands? We are attached to something that remains inaccessible to us; we are rooted in our "uprootedness". This passive relation to one's name forces the subject out of its own center. The subject is thus "attached to something to which it does not find access and from which it cannot rid itself, because it is that to which it owes its singularity."[3] This ambiguous and uncomfortable situation also characterizes, I believe, the Western philosophers' relation to philosophy.

Our Chinese colleagues find themselves in a similar but somewhat different predicament: while their academic activity also derives meaning from the framework within which they operate, they are aware that one of their forefathers was an adopted child. They know that even after a century, Western philosophers often do not consider them family members of equal standing. Some of them reject the adoption and prefer to function without the name and demands of "philosophy". Fu Sinian once remarked in a private letter to Gu Jiegang: "I do not approve of Mr. Hu Shi's designation of the records on Laozi, Confucius, Mozi et al. as the history of philosophy. China did not originally have a so-called philosophy, thank god for giving our tribe such a healthy practice."[4] But the majority of Chinese colleagues, following Feng Youlan or Hu Shi, propose that the ancient masters do belong to the great philosophical family. Some among that majority demand or predict that philosophy family will adapt itself to its adopted children by becoming broader and more pluralist.

Another difference is that "philosophy" in China probably has fewer proper name qualities than in the West. Indeed, it tends more towards a generic noun. Since it became part of the expression "Chinese philosophy", the name "Philosophy" in itself has lost some of its sensitivity in China to the name "Chinese": while the former may retain something foreign, the latter indicates home. "Chinese" more clearly contains characteristics of a proper name than the term "philosophy". Nationality is the name of one's group.[5] Again, there is an attachment to being American or European, French or Chinese, although we do not know what exactly these names mean. In his analysis of attitudes towards national feelings in terms of attachments to proper names, Visker identifies two opposite attempts to re-center the de-centered subject. The former is the sort of nationalism (or other types of particularism) that tries completely to fill the emptiness that comes with a name. It admits that people are attached to something and believes that they can get total access to it. Confident statements about the essence of being Chinese are instances of this strategy. The opposite attempt can be associated with universalism, which sees the particular name as something irrelevant, since it is arbitrary and impossible to uniquely describe. In their opposition to the essentialist claims of particularism, universalists stress the fact that a Chinese native simply does not exist, thus rejecting expressions of particularistic attachment as nationalistic delusions. Both are attempts--very common but misguided, according to Visker--to regain control, to undo the uncomfortable position of *finding oneself* attached to something to which one does not totally know, something one has not actively attached oneself.

The description of "Philosophy" as a proper name is not proposed here as a theory on names, but rather as an analysis of attachment. A proper name--one's family name or nationality--can be seen as paradigmatic for something that is both sensitive and yet relatively meaningless, such as one's gender, race or species. We are attached to it without knowing exactly what it is. To the, admittedly minor, extent that "(Western) Philosophy" and "Chinese (Philosophy)" function like proper names, we belong to them as to our family or tribe. This type of belonging, combining familiarity with the ultimately unfamiliar, can shed light on the sensitivity of the question.

A first characteristic of a family or tribe is that its common norms and daily habits are largely implicit. The parochial context predates and shapes the subject; few things are more irritating for an outsider than these meaningless habits. Implicit views of philosophy, as one largely acquires them during one's academic training in a particular setting, are like habits. Most philosophers in the West do not reflect at length about the definition of philosophy before excluding the Chinese masters. This rejection belongs to the background of philosophical activity, while its acceptance has largely lived an equally implicit life in China. Many Chinese scholars, sinologists and some Western philosophers are vexed by this implicit exclusion of Chinese philosophy on the basis of what they consider exclusively Western and even modern criteria.

But when contemporary Western scholars seriously reflect on the meaning of philosophy, as philosophers occasionally do, they tend to disagree with these implicit norms and with each other. In their reflections, a second characteristic of family bonding is often revealed, namely emotional commitment, predominantly pride. For instance, Husserl, Heidegger, Derrida, Deleuze and Guattari, each in their own way, seem to be thinking of philosophy as a tribal activity, something particular to their own culture. Even though they consider philosophy universal in its ambitions, claims, interest, relevance or historical evolution, they are fascinated by the early Greeks as by their own ancestors.[6] They are proud of philosophy in a way that a Chinese may be proud of Shadowboxing. And they reject the idea of an ancient "Chinese philosophy" just as Chinese people would deny that the West has always had its own *Tàijíquán*. Scholars of Chinese thought tend to be more proud of the Chinese intellectual heritage--whether or not labeled as philosophy--than about philosophy.

This combination of implicit ethnocentrism and explicit cultural pride may sound like a comfortable position. But the analogy with the proper name further suggests a third characteristic, namely a dimension of strangeness in one's own home. Belonging to a certain family or tribe is beyond one's personal control: not only is it a given and not-chosen fact, its meaning is also largely determined by others. From very early on in life, one is identified by others as belonging to that family. The fact that we have not consciously and carefully chosen a certain family does not make the bond any weaker. On the contrary, consciously chosen bonds--marriage or adoption--often turn out to be the weakest in a family. The emotional commitment that ensues from this bond is complex. Pride is only one possible part of it and a rather intriguing one. But there are often other emotions involved in one's belonging to a tribe, such as love, concern, but also embarrassment, shame or even revolt or guilt. Without having chosen to be American or Chinese, one nevertheless feels attached to one's nationality: proudly or shamefully, gratefully or reluctantly, or in a mixture of all these and other emotions.

The strongest type of attachment, fourthly, is probably not with the family in which one is born, but with one's own children. Although parents nowadays can choose to have children, they cannot (yet) determine how the child will be. However it turns out, parents tend to love it dearly. They know that these feelings do not depend on a judgment concerning the child's character or features, but on the mere fact that this child happens to be theirs. Since parents know that their attachment is deeper than all the good reasons they can give in support of it, they can accept the neighbor's relative indifference towards their child. Though they may occasionally expound on the many reasons for their pride, they also consider it a matter of good taste not to overdo this. One can be impressed by one's own tradition and give descriptions of its merits, but recognition and admiration by others cannot be forced. There should always be some acceptance of the failure of argumentation in this matter. Overly self-confident statements on the nature of Chinese philosophy and insistence on its absolute superiority in the world are not only a breach of good manners, they indicate also one's incapacity to stand the predicament of being, in Visker's terms, de-centered. Milder and tentative reflections suggest, paradoxically, a more confident acceptance of this predicament.

Fifth, besides a lack of control over one's emotional entanglement and the limits of argumentation, family relations are also characterized by a failure to fully understand. Deleuze and Guattari explicitly distinguish their reflection on the nature of philosophy from hurried thoughts on the topic, when "one kept asking the question, but too indirectly or obliquely, too artificially, too abstractly, and one expounded it, dominated it, in passing rather than being grabbed by it... One was too eager to do philosophy, so that one failed to ask oneself what it was." The reflection they undertake is not young or overly confident, but comes with old age, occurs at midnight, when one wonders: "But what is it that I have been doing all my life?"[7] Perhaps because "philosophie" in French is a female noun, the authors' approach reminds one of a loving and lucid husband who, after several decades of marriage life, still wonders about the peculiarities of his wife's character, the mysteries of his most intimate companion. Philosophy loses her air of transparency as one really tries to see through her mysteries. According to Derrida, philosophy is never a given: despite the fact that philosophy is from our soil, it has always retained something foreign: "Under her Greek name and in her European memory, she has always been a bastard, hybrid, grafted, multilinear, polyglot...".[8] Concise definitions and general statements in footnotes or prefaces concerning the definition of philosophy are usually no indication of a close acquaintance with her.

And finally, we tend to forget that philosophy is a "love" affair that one has with "wisdom". Love affairs are not always as innocent as the life-long fascination with one's partner: they make philosophers jealous, uncertain and unfair towards others. Although the *philo* for *sophia*--the *ai* 爱, which does *not* occur in Chinese neologisms for "philosophy"--is usually understood as a continuous search for wisdom or some form of blissful contemplation, it may also be seen as a source of painful contention and unfair exclusion. It is easy to recognize the threat posed by the enormous Chinese corpus of texts to the average Western professor who will never master its difficult scripts. Like a jealous husband, he rejects the Chinese rival without knowing him. This mechanism of exclusion on a more philosophical level is analyzed by Wu Xiao-ming as the "relation of philosophy with the irreducible other that it nevertheless endeavors to reduce."[9] The aim of Western philosophy is to determine its own identity by excluding the other: China. Chinese thought is presented as non-philosophy, the limit of philosophy, its proper other. Being "the only discourse that has ever intended to receive its name from itself,"[10] philosophy thus re-appropriates the other as exactly that which is excluded.

The six family features which I have identified with attachments to "Chinese" and "philosophy"--implicit norms, parochial pride, lack of control, limits of argumentation, lack of knowledge and jealousy--are only part of a larger picture. Of course, the question of the legitimacy of Chinese philosophy should not be reduced to that: rational arguments as those presented by Tang Yijie and Roger Ames, retain their relevance, as long as one respects their limits. Even though the members of this meeting here probably all agree on the legitimacy of Chinese philosophy, we also belong to different branches of the family of philosophy so that part of what happens here is not rational understanding and misunderstanding or argumentative agreement and disagreement, but also polite disinterest or failure to see the relevance of someone's approach. Although increasing cultural contacts may allow Western and Chinese scholars to become more familiar with each other, and thus perhaps--not necessarily--to understand and appreciate each other better, there will always be some attachment to tribal habits as there is to one's own children. The lack of a perfect mutual understanding may be counterbalanced by some understanding of why we do not totally understand each other. Here too, we can learn from Confucius' first saying in which he urges one to "behave like a gentleman, if one is not understood or appreciated by others."

NOTES

1 See Feng Youlan 冯友兰, *Zhongguo zhexueshi xinbian* 中国哲学 新编 (A New Edition of the History of Chinese Philosophy): Vol. 7 (Taibei: Landeng, 1991), p. 209.

2 See Visker, R., *Truth and Singularity: Taking Foucault into Phenomenology* (Dordrecht: Kluwer, 1999), p. 19, using Jacques Lacan.

3 See Visker, *Truth and Singularity: Taking Foucault into Phenomenology*, pp. 1, 11-13.

4 See Fu Sinian 傅斯年, "Yu Gu Jiegang lun gushishu" 與顧頡剛論 古史書 (Debating Books on Ancient History with Gu Jiegang), in *Fu Sinian quanji* 傅斯年全集 (Complete Collection of Fu Sinian): Vol. 4 (Taibei: Lianjing, 1980), 454-494, p. 374.

5 See Lyotard, J.F., "Le nom et l'exception", in H. Nagl-Docekal e.a. (ed.), *Tod des Subjekts?* (München: Oldenbourg Verlag, 1987), 43-53, p. 51.

6 Husserl characterizes philosophy as the disinterested pursuit of "theoria" for its own sake and, therefore, denies its existence in any other

ancient culture, including the Chinese. See his, "The Vienna Lecture: Philosophy and the Crisis of European Humanity", appendix of *The Crisis of European Sciences and Transcendental Phenomenolohy: an Introduction to Phenomenological Philosophy,* trans. D. Carr (Evanston, Northwestern University Press, 1935, 1970), pp. 279-80. See also Heidegger, *Was ist das – die Philosophie?*, p. 13 and Deleuze & Guattari, *Qu'est-ce que la philosophie?*, p. 92.

    7 Deleuze & Guattari, *Qu'est-ce que la philosophie?*, p. 7.

    8 Derrida, Jacques, *Le droit à la philosophy du point de vue cosmopolitique* (Verdier: Editions Unesco, 1997), pp. 1, 33.

    9 Wu, "Philosophy, *Philosophia*, and *Zhe-xue*", p. 409.

    10 *Ibid.*, p. 431.

REFERENCES

Defoort, C., "Is There Such a Thing as Chinese Philosophy? Arguments of an Implicit Debate", *Philosophy East and West* 51.3 (2001), 393-413.

Deleuze, G. & F. Guattari, *Qu'est-ce que la philosophie?* (Paris: Les éditions de minuit, 1991).

Derrida, Jacques, *Le droit à la philosophy du point de vue cosmopolitique* (Verdier: Editions Unesco, 1997).

Feng Youlan 冯友兰, *Zhongguo zhexueshi xinbian* (A New Edition of the History of Chinese Philosophy), vol. 7 (Taibei: Landeng. 1991).

Fu Sinian 傅斯年, "Yu Gu Jiegang lun gushishu" (與顧頡剛論古史書) (Debating Ancient Chinese Historical books with Gu Jiegang), 傅斯年全集 (Complete Collection of Fu Sinian), (Taibei: Lianjing, 1980), vol .4, 454-494.

Husserl, E., trans. D. Carr, "The Vienna Lecture: Philosophy and the Crisis of European Humanity", the appendix of *The Crisis of European Sciences and Transcendental Phenomenolohy: an Introduction to Phenomenological Philosophy* (Evanston: Northwestern University Press, 1935, 1970), 269-289.

Lyotard, J.F., "Le nom et l'exception", in H. Nagl-Docekal e.a. ed., *Tod des Subjekts?* (München: Oldenbourg Verlag, 1987), 43-53.

Visker, R., *Truth and Singularity. Taking Foucault into Phenomenology* (Dordrecht: Kluwer, 1999).

Wu Xiao-ming, "Philosophy, *Philosophia*, and *Zhe-xue*", *Philosophy East and West* 48.3 (1998), 406-452.

Some Progressive and Problematic Features of Current Philosophy in China

Zhao Dunhua

Brief Review and more Recent Progress

By "current philosophy in China" I mean philosophical studies since 1980s when China adopted the policy of reform and opening. To appreciate the progress of philosophy in those years, it is helpful to review contemporary Chinese philosophy in the previous decades. The beginnings of contemporary Chinese philosophy was characterized by its creativity, variety and fruitfulness. I consider this the second, "golden stage" of Chinese philosophy, being second only to the "one hundred schools" stage more than 2,200 years ago. Active figures in the period between 1920s and 50s, such as Hu Shih, Feng Youlan, He Lin, Cha Hong, Zhang Dailian, etc., are founders of contemporary philosophy in China. All of those masters and the later Neo-Confucians in Hong Kang and Taiwan, by combining the heritage of traditional thoughts with newly introduced ideas of Western philosophy, laid a firm and broad foundation for philosophical studies even until nowadays. This philosophical prosperity disappeared, however, in the 1950s when Marxism became the dominant ideology of China. Marxism in China in the time between 1950s and 80s, like in the Soviet Union, was distorted as "Communist Party philosophy" and "Communist Party philosophy is simply the philosophy of struggle." This kind of philosophy climaxed in the Cultural Revolution, as expressed in the propaganda slogan: "Endless happiness in the struggle against heaven! Endless happiness in the struggle against earth! Endless happiness in the struggle among people!" (all quoted from Mao's sayings)

The new policy since 1980s has rendered Chinese scholars more flexible in thinking. Philosophy is going forward along with the economic and social progress in China. The following progressive features are to be noticed:

(1) Marxist philosophy is grounded on its own basis. People are no longer content with the system of "dialectic materialism and historical materialism", which was first outlined by Stalin in *History of the All Union Communist Party (Bolsheviks): Short Course*,[1] and fixed its 'orthodoxy' in a text book. In order to get out of the shadow of Stalinism, some Chinese Marxists propose "humanist philosophy" or "practical materialism" to highlight the essentials of Marxism; some interpret Marxism mainly as a political and moral philosophy, with the central problem how to get rid of the alienation not only in capitalism, but also in socialism; some believe that the reasonable ground

of Marxism can only be founded either in the original texts of Marx, or in the dialogues with the "Western Marxism". In other words, the right way of doing Marxist philosophy is either "going back to Marx" or "being contemporary with Marx". In studies of Marx's texts and Western Marxism, those questions raised in the Western scholarship become hot points for debate. Is "dialectic of nature" a legitimate concept? How far does Marx differ from Engels and Lenin? How is Young Marx related to Later Marx? Is "praxis" an ontological notion for Marx? Did Marx provide a materialist worldview? Needless to say, debates around those questions manifest difference not only in exegesis, but also in ideology. Leftists (old and new) and rightists (old and new) give conflicting answers to those questions. Sometimes the Party leaders are concerned with, even occasionally interfere in the seemingly academic debate. Even though scholars were rarely punished for their opinions in the ideologically flavored debate, we should not satisfy ourselves with the minimum degree of freedom. Further progress is to be made for free expressions in all academic affairs.

(2) Specialists in Chinese traditional philosophy and Western philosophy are liberated from the bondage of materialistic model of interpretation. This model was set up by Zhdanov who was the Party Secretary in charge of ideology under Stalin. In 1948, he defined the history of philosophy as "fighting between two campuses, the materialists and idealists, usually, the former are progressive and the latter counter-revolutionary". His definition dominated Chinese philosophers for more than 30 years. Western philosophers, except for Hegel, Feuerbach, and those few who were praised by Marx and Engels, were accused of counter-revolutionary idealism. Classical philosophy was interpreted as nothing but footnotes of Marxist works, and contemporary Western philosophy was condemned as ideology of the decadent, impotent and decaying bourgeois. In the same model, all concepts of Chinese traditional philosophy were divided into the dichotomy of two categories, i.e., "matter" (or "existence") and "spirit" (or "thinking"). By the criterion looking to see whether the alleged "matter" is prior to "spirit", the label of "materialist" or "idealist" was imposed on all Chinese philosophers. After abandoning Zhdanov's definition in the early 1980s, some dramatic changes have been undertaken. Western philosophy and Chinese traditional philosophy have become independent disciplines. Chinese and Western philosophers in the past are studied in detail and evaluated on the basis of their own, not in accordance with their relation to Marxism or materialism in general. Their thoughts are accepted as the precious heritage of human culture and living elements in modern life. The three mainstreams of Chinese traditional philosophy, Confucianism, Taoism and Buddhism, are pervading all cultural discourses, from academic studies of humanity to the medium and folk culture. Among Western philosophers, the figures of the "cultural fever" are contemporary Continent philosophers such as Sartre, Nietzsche, Freud, and Heidegger, Foucault, Derrida in the sequence of time from early 1980s to nowadays. Western classical and modern Analytic philosophers, such as Plato, Aristotle, Kant, Hegel, Wittgenstein, are studied mostly for the interest of academic research.

(3) Philosophical studies are expanded to be a comprehensive field. In the discipline catalog made by the Ministry of Education, Philosophy is a discipline of the first order, including 8 disciplines of the second order: Marxist philosophy, Chinese philosophy, foreign philosophy, ethics, aesthetics, logic, philosophy of science and technology, religious studies. This division is not very reasonable; it can nevertheless show how comprehensive philosophy in China today is. By analyzing the comprehensiveness, we can understand its pro-active status.

First, philosophy departments in China often are large in scale; there are in average about 50 faculties and hundreds of students on different levels, from B.A. to Ph.D., in a philosophy department. Those departments cover the specialties which usually are in several departments or schools in the universities in the West. For example, Marxist studies in political science, Chinese philosophy in sinology or Eastern studies, aesthetics in literature and religious studies belonging to an independent department. This difference explains the reason why philosophy departments in China are usually (not always) larger than those in the West.

Second, religious studies are affiliated with philosophy, yet not limited to the philosophy of religion. For the purpose of the interdisciplinary studies of religion, Peking University established the first department of religious studies among state universities in China (mainland, Taiwan and Hong Kong) in 1995. Due to the fact that the discipline of religious studies is a division of philosophy, the department of religious studies is affiliated with the philosophy department. This mode of the two joint departments at Peking University was soon adopted by other universities. By now about 20 universities established departments or institutes of religious studies within a philosophy department. The prosperity of religious studies in philosophy is caused partly by the national interest in religious culture and of Christian studies.

Third, Marxist philosophy parallels other disciplines of the second order. This means independence of each philosophical discipline from others. Admittedly, the independence can be both advantageous and disadvantageous. Its advantage allows Western philosophy and Chinese traditional philosophy not to obey Marxism. They can be developed by and for themselves. It is disadvantageous, however, when the independence results in separation of different disciplines of philosophy. Philosophy in China now is like Shakespeare's King Lear who divided his kingdom into three parts occupied by each of his three daughters, and nevertheless found no place of his own. The current Chinese philosophers are not doing philosophy in general, but are experts in one of those eight disciplines. Experts in Marxist philosophy need not study Western philosophy. Even in considering "Western Marxism", the background knowledge of contemporary Western philosophy often is not available. Experts in the history of philosophy specialize in one philosopher or one philosophical school either in China or in the West, but do not often cross the boundary between China and West to do comparative studies. Many experts in ethics or aesthetics do not have sufficient knowledge of Western or

Chinese philosophy; many experts in logic consider analytic philosophy to be a foreign field; and many experts in philosophy of science take "dialectics of nature" as their major, and treat logical positivists, Popper, Kuhn, etc., as Western philosophers belonging to the subject matter of another discipline. I share with some Chinese intellectuals the worry that the separation of disciplines has impeded the exchange and dialogue which are essential to, and necessary for, philosophical development.

PROBLEMATIC ISSUES

In order to warn of the danger of the self-isolation of each discipline, I organized a topical discussion. As a result, six articles under the heading "Contemporary China's Philosophy: From Dialogue to Innovation" was published in *Social Science in China* (the only English journal in mainland China). In the Editorial, I wrote:

> Due to the lack of a fruitful dialogue, Chinese philosophers in each discipline have encountered a number of tricky problems. For example, Marxist philosophers have come up against the following questions. Is Marxism merely a revolutionary ideology that contends with the Western philosophical tradition, or does it result from the historical development of Western philosophy? Is contemporary "Western Marxism" truly a continuation of Marxism, or just a distortion of it? Are Western philosophers after Hegel able to provide rich resources for the further development? Current studies of traditional Chinese philosophy are asked to deal with some key questions about the nature, subject matter and methodology of this discipline. Was there philosophy in the genuine sense of the word in the ancient China? Is Chinese philosophy "westernized" philosophy in disguise? Is it possible to do comparison of philosophies without an oriental or an occidental bias, and if so, how this to be done? Chinese studies of Western philosophy have been recently challenged by the difficulty of translation of a few key terms. In the late few years, dispute has focused on the meaning of Being (and its equivalents of *to on, esse, Sein, étant* in the European languages). Can "Being" be translated unequivocally into one Chinese word, or it is a concept with many meanings correlating to several words in Chinese? If the former is the case, which one in Chinese is correlated to "Being"? "Existence" ("*cunzai*"), "is-ness" (*shi*), and "there-is" ("*you*") are all candidates, but which one is most fitting? If the latter is the case, how do we understand the unity of metaphysical thinking in different contexts? Those are questions relevant not only to the translation of Western philosophy, but also to

understanding of ontology in ancient China and Marxism. The fact that there is no correlation of "Being" to a single Chinese term is taken as an evidence of the non-presence of ontology ("science of Being") in ancient China. The equation of *"Sein"* with *"Existenz"* by Engles[2] has tempted some Chinese to reconstruct Marxist ontology ...... In view of the complexity and profoundness of those questions, answers cannot be given in a satisfactory manner within the confines of the second-order disciplines. This situation show the urgent need to break down the isolation of Marxist philosophy, Chinese traditional philosophy and Western philosophy in China's philosophical studies. [3]

I cannot give solutions in this paper to the above questions. What I intend is to indicate some developmental directions in the conflicting trends as shown in various disputes among Chinese philosophers today. The conflicting trends can be classified in four headings: (i) convergence and divergence, (ii) universalism and particularism, (iii) ideology and its critique, (iv) local and worldly philosophy. Let me examine those issues one by one in the following.

CONVERGENCE AND DIVERGENCE

Zhungzi said, "From the view point of difference, liver and gallbladder in the body are like two distant countries; from the view point of similarity, all things are one and the same."[4] Those words illustrate a paradox of comparative philosophy: whether the convergence or divergence approach is to be adopted. Since the time of Hegel, the divergence approach has been prevalent in West. The difference between Chinese and Western philosophies was sometimes exaggerated to the extent that no Chinese thought could meet the criterion which specifies certain Western thought as philosophy. Due to the occidentalist presupposition, the question whether there was philosophy in the ancient China has been raised frequently among sinologists.

Strangely enough, the same question has been raised by Chinese philosophers themselves, as a reaction to the occidentalist notion of philosophy. When Derrida visited China in 2002, he said to the public, "China had no philosophy, but only thinking." This is praise for China in accordance with the deconstruction of philosophy by his discourse ("thinking" this time). But his praise misled some specialists in traditional Chinese philosophy to reach the conclusion that "Chinese philosophy" is not a legitimate concept. They argued that Chinese and Western thoughts are so divergent that the two differ in their essential nature, mentality, or mode of life. According to them, philosophy was a creation by Westerners to express their thinking and living experience; as such it is characterized by logical thinking, conceptual analysis, dichotomy of binary concepts, and request for Truth and exact knowledge. None of those directed Chinese thought; the contrary was true for the ancient Chinese. In the debate some defended the legitimacy of Chinese philosophy by auguring that this is a philosophy with Chinese characteristics; that we should get rid of the westernization of philosophy; that we Chinese should "think our own thoughts and think by ourselves."

In my opinion, both parties in the debate on the "legitimacy of Chinese philosophy" share common presuppositions that Chinese and Western thoughts differ in essence; that there is an essence which accounts for what is the "Chinese thinking" or the "Western thinking". The two parties disagree only on the question whether the alleged Chinese essence was philosophical or not. The crucial point is that the presupposed contrary essences simply did not exist in Chinese and Western philosophy. Oppositions between logical and figurative thinking, conceptual analysis and overall synthesis, dichotomy and unity, exact knowledge and enigmatic discourse, orientation to Truth and focus on Morals, are neither necessary nor sufficient to differentiate Chinese and Western philosophy. Most pre-Socratic and modern philosophers like Pascal, Nietzsche, or Confucius and Laozi, all gave rise to many enigmas, while Mencius, Mozi, Xunzi are as logical as Plato and Aristotle. Augustine and Dong Zhongshu had a common style of writing on an overall world view, yet both were interested in analysis of terms. Zhu Xi and Aquinas were both synthetic and analytic. Needless to say, most great philosophers, no matter whether they are Chinese or Westerners, were concerned both for Truth and Goodness. In other words, the "essence" of defining Western philosophy is applicable to the Chinese, too; and vice versa.

I do not thereby deny the respective unities of Chinese and Western philosophy. Each unity is not, however, caused by a distinctive essence, but by the systemization of its history. In the Western world, systematic accounts of history of philosophy began in the second half of 17th century, in the writings of Geirge Horn of Leyden, Thomas Stanley and Jacob Brucker, etc. Hegel came later on the scene, but set up a model for the unity of philosophy through its history. The systematic account of Chinese philosophy did not appear until Hu Shih and Fung Youlan undertook this task in 1920s. It was by accident that both studied in the U.S., and they wrote history of Chinese philosophy when coming back. This fact does not mean that studies of the history of Chinese philosophy were "westernized" from the very beginning. The Western influence, if there were any, was simply on the making of unity of Chinese philosophy through writing its history. Wang Guowei, a founder of the modern Chinese academics, said correctly that even in the time when there was no name of philosophy, it was actually present. The actuality of Chinese philosophy needs to be fixed by disciplinary studies. Chinese philosophy became a discipline recognized by international academic circles only when historical materials were gathered and arranged into a unity. But this does not mean that there had been no Chinese philosophy before its unitary history was written. Likewise, Western philosophy had existed long before the writings of its history in the 17th century.

It is worth noting that writing the history of philosophy is an historical reconstruction, and it abides by the interpretation of hermeneutics.

An historical reconstruction is relative to social conditions and theoretical circumstances, but is not an arbitrary interpretation; there are "good" and "bad" interpretations. As far as convergence and divergence approaches are concerned, there is no a prior reason why the former is better than the latter. Zhdanov's mode of the history of philosophy, as mentioned above, made all philosophical theories converge on Engels' distinction between matter and spirit. Convergence approaches of this kind failed, but this does not prove the correctness of the divergence approach which has been pervasive in the domain of comparative philosophy. On the contrary, I believe that in current situations the convergence approach is better or more reasonable than the divergence one. I will explain the practical as well as theoretical reasons why this is so.

PARTICULARISM AND UNIVERSALISM

When Max Weber criticized Chinese culture in terms of particularism in contrast with the universalism of Puritanism, he could never imagine that his assessments would be reversed after 80 years. While universalism is denied as a Western prejudice by postmodernism, particularism is hailed as a high value for Chinese identity. Particularism of this kind is dressed with a new cloth, being called "Chinese characteristics". Since the Party claimed socialism with Chinese characteristics as its course and doctrine, the label has been popularized by bureaucratic intellectuals as a symbol of "political correctness", as a cheap tag stuck on every discipline and social domain. We have now: market economy with Chinese characteristics (abbreviated as Cc hereafter), Marxism with Cc, economics with Cc, jurisprudence with Cc, legal science with Cc, social science with Cc, political science with Cc, and philosophy with Cc, of course.

It is reasonable for a nation to adopt socio-political policy with its own characteristics, but it is quite unusual for social scientists and philosophers to be proud of scholarship with a particular national characteristic, and not seek for universalized knowledge. I once compared the Chinese with Jewish thinkers: both have old traditions and cultural identities. Jewish thinkers, by contrast, inspired by a sense of a worldly mission, always aim at universal truths. If they were devoted to theories with "Jewish characteristics", there would be no Marxism, no Freudianism and, no Einsteinian relativist theory for all human beings.

The particularism pervading Chinese academics is related to the cultural relativism which is developed into a kind of ethnic nationalism in many developing countries after the Second World War. As Anthony Smith observed, ethnic nationalism of this kind is characterized by the formation and persistence of collective cultural identity, the myth of common ancestor and descent, the sentiment of ethnic centrality and superiority, the mobilization of mass against colonization, and the traditionalism of the elite.[5] We are witnessing all of those characteristics in the "philosophy with Chinese characteristics".

Conservatives in Chinese traditional philosophy have attempted to prove the uniqueness of the "Chinese mentality" with the alleged evidences of "unique origin" of the Chinese people more than two million years ago, and "continuous progression" of the Chinese civilization in more than ten thousands years. In order to emphasize the modern role of Chinese traditional philosophy, they try to justify its superiority over Western philosophy by spreading an arrogant prediction that the 21st century is the Chinese one, or the ungrounded news that many Nobel winners gathered in Paris had published a declaration that human beings would not be able to survive without Confucius' thought. To my and many others' ears the most beautiful song in our age is: "We are the world; we are the children." But what we are hearing is the incongruous sounds: "We are the Chinese; we are the oldest."

Leftists of Marxist philosophy employed "Chinese characteristics" as the latest means to prevent the bankruptcy of socialism as happened in the Soviet Union and the eastern block. They see globalization as a new conspiracy of imperialism to exploit and oppress developing contraries. To resist it, they combine the Marxist doctrine of class struggle with the "post-colonist theory" to mobilize the masses. Ironically, those Marxists seem to forget that Marx in "The Manifesto of the Communalists" spoke of the counter-globalization as "the great chagrin of Reactionalists", as "one-sidedness and narrow mindedness". He also praised the role played by the bourgeoisie in globalization: "The cheap prices of its commodities are the heavy artillery, with which it batters down all Chinese walls", "It compels all nations, on pain of extinction, to adopt the bourgeoisie mode of production …so it has made barbarian and semi-barbarian countries dependent on the civilized ones, nations of peasants on nations of bourgeoisie, the East on the West", "from the numerous national and local literatures, there arises a world literature."[6] Those seemingly "politically incorrect" words were nevertheless written by Marx, many of whose followers have committed a sin against Marx's ideas of globalization.

Fashionable learners of Western philosophy are enthusiastic over the post-modernist critiques of the Western tradition universalistic claims to Truth, "logocentrism" and absolutism. All of those suggest approval of cultural particularism and a relativism of value and truth. They are proud to find some post-modernists appeal to Chinese traditional thought for their particularist and relativist approaches. The dictum "the Western post-modernism is the Chinese pre-modernism" suggests the inner link between the critical radicalism in the West and the traditional conservatism in China.

Most schools of Western and Chinese philosophies and Marxism all claimed a universalism of each own. Such conflicting claims does not justify the post-modern assumption that universalism is simply a prejudice or an illusion. Rather, the universalistic philosophers are called to commit themselves to dialogue with one another. Only through and by effective dialogues can some universal consensus be reached. What is important is to realize that universalism is not something ready at hand, but a matter of reconstruction, a potentiality to be realized, and a consequence of collaborative dialogues. I share with many scholars the viewpoint that the universalistic potential of Chinese philosophy is important not only for the Chinese, but also for all humans. It cannot be indifferent to all of us whether human right and democratic institutions are nothing but the prejudice of a particular civilization in a certain historical stage, or if they are based on intellectually shared convictions.

IDEOLOGY AND ITS CRITIQUE

In the above we have seen how leftist Marxism, counter-globalization, post-modernism, ethnic nationalism, and traditional conservatism have merged together to satisfy the need of the ideology of neo-totalitarianism. In the debate against this sort of ideology, some intellectuals have been engaged in liberalism, Enlightenment, cosmopolitanism, and anti-traditionalism. On the one side, current Chinese philosophy is seen as a battlefield of ideology between those conflicting -isms. On the other side, many Chinese philosophers adopt a non-ideological position and want to do "pure" philosophy. As a consequence, they withdraw into an ivory tower, doing the exegesis of philosophical texts without reference to public affairs. "Pure" philosophy has caused common people to question the use of philosophy. Western philosophers often meet this challenge with the dialectics of "nothing but everything"; similarly, Chinese with that of "great use of no use". But the equivocation of meaning cannot conceal philosophy's crisis in the public trust and in social functioning.

China is now undertaking an epoch-making transformation in all domains of social life, in economy, politics, education, folk culture, etc. In this crucial time, social injustice and violence, defrauding, corruption, environmental pollution, abuse and misuse of power are common in social life. Chinese intellectuals and philosophers in particular should occupy themselves with the question of how to participate in modernity: a question which seems to be out-dated in the West, but is really up-to-date and urgent in China.

The philosophical concern with public affairs cannot but be involved in ideology. Although the term "ideology" has a bad reputation at present, by no means are all ideologies equally bad; most probably some are better than others. For example, the ideology of democracy has admittedly suffered with many defects and demerits, it can still be evaluated as "the best choice we have to make in order to avoid otherwise worse solutions." The choice is always difficult to make in the battlefield of ideology. There is no a priori reason why nationalism is better than cosmopolitanism, and vice versa; or, why liberalism is better than Marxism, and vice versa, etc. Whatever choice is made, a critique of the ideology should be presented. Critical Theory pointed out the dilemma that the critique of an ideology is already embedded in another ideology. In the Chinese context, the critique should be carried out not only upon the condemned "worse" ideology, but also upon the preferably "better" one. Due to the complexity, difficulty and breadth of social problems in Chinese modernization, no single set of ideology can be chosen once and for all to solve all problems. Reasonable choices have to be made to deal with concrete problems in their circumstances. Marxism, for example, might have

been proven to be wrong on certain problems; it does not, however, completely lose its potential effectiveness to solve other problems; nationalism can be
used for the domestic solidarity, yet poision international relation, etc. The
plural use of ideologies will change their relations. The struggle for ideological dominance is expected to be compromised in order for certain problems
to be solved. Needless to say, philosophical dialogues can play active and
even decisive roles in such change. The task of Chinese philosophy today, in
my opinion, is not to follow the fashion of de-ideologization in the Western
world, nor to sustain the ideological struggle for an out-dated Marxism, but
to integrate all useful elements from different ideologies by critical reflection
and fruitful dialogue.

LOCAL AND WORLDLY PHILOSOPHY

Philosophy usually has been classified into German and French (or
Continental), British and American (or Anglo-Saxon) philosophy, as well as
Indian, Japanese, Arabic and Chinese philosophy, etc. The national or geographical mark for philosophy implies an ambiguity between a local philosophy and philosophy in a location. I thus distinguish between Chinese philosophy and philosophy in China. Given the far-reaching and fundamental
changes in China brought about by Western civilization and Marxism in the
past century, a purely "Chinese" philosophy in the local sense of the term
no longer exists today; philosophy in the present China consists of Chinese,
Western and Marxist philosophy.

In the above I have illustrated some problematic features of philosophy in China in conflicts, contradictions and debates. Those also show a rich
diversity and variety. As almost all local philosophies have been introduced
and absorbed in China's philosophy, it becomes one of the most promising
arenas for worldl philosophy. The phrase "world philosophy" was given by
Fung Youlan in an article published in *The Philosophical Review* in 1948. He
predicted there that "in my view, the world philosophy to come must contain
more rationalism than Chinese traditional philosophy, and more mysticism
than Western philosophy." [7] He was talking about "world philosophy" in the
sense of comparison and blending of Chinese and Western philosophy. After
more than half a century, we are prepared to do world philosophy in this
way.

As a matter of fact, much stress has been laid on foreign language
teaching in China over the past decades, and departments of philosophy have
popularized the study and teaching of foreign philosophy. English is more
popular in China than Chinese is in English speaking countries, and the Chinese know much more about Western philosophy than Westerners do about
Chinese philosophy. Knowing both sides well, Chinese philosophers are in
a privileged position to do comparative philosophy. Indian philosophers, of
course, have enjoyed also such a position for many years. Nevertheless, the
common ground of the Indo-European languages has obscured some fundamental differences between Eastern and Western philosophy. By contrast, I

am confident that similarities and differences in question emerge more clearly in comparative studies of Chinese and Western philosophy.

The orientation towards worldly philosophy does not exclude Marxism, but accords with Marx's notion of philosophy. Marx in his youth predicated the future of philosophy in these words: "Philosophy then ceases to be a particular system in relation to other particular systems, it becomes philosophy in general in relation to the world, it becomes the philosophy of the contemporary world ... it is the living soul of culture, that philosophy has become worldly and the world has become philosophical ... and become citizens of the world."[8] According to the young Marx, the world philosophy is philosophy in general, not a particular system vis-á-vis other particular systems. World philosophy is general in the sense that it is not only inter-disciplinary but also cross-cultural, going beyond various barriers set by local philosophies.

The potentials for comparative philosophy and Marxist philosophy in China to become world philosophy can be realized only if certain conditions be fulfilled. Those conditions include, as said above, shifts from the 'divergence' approach to a 'convergence' one, from a narrow-minded particularism to a broad vision of universalism, from the nationalist totalitarian ideology to its critique, and in addition, to closer cooperation with the international community of philosophers.

NOTES

1 *History of the Communist Party of the Soviet Union*, Ch. 3, Sect. 4, Moscow, 1945.

2 "Wenn wir vom Sein sprechen, und bloss vom Sein, so kann die Einheit nur darin bestehn, das alle die Gegenstande, um die es sich handelt—sind, existieren."*Marx Engels Werke*, vol.20, (Berlin: Dietz Verlag), s.40.

3 *Social Science in China*, vol. xxvi, no.1, spring, 2005, pp. 110-11, with some revision.

4 *The Book of Zhuangzi*, ch.5, sect. 2, translation of my own.

5 A. D. Smith, "The politics of culture: ethnicity and nationalism', in *Companion Encyclopedia of Anthropology*, ed. by Tim Ingold (London: Routledge, 2002), pp.706-33.

6 *Marx- Engels Collected Works*, vol. 6 (Moscow: Progress Publishers, 1976), p.488

7 Translated from the Chinese version in Fung Youlan's *Collected Works from Sangsongtang*, vol.11 (Henan People's publisher, 1898), p.593.

8 *Marx- Engels Collected Works*, vol. 1 (Moscow: Progress Publishers, 1975), pp.195-6.

Chapter 5

Dialogue Between Eastern and Western Mathematics and Medicine

Sasaki Chikara

The papers of Professors Tang Yijie and Roger T. Ames suggest that the modern Japanese experience of philosophizing in the Western way after the Meiji Restoration may be quite useful for the future construction of truly oecumenical philosophy in East Asia.

As is pointed out, the Chinese word '*Zhexue*' was coined by the Japanese scholar Nishi Amane (1829-1897) soon after the Meiji Restoration. Since then, before World War II, Nishida Kitaro (1870-1945) made a great effort to form a style of philosophy appropriate for the Japanese spiritual soil, the fruit of this endeavor being a form of philosophy mixing German idealism and Zen Buddhism. After World War II, the philosophical system of my colleague at the University of Tokyo, Hiromatsu Wataru (1933-1994) tried to construct a radical Marxist philosophy following the German philosophers Immanuel Kant (1724-1804) and Ernst Cassirer (1874-1945), and the Austrian physicist-philosopher Ernst Mach (1838-1916).

Before the acceptance of the Japanese word for philosophy by China during the 1880s, however, the Jesuit missionary Giulio Aleni (1582-1646) had used his own term for the Western discipline 'philosophia' in his *Xixue-fan* of 1632, according to Dr. Chen Jidong. Also it is known that Joseph Edkins (1823-1905) transformed the term for philosophy into *Lixue* in his *Xixue lüeshu* of 1886. But, it was very hard for the Chinese people to implant the Western way of philosophizing even then. Only with the establishment of the Republic of China did they make philosophy a legitimate discipline with the term '*zhexue*'. I hope that a creative form of philosophy will be established on Chinese soil in the near future.

A NEW TASK FOR THE HISTORICAL PHILOSOPHY OF SCIENCE: FROM THE PHENOMENOLOGY OF EXACT SCIENCES TO THE THEORY OF MEDICINE

In what follows, I will try to shed light not on general philosophy but on philosophy of science, in particular, the philosophy of mathematics and of medicine. My serious philosophical readings began with phenomenological works written by the German philosopher Edmund Husserl (1859-1938) concerning the foundations of mathematics. I was trained at Princeton University under Prof. Thomas S. Kuhn (1922-1996), who proposed a new view of philosophy, now called "historical philosophy of science" in contrast to the logical philosophy of science proposed by Rudolf Carnap (1891-1970), which flourished in the first half of the twentieth century. Under the guidance of Professor Michael S. Mahoney, a disciple of Prof. Kuhn, I obtained a Ph.D. degree for "Descartes's Mathematical Thought."

Phenomenological studies have not been confined to foundational research on mathematics, with which Husserl was familiar. Their subjects included also psychiatry, among others, proposing an alternative understanding of mind-body problem. Beyond these, I would like to suggest that phenomenology should contribute to reflection on the theoretical and practical aspects of ordinary medicine. Especially, we should study the effectiveness of traditional Chinese medicine in a critical manner from the phenomenological point of view.

As is well-known, in his later years Husserl himself began to emphasize the historical approach. One such examples was the posthumous 1939 essay "Die Frage nach dem Ursprung der Geometrie als intentionalhistorisches Problem," in *Revue internationale de Philosophie*, 1. Jahrgang, No. 2, S. 203-225: Reprinted in *Husserliana*, Bd. VI (Hague: Martinus Nijhoff, 1962), S. 365-386. I learned from this view and connected it to Prof. Kuhn's "historical philosophy of science" for my own study of the history and philosophy of mathematics. From Kuhn's standpoint , the philosophy of medicine has remained an uncultivated domain of research. Especially, there is a need for a comparative study of Eastern and Western medical thought, particularly that of China, ancient Greece and modern Europe.

DIALOGUE BETWEEN EASTERN AND WESTERN SCIENTIFIC THOUGHT: A LESSON FROM LEIBNIZ

In recent years, comparative studies of Western and Eastern scientific thought have been fashionable. I understand that quite recently Geoffrey Lloyd of Cambridge University and Nathan Sivin of the University of Pennsylvania have been developing a project of the comparative study of Western and Eastern scientific thought, for example in the book under the title *The Way and the Word: Science and Medicine in Early China and Greece*, published with Yale University Press in 2002, and G. E. R. Lloyd, *The Ambitions of Curiosity: Understanding the World in Ancient Greece and China*, published with Cambridge University Press in 2002. The great Joseph Needham (1900-1995) would have encouraged this kind of historical study.

However, the aforementioned books have not proven quite satisfactory. A monograph entitled *Leibniz and China: A Commerce of Light*, by Franklin Perkins was published was by Cambridge University Press in 2004. I recalled Leibniz's (1646-1716) book *Novissima Sinica*, (in English *The Newest Things Chinese)*, published in 1697, with a second edition in 1699.

In order to attempt a comparative study of Chinese and European thought in general, we should refer first of all, to Leibniz's preface to the *Novissima Sinica*. Leibniz, saw the most sophisticated forms of culture flowering in the two extremes of the Eurasian continent, i. e., in Europe and China. The two civilizations are balanced as a whole, at times Europe alternating between superior and inferior in relation to China. On the one hand, Europe is superior in the theoretical disciplines, e. g. logic and metaphysics, and especially the mathematical sciences. Leibniz states: "The Chinese are thus seen to be ignorant of that great light of the mind, the art of demonstration, and they have remained content with a sort of empirical geometry, which our artisans universally possess."[1] In addition to this, moreover, he pointed out that China is inferior to Europe in the art of war. On the other hand, Leibniz asks rhetorically: "But who would have believed that there is on earth a people who, though we are in our view so very advanced in every branch of behavior, still surpass us in comprehending precepts of civil life?" He answers: The Chinese "surpass us (though it is almost shameful to confess this) in practical philosophy, that is, in the precepts of ethics and politics adapted to the present life and use of mortals. Indeed, it is difficult to describe how beautifully all the laws of the Chinese, in contrast to those of other peoples, are directed to the achievement of public tranquility and the establishment of social order, so that men shall be disrupted in their relations as little as possible."[2] I suppose Leibniz's observation was quite insightful and can be still applied, at least in part, to the contemporary world at the beginning of the twenty-first century in which brutal wars of invasion are initiated.

According to Perkins, the author of the above monograph *Leibniz and China*, Leibniz became interested in Chinese science and medicine from 1671 when he wrote a plan for a German academy. He wrote a letter to the French Jesuit missionary Joachim Bouvet (1656-1730) in 1697:

> I come to physique and I understand presently under this name all the experimental notices of corporeal things for which one still cannot give the reason by geometrical principles or mechanics. Therefore these cannot at all be obtained by reason and a priori, but only by experience and tradition; and I do not at all doubt that the Chinese surpass us much on this point, because their experience is longer and their tradition less interrupted and more polished than ours.[3]

"Ours" in the quoted passage refers to "the Christianized Europeans." In Leibniz's opinion, European knowledge is more easily learned, both because it is based more on reason and because it is more public; while Chinese knowledge is based more on experience, held by men of the professions, and passed on by tradition. What Leibniz seeks to learn from the Chinese is directed both by his epistemology and by his evaluation of the complementary strengths of European and Chinese knowledge. He sets up an opposition between the simple recording of experiential data and the use of necessary truths, putting China on one side and Europe on the other. The importance of experiential data for an uninterrupted long period is especially recognized in Chinese medicine.

Today, everybody understands the importance of ecological thought and of the approach through natural history in biological research. They are characterized as views of nature complementary to the understanding through modern mathematical physics in the macrocosmos. What scientific knowledge is complementary to modern European medicine in the domain of the micro-cosmos? At least one of the candidates must be Chinese traditional medicine. It literally represents a complementary alternative medicine (CAM), another way to the art of healing. It should be reconsidered and reconstructed as an evidence-based medicine (EBM). Our historical and philosophical studies of medical thought should provide a help in this direction.

Thus far my sketchy view on the relation between traditional Chinese and modern European scientific thought is inspired by Leibniz. I insist that it can be applied to Chinese and European mathematical thought. Our problem is how it can be applied.

THE PRESENT STAGE OF THE HISTORICAL PHILOSOPHY OF MATHEMATICS

Before arguing for the need of a dialogue between Eastern and Western medical thought, I will briefly sketch the present stage of the historical philosophy of mathematics. Hitherto the historiography of mathematics had concentrated regionally on Western Europe and, then, for the past thirty years on the Islamic world, thanks mainly to Prof. Roshdi Rashed. The historical study of mathematics in East Asia had been relatively underdeveloped. However, to order to establish a truly ecumenical history and philosophy of mathematics, one of the desiderata in the twenty-first century must be the establishment of the critical historiography of the history of mathematics in China and Japan.

It must be remembered at this juncture that European mathematics in the seventeenth century was not simply the mathematical knowledge which had flourished in Western Europe, but rather the mathematics which should be named "Eurasian mathematics," containing speculations on the philosophy of mathematics in ancient Greece, the art of numerical calculations in India, algebra in the Islamic civilization, and their introduction and fermentation in medieval and Renaissance Europe for several centuries.

We occasionally assume that before ancient Greece there existed only an underdeveloped and deformed kind of mathematical knowledge, namely, Babylonian and Egyptian mathematics. According to the so-called 'ortho-dox' understanding of the history of mathematics, full-fledged mathematical knowledge began to flourish after the formation of the axiomatic method in mathematics, of which a representative work was Euclid's *Elements*. The rea-son to think so was that the axiomatic method in mathematics was so crucial and important in the history of mathematical knowledge. But, we should not simplify and overemphasize history. To consider the axiomatic or synthetic method as the unique mathematical method may lead to neglecting or ignor-ing the inventive or analytical aspect in the process of the formation of math-ematical knowledge. The inventive or analytical aspect is more closely related to the actual and practical dimension of mathematics.

Thus, I believe an image of the history of mathematics as a single lineal development from ancient Greece to contemporary mathematics is a kind of myth. In this image, mathematics developed from a premature version in Babylonia and Egypt to a mature and full-fledged form in Greece. And this successful ancient Greek mathematics was transmitted from Alexandria, a center of Hellenistic civilization, to Bagdhad, a center of the Islamic world of which the official and scientific language was Arabic. Thus during the Renaissance of the twelfth century Greek mathematics was translated from Arabic terms into medieval Latin, and then was totally restored and spread in modern Europe.

But, here we should ask: How was Arabic mathematics formed? Its main sources were ancient Greek mathematics and the Indian art of calculations; in other words, Arabic mathematics consisted of Hindu-Arabic numerals, *al-jabr;* the practice and theory of equation and demonstrative mathematics originated from Greek mathematics. Prof. Roshdi Rashed, today's authority on the history of Arabic science, occasionally contends that Arabic mathematics was truly an international mathematics. Arabic mathematics greatly transformed European mathematics after Leonardo da Pisa (Fibonacci) (ca. 1170-after 1240). Mathematics in Europe after the twelfth-century Renaissance was, in fact, not simply, Arabic or European, but "Eurasian mathematics."

I have introduced this in part in *Descartes's Mathematical Thought*, (Kluwer, 2003), namely, that modern European mathematics is in reality "Eurasian mathematics." Further, I contend that traditional Chinese mathematical thought and Greek mathematical thought are mutually "incommensurable," to use a concept Kuhn, regarded as the most crucial in his historical philosophy of science.

In my opinion, to understand that modern European mathematics was actually "Eurasian mathematics" is not sufficient for historians of mathematics in an age of unprecedented globalization in the twenty-first century. We have to include the mathematical thought of traditional China and Japan in the history of mathematics in the twenty-first century. Without such an intellectual endeavor, we will not be able to have a truly ecumenical historiography of the history of mathematics in the twenty-first century.

To compare European, in fact Greek, mathematical thought with traditional Chinese mathematical thought, we would present a typical image of doing mathematics in ancient Greece: The Greek idealized mathematical objects and provided demonstrations with systematic axiomatic method. On the other hand, the traditional Chinese treated concrete mathematical objects with practical algorithmic calculations. The Greek emphasized a theoretical aspect of mathematics while the Chinese never forgot its practical aspect. To argue that Chinese mathematical thought and European mathematical thought are mutually incommensurable is to insist that Chinese mathematical thought isn't inferior to European mathematical thought. To reconfirm this belief, we should recall what Joseph Needham has said:

In taking our leave of the twenty centuries of autochthonous

Chinese mathematics we may cast a brief backward glance over the successive periods and their qualities. The two dynasties which stand out for mathematical achievement are the Han and the Sung. For the 1st century, the time of Lohsia Hung and Liu Hsin, the *Chiu Chang Suan Shu (Nine Chapters on the Mathematical Art)* was a splendid body of knowledge. It dominated the practice of Chinese reckoning-clerks for more than a millennium. Yet in its social origins it was closely bound up with the bureaucratic government system, and devoted to the problems which the ruling officials had to solve (or persuade others to solve). Land mensuration and survey, granary dimensions, the making of dykes and canals, taxation, rates of exchange,--these were the practical matters which seemed all-important. Of mathematics 'for the sake of mathematics' there was extremely little. This does not mean Chinese calculators were not interested in truth, but it was not that abstract systematised academic truth after which sought the Greeks.[4]

Needham seems to have insisted that the Chinese people have been by nature pragmatists. In order to ascertain such a rather epistemological observation, we, historians of mathematics, have to proceed to establish our accurate historical image of traditional Chinese mathematics. We have to present, first of all, critically compiled historical documents of traditional Chinese and Japanese mathematics in European languages, following the leads of Mikami Yoshio (1875-1950) and Joseph Needham. The recent publications of *The Nine Chapters on the Mathematical Art* by Shen Kangshen, John N. Crossley, and Anthony W.-C. Lun with Oxford University Press and Science Press, Beijing, in 1999 and *Les Neuf Chapitres: Le Classique mathématique de la Chine ancienne et ses commentaires* by Karine Chemla and Guo Shuchun with Dunod, Paris, in 2004 are good symptoms. Chinese mathematics with a highly pragmatic character may provide original mathematical thought in contrast to the axiomatic mathematics in ancient Greece. The critical editions of the works by Seki Takakazu (?-1708) and his most talented disciple, Takebe Katahiro (1664-1739), should be published with translations and detailed commentaries in European languages. The traditional Japanese mathematics in the early modern period after a drastic reform by Takakazu must be the highest form of indigenous East Asian mathematics, comparable only with modern European mathematics after François Viète (1540-1603).

THE BLOCKADE OF MODERN EUROPEAN MEDICINE AND THE IMPORTANCE OF CHINESE MEDICAL THOUGHT FOR THE CONTEMPORARY WORLD

Modern European medicine is considered to have started with William Harvey's (1578-1657) and René Descartes' (1596-1650) doctrine of the circulation of blood. We may not characterize Harvey's medical thought as "mechanical," but Descartes certainly entertained a "mechanical" view of the human body in one sense. However, there remains doubt over insisting that Descartes's was dogmatically and categorically "mechanical."

Today's art of cure in Western medicine is "vulgarly" regarded to consist of two components: chemical drugs and surgery. The uncritical belief in modern European medicine had its roots deep in people in the nineteenth and twentieth centuries when infection through bacteria began to be overcome on a broad scale. As the frontier of diseases changed after World War II, modern European medicine began to be regarded to having a certain blockage. This recognition was related to the fact that curing liver disease and various kinds of cancer became important tasks of medicine.

Modern European medicine is based on "universal" natural laws provided by modern natural sciences which developed drastically since the seventeenth century. The main trend of natural sciences in modern period has been mechanical. On the one hand, this direction of medicine should be developed highly. At the same time, on the other hand, an alternative way must be sought. A dialogue between Eastern and Western medical thought may be not simply theoretical but also practical. We have to seek the practical purposes very concretely: First, the rehabilitation of medical practices along the way of traditional Chinese medicine based on legitimate foundations; and second, the establishment of Chinese and Western Combined Medicine in the contemporary world, especially in East Asia.

These purposes must be accomplished through the spirit of Leibniz, who called for the mutual exchange of Chinese and European culture. A serious dialogue between traditional Chinese and modern European medical thought, and scientific thought in general, is called for by Leibniz's encouragement of the promotion of commerce between Chinese and European knowledge: "A commerce, I say, of doctrine and mutual light."

NOTES

1 Donald F. Lach, *The Preface of Leibniz' Novissima Sinica, Commentary, Translation, Text* (University of Hawaii, 1957), p. 69.

2 *Ibid.* pp. 69-70.

3 Franklin Perkins, *Leibniz and China: A Commerce of Light* (Cambridge University Press, 2004).

4 Joseph Needham, *Science and Civilisation in China*, Vol. 3: *Mathematics and the Sciences of the Heavens and the Earth* (Cambridge University Press, 1959), p. 153.

The Complementarity of Science and Religion

Meville Y. Stewart

INTRODUCTION

We are living in a day of unprecedented scientific exploration, discovery and achievement.[1] Astronauts were sent up into space here in China, and a week later landed safely in the desert to the north in Inner Mongolia. According to the *China Daily*, scientists are predicting that the Arctic polar region may have no ice at all in 55 years.[2] Nearly four years ago, a feature article in *Time* magazine on "How the Universe Will End" provided a graphic flow-chart account of how the cosmos started and how scientists see it as finishing in a Dark Era, comprised "...mostly of photons, neutrinos, electrons and positrons wandering through a universe bigger than the mind can conceive...[They went on to say] From here into an infinite future, the universe remains cold, dark and dismal." Scientific prognosticians paint a rather dismal picture for the human race and its planet Earth. Many think that the sun will eventually fade into a ball a little bigger than our "home planet" and if humanity is going to survive it will be by some vestigial remainder aboard a "galactic ark" searching some distant planet for possible human habitation, with its human occupants passing through generations on a seemingly endless journey to a still more distant site than our nearest star (next to the sun), Proxima Centauri, some 4.3 light years away.

But scientific predictions relating to our planet are not in some respects worse than those found in the Christian Scriptures. Paul talks about a complete dissolution of the present heavens and earth in his account of the unity of the eschatological complex of events Christians see as attending the Second Coming of Christ.[1] The picture is of an earth-shaking, breath-taking final consummation so as to make way for another era, the coming of the Millennial Age, or as some see it, the final consummation of the Kingdom of God.[2]

There is an obvious difference between the two accounts, the former is an hypothesis (*jia shuo*) offered as an explanation of the direction scientific data takes us presently with regard to the destiny of our planet. The latter is predictive account of the future contained in the Scriptures, some of which date back at least two thousands years to the prophetic forecasts of Paul, Peter and John, and even further, if one takes Old Testament prophecies as at least hinting eschatological disclosures. The former is offered as a possible and some think plausible scientific hypothesis, the latter is viewed as a foretelling of the future, based on what is taken as a revelation of God communicated to persons chosen to be recipients of divine revelation.

There is little doubt that these two accounts intersect at least in one way, they both are predictions of future sets of states of affairs. The one says the universe will cool down, the other that it will heat up eventually to the point that our earth will be consumed. One claims to explain facts of an empirical sort, the other takes the data (*shi shi*) of Scripture seriously. For some, probably many today, that, at least prima facie, is where the intersection ends. The methods are on many accounts, putatively completely different. The scientist works with what has become known as scientific reasoning and the scientific method (*ke xue fang fa*), and the latter, for some representatives at least,[3] works with reason as a tool for understanding and interpreting the Biblical record. But there is another alleged difference that some see as irrevocably polarizing the two, and that is the claim that scientific practices of inquiry starts with assumptions that are minimally voluntaristic. By contrast, the religious requires that faith if not primary, is certainly necessary, and for some it is an appropriate posture to assume before God. For the theist the New Testament author John declares that, "without faith, it is impossible to please God, for those that come to him must believe that he is."[4] Neither time nor space allow expansion of the various ways this has been understood in the history of the Christian Church. In contrast, notwithstanding Bertrand Russell's admission that the scientist too must work with some element of faith (regarding basic assumptions, since there has to be a beginning to justification of beliefs), it will suffice our interest here to note that the religious mind typically offers more robust renditions of faith, and always gives it greater centrality, than the scientist.

But our project in this paper is not so much to draw contrasts and differences. It seems that those of the scientific community as well as those representative of the religious community, have been quite diligent if not overly solicitous in their various attempts at flagging disparities. There is little doubt that there are differences as to method, subject matter and objectives. In spite of these differences, some of which will be noted along the way, there are also analogues and in some instances, maybe even close parallels. Arguably, the two areas of inquiry involve practices of inquiry[5] that in significant ways may be taken as analogous. They are analogical in their respective (1) use of paradigm, (2) models of explanation; (3) methods of reasoning; and (4) interest in meaning and rationality. I shall moreover argue that the scientist who begins his/her scientific practice of inquiry with an attempt to avoid making ultimate assumptions regarding origins, not only operates with the presumption of a naturalism/atheism at root, but that his/her beginning may bear some resemblance to the theist's starting assumption that there is a God.[6] I shall also argue that neither one can approach science objectively, i. e., with a neutral point of view or perspective, and furthermore that both sides to scientific disputes should acknowledge their starting assumptions as involving bias, and they should therefore proceed not only with a recognition of this fact, but with a friendly mode of exchange open to communicative rationality. In the arena of the academy, and wherever the public square obtains, there should be a free exchange of ideas and hypotheses with the aim of pursing truth and meaning. There should be a common recognition that science and religion are topics of common interest and concern to all members of a pluralistic society and world to which all share a common goal, the common good, thereby effecting at least potentially a convergeance of fact and value.

In the following, I shall contend that in spite of many differences, science and religion bear significant affinities in their repective uses of paradigm (*fan shi*), explanation (*jie shi*), and reasoning processes (*tui li guo cheng*), and in their overall concern for rationality (*li xing*). Regarding the last, I shall also argue, that they share a common interest in the quest for truth and meaning. Our objective here is to see these affinities, not in expansive detail, but in brief array.

PARADIGM IN SCIENCE AND RELIGION

Generally speaking, there are three basic positions regarding the relationship between religion and science: (1) they are in conflict *(chong tu)*; (2) they are compartmentalized (*fen li*); (3) they are complementary (*bu chong*). The first sees the two as a polarity. When the objects, aims, or methods are conceived of such that they intersect or overlap in terms of what they claim, then the possibility of conflict quite naturally arises. It is the third category that I wish to look at more closely in the following.

We will begin with a brief introduction to paradigm (*fan shi*) and paradigm shift (*fan shi zhuan huan*) as these concepts are etched out by Thomas Kuhn in *The Structure of Scientific Revolutions*. Kuhn's formulation of the concept of paradigm has itself undergone a shift, from an equivocal rendition in the first edition of his work, to a distinction between the two senses attributed to the term, a narrow sense that sees paradigm as "exemplary problem solutions," and a wider sense which gathers together all of the "components of scientific consensus" and bears the name, "disciplinary matrix." The latter includes the various scientific values such as "accuracy, consistency, fruitfulness, scope and simplicity." In our comparative account of the scientific and religious uses of paradigm, I will at times work with the wider notion of disciplinary matrix since it helps overcome the tendency toward discipline-compartmentalizaton. And I will not attempt a full expansion of the notion of paradigm. It will suffice to understand it. Our focus will be more particularly upon the components of scientific consensus embraced in the notion as Kuhn specified it.

Lists vary from one scholar to another. David Lewis advances four criteria for selecting the "best theories," "truth, simplicity, strength, balance."[7] Kuhn's list overlaps some of Lewis's items, but even his account is not hard-and-fast secure,-- not for other scientists, and interestingly, not for Kuhn. His track record has "charted historical variations" as to what sorts of empirical information were expected of scientific theories. Moreover, for Kuhn, with new paradigms there may be "shifts in criteria determining the legitimacy both of problems and of the proposed solutions."[8] So there are different lists of criteria, or could be, and different glosses on the criteria themselves. But it isn't necessary to offer a complete list of the possible criteria out there. All we need do is offer a summary account of Kuhn's criteria associated with paradigm shift, so as to have a working account of how one approach may be viewed in comparison to religious understandings and uses.

Kuhn's list of criteria in terms of which competing paradigms are appraised in the process of a possible paradigm shift includes: (1) accurate prediction (*jing que de yu yan*) of empirical phenomena; (2) consistency (*yi guan xing*); (3) fruitfulness (*fu you cheng guo*); (4) scope and simplicity (*shi ye he jian yi xing*). One element of the first is "theory effectiveness" in giving us information. But there are other factors related to theory effectiveness, such as, How does the theory in question combine with "theories outside the context" of the question(s) at hand? The general idea is, the theory under consideration provides "accurate prediction, and so is "theory effective" in giving us information.

The second is consistency (*yi guan xing*), that is, the various central elements of a paradigm under consideration work together in a coherent, continuous fashion. The third, fruitfulness (*fu you cheng guo*), brings into view workability, applicability, and results with regard to a paradigm. Finally, a paradigm's scope and simplicity (*shi ye he jian yi xing*) are explored. Here, the question is,-- What is the range of data the new paradigm explains? How many anomalies does it resolve or explain? And perhaps the more problematic of the two, is simplicity. Even if all scientists agreed as to what this criterion means, simplicity "is a human, historically conditioned one."[9]

For each of our sub-topics, we will look at how the topic relates to the scientific, and then the religious, following the order indicated in the title of our study. To keep matters rather simple, I would like to view the notion of paradigm shift in the sciences by taking as an example, Dr. William Harvey's discovery of the flow of blood as an instance of paradigm shift from an earlier paradigm embraced by Galen and other medical scientists of Harvey's time, and then discuss an analogous use of this category in religious discourse.[10]

From the historian's point of view, the story about the lives and events that comprise the context in which Harvey's great discovery took place, from beginning to end, begins at the University of Padua. There, Vesalius, Columbo and Fabricanius, Harvey's predecessors made their marks: Vesalius with the publication of *De Fabricia,* a foundational work in anatomy, Columbo, for his discovery of pulmonary circulation, Fabricio (Harvey's mentor), for his description of certain valves in veins. But the piecemeal progress and influence of these great figures in the history of medical science were eclipsed by their successor, Dr. William Harvey. With the publication of his now classic, *De Motu Cordis.*[11]

Chapter Five of DMC gets to the "heart" of the matter. After having provided the reader with what T. Ghiselin terms a "comparative foundational anatomy,"[12] Harvey sketches an account of the "actions of the heart."[13] The description Harvey offers, the details of which are omitted here, pictures two movements of the heart in less than three pages of the DMC working with a mixture of mechanical descriptive language and teleological discourse. Both are conspicuously present in his DMC.

His account meant the introduction of a new paradigm—a paradigm shift in marked contrast to that of his predecessors, most notably Galen. And while he credited Galen and others with having given a reliable account of the anatomy of the heart and its vessels, he opined that a true understanding of the function of the heart hinged on an acceptance of his paradigm. And while he did not give a full and final account of all the data, he did give a more complete and plausible account of much of the data up to this point in medical history.

What is of chief concern here is Harvey's belief that a paradigm satisfy a number of criteria. And while he didn't put together a formal list like the one Kuhn proposes in connection with his notion of inter-disciplinary matrix, his record shows approximations to each criteriological point in Kuhn's list.

Following Kuhn, Harvey believed that his new account provided accurate prediction and so was in Kuhn's language, theory effective in giving us information. He thought that his new paradigm gave account/explained the mass of data he had collected in his laboratory observation of cadavers. His picture of the structural pattern of cuspids, as in his description of the sigmoid valves, and his succinct rendition of the various chambers of the heart provided an informational disciplinary matrix which answered central questions regarding the flow of blood.[14] His new paradigm also pivoted on the notion of consistency. The various central elements of his theory worked together in a coherent, continuous fashion. The functioning of the right side of the heart worked together with the left in one heart beat. It was for Harvey an obviously coherent picture.

And what of fruitfulness, workability, applicability and results (*fu you cheng guo, ke cao zuo xing, ke ying yong xing*)? To put it simply,-- Does the paradigm work? This too is present in his account. A teleological gloss is weaved into and with mechanical elements of the hypothesis. His emphasis upon diastole and on a closed circulatory system was in direct contrast to the view of his contemporaries. He saw his paradigm as the way the heart functions/works, and that his view of the circulatory system was taken as essentially correct, and so would yield helpful information for those in the medical sciences. It was indeed more helpful than the current view which saw the heart as an organ that merely sucks in blood.

As for scope and simplicity, Harvey saw his discovery as having implications for all that pertained to heart physiology and function in particular. It was indeed a simple theory, the description of which barely took up three pages. That pericope set forth a paradigm that has remained basically in tact to the present, of course with various elaborations and refinements.

Interestingly, the central criteria listed by Kuhn, at least in a preliminary way, bear some analogy to paradigm and paradigm shift in the religious as well. For many, but possibly not for all, [15] one may observe paradigms and paradigm shifts with regard to religious and philosophico-religious sets of beliefs. For example, T'ien-T'ai philosophy (of which there are religious readings) is one paradigm within Madhyamika Buddhism.[16] It is a particular interpretation within this tradition that gives account of data[17] shared by the

larger school of thought. Conceivably, an individual might move or experience a paradigm shift from one school within the larger school of Madhyamika Buddhism (da cheng fo xue) to T'ien-T'ai philosophy (*tian tai zong*),
say after having read Paul Swanson's book on the subject, and after having
done some research. As interesting as it might be to pursue this sort of shift,
I would like to share a personal narrative that describes what I take to be a
religious/philosophical paradigm shift that I underwent.

More than fifteen years ago, I held to a thorough-going Calvinism
that included a variant form of soft-determinism (*ruo jue ding lun*). I held to
a divine predestination thesis that not only ranged over the general outline of
history from beginning to end, but over human destinies, extending to every
particular of a person's life. But I also held that this belief was not incompatible with the belief that some sense could be given to my being free and morally responsible for my actions. Choices were the result of my genetic code,
my background, the total causal picture that made up my past. But when it
came to personal choices, I held to a measure of freedom, at least in the sense
that the causal path leading to "free choices" passed through me. About five
years later, some of my core beliefs[18] went through a critical process of evaluation and examination, as I began to explore another paradigm. It was during
the summer when I was working on an early draft of my dissertation. Bus trips
to the University provided opportunity for reading, and the book I had chosen
was David Ray Griffin's *God, Power and Evil*. Questions concerning God's
agency and human agency were raised by Griffin in a way I hadn't thought of
before. My reading of the Epistle to the Romans at the time seemed initially
to help me retain my grasp of the accepted paradigm. But eventually, I came
to hold a belief that persons have moments when they are free in a way that is
incompatible with the determinist thesis I had held. I began to piece together
another paradigm which included the belief that some choices are not necessitated by antecedent causes and conditions. The new paradigm isn't even
now without its anomalies.

Now I have to explain or give account of my use of terms associated with the scientific understanding of paradigm and paradigm shift, and
criteria (*biao zhun*) appealed to in appraising competing paradigms. I've not
claimed that these terms are exact equivalents in the two realms in question.
Our practice of inquiry here involves a drawing of analogous senses of key or
pivotal terms.[19] For me, paradigm may be a specific set of beliefs comprising
a matrix in terms of which facts of experience, and the data of Scripture are
explained. Originally, I thought that everything was a result or an outcome
of antecedent causes and conditions, ultimately ending with God as overall
Sovereign. While the new paradigm includes a belief that God is ultimately
Sovereign, I don't' hold that He holds sovereign sway over every choice that
I make. While he remains sovereign, there are choices that I make that are
creaturely-sovereign. And because of this move, I believe that the new paradigm has a greater power of explanation,[20] because I believe that the new
paradigm absolves God from a blame that I think is difficult to absolve him
from on the older paradigm. As a manner of speaking, an anomaly has been

taken care of. But there is a new one. I don't know how to explain how it is that my free choices, which are here free in the sense that my choices are not necessitated by antecedent causes and conditions, can really be "mine."[21] To use Campbell's distinction, the choices that are free issue from the "free self *(zi you de zi wo)*," but those which issue from my causal background and desires, issue from the "character self *(zi ran de zi wo)*." So it appears that when I am free, I am really not acting "out of character." But I prefer the new paradigm because I think that the shift handles a more difficult anomaly than the one it generates.

Here it isn't necessary to show how each item in Kuhn's list apply to my case of paradigm shift. I think that it is easy to show that they do. That is, I take the new paradigm to be a more accurate picture than its predecessor, and more consistent, and clearly leads to greater fruitfulness, since I see free actions as mine and as episodes for which I have made a choice and bear responsibility, not God. As for scope, though it is very limited in respect to the number of actions to which one of the beliefs (of the paradigm) ranges over, namely free actions, since I hold like many others who espouse this view, that the number of such actions are very limited indeed (most of my choices issue as Campbell argues from the character self). But it is accompanied by another belief in the paradigm, which is a revision of the former, and which qualifies and so limits the Sovereignty of God *(shang di de tong zhi quan)* in a way I think compatible with an the notion of an Ultimate Sovereign. So the new paradigm is superior in the sense that it satisfies all of the criteria in a way that the earlier one doesn't.[22]

In the next section, we will turn to what may be called a particular element of a paradigm, namely, its explanatory power. The rubric just discussed is not thus a separate topic. The one that follows is a specialized/particularized focus on the role and effectiveness of paradigm as a device used to give account of sets of selected data.

EXPLANATION IN SCIENCE AND RELIGION

What is the problem or issue here? (*Wenti shi shen me?*) Our concern here is with the explanatory power (*jie shi de li liang*) of a paradigm (*fan shi)*. It is that which relates to a paradigm's fruitfulness and workability. We touched on it above in connection with a critieria. It is expanded upon here, because discussions in philosophy of science give it special attention. One of the issues for the scientific and the religious is the plurality of views of explanation that are out there. Our attention will be given to the scientific array of options first.

The scientific accounts of explanation range from more traditional Formalist/Normative theories to the more recent Contextualist views of those who espouse what are called "Hermeneutical theories."

Formalist/Normative accounts have two central concerns, (1) the rationality of science, which attends to the question,-- Is science rational?, and a focus relating to our present topic of inquiry, What is the explanatory power/

force of a scientific explanation? Karl Popper's Formalist model is briefly described thus in his *The Logic of Scientific Discovery*: "To give a causal explanation of an event means to deduce a statement which describes it, using as premises of the deduction one or more universal laws, together with certain singular statement, the initial conditions."[23] Thus the only satisfactory explanation is one where the *explanandum* (what is to be explained) follows deductively from the lawlike portion of the *explanans* (the explanation). This is known as the deductive-nomological explanatory model. For Popper, since this procedure did not rest or depend upon any metaphysical or theological/religious claims or assumptions, it doesn't matter whether the explanation is in any way ultimate.

Carl Hempel's model bore similarities to Popper's, but there were some changes. For Hempel, four conditions had to be satisfied according to his nomological model: (1) the *explanandum* must be a logical consequence of the *explanans*; (2) the *explanans* must contain general laws; (3) it must have empirical content; (4) the sentences constituting the *explanans* must be true. His proposal generated six problems, one of which is especially relevant to our study, viz. the claim that there must be observation sentences. It is a claim similar to contention of the Vienna Circle/the Logical Positivists, that if an empirical claim is made, there must be statements that are at least in principle verifiable by way of observation.[24]

More recently, science and philosophy of science have witnessed a contextualist shift from the Formalist theories of Popper and Hempel to the hermeneutical (*jie shi xing de*) account of theorists like Thomas Kuhn, outlined in his famous, *The Structure of Scientific Revolutions*. With the fall of Logical Positivism (*luo ji shi zheng zhu yi*) and the rise of the later Wittgenstein,[25] philosophers of science began to pay attention to the actual process of scientific discovery. Others helped this along, such as Stephen Toulmin, who continued to speak of the "logical character of laws," while also allowing that science in the more general sense is a "process of understanding that addresses the question,--How can a class of phenomena be accounted for in terms of some principles?" It was his emphasis which some think served as a clarion call to this new emphasis in science and philosophy of science. He held that there is no "universal recipe for all science and all scientists."

Enter the stage, Thomas Kuhn, one of the most influential authors in philosophy of science at the end of the 20th and beginning of the 21st centuries. In the light of his contextualist shift, explanation is relativised and becomes an element in the broader hermeneutical task that is science. It is his view that the scientist can no longer elucidate an abstract and authoritative structure, thereby capturing the essence of explanation in all its instances. His account, shifting itself from an earlier paradigm notion, to an interdisciplinary matrix idea, moves away from the authoritative role of science, precisely because it isn't possible to capture the essence of explanation in all of its instances. At best, it can only lead a reader into a given scientific explanation, and thereby convey what its models are and how it proceeds and puts the world together. What he ends up isolating through the notion of paradigm and disciplinary matrix more precisely are five sub-notions that we expand on here because of the special relevance they sustain to points drawn with regard to scientific explanation, and later religious explanation: (1) shared symbolic generalizations (of various theories); (2) model agreement (models may agree in the sense that they serve as heuristic devices for further investigation; (3) values-interdisciplinary matrixes should be accurate, consistent, wide in scope, and be simple and fruitful (the criteria we noted earlier in connection with paradigm in particular); (4) metaphysical principles-the scientific community will agree on certain untestable assumptions (*bu ke zheng shi de jia shuo*) which play an important role in determining the direction of research; (5) exemplars, or concrete problem situations--here his notion of interdisciplinary matrix emerges more clearly as the scientific community comes to agree what problems persist and ways they may be resolved.

Though paradigms in the sciences abound, one only will be alluded to to illustrate explanation in the sciences, the Big Bang Theory (*da bao zha li lun*). A hint at its discovery was a discovery by an American astronomer Vesto Melvin Slipher, who in 1914 announced at an American Astronomical Society in Evanston, Illinois, what he thought was an astounding discovery, namely that all of the galaxies he had been studying at the time, about a dozen, were receding from the earth an incredible rates of speed, "some up to 2 million miles per hour."[26] By 1925, he increased his study to include 45 galaxies. We don't need to elaborate on this model further, since its impact on the contemporary scientific community is well known. Few now doubt the credibility of this paradigm and its explanatory power in astrophysics.

A helpful book on the subject of religious explanation (*zong jiao xing de jie shi)* as it compares to the sciences is Philip Clayton's, *Explanation from Physics to Theology*.[27] Clayton lists several sorts of explanation that might be viewed as falling under the religious, (1) private explanations, (2) communal explanations, and (3) intersubjective explanations (*jiao hu zhu ti xing de jie shi*). It is the third that I wish to expand briefly here. The third claims to be intersubjectively valid, that is, the sort of validity claimed is held to be accessible to all who are willing to examine the evidence. The strongest sort would be someone who believed that he/she could prove his religious beliefs. Such an approach might work with the tools of natural theology. While I might want to claim that proofs of the sort mentioned might be possible, I hold that this is possible only when a disputant agrees with the truth of the premises, and the argument offered exhibits a valid deductive inference pattern.[28] Central to the third sort of religious explanation is the notion of rationality. For Clayton, and for many others who hold to religious beliefs, this is a pivotal notion.[29] Clayton holds that three conditions must obtain for rationality to be preserved: (1) external reference or intentionality (*yi xiang xing)*--that explanation be inter-subjectively accessible to those beyond the believing community; (2) truth--sound religious explanations must be true; (3) validity/rationality--such explanations must be accessible to others who use reason.

That there are paradigms in religion and theology is without question. That there are similarities to the scientific needs to be shown. Clayton's three conditions with regard to religious explanation arguably contain elements resembling features we covered in the scientific. Since contemporary accounts of the scientific, especially contextualists like Kuhn, openly deny that scientific models of explanation are true, but rather may exhibit at best a workability, I will focus here only upon the rationality requirement. Many Christian theists, notably philosophers such as William Alston, Alvin Plantinga and Richard Swinburne strongly argue for the rationality of religious belief, specifically the belief that God exists, more precisely the God of the Christian faith.[30] Their contention is that there is an intercommunicative rationality, i.e., a rationality accessible to all who work with the basic tools of inductive and deductive logic.

Moreover, this belief is held to offer explanatory power with regard to origins. Robin Collins, for example, appeals to findings in recent science which he takes as "strongly suggesting that the universe is finely tuned in a manner suited to human existence.[31] If one looks at the evidence, he contends, one can't deny the plausibility of his inference that the universe exhibits design.

But many of the recent works and thinkers sympathetic to the Christian view spend little time detailing how the natural order came into being. That's partly accounted for by an admission that the Biblical account doesn't give us much to go on in this regard. Though there is according to some a rough account of the chronological ordering of that origin, there is little more than the affirmation in Hebrew verse that God is the Ultimate Source of its origin. But there is almost nothing as to how God created when he did. That is, his *modus operandi* isn't detailed, at best only suggested.[32] The main point here then is, there are significant limitations as to how much explanation is offered. But the central hypothesis is itself limitless in its power for science. Alfred North Whitehead declared as much when he said that all of Western science owed a tremendous debt to the Christian life-and-world view, precisely because it begins and proceeds with the claim that a rational God brought into existence a universe that exhibits an order and rationality he imposed on that creation. Moreover, the divine image, spelled out by Paul in the New Testament in terms of knowledge, holiness and righteousness, carried the inference that humans by reason of capacities attaching to that image had the capability of discerning that order and rationality.[33] It is a capacity for many theists, available to all who will pursue the objective.

It is my contention that there are many religious believers, some of which are well-trained scientists, who strongly hold (1) that religious claims are rational in a way accessible to others outside the religious community. And further, that claims relating to origins, specifically claims that center on God as the Ultimate Origin of the universe has the potential of an expansive explanatory power extending to various practices of inquiry extending to various disciplines, hence the propriety of calling it an interdisciplinary matrix with multifarious corresponding powers of explanation. Moreover, I am contending that the scientific realm is not antithetic to the religious, not even tangential, or minimal, but that there is a strong robust sense in which the two areas of inquiry intersect. Our basic conclusion here is, there is a shared sense of rationality *(li xing)* in both scientific and religious explanatory paradigms/interdisciplinary matrixes. But the discussion which follows allows us to draw this out in further detail another way, through a consideration of reasoning in science and religion.

REASONING IN SCIENCE AND RELIGION

For this focus, I work with a recent publication on the topic, *Understanding Scientific Reasoning*.[34] I turn to this study, partly because the authors' design is to give a good clear account of scientific reasoning as it is currently conceived. The study in question comprises 320 pages of carefully detailed discussions of the various components of scientific reasoning. We can only hope to select some of the main points and discuss them in summary fashion. There is thus a risk potential because of this incompleteness, the story may at significant points bear deficiencies. Nevertheless the task may have warrant if in some small measure it helps provide grist for the claim that there are affinities between the two disciplines regarding their respective reasoning methodologies perhaps thereby suggesting the possibility of an interdisciplinary reasoning matrix.

For the authors, finding out how scientific reasoning works "is a matter of learning how to understand and evaluate reports of scientific findings we find in popular magazines, national newspapers, news magazines, and some general professional publications."[35] They borrow then from the tools of reasoning in general, "studies in the nature of science and philosophy of science, the study of logic by philosophers, the study of human reasoning by cognitive scientists, the study of proability and statistics by mathematicians, and the study of decision making."[36] This, they take to be a fair sampling of the various sciences that use what they call "scientific reasoning."[37]

Scientists are pictured as "exploring how the world works." And as such, they are putatively engaged in "careful and deliberate interactions with the world. They do experiments and make observations, some of which are designed to help them decide which of several possible ways the world might work is most likely the way it really does work."[38] It is this feature that signals on their account, the difference between the scientific tradition, and the religious. The latter are pictured as understanding the world through the interpretation of sacred texts or from some literary text, such as a novel. Several distinctions need to be drawn here that might be helpful. The USR text draws a sharp contrast between scientific traditions and the religious that hinges primarily upon the sources of information. And while there is little doubt that much that is religious lends some support to this claim, there is a lot that doesn't. Hence the account is grossly incomplete if not inaccurate as a general description of the religious in particular. Current literature on origins, for example, in particular philosophy of religion, and cosmological arguments for the existence of God yet more specifically, do not generally access sacred texts. Perhaps more incisive with regard to sources and method, there is rather a general confinement to the natural light of reason, the tool of the natural theologian. And while scholars like Marilyn Adams sometimes access the sacred text as she does when dealing with the problem of evil, this is atypical rather than usual fare.

Another point needs to be address at the start. The authors observe that there is often a reference in the literature to the scientific method, as thought it were a monolith, a singular model. But nothing could be further from the truth, as we saw when we attended to Thomas Kuhn's multivarious inter-discipinary matrix notion. What is of special interest to note, for our purpose of finding similarities in respect to scientific reasoning and the religious use of reasoning, is a short discourse on "analog models." For the authors of USR, analog modes are useful as tools for understanding a new model of explanation, but they are not very open to analog as a way of working across disciplines, especially moving from the scientific to the religious. This was not even on the horizon.

Their path to understanding scientific reasoning moves from theoretic models to hypothetical reasoning, which in turn offers us explanations of data from the real world. This perhaps, is as close as they come to offering a succinct, abstract on the reasoning we're after. This is a surprising note, in view of sentiments expressed to the contrary by the likes of anti-realist authors Thomas Kuhn, Willard van Orman Quine, and more recently, Hilary Putnam.[39] What is the reader to make of it? My initial reaction was, the authors were either reminiscing the past, or refusing to take the road down which contextualists have travelled. And I suspect that many scientists are similarly persuaded that Kuhn is too avant-garde for their tastes. So my suspicion is scientists are not enamored of Kuhn and his move away from the optimism/realism of Formalist/Nomological theorists like Popper and Hempel. Science remains a sacred terrain wherein great theoreticians continue to construct abstract hypothetical pictures of the way the world really is. They are still hopeful that their scientific paradigms approximate reality, or are more and more closely approaching that end.

When it comes to giving account of and appraising theoretical hypotheses, six steps are listed as follows:

Step 1. *Real World.* Identify the aspect of the real world that is the focus of study in the episode at hand. These are things or processes in the world that can be described mostly in everyday terms together with a few widely used scientific terms. Do not use terms introduced to characterize particular models to be evaluated.

Step 2. *Model.* Identify a theoretical model whose fit with the real world is at issue. Describe the model, using appropriate scientific reasoning as needed. A diagram may be helpful to presenting a model.

Step 3. *Prediction.* Identify a prediction based on the model of experimental setup identified, that says what data should be obtained if the model actually provides a good fit to the real world.

Step 4. *Data.* Identify the data that have actually been obtained by observation or experimentation involving the real-world objects of study.

Step 5. *Negative Evidence.* Do the data agree with the predictions? If not, conclude that the data provide good evidence that the model does not fit the real world. If the data do agree with the prediction, go to step 6.

Step 6. *Positive evidence.* Was the prediction likely to agree with the data even if the model under consideration does not provide a good fit to the real world? This requires onsidering whether there are other clearly different, but also plausible models that would yield the same predictions about the data. If there are no such alternative models, the answer to the questions is "No." In this case, conclude that the data do provide good evidence that the model does fit the real world. If the answer to the above question is "Yes," conclude that the data are inconclusive regarding the fit of the model to the real world.[40]

The above is a program for evaluating scientific theoretical hypotheses. There are two parts, comprising steps (1)-(4), which help the reader identify the basic components in an episode, and the second part, steps (5) and (6) which help the reader evaluate the episodes in question. The order that is given is not, however, in concrete, it is just a listing for a procedure that could be followed. It should be noted further, that the program is only a guide for evaluating reports of scientific findings.

Several comments are in order here. First, the whole model works with a realist rather than anti-realist approach to science. The language employed suggests that there is a real world out there which our scientific hypotheses might come to approximate or reflect. While I favor a realist view myself, the proposal certainly doesn't reflect the direction of some of the recent philosophers of science such as for example, Thomas Kuhn.

However, I want to suggest that the realist line isn't a liability, but rather an asset,[41] since the theist wants to maintain not only that there is a real universe out there, but that humans have been given the capacity to observe, understand and appreciate this world, which opens the door not only to scientific discovery, but perhaps knowledge as to human origins. After all, "mapping the universe is about finding its origins. If we can't understand where the universe came from, then we can't understand where we came from."[42] I wish to argue that when it comes to origins, the Christian hypothesis is open to the 6-step process outlined above, and that given the data, and the information contemporary philosophers of science and scientists of a Christian orientation have to offer in response to the origins question just might be worth considering. Suppose, for example, the non-theist naturalist were to be confronted with the following pattern of reasoning. The form should immediately strike a familiar note with those familiar with first-order logic, and a few rules in modal logic.

There are only two possible answers to the origins question. Either the universe itself or something in it is eternal in the past, and so it (the universe) had no beginning, or it came into being by divine fiat. My argument runs something like the following. I'll call it my "Eternity Argument," EA.[43] It begins with the premise,

(1) Something exists.

The second premise is,

(2) Necessarily (if something exists, then something exists eternally in the past).

Therefore,

(3) Something exists eternally in the past.

The first premise I take to be uncontroversially true. It is a fact of experience. If there is a reader of this argument, or someone listening to its being read, the first premise is obviously and without controversy true.

The second premise is the conditional,-- Necessarily (if something exists, then something exists eternally in the past). It has the necessity modal functor ranging over the entire conditional. If we remove the modal functor by invoking a rule in modal logic,[44] we have a simple Modus Ponens, and so the argument is clearly valid. We need now to look at establishing the truth of premise (2). Let's assume that the world we experience from day to day is real. Were we to construct a rudimentary cosmogony for this world, there are four main options:

(A) God alone is eternal, and he is the efficient cause of everything that exists contingently.

(B) God and the world (by "world" I mean, "All that is the case contingently) exist eternally in the past.

(C) The world (as a whole) or something in the world is eternal in the past.

(D) Everything that exists comes into being out of nothing.

No doubt there are variations of these options, and some could be more finely tuned. Nevertheless, we have before us the main candidates available for the cosmogonist. Since (B) is a variant of the God exists hypothesis central to (A), we need not pay attention to it here.

(D), if true would violate the principle, *Ex nihilo, nihilo fit* ("out of nothing, nothing comes," hereafter ENNF). Now Willard Van Orman Quine views ENNF in *The Web of Belief* as a "limiting principle, and describes "limiting principles" as being "broadly philosophical in tone, that disallow one or another general sort of scientific hypothesis."[45] He contends that the principle "narrowly escapes" rejection because some who hold to steady state theory[46] argue that hydrogen atoms pop into existence out of nothing at all! This theory is contrasted with the "explosion theory," which invokes ENNF. The upshot for Quine is, though the former theory has lost to the latter, ENNF has been shown to lack self-evidence.

Perhaps a stronger reading of the principle will give us the self-evidence Quine sees the original one as lacking. Let us say that out of nothing nothing comes means, out of *absolutely* nothing, nothing comes. Arguably, on the steady state hypothesis, if hydrogen atoms are popping into existence, perhaps there are factors figuring in the phenomena which we cannot observe or measure, which cause[47] the atoms in question to appear. After all, the universe is assumed to exist in the steady state theory. But if we begin with absolutely nothing, then intuition tells us, out of nothing—absolutely nothing, nothing comes, which we may now take to be a genuine limiting principle. Let us call the first reading, $ENNF_1$, and the second, $ENNF_2$. Now $ENNF_2$ as a genuine limiting principle, eliminates (D). The remaining options may then be expressed in the following conditional:

(4) If there is a real world, then God or the universe or something in the universe must exist eternally.

Since all of the possibilities as to cosmogonic origin are included in the consequent, we may prefix (4) with a necessity modal functor as follows:

(5) Necessarily (If there is a real world, then God or the universe or something in it exist eternally. What have we established so far? For starters, if we use possible world semantics,[48] our argument precludes from the class of possible worlds, where contingent propositions may be said to be true (in the sense that they correspond to possible sets of states of affairs), worlds as wholes coming into existence, and non-eternal worlds empty of individual parts that are eternal, hence only those worlds where contingent propositions are true are possible, which are eternal as wholes, or if the world in question lacks eternal existence as a whole, then the possible worlds must each contain parts that are eternal. We should carefully note that we are talking about a subset of possible worlds, viz., worlds where contingent propositions may be said to be true, or where contingent propositions would exist. There is another set of possible worlds where analytic truth exists. Of course this set includes all possible worlds, since such truths exist in all possible worlds. To keep clear this distinction relative to possible worlds, I shall refer to the former set of possible worlds as S_1 and the latter as set S_2. Then necessarily, a world is possible in S_1 just in case it, the world, or something either internal or external to the world in question is eternal. Or, it is not possible that there be something contingent without there being something eternal.

The above cosmogonic task is actually more ambitious and comprehensive than we need for our purposes in this paper. More refinements could be added, such as a qualifier applied to the eternal existence in question, since the argument really should direct us to existence eternally in the past. What it points us to regarding origin options is two alternatives only, either there is a God, or the universe is eternal in the past. The latter might be evidence for a stronger claim still, that the universe alternative implies an eternal universe. One could then add other predicates that ordinarily apply to the God of Christian theism such as mystery, rationality, etc. Then the Christian cosmogonist might be thought to have the naturalist in a corner. The options for cosmogony narrow down, from two distinctly disparate starting alternatives, to one clearly theistic, and the other resembling in analogous ways its counterpart.

All of which should evidence the claim that the religious defender, just might be viewed as making good use of standard methods of scientific reasoning, such as deduction, induction, and the like. But over and above this, the argument above just might satisfy the steps outlined in connection with hypothesis evaluation in the USR volume.

TRUTH AND MEANING IN SCIENCE AND RELIGION

Here there is really a need for an expansive account of the concepts, truth and meaning in science religion and philosophy. Philosophers, and philosophers of science for decades if not centuries have argued and defended various theories, including coherence, correspondence, pragmatic, semantic, redundancy, and so on. Space does not permit an examination of each. It will suffice here to note that I tend to favor an approach to truth which lists three tests as maybe together comprising a full-orbed account of the nature of truth. Simply stated, truth is a property of propositions, and coherence is a *prius* to a propositions corresponding to sets of states of affairs in the world, if one takes the straightforward "external world" notion listed in the six steps of the USR volume.[49] .Finally, I think that if a proposition is coherent, and it corresponds to the way the world is, then it is going to have some sort of applicability/ pragmatic value. I take this to be the way to look also at hypotheses and paradigms/interdisciplinary matrixes, and explanations of paradigms/disciplinary matrixes.

As for meaning, the religious, from my perspective, the Christian hypothesis[50] seems to hold real promise for meaning and explanation when it comes to understanding the reason(s) for human existence. No doubt there are those who have contrived naturalistic models for meaning, but they are all relative to those who construct them and the cultural context which helps give them rise. Of course religious beliefs/models/paradigms are also relative in this way, and with the others in a person-relative way, and a person-variable way.[51] But none of this relativity entails an ultimate meta-relativism. Clearly, on a Christian worldview, God gives the creature meaning and value, because he provides a meta-ethical base for both. And while notions of good and just are prevenient on earlier predicates of the divine,[52] there is a sense in which the creature may find meaning and purpose in such an hypothesis. *Prima facie*, it certainly seems to hold more promise than any naturalistic metaphysical rivals.

CONCLUSION

Our conclusion is that the religious is not as antithetic to the scientific as might initially appear to many interested in the latter, but not in the former. Perhaps there is more promise to practices of inquiry into the religious than many naturalists have heretofore thought, if current literature is any index. Certainly, if the scientist is going to serve the common good, there ought to be an openness to whatever paradigms/interdisciplinary matrixes, explanations that are out there. Moreover, premature hasty rejection without careful scrutiny bears no fruit for anyone of any persuasion. That is why the university, the public square, and most definitely the news media, need to allow all options a fair and careful hearing/reading. Such an intercommunicative openness to healthy and careful critical rationality may produce not only more understanding, but better communication and perhaps a better grasp of truth, meaning and value for the human family worldwide. This is an objective clearly in line with the notion of harmony and prosperity for all peoples and nations, which is central to the Beijing International Forum's theme.

NOTES

1 Some hold that there is to be more than one return of Christ, one before the Millennium, and another at the end of the Millennium, some even another.

2 Some Christians hold that Christ is going to return to bring to pass a secret rapture, while others hold that his return is going to usher in the final state of everlasting felicity and though it will involve a rapture, it will not be secret.

3 It is just about as difficult to find a consensus among Christian theists, as it is scientists these days. Some within the Christian tradition skewer reason, holding it detrimental to Christian virtue, and the spirit's proper posture before the Creator, notably some of Kierkegaardian ilk.

4 Anselm of Canterbury (1033-1109 A.D.), held that one must *believe* in order that one may understand (his famous Latin dictum runs, *credo ut intelligam*, I believe in order that I may understand). Arthur Holmes, now retired from teaching, authored a book, *Faith Seeks Understanding*. The key persons who gave birth to the Society of Christian Philosophers (SCP) decided to call the journal of that Society, *Faith and Philosophy*, not the other way around. For some at least, there appears to be a *prius* of faith.

5 I am indebted to Professor Nicholas Wolterstorff for his account of this concept in a paper he delivered at the Society of Christian Philosophers symposium held at Fudan University, October 15-19, 2005. See his unpublished paper, "Religion in the Academy and in the Political Order."

6 Some think of starting points as *assumptions* in the sense that they are pre-critical.. My former mentor, Cornelius Van Til spoke of them as *presuppositions*. Though many think of them as pre-critical sorts of beginnings, sometimes they are really carefully crafted statements. For some theists they are carefully selected, as we see in the case of Van Til). For Alvin Plantinga, the Christian's belief that God exists is viewed as a *properly basic belief*. See his, *Warranted Christian Belief*, which is in English and Chinese editions.

7 Bas C. Van Fraasen, *Laws and Symmetry*. Oxford: The Clarendon Press, 1989.

8 Thomas Kuhn, *The Structure of Scientific Revolutions*, p. 109.

9 Bas Van Fraassen, *Laws and Symmetry*, p. 56.

10 In an earlier paper, this comparative study is elaborated in greater detail, "Paradigm in Science and Religion," and is available in Chinese only in, *A Dialogue Between Science and Religion*, Melville Y. Stewart and Kelly James Clark, editors, Xiamen University Press, 2003.

11 The full title is, *Exercitatio Anatmica De Motu Cordis et Sanguinis in Animalibus*, which translated is, *An Anatomical Study of the Heard and Blood in Animals*. The shorter title, *De Motu Cordis*, translates, *The Motion of the Heart*, and hereafter I will refer to it as *DMC*.

12 In his essay, "Harvey's Quantitative Method," Michael T. Ghiselin claims that the *DMC* is an outstanding example of the hypothetico-deductive system, p. 326. He defended his claim against challenger Paul Farber in a letter to the *Bulletin of the History of Medicine*, Vol. 41, 1967, p. 78. See my article for further details.

13 In the Leake translation of *DMC*, three different terms are used, *motion, movement* and *actions*. All three terms appear to have an equivalent meaning. It seems that Harvey had in mind the chief role of the heart, and the term in Leake's translation used to reflect this is, *function*.

14 I am indebted to my son, Steven Allen Stewart, for reading sections dealing with medical particulars pertaining to the heart. He is a specialist technician and assists in heart surgeries that involve introducing mechanical devices. Some inaccuracies were avoided because of his editing.

15 Conceivably, some remain in a religious tradition and entertain a general posture that isn't very much open to change. One might imagine, for example, a person growing up in the Russian Orthodox Church, and remaining in this tradition for his/her entire life. This tradition doesn't generally advocate reformation or radical revision. The Seven Councils of the Church, and Church's tradition are viewed as essentially unalterable and without revision. Hence it is unlikely that such a person would ever experience anything like a religious paradigm shift.

16 Another, perhaps more popular variant is, *Mahayana* Buddhism.

17 *Data* may have a different sense here from its use in scientific contexts. Moreover, I am inclined to the view that beliefs can serve as *data*, as Nicholas Wolterstorff suggests in his book, *Reason Within the Bounds of Religion*. He calls them *data beliefs*. They are not a specific *kind* of beliefs, but a specific *role* that beliefs as beliefs may be viewed as having.

18 Along with Nicholas Wolterstorff, I hold that beliefs can function in three ways: (1) control core beliefs; (2) data beliefs; (3) data background beliefs. I've given a brief account of (2) in footnote 21 above. *Data background beliefs* have the role of helping me gather the data that I in fact gather. And *control beliefs* have two functions, they guide me in the *generation* of other beliefs that I may or may not add to my overall superstructure of knowledge, and they help me in the sorting out of beliefs that might be under scrutiny for inclusion in that superstructure.

19 The notion of analogy for me here, is analogy of proportionality rather than attribution, because the former allow for some point or element of *univocity* with regard to both analogues, whereas attribution doesn't.

20 My focus here on the *explanatory power* of a paradigm will come up in greater detail when the primary focus is upon the notion of explanation itself in the next section.

21 I am aware that one may construct a new explanatory model here,

one that works with the self as the first cause in the causal chain. But this move doesn't seem to help me in affirming that such choices are really me, for the reason that they do not result from my likes and dislikes, my desires and wants. For if they did, then they would be caused.

22 For those who like my friend, Yue Feng, can speak and read Russian, see my article, *Искупление* (*The Atonement*), "Свобода, Необходимость И Искупление" ("Freedom, and the Necessity of the Atonement"), published by St. Petersburg School of Religion and Philosophy Publishers, 2000, edited by Melville Y. Stewart and Natalia Pecherskaya. In this essay, two positions are contrasted, Calvinism and Arminianism, with their respective strengths and weaknesses. And I argue that if on the one hand, God's Sovereignty is in view, it cannot be compromised, but if on the other, human free choice is in view, then freedom of choice is essential, if humans are to be held responsible by this Sovereign Agent. Moreover, I argue that sovereignty is not genuine or authentic unless there are *free* agents. On some issues, particularly the one relating to the choice of salvation, neither paradigm is without its problems (perhaps we can call them *anomalies*). At this point, the present *disciplinary matrix* has a perceived strength the other does not.

23 Karl Popper, *The Logic of Scientific Discovery*.

24 The Logical Positivists held that factual claims such as, *It is raining*, must be reducible to *protocol statements*, and these in turn must be verifiable by *simple observations*. The first formulation (in A. J. Ayers book, *Language, Truth and Logic*) of what became known as the Verification Principle, was revised to allow a more liberal reading of verification, where verification was expanded to include what is verifiable *in principle*.

25 By the Later Wittgenstein, I mean the views of Ludwig Wittgenstein that appear in his *Philosophical Invetigations*.

26 Stephen M. Barr, "The Big Bang," Chapter 6 in *Modern Physics and Ancient Faith*. Notre Dame: The University of Notre Dame Press, p. 38.

27 Philip Clayton, *Explanation from Physics to Theology, An Essay in Rationality and Religion*. New Haven, Yale University Press, 1989.

28 The criteria are more complete actually. I follow George I. Mavrodes' account of a proof (in *Belief in God, a Study in the Epistemology of Religion*, Chapter 11, pp. 17-48) as including: (1) the deductive form is valid; (2) the premises are agreed upon as being true by the disputant in question; (3) the argument does not beg the question.

29 Here one might wish to distinguish various accounts of the rationality of faith, notable among which are Alvin Plantinga, in his 3rd volume on epistemology, *Warranted Christian Belief*, Oxford: Oxford University Press, 2000, and Richard Swinburne and his study of epistemological theory, *Epistemic Justification*, Oxford: Oxford University Press, 2001. Whereas Plantinga argues for a *de jure* rationality of properly basic Christian beliefs, Richard Swinburne wants to go beyond *de jure* rationality adding on *de facto* rationality, the idea that Christian belief claims are *probably true*. An alternative to both is the *reliabilist epistemology* of William P. Alston, who argues for a perception account of God that resembles his general theory of perception,

see his, *The Reliability of Sense Perception*, Ithaca: Cornell University Press, 1992.

30 I should add that the arguments of both Plantinga and Swinburne could just as well be applied to the religious systems of the Jewish, Islamic, or other theistic views of the world.

31 See *Philosophy of Religion*, Melville Y. Stewart, Xing Taotao, editors, Beijing: Peking University Press, 2005, pp. 161-180, and especially pp. 179 181 for an extensive bibliography of studies which relate to this sort of claim.

32 Arguably for some, that the Scriptures state in Genesis 2:7, that "God took of the dust of the ground, and breathed into it, and it became a living soul (ש פ נ)," suggests for some the possibility that humans do in fact have an affinity with the animal world, and that evolution of some sort might be hinted at as being employed in the creation of humans.

33 Alvin Plantinga would add that this capacity, though affected by a fall, can be reliable, if *instigated* by the Holy Spirit, resulting in a belief-forming mechanism that functioning property, in an environment friendly to the objective of forming beliefs that are rational and true, can achieve that objective.

34 *Understanding Scientific Reasoning*, 5th edition, Ronald N. Giere, John Bickle, Robert F. Mauldin. Belmont: Thomson Learning, 2006, hereafter, *USR*. The date of copyright is curious, since the book is now in print. It is good to be up to date, and even better to have something on scientific reasoning that anticipates the *future*!

35 *USR*, p. 5. Their reason for taking this simple approach is the claim that if one were to try to follow the professional discussions one would have to be a scientist and have a "touch of genius" as well.

36 Ibid., p. 6.

37 Ibid., p. 6.

38 Ibid., p. 19.

39 Putnam has shifted from an earlier realism to a view that falls just short of anti-realism, favoring an internal realism, p. 760, Robert Audi's, *The Cambridge Dictionary of Philosophy*, Second Edition, Cambridge: Cambridge University Press, 1999.

40 Ibid., pp. 34, 35.

41 While it is an asset, Kuhn's approach is also an option for the theist, since he wants to work with an interdisciplinary matrix, and this just might allow some room for the religious sort.

42 Ibid., p. 54.

43 My version of the EA argument is a brief account of a longer and more complete version that appears in Russian in the *Proceedings of the First International Conference*, held at St. Petersburg, Russia, 2000.

44 Brain F. Chellas, *Modal Logic, An Introduction*. Cambridge: Cambridge University Press, 1980, p. 6. The rule is the Necessity Elimination Rule in System S5.

45 Willard Van Orman Quine, *The Web of Belief*, 2nd ed., New York,

Random House, 1978, p. 46. ENNF is a traditional philosophical maxim often invoked in Christian accounts of creation. Scholastic Protestants held that ENNF is a limit of natural reason, and supplemented it with the idea that without the creative activity of God, nothing would come into existence. The exception is the *ens perfectissimus* (God), and so he can give being to a finite universe. Arthur A. Muller, *Dictionary of Latin and Greek Theological Terms*, Grand Rapids, Baker Book House, 1985, p. 108.

46 Steady state is a cosmological theory involving the claim that the average density of matter doesn't fluctuate with either space or time, even with the expansion of the universe. The theory requires that matter be "continuously created." *McGraw-Hill Dictionary of Scientific and Technical Terms*, 2nd ed., New York, McGraw Hill Book Company, 1969, Daniel N. Lapedes, Editor in Chief.

47 We are invoking another "limiting principle" here, "Every event has a cause." Quine talks about this as also lacking the "necessary" self-evidence he wants in *The Web of Belief*, p. 47.

48 For an interesting challenge to modal realists who accept the existence of possible worlds, see Charles S. Chihar's, *The Worlds of Possibility*, Oxford, Clarendon Press, 1998, where he argues for modality without a possible world metaphysic. There is no attempt to settle this dispute here. I merely entertain possible world semantics as one way to develop the issue at hand.

49 Bertrand Russell developed at least six different versions of the correspondence theory, and each had its problems. I only wish to claim here that I think that some version of it is arguable, and further that it lies at the root of a propostion's working.

50 Those of alternative religious persuasion could interpolate their own preference as to the religious.

51 A belief is *person-relative* in the sense that *one person may believe proposition A, and another no*t. And they are also *person-variable* in the sense that *at time t_1, person M may believe proposition A, but at another time t_2 not.*

52 The notions of *good* and *just* are prevenient on earlier notions instantiated in God, and these are or have to be truncated notions. That is, God cannot be just without persons toward whom he can be just, hence on a view where God is viewed as existing before creation (and hence there is a sense in which God is related to time on this view), he can't be actually good and just toward anyone, but only dispositionally so, and so potentially so, not *actually so.*

Part II

Dialogue between
Confucianism and Christianity

Chapter 6

An "Anthropocosmic" Perspective on Creativity

Tu Weiming

In his seminal study on the intellectual foundations of China, Fritz Mote makes a strong claim:

> The basic point which outsiders have found so hard to detect is that the Chinese, among all peoples ancient and recent, primitive and modern, are apparently unique in having no creation myth; that is, they have regarded the world and man as uncreated, as constituting the central features of a sponta- neously self-generating cosmos having no creator, god, ulti- mate cause or will external to itself.[1]

He further claims that "[t]he genuine Chinese cosmogony is that of an organismic process, meaning that all of the parts of the entire cosmos be- long to one organic whole and that they all interact as participants in one spontaneously self-generating life process." In Joseph Needham's analysis, the Chinese cosmological thinking presupposes "an ordered harmony of wills without an ordainer." [2]

I have modified this interpretive stance in my essay on "The Continu- ity of Being: Chinese Visions of Nature."[3] By focusing on the Confucian ideal of forming one body with Heaven, Earth, and myriad things, I argue that the distinctive feature of Chinese cosmology is not the absence of cosmogonist concerns, but faith in the interconnectedness of all modalities of being as the result of the continuous creativity of the cosmic process.

With this introductory note, I would like to pursue the intersection of two lines of thinking--Heaven and the human in Confucian cosmology. Heaven is intimately related to the story of the earth. The earth, as the habitat of all known creatures, is the proper home for us. Even if we can imagine a spiritual sanctuary radically different from the world on this earth, such as the Kingdom of God or the other shore, the earth is a lived reality that defines our daily existence here and now. A great manifestation of Heaven's creativity is the plenitude of the earth. A passage in *Zhongyong* 中庸 (centrality and com- monality) captures this aspect of Heaven quite remarkably:

> The sky now before us is only this bright, shining mass; but when   viewed in its unlimited extent, the sun, moon, stars, and constellations are suspended in it and all things are cov- ered by it. The earth before us is but a handful of soil; but in its breadth and depth, it sustains mountains like Hua and

Yue without feeling their weight, contains the rivers and seas without letting them leak away, and sustains all things.

The mountain before us is only a fistful of straw, but in all the vastness of its size, grass and trees grow upon it, birds and animals dwell on it, and stores of precious minerals are discovered in it. The water before us is but a spoonful of liquid, but in all its unfathomable depth, the monsters, dragons, fishes, and turtles are produced in them. And wealth becomes abundant because of it. [XXVI:9]

In this view, sky, earth, mountains, and rivers are vital energies displaying the stupendous power of Heaven's life-generating process. There is nothing in the world that is not a demonstration of Heaven's creativity. Human beings, animals, grass, and plants are obvious examples. Even rocks and soil are no exception. All modalities of being are interconnected in this ceaseless evolution. The relevance of *qi* (vital energy) to this cosmological model is obvious. This may have prompted Carl Jung to characterize the cosmos in the ancient Chinese mind as "a decidedly psychophysical structure" in 1949.[4] Although this is not the place to delve into a discussion of the methodological implications of *qi* as psychophysical stuff, it entails a complex world view not conducive to mechanistic and theistic explanations. Carl Jung's idea of "synchronicity" may be idiosyncratic, but it suggests an approach to Heaven much more sophisticated than most forms of causality.

What is the significance for conceptualizing Heaven's creativity as a life-generating process? For one thing, it is compatible with either the "Big Bang" or the "steady state" cosmogony. Assuming that the "Big Bang" is the most persuasive current astronomical interpretation of the origins of our universe, Heaven emerged as the result of billions of years. When the earth evolved, the virtue of Heaven as a life-generating creativity became particularly pronounced. The idea of the "steady state" is congenial to Heaven in an evolutionary process. There may have been ruptures, certainly discontinuities, but, by comparison, they were no more than tiny bangs. And, as far as we can tell, despite these tiny bangs our universe was formed in such a way that the story of the earth (the delicate equilibrium that engenders and sustains numerous life forms) is unique to us. Surely, in principle, we cannot and should not rule out the possibility that, as our scientific knowledge is extended, we may discover life forms on other planets and thus we must remain open to the mystery of the origins of life anywhere as well as here on earth.

The cumulative knowledge resulting from the investigation, interpretation, and imagination of astronomers and other scientists points to a natural process that for the most part is not at all connected with the advent of the human. The anthropomorphic or anthropocentric reading of this process seems fundamentally flawed and an unexamined assumption that the whole dynamics took place for the sake of the human is untenable. Heaven is for all beings. It does not seem to have a particular design for the human. Strictly speaking, there is no indication that Heaven has a particular purpose in mind.

The assumption in the ancient Chinese texts is that Heaven does not exist for the sagely king Yao; nor does it perish because of the tyrannical Zhou speaks to this.

Historically, the idea of Heaven emerged in China in the Western Zhou around the first millennium B.C. Ostensibly, it was a replacement for the anthropomorphic Lord-on-High, the deified ancestor of the previous Shang dynasty. Heaven continued to assume some anthropomorphic characteristics during the time of Confucius. The master believed that Heaven willed that his mission to humanize the world would not perish. He also remarked that no one but Heaven understood him. In Mencius' time, the anthropomorphic theme persisted. However, the conviction that human nature is conferred by Heaven granted humanity an access to Heaven's creativity and a self-knowledge that is potentially omnipresent and omniscient. From the eleventh century on, Neo-Confucian thinkers made a definitively naturalistic turn by focusing on the Heavenly Principle (*tianli* 天理) which, as the underlying pattern of all things, does not seem to have a will of its own. Understandably, in the 17th century, Matteo Ricci's theological strategy to convert the Chinese to Catholicism was to critique the idea of principle as the ultimate basis for the order of things and to urge Confucians to return to the idea of the Lord-on-High, which later became the standard translation of God.

My approach to Heaven in our discussion on creativity is based on an anthropocosmic vision. It is, on the one hand, recognition that Heaven, as the result of human conceptualization, interpretation, and imagination, is inescapably anthropological. Yet, on the other hand, as the generative force that has created all modalities of being, Heaven cannot be confined to an anthropocentric picture of the universe. An anthropomorphic depiction of Heaven is also incomplete because, as the Big Bang and evolution clearly indicate, billions of years prior to the birth of Planet Earth and millions of years before the first appearance of life on earth, there were no traces of any human shape or form at all. However, we should not rule out the possibility that Heaven as a life-generating creativity may have been present all along. Then, why can't we simply define Heaven in purely naturalistic terms as the cosmic process then? The advent of the human does make a difference. The anthropocosmic idea addresses the interplay between Heaven's creativity as expressed in the cosmological process and humans' creativity as embodied in Heaven's life-generating transformation.

The myth of Yu 禹 is pertinent here. The Chinese counterpart to Noah's story is a demonstration of human courage, ingenuity, and hope. Sage King Yu, charged with the responsibility of contending the major catastrophe threatening to human survival, was not escape but management. Having learned the futility of his father Gun 鯀 whose damming method worsened the situation and was banished for his failure, Yu, fully accepted Sage Kin Yao's 堯 order, approached the Flood with a well-thought-out plan. He first studied the cause and surveyed the typography of the whole land. Having gained thorough knowledge of the overall damage, he set out to deal with the disaster. He mobilized tens of thousands of laborers to develop a drainage scheme, and step by step allowed the water to flow through numerous channels to the major rivers and eventually to the ocean. His persistent effort not only solved the program but also created an elaborate irrigational system. He worked patiently, selflessly, and effectively at the project and it worked. For nine years he never relaxed for a moment. It is said that "he racked his body and wearied his mind, living outside his home for thirteen years, not daring to enter his house even when he passed its gate."[5] What Yu demonstrated was the human spirit at its best: thoughtfulness, leadership, sacrifice, and compassion. His creativity changed the course of nature and enabled human beings to survive and flourish.

In this view, human beings are not merely creatures, but co-creators of the cosmic process. They actively participate in "the great transformation" (*dahua* 大化). Symbolically, since our understanding of Heaven as creativity is an integral part of our own creative imagination, we must take responsibility for this anthropocosmic interplay. In the language of the Book of Change, the cosmos is never a static structure but rather is a dynamic process. In its constant unfolding, it always generates new realities by creatively transforming the existing order, laden with inconsistencies, into an ever-innovating congruent process. By implication, self-cultivation, a form of spiritual exercise, emulates Heaven's creativity.

Heaven's creativity that is embodied in the human as well as Heaven's creativity in itself is open, dynamic, transformative, and unceasing. So far as humans are concerned, it is also indwelling. Whether we came into being by the mysterious design of a transcendent reality, the "wholly other," or by a persistent evolutionary process, we find an intimate niche in the cosmos as our ultimate source and meaning of life. It is worth noting that this Confucian position is significantly different from conceptions of an anthropocosmic relationship defined in terms of rupture and discontinuity. [*Zhang Zai* 張載] Confucians assume that we are here not as mere creatures passively submitting to an absolutely incomprehensible power or a radically different divinity, but as co-creators endowed with the intelligence and wisdom of apprehending Heaven as creativity in itself.

I believe that from the idea of co-creator we can extrapolate a further implication of the anthropocosmic interrelatedness. We are entrusted, individually and communally, with the duty to realize through self-cultivation both our aesthetic ability to appreciate the wonderful presentation of Heaven's resourcefulness and our moral power to actively continue Heaven's great work. The ancient Chinese saying, "Heaven engenders; human completes" (*tiansheng rencheng* 天生人成), accurately represents the spirit of this "anthropocosmic" vision.

We may have encountered a serious conceptual difficulty, if not a major methodological confusion here. If Heaven has entrusted us with the duty to realize ourselves in cosmological as well as anthropological terms, how can we escape the anthropomorphic reading of Heaven's will? If we simply assign ourselves the divine mission to complete Heaven's great work, how can we justify in attributing such obviously human desire to Heaven? Our naturalistic impulse compels us to purge all anthropological intentions in our cosmological narrative. If we follow this line of thinking, it is inconceivable that any psychosocial terms, such as "we are entrusted with the duty," have a place in it. However, Confucian humanism is not only naturalistic but also spiritual. The whole idea of Heaven-human mutuality or mutual responsiveness is predicated on the assumptive reason that there must be an intelligible way of defining what form human creativity actually takes. If Heaven's creativity is a life-generating process, in what sense can human creativity be understood as a crystallization and continuation of that process? The aesthetic and ethical implications of "Heaven engenders and human completes" are too rich and complex to explore here. Suffice it to simply mention that the human capacity to appreciate nature and to nurture a fiduciary community as the human counterpart to Heaven's creativity is thought to be an exemplification of this Heaven-human relatedness.

Of course, we can interpret the human embodiment of Heaven's creativity differently. There is room for a multiplicity of interpretive strategies. We may, for example, consider destructiveness as an integral part of creativity. The apocalyptic vision of cataclysm in which evil forces are destroyed entails the annihilation of age-long civilizations as well is certainly one of those alternatives. Confucians opt for the enduring significance of "human symbolic activity"[6] and the preservation of the cumulative traditions of literature, history, philosophy, arts, and the elaborate constructions of economic, political, social, and cultural institutions as a demonstration of Heaven's creativity in humans' conscious and unconscious endeavors. Despite the possibilities of natural and man-made disasters, humans are capable of and engaged in a continuous effort to build and rebuild physical and symbolic structures. Contrary to the Daoists' perception that any artificial manipulation of the natural process eventually leads to self-destruction, Confucians take a positive attitude toward all human creations, especially those in harmony with Heaven's life-generating functions.

Heaven so conceived is omnipresent and omniscient, but not omnipotent. To insist on Heaven's omnipotence is to accord the cosmic process an all-embracing power of self-adjustment without any reference to the centrality of human participation. An unintended negative consequence of this is an abdication of human responsibility in the maintenance of universal order. Human beings can, through their own personal cultivation, actively take part in Heaven's creativity. They are also capable of committing grave mistakes contrary to the Heavenly virtue of generativity and vitality, damaging to themselves and detrimental to the environment around them. Human beings can survive all natural catastrophes, but they may be destroyed by their own doing (we cannot escape human disasters, 自作孽，不可活.) The contemporary significance of this line of thinking is obvious: man-made disasters, beyond Heaven's power to prevent them, are the real reason for raising doubts about the viability of the human species.

Human nature, like all other modalities of being, is endowed by Heaven. Yet the uniqueness of being human is our inner ability to learn to follow the Way. We are capable of educating ourselves to become worthy partners of the cosmic process. We are empowered to apprehend Heaven through our self-knowledge. As Mencius avowed, if we can realize the full measure of our heart-and-mind, we will know our nature; if we know our nature, we will know Heaven. Surely existentially we cannot fully realize our heart-and-mind, thus, in practical terms, it is unlikely that we will ever know our nature in itself and, by inference, it is unlikely we will ever know Heaven in its entirety. But, in theory and, to a certain extent in practice, we can be attuned to the Way of Heaven; specifically a sympathetic resonance with the cosmic process ("the flowing agency of the great transformation") is realizable through our persistent self-cultivation. This involves not only the cognitive recognition of the mind but also the experiential embodiment of the heart [*tizhi* 體知, *xin* 心 as heart-and mind].

The highest manifestation of Confucian self-realization is the "unity of Heaven and humanity" (*tianren heyi* 天人合一). The authentic possibility of mutual responsiveness between the human heart-and-mind and the Way of Heaven is implied in such a unity. It is vitally important to acknowledge the asymmetry in the Heaven-human relationship. Heaven is creativity in itself and human beings learn to be creative through self-effort. Heaven's genuineness is naturally brilliant, whereas human beings at their best struggle to become true to themselves by means of their knowledge and wisdom. Nevertheless, as co-creators of the evolutionary process, human beings can carry Heaven's Way in the world. Indeed, they are obligated, by their own nature, to realize Heaven's Way in their lifeworld. In so doing, the Way is no longer out there as mere transcendence with no intimate relationship to human existence here and now. Rather, it is embodied in the common experience of everyday life, making ordinary people, without necessarily being aware of its far-reaching implications, personally connected with Heaven.

Of course, there is a transcendent dimension of Heaven that we can never fully conceptualize, but Heaven is also immanent in human nature, not merely a laden potential but a lived reality. Indeed, human beings can assist in the transforming and nourishing functions of the cosmic process [Doctrine of the Mean] and, by implication, help the Heavenly Way prevail in the world. This may explain why Confucius affirmed that "human beings can make the Way great; the Way cannot make human beings great!" (Analects)

The godlike power of the human implicit in this intriguing statement entails neither anthropocentrism nor anthropomorphism. Although Confucians regard humans as preeminent, they do not view the cosmos exclusively from the human point of view. They occasionally attribute human characteristics or behavior to nonhuman things, but, in general, they do not depict Heaven in human terms. However, humans are supposed to emulate Heaven and to learn from Heavenly patterns for the sake of self-realization. Notwithstanding that the rich endowment of human nature and the Way are accessible to all human beings, the task is painfully difficult. Only with awe-inspiring effort can one truly bear witness to the Way. Mencius made this explicit in an apparently anthropomorphic assertion:

Shun rose from the field; Fu Yüeh was raised to office from among the builders; Chiao Ke from amidst the fish and salt; Kuan Chung from the hands of the prison officer; Sun Shu-ao from the sea and Po-li Hsi from the market. That is why Heaven, when it is about to place a great burden on a man, always first tests his resolution, exhausts his frame and makes him suffer starvation and hardship, frustrates his efforts so as to shake him from his mental lassitude, toughen his nature and make good his deficiencies. As a rule, man can mend his ways only after he has made mistakes. It is only when a man is frustrated in [his] mind and in his deliberations that he is able to innovate. It is only when his intentions become visible on his countenance and audible in his tone of voice that others can understand him. As a rule, state without law-abiding families and reliable Gentlemen on the one hand, and, on the other, without the threat of foreign invasion, will perish. Only then do we learn the lesson that we survive in adversity and perish in ease and comfort. [Mencius, VIB:15]

Since the realization of humanity has cosmological as well as anthropological significance, it is never an easy task. The human aspiration to uniting with Heaven is not a demonstration of hubris. Nor is the human hope for Heaven's responsiveness a justification for self-aggrandizement. The promise of full humanity is only realizable through a total commitment: "the profound person cannot but be broadminded and resolute, for the burden is heavy and the way is long. He takes humanity as his personal vocation, how can we say that burden is not heavy? He does not let go until he dies, how can we say that the road is not long?" [Analects]

The paradox is that, on the one hand, Heaven is the ultimate authority for human worth and the primary source of human life and, on the other, the active participation of the human is essential for the completion of Heaven's great work. One can certainly contend that this human concept of Heaven is inescapably anthropocentric and anthropomorphic. In the last analysis, however, an anthropological characterization, no matter how sophisticated, is inadequate to capture the cosmic dimension in the Confucian sense of humanity. The Classic of Change is primarily a cosmological text, but it is also a book of wisdom profoundly meaningful to those who put into practice in their lives its insightful observations about "the design of Heaven and the pattern of earth" (*tianwen dili*).

The fundamental flaw of the anthropocentric interpretation and the inadequacy of the anthropomorphic interpretation of Heaven is failure to account for the Big Bang and the evolution of the earth, both predating the advent of the human. Surely Heaven in the human imagination is intimately related to the anthropological world, but the same human imagination can rise above the anthropocentric and anthropomorphic predicament and recognize that Heaven is also connected with evolution and the Big Bang in a mysterious way beyond current human comprehension. As Heaven's creativity unfolds in front of our eyes, we cannot but acknowledge that it embraces a much larger universe than the human world. The anthropocentric reading of Heaven is cosmologically untenable. It is also a limited and limiting understanding of human creativity and imagination.

The anthropomorphic depiction of Heaven is more complex. By attributing the human form to Heaven, we obviously fail to appreciate the mystery of Heaven as creativity in itself and the simple fact that such creativity is essentially impersonal and non-human. Also, in so doing, we are unable to account for Heaven's "great transformation" and the way it generates the myriad things. Yet since humans are Heaven's partners and co-creators, understanding Heaven in anthropological terms is unavoidable and often necessary. Furthermore, Heaven is a creation of the human imagination. Since Heaven and the human are dynamically interacting, an anthropomorphic reading of Heaven's activities is conceivable, occasionally even desirable. Nevertheless, anthropomorphism, in theory and practice, only superficially grasps Heaven's all-embracing fullness.

What are the implications of this mutuality and mutual responsiveness between Heaven and the human? First of all, we assume that both Heaven and the human have been undergoing a persistent transformation. Surely, Heaven is creativity in itself, but it is also an emergent state that is conceptualized and experienced by humans as the ultimate source of their existence and the ultimate meaning of their lives. Although the images and pictures of Heaven are manifestations of human creativity, Heaven as such can never be fully comprehended by the human mind. Despite human accessibility to Heaven, human aesthetic and ethical symbolizations of Heaven are always inadequate and incomplete. Heaven and the human are both dynamic processes rather than static structures. The dialectic interplay between them makes the evolutionary, indeed co-evolutionary, process more complex, giving rise to rich and diverse realities and possibilities. Although we know Heaven to the extent that it involves itself in human affairs, we can never grasp the full measure of its creativity. We can imagine that Heaven was intimately connected with evolution before the advent of the human. It may have been present in the Big Bang that created our universe. We should not rule out the possibility that, as our intelligence advances, our knowledge about the Big Bang will increase and our formulation of the theological question will change. At the present juncture, we are not strictly agnostic, but we accept a healthy dose of agnosticism.

So far as our intimate relation to Heaven is concerned, we know experientially and empirically that Heaven is omnipresent and omniscient The all-present and all-knowing Heaven is not an outside observer but an inside participant. Heaven engenders new realities and possibilities by its very presence and knowledge. By emulating Heaven, human beings learn to be present everywhere and to try to know everything. They acquire that capacity through sympathy as well as rationality. Without sympathy, they cannot experientially understand each other, let alone other modalities of being that are structured different from their own species. The human capacity to cultivate a sympathetic resonance with the myriad things is predicated on the innate quality of human nature to sympathize as well as on the learned ability to develop an ever-expanding network of relationships.

It is a truism that human beings are characterized as biohistorical beings. The Confucian perception is in perfect accord with Gordon Kaufman's view that human beings' "deep embeddedness in the web of life on planet Earth while simultaneously attending to the significance of our radical distinctiveness as a form of life" with an important caveat.[7] They are also aesthetic, ethical, social, political, and metaphysical beings. Surely, through biological evolution and historical development, human beings become increasingly sophisticated in using symbols to guide their responses to the environment around them. Aesthetic, ethical, social, political, and metaphysical aspects of the human are inevitably intertwined with human historicity. Genetically, the dialectic interaction between the brain and language may have enabled humans to imagine, picture, and comprehend all that is relevant in their lifeworld. However, if we insist that this is the whole story of human evolution, it is, at best, one-sided. Whether or not the human heart-and-mind and body are reducible to the functions of the brain and language is far from settled.

Confucians, especially those who followed Mencius, contend that the heart-and-mind and the body are innately endowed with the ability to experience and creatively respond to the surroundings and the world at large. They do it specifically rather than generically, but, in practical terms, their general capacity to do so is never in doubt. Since this capacity is already in place at the pre-verbal stage, the possibility of extra-linguistic experience is imaginable. Even if we prefer to characterize all conscious and unconscious activities as functions of the brain filtering through symbols, it is ill-advised to subsume the heart-and-mind and the body under the category of the brain.

The body itself offers a useful example. It is not a given, but an attainment. As an attainment, it is not merely the result of sociality but also the result of persistent conscious effort. Actually, its individuality is profoundly personal, although it is empirically visible and publicly accountable. As Eliot Deutsch insists, we do not own our body, we become our body. Mencius offers a classical articulation of this insight: "Our body and complexion are given to us by Heaven. Only a sage can give his body completion." [Mencius, VIIA: 38] On the surface, this clearly indicates that the body is not only biophysical, but also social and cultural. Yet, the process of becoming our body presupposes that social and cultural conditioning must be predicated on the physical constitution of the body which is not merely symbolic. Actually, we do not think merely with our brain. Since thinking necessarily involves feeling, we often think with our heart-and-mind and with our body. Embodied thinking is particularly significant in aesthetics and ethics. In aesthetic and ethical praxis, thinking and doing are inseparable. Bodily sensations, such as sight, sound, smell, taste, and touch, are often integral parts of an apprehending process. Without them, an aesthetic or ethical act may be reduced to a flat and impoverished abstraction.

We should not confuse the genetic reasons for the maturation of the modern person, which are attributable to the increasing sophistication of the brain, with the structural features of the body and the heart-and-mind. As human beings in the modern and postmodern world, we are in possession of a quantity of data, information, and knowledge that is unprecedented in human history. Science, technology, the market economy, tourism, migration, disease, drugs, violence, and terrorism, not to mention environmental concerns, prompted global interconnection, intercommunication, interchange, and interaction that only a few decades ago was beyond our imagination. Although we celebrate the mysterious creativity that enabled human beings to emerge as self-conscious biohistorical beings, we are also wary that the rich experience of face-to-face communication, the art of listening, and learning from the wisdom of the elders are relegated to the background.

As the viability of the human species is problematical, we begin to seek the wise counsel of ancient sages and contemporary spiritual leaders. As Ewert Cousins observes, given the current human condition, the earth is our prophet and indigenous peoples can teach us the simple way to coexist with nature. If we do not confuse data with information, information with knowledge, and knowledge with wisdom, we must recognize that the appearance of the Enlightenment that initiated the modern age of reason is a double-edged sword. It is a marvelous manifestation of human creativity. But it has also unleashed terrible, destructive power. We must acknowledge that creativity is often accompanied by annihilation, violence, and devastation. This is true with the Big Bang, evolution, and the emergence of the human.

As we begin to reflect and meditate on the meaning of being human in the current situation, our attention is drawn to the spiritual leaders, those Karl Jaspers refers to as "paradigmatic personalities," such as Socrates, Plato, Moses, Laozi, Confucius, Buddha, Jesus, Mohammed, and others. The ethic they teach us is not confrontation, violence, destruction, or war, but self-knowledge and communal solidarity through peace, agape, love, justice, wisdom, civility, trust, and compassion. What is the relevance of their teachings to us in a world full of tension and conflict?

There is an explicit way that the Confucians understand Heaven as creativity in itself. As the Book of Change specifies, the creativity that Heaven exhibits is a life-generating process. We may imagine that the destructive power, as manifested in the Big Bang , the evolution that brought about the planet Earth, and the floods, earthquakes, volcanic eruptions, and typhoons that continue to destroy life on earth, is an integral part of Heaven's creativity. But what Confucians observe is an organismic cosmos, ceaselessly evolving and dynamically transforming. As a complex adaptive system of vital energies, it never loses its life-supporting equilibrium. So far as we can tell, the Big Bang and the evolution that eventually provided the conditions for the human form to come into view were characterized by explosive forces and incessant disruptions. Without them, planet Earth could not have evolved. Similarly, the evolution on earth was by no means a smoothly calibrated gradual process. Indeed, it was marked by catastrophic events that made many life forms extinct. Without such imbalance and disharmony, the advent of the human is inconceivable.

Nevertheless, Heaven's creativity as a life-generating process, despite the unpredictable forces that occasionally destroyed its stability and caused it to be imbalanced, is never permanently disoriented. At a minimum, it will not become a life-destroying process. Confucian faith in the predictability of the "great transformation," far from being a naive assertion about the balance and harmony of nature, is predicated on empirical knowledge and historical memory. The Confucian observation of the constellations, seasons, weather, ebb and flow of the oceans, and a host of other factors, convinces them that, despite surprising events such as violent seismic changes, the general pattern of the earth as a self-organizing system is steady, resilient, and balanced. Indeed, without such a delicate equilibrium, human survival is not possible.

Needless to say, humans are not satisfied with mere survival. As meaning-given and value-creating beings, we constantly strive for higher attainments in all our cognitive and affective endeavors. A precondition for our flourishing is the continuous wholesomeness of the Planet Earth. We are critically aware that as the result of the Big Bang and the evolution that have brought our earth into existence, the danger of what we take for granted, like numerous stars and galaxies, instantaneously disappears is imaginable. We are also critically aware that, so far as our universe is concerned, there is no limit in time and space to our creativity. For the Confucians, an essential reason for humans to act rationally, responsibly, and humanely is their faith in the delicate equilibrium of their microcosm. By emulating the macrocosm of Earth and Heaven, they try to make their self-organizing system adapt to new challenges by maintaining its stability, resilience, and balance.

NOTES

1 Frederick W. Mote, *Intellectual Foundations of China*, Alfred A. Knopf, 1971, pp.17-18.

2 Ibid., p.20.

3 Tu Wei-ming, *Confucian Thought: Selfhood as Creative Transformation* (State University of New York Press, 1985), pp. 35-50.

4 Mote, *Intellectual Foundations of China* , p. 20.

5 Sima Qian 司马迁, Shij 《史记》, *Record of the Grand Historian*, (北京: Zhonghua shuju, 1972), pp. 50-51; trans. Willaim Nienhauser, *The Grand Scriber's Records, Volume I: The Basic Annals of Pre-Han China*, New York: Columbia University, 1994, pp. 21-22.

6 Gordon Kaufman, *Creativity* , Fortress Press, 2004, p. 84.

7 Ibid., p. 42.

Ancient Hebrew and Early Confucian Conceptions of Divinity: A Comment on the Paper of Tu Weiming

Kelly James Clark

Hebrew monotheism developed within the ancient Near Eastern context of widespread polytheism. In the Hebrew narrative we find the authors struggling to define and refine their understanding of divinity within this context. Within these narratives we find the ancient Hebrews variously believing in one God, believing their God to be one of many other tribal or national deities, and following other gods. By the time of Isaiah, however, radical monotheism is asserted; this would come to characterize Hebrew theology and its descendants, Christianity and Islam.

In ancient China, Shang and Zhou theology likewise developed within a polytheistic context which included a variety of ancestral, tribal and nature deities. During the Shang dynasty, *Di* or *Shangdi*, held a position above the various deities and extended the domain of the divine from the Shang tribe to the universe. During the Zhou dynasty, *Shangdi* underwent a partial name-change to *Tian*.

THE GOD OF ABRAHAM AND ISAIAH

The evidence for Hebrew polytheism is threefold. First, there are many indications of polytheism within the Hebrew bible itself. Second, recent archaeological discoveries attest to the diversity of deities countenanced in Israel. And, finally, there is post-exilic archaeological evidence that during the diaspora the Hebrews worshipped goddesses and other Babylonian deities. This essay will focus on the indications of polytheism within the Hebrew narrative itself.

Abraham was from Mesopotamia, a land and culture that countenanced countless gods. Each of these gods or goddesses had its own name and its own sphere of activity including professions, portions of nature, or cities. Local gods or goddesses could be found in every city. Because of the distance people felt between themselves and the major deities, they cultivated a more personal relationship with their own, angel-like, gods. Yahweh becomes the God of Abraham and, for his descendants, the God of their Fathers (Abraham, Isaac and Jacob). Given the ancient Near Eastern context of many relatively local and even personal deities, the claim to be their God is more redolent of henotheism than monotheism.

The Hebrew narrative includes many references to other gods, such as Baal, Ashtoreth, Molech and Chemosh and their seductive power over Israel.

The Hebrews are constantly reminded that their god is Yahweh and warned to resist the temptation to follow other gods. The first commandment, "You shall have no other gods before me," makes little sense if the Israelites believed that there were no other gods to tempt them. This commandment does make sense given the narrative: when the Israelites felt abandoned by Yahweh or when they believed their prayers were unheeded, they turned to other gods.

Isaiah, however, asserts the familiar monotheism of the Judeo-Christian-Muslim traditions: Yahweh is God and there is no other. Ethical monotheism asserts Yahweh alone as the source of righteousness that rains down on the earth. What the earlier books sometimes treated as gods on a par with Yahweh are now considered mere idols—no more than the stone, metal or wood that is their stuff.

THE CONFUCIAN GOD

There is an increasing tendency among sinologists, especially philosophers, to claim that ancient China had no concept of a personal deity. Hall and Ames contend that while *Tian* may have been religiously significant, there is no evidence that *Tian* was believed to be a personal deity. Gernet goes even further, contending that the ancient Chinese had no notion of transcendence whatsoever. He contends that the Chinese never imagined a spiritual substance distinct from the material nor did they conceive of a world that transcended this world of appearances and transitory realities. The purpose of this section is to offer a corrective to these sorts of reading of the ancient Chinese traditions.

The Shang affirmed a high God (*Di* or *Shangdi*) who reigned supreme over a host of lesser Powers and spiritual beings, including ancestors. The hierarchy of these spiritual beings is modeled in accordance with secular political bureaucracy. Although ancestor worship was widely practiced in ancient China, this may be due more to the exalted status of *Shangdi* than to the divine status of ancestors. For example, because Shang kings considered *Di* the most awe-inspiring and powerful Supreme Being, they did not dare to approach *Di* except through the medium of ancestral spirits. There is simply no archeological evidence to support the speculative claim that *Di* might be the First Ancestor who became the Shang 'tribal' God.

The Zhou dynasty more typically but not exclusively uses the term *Tian* in reference to the divine. Most historians have given up the fashionable claim that, contra the anthropomorphic *Shangdi*, *Tian* is an impersonal, natural force. In those portions of the Shujing that have been authenticated as the most trustworthy products of the Western Zhou dynasty, references to *Shangdi* and *Di* repeatedly appear, often in the same context as *Tian* and, moreover, *Tian* is often a synonym for *Shangdi* and *Di*. The Da Gao contains the earliest reference to the foundational Zhou doctrine of *Tian ming*. The divine reappointment of the dynastic house was considered a moral rebuke of the Shang and an affirmation of the virtue and wisdom of Kings Wen and Wu, the founders of the Zhou dynasty. Thus the mandate of heaven provided a legitimation of the overthrow of the Shang and the moral establishment of the Zhou. Youthful King Cheng, considering himself the "servant of heaven", accepts the divine charge to restore tranquility to his kingdom. But his advisors, noting the difficulty of the mission and the troubled state of his people, recommend ignoring heaven's mandate. But King Cheng determines not to disregard the voice of Heaven. Heaven then assists King Cheng by purging his kingdom, creating loyalty to the king among the people, restoring peace and tranquility, and providing the moral enlightenment of the country.

With respect to Zhou theology, there is much to be noted here. First and foremost, within a single paragraph we find the interchangeable use of *Shangdi* and *Tian*. In this important document, the mandate of heaven is also the charge of God. *Tianming* is *Shangdi ming*. There is no contrast between *Tian* and *Shangdi* here. Even if the term *Di* were nowhere to be found in this section, *Tian* functions in precisely the personal and providential way of *Di*. Given the divine authority of the mandate of heaven and the righteousness of Heaven's judgment, it is not surprising that King Cheng declares: "The decree of Heaven is not to be changed". Indeed, it is to be revered and obeyed. The words 'Shangdi' and 'Tian' connote a political ruler of the universe, to whom subordinate earthly kings and lesser deities owe reverence and obedience. *Tianming* connotes a sacred relationship between Heaven and his people; the earthly kings, as Heaven's emissaries, exercise their benevolent rule on the people which are Heaven's own possession or direct subjects. The concept of deity then, both in the Shang and Zhou dynasties, is of a personal, moral and political God.

SIMILARITY AND DIFFERENCE

The similarities between Hebrew and ancient Chinese theistic development are quite remarkable. Both traditions affirmed, or came to affirm, a single, ultimate and personal source of value and power; both beings were deemed worthy of worship. Of course, the Hebrew tradition took the decisive steps to philosophical monotheism that the Chinese tradition did not. The nature and ancestral deities linger in ancient Chinese religion while the pantheon of deities in the early Hebrew historical narratives cannot survive the withering monotheism of Isaiah. But even though the nature deities, ancestors and spirits linger in the Zhou period, they are clearly subservient to supreme Heaven. So, although ancient China remained polytheistic, it was functionally monotheistic: *Tian* is the only deity referred to in the Shujing; the lesser deities have become theologically inconsequential. And, although ancestor worship persists, it is clear that its practitioners know where the ultimate Power lies.

We need not have restricted our defense of Confucian theism to the Early Zhou period. There are, contra Mote, pre-historical creation myths in the ancient records and some in the Shijing. There are many passages of the Analects that conceive of *Tian* as both transcendent and anthropomorphic; and, if portions of the Shujing are reliably dated to times and places two or three hundred years after the death of Confucius, the identification of *Shangdi* and *Tian* is still maintained in the post-Confucius era. For example, when the mythic king Shun ascended to the throne, "He sacrificed specially...to *Di*, sacrificed purely to the six objects of Honor; offered their appropriate sacrifices to the hills and rivers, and extended to his worship to the host of spirits". Special homage is offered to *Di* but worship is also extended to the lesser "deities" (of the hills and rivers and hosts of spirits). It is also recorded that every fifth year, he offered "a burnt offering to Heaven". So a post-Confucian text understands *Di* and *Tian* in exactly the same manner.

Tu Weiming rightly rejects Motes's unsubstantiated claim that the Chinese had no creator, god, ultimate cause or will external to itself. Mote and many other sinologists have an unfortunate tendency to refer to "the Chinese" as though there were a single Chinese mind on these matters. Needham makes a similar claim about the Chinese who believed in "an ordered harmony of wills without an ordainer." But "the Chinese" is a myth. Simply put, Chinese thinkers are as diverse as their Western counterparts; indeed Confucius's philosophy was just one among countless many. One such prominent school, that finds clear expression in the oracle bones, pottery shards Shujing, Shijing, Analects, and post-Confucius texts, includes belief in a transcendent, personal deity. I doubt that anything can be meaningfully said of the ancient Chinese, especially in the Era of One Hundred Schools. Indeed, I believe that very little can be said of the Confucian view on most doctrines. Again, I am not stating that the theistic tradition better represents the Chinese mind than the naturalistic tradition; but the theistic tradition is the dominant intellectual tradition in the Shang and early Zhou periods and finds clear and remarkable expression for nearly a millennium thereafter.

CONCLUSION

Confucianism is often declared a humanism with Judeo-Christian traditions being considered religions that are more other-worldly. But both traditions maintain their respective high deity's deep and abiding commitment to human welfare. And there is little discussion of the afterlife in the texts we have examined. What Professor Tu asserts of the Chinese is equally true of the ancient Hebrews: "Heaven is intimately related to the story of the earth. The earth, as the habitat of all known creatures, is the proper home for us. Even if we can imagine a spiritual sanctuary radically different from the world on this earth, such as the Kingdom of God or the other shore, the earth is a lived reality that defines our daily existence here and now." How humans should live in harmony and flourish in the here and now is the concern both of the people and of their gods. Both Christianity and Confucianism are deeply humanistic (without being anthropocentric).

This is evident as both deities are moved to act decisively upon hearing the cries of the oppressed. In the book of Exodus, Yahweh speaks to Moses of Israel's suffering servitude in Egypt: "I have indeed seen the misery of my people in Egypt. I have heard them crying out because of their slave drivers, and I am concerned about their suffering. So I have come down to rescue them from the hand of the Egyptians and to bring them out of that land into a good and spacious land, a land flowing with milk and honey". Yahweh releases them from slavery and leads them to a land where they are ruled in righteousness. This pattern is echoed in "The Announcement of the Duke of Shao." After the Shang rulers allowed their state to fall into disharmony and disarray, an outpouring of despair moved Heaven to compassion: "The poor people in such a case...made their moan to Heaven....Oh! Heaven had compassion on the people of the four quarters; its favouring decree lighted on our earnest founders". Heaven responds by empowering the righteous Kings Wen and Wu to lead the oppressed out of Yin and into a land ruled by righteous kings. Neither Tian nor Yahweh are conceived as distant, unresponsive kings who unfurl their plans without regard for the welfare of their people. They may rule from Heaven on high but both Yahweh and *Tian* act decisively in response to the suffering of the poor, the children and the oppressed.

Is the Confucian Concept of "Heaven" still Relevant Today? A Comment on the Paper of Tu Weiming

Li Chenyang

Professor Tu's anthropocosmic approach has been one of the most important contributions to Confucian studies in recent years. As a central banner in the field, this approach has exerted a tremendous influence in the articulation of the Confucian stance on a variety of contemporary philosophical issues such as global ethics and environmental philosophy. Today, Professor Tu presents us with a forceful argument that the Confucian anthropocosmic conception of Heaven is more compatible with what we know today about the origin of the universe.[1] He makes a convincing case that anthropocentric or anthropomorphic readings of the cosmological process are no longer tenable and that alternatives, such as his anthropocosmic model, must be taken seriously. While I find Professor Tu powerfully convincing, my primary role here is not to praise his paper, but to raise questions. Let me respectfully raise some concerns with his paper. My question is primarily with the notion of "Heaven." What I am going to say here includes some minor questions for clarification purposes and a major question about the suitability of the notion of "Heaven," which is a key concept of Professor Tu's paper.

Professor Tu's notion of "Heaven" comes from the Confucian lineage, with important modifications. Whereas "Heaven" in Confucius and Mencius has more or less an anthropomorphic theme, Professor Tu's "Heaven" makes an anthropocosmic turn away from the anthropomorphic view. Whereas "Heaven" in Song-Ming Neo-Confucianism made a definitively naturalistic move (one could argue that this move was first made by Xun Zi long ago), Professor Tu's "Heaven" is also laden with human participation. Therefore, in a qualified sense, we can say that Professor Tus' notion of "Heaven" stands in between classic Confucianism and Neo-Confucianism, if we see humanity as situated somewhat between the divine and pure nature. While readily acknowledging the advantages of Professor Tu's concept of "Heaven" over the previous two, I am a bit unclear about what Professor Tu means by "Heaven." At times, it appears to refer to creativity itself. For instance, he uses expressions such as "Heaven as creativity," "Heaven as a life-generating creativity," and "Heaven as creativity itself". At other times, "Heaven" seems different from creativity, as Professor Tu uses expressions like "Heaven's creativity," and "Heaven as a creation of the human imagination". Obviously, if "Heaven" is creativity, it would be redundant to say "creativity's creativity" as in "Heaven's creativity." It thus appears that Professor Tu uses "creativity" as two senses. If so, I would like to learn the relation between them.

Second, Professor Tu claims that "Heaven...is omnipresent and omniscient, but not omnipotent" (p.149). Besides that his use of the "omni-" prefix is immediately reminiscent of anthropomorphic theologies, which Professor Tu rightfully rejects, it is not clear what he means by saying that Heaven is omniscient. "Omniscience" means "all-knowing." In what possible sense we can meaningfully say that creativity, which would be Heaven, knows all about everything? Professor Tu claims that "So far as our intimate relation to Heaven is concerned, we know experientially and empirically that Heaven is omnipresent and omniscient" (p.152). Do we really know that Heaven is omniscient? (With all due respect, this does sound like my Christian friends who would say things like "Of course God exists; we all know that God exists." While they are too polite to say to me, as they would among their fellow Christians, that "only the foul think that God does not exist," they cannot provide me with any convincing proof that God indeed exists.) Why would Professor Tu make such a claim? What support does he have? I would appreciate being enlightened on this.

The second part of this commentary concerns the relevance of the concept "Heaven" to public discourse today. Let me make it explicit at the outset that I am not decidedly opposing the use of the concept of "Heaven." I am here not so much advocating the termination of the concept of "Heaven" in the discourse of Confucian theology/philosophy as to raise the question for Confucian scholars to examine it. In Professor Tu's paper there are suggestions that "Heaven" is a creative process, not an entity, spiritual or otherwise. The emphasis of "Heaven" as process and creativity bears a direct similarity to the concept of "God" in Christian process theology. Process theology holds that God is not omnipotent and does not exist as an entity separate from the human world; rather it exists through human experience and the transformation of the world. According to this view, God is present in the dynamic process of events in the world as a creative pattern of process reality.[2]

In what way is a Confucian concept of "Heaven" still relevant to our public discourse today? Professor Tu's concept of "Heaven" is no longer the concept used by Confucius and Mencius. It no longer has the kind of anthropomorphic appeal to followers, in ways similar to how "God" in Christian process theology has lost His/its traditional anthropomorphic appeal and the powers traditionally attributed to Him/it. Such a concept of "Heaven" appears to be more a relic notion like "God" in Christian process theology than a meaningful philosophical notion. Is it now high time to drop it from our public discourse altogether? One may worry that, without "Heaven" Confucians may be seen as "godless people." But so what? In a sense, many process Christian have finally realized that they are, after all, also "God-less" in the sense of traditional Christian God, which has been believed to be anthropomorphic, omnipotent, and essentialistically unchanging .

If "Heaven" is creativity itself, if it is the creative process of the world in which humans are a principal player, how is such "Heaven" different from the Tao/Dao? At times, Professor Tu makes a connection between "Heaven" and the "Way" or Dao. For example, he writes, "as co-creators of the evolutionary process, human beings can carry Heaven's Way in the world," and "human beings can assist in the transforming and nourishing functions of the cosmic process and by implication, help the Heavenly Way prevail in the world" (p.150). Reading these statements, one cannot help but wonder what difference it would make had the word "Heaven" been dropped in this discourse. With a capital "Way" or "Dao," would not these statements without "Heaven" function the same way as with the word "Heaven"? Given that the concept of "Heaven" is laden with an anthropomorphic ambiguity through history as Professor Tu rightfully indicates, would not we be better off simply to use the concept of "Dao" to denote the incessant, profoundest, and ultimate creative process of the universe? Perhaps I am missing something very important here. Perhaps the concept of "Heaven" is indispensable for a new Confucian theology/philosophy. If so, I would like to take this valuable opportunity to hear Professor Tu's insight.

NOTES

1 Professor Tu specifically mentions its compatibility with the "Big Bang" or the "steady state" cosmogony. The "steady state" theory is no longer accepted by most cosmologists, particularly after the incompatible discovery of cosmic background radiation in 1965, which scientists generally believe has confirmed the "Big Bang" theory.

2 I am not suggesting that Professor Tu has borrowed from Christian process theology. Chinese classical thought such as the *Book of Change,* which Professor Tu quite appropriately quotes in his paper, has extremely rich resources in the regard. Furthermore, I do not feel anything inappropriate to borrow from other cultural resources, for I would definitely welcome other cultural traditions to borrow from Confucian theology. The issue of whether Professor Tu's interpretation of Confucian concept of "Heaven" resembles "God" in Christian process theology is beside the point here.

A Comment on the Paper of Tu Weiming

Tran Van Doan

It is my great pleasure and honor to reply to Professor Tu's very thoughtful paper on the much discussed but still unsolved concept of creativity. It is beyond doubt that the depth and breath of his view (and of the problem itself) require a more encompassing and detailed discussion that is impossible for a short comment, and perhaps, beyond my reach. Therefore, I would like to ask your permission to limit my comment to a single aspect, namely on his proposed understanding of human creativity as "a life-generating process" and on his insistence on the Confucian creativity as a human activity of "self-organizing ... adapt[ing] to new challenges by maintaining its stability, resilience and balance."

TU'S THESIS

Human intellectual history is beset with the question of human origin: whether man is created by God, or by evolution (Darwin)? The answer to this question is by no means final. Each kind of answer becomes again a new enigma, and the arguments pro or contra contain in se an innumerable hubris of which advanced sciences could hardly give a clear and final picture. Professor Tu's anthropocosmic view is an attempt to overcome the difficulties of both the cosmic (natural) and anthropocentric (human) view. Creativity is understood, in consistency with Tu's interpretation of Chinese cosmology, as "the interconnectedness of all modalities of being" in the cosmic process. With such an anthropocosmic view of creativity, Professor Tu claims to be able to dissolve the contradiction between the cosmic view and the anthropomorphic view of Heaven.

Professor Tu's argument for the anthropocosmic view consists of a critique and a reconstruction of the Confucian creativity in terms of modern physics. First, Tu criticizes the view that man is created according to the form (model) of nature, and he objects to the anthropomorphic and anthropocentric view of nature. In his view, the problems of the former view make it essentially untenable, simply because creativity could not be possible in terms of mechanistic and organic function. The problem of the latter view is its too narrow understanding of creativity as a specifically human capacity, and as such excludes all others (the myriad things) from this property. Tu argues: "Heaven is for all beings. It does not seem to have a particular design for the human."

Second, if all things possess the creative capacity, then the most foundational question should be how creativity is possible. The model of modern physics is taken to support the Confucian understanding of creativity. According to Tu, modern physics -- with the theory of the "Big Bang"-- is characterized by two essential features: its claim of creativity as a life-generating process, and its "steady state." Tu wrote: "Heaven emerged as the result of billions of years ... of life-generating creativity" , and "The idea of the "steady state" is congenial to Heaven in an evolutionary process.

Tu's arguments are well developed with his investigation into the history of the concept of Heaven and its principle. The ideas of "co-creator" and "inter-connectedness" are correctly based on the earlier Chinese philosophy (and cosmology) of The Three Elements (*San-tsai*), as well as its corollaries like the principles of "Unity of Heaven and Humanity" (*tianren heyi*) and "Heaven engenders; human completes" (*tiensheng rencheng*).

APPRAISAL AND QUESTIONS

The question raised and the answer given by Professor Tu are, no doubt, the most debatable issues so far, but as far as I understand, they are far from conclusive. The point I wish to raise here is a human approach to the problems: one tries to understand the Heaven in accord with the human way of living, copulating, birth-giving and life-preserving. Such an approach is hardly considered scientific investigation; it is understanding in the widest sense.

If so, then the most frequently taken approach is the so-called anthropological way of thinking and not the reverse, namely, the naturalistic approach (or the cosmic approach). Though Ptolemus, Aristotle and some medieval philosophers have wondered about nature, their "approach" was clearly human. So, one may say that the cosmic approach began (most probably) with modern philosophy and sciences. Copernicus, Galileo and Newton have attempted to give independence to sciences: natural laws are no longer divine laws, and they are fully autonomous. However, both anthropological and cosmic approaches could not give a complete picture of reality. If I do not mistake Professor Tu's idea then, the flaws of these two approaches are visible in their main tenets: (1) the belief in man as a micro-cosmos, therefore, cosmos per analogiam is a magnitude of man; (2) since human generation is known and judged by a web of causal relations, the principle of causality must serve as the guiding principle for the search of human origin; (3) the anthropological approach analytically contains the belief that the cosmos bears the same form of man (anthropo-morphism), and man must be the center of the cosmos (anthropocentrism). Of course, it is easy to refute such views, simply by a reverse logic: man as a micro-cosmos must be a part of the macro-cosmos, and not the reverse, and in this sense, per analogiam, must be similar to the cosmos.

Both arguments must clear the following obstacles:

The first is the problem of cosmos itself. So long as this problem is unsolved, both the anthropological and cosmic approaches cannot be taken for granted. That means, creativity cannot yet be explained in terms of creatio ex nihilo (imago Dei) or creatio ex fantasia (imago hominis). Both cosmic and anthropocentric approaches are, therefore, insufficient to give a satisfactory answer to our question. It seems that we scratch where we do not itch. Now, it is clear that the main and first question would be centered on the cosmos itself: what is it, how does it come into its present form, how is it "living" (functioning, acting, interacting), what are its laws, and the like. Evidently, a thorough investigation of cosmology must be a prerequisite for any understanding of creativity. The question of human freedom comes only after.

Second, if human follows the same laws, bearing the same nature as cosmos, how then can we explain human freedom of not following natural laws and human capacity to change the world, to destroy nature? Is man the real master of nature or, just a simple and humble creature among others?

There is no need to note here the similarity between Fritzof Capra, the author of the much appraised but also very controversial *The Tao of Physics* and Professor Tu. Both attempt to find the common between modern physics and Chinese philosophy. If Capra takes the Taoist philosophy to reinterpret modern physics then Tu does the reverse. He takes the theory of the Big Bang to give light to the conception of creativity in Chinese philosophy. This is a good approach so far as we know.

The problem, however, is whether there is any compatibility among these two different kinds of "sciences"? In my view, the Chinese approach is, in its essence, still anthropomorphic, while Capra's approach is not a scientific investigation, but a proposal to approach science from a different aspect, much different from the cosmic one. So, it would be quite plausible to say that both the approaches of Professor Tu and Capra could be helpful in understanding creativity in accordance with our Chinese view, but have less effect in engaging in creative work.

The next question would be whether the theory of Big Bang and Black Hole is definitive, or whether it still remains as a hypothesis. We know that this theory is only an extension of the theory of general relativity of Einstein, which is perhaps only one of the most plausible ways to the explore the mystery of the universe. We know, Einstein's general theory of relativity, in the description of Stephen Hawking, "predicted that space-time began at the big bang singularity." It would "come to an end either at the big crunch singularity (if the whole universe collapsed), or at a singularity inside a black hole (if a local region, such as a star, were to collapse)." (*A Brief History of Time*, p. 115). Einstein's insight leads to the hypothesis that the cosmos has no beginning and no end: "Does the universe in fact have a beginning or an end?" (id). But people like Hawking, Ellis, and Penrose could not claim to possess the last answer. It is by no means definitive. (See Steven W. Hawking, George F.R. Ellis, "The Cosmic Black-Body Radiation and the Existence of Singularities in our Universe, *Astrophysical Journal*, 152 (1968), pp. 4-36). Despite Einstein, the question of the origin and the fate of the universe continues on as still unanswered. All approaches, so far, are different hypotheses indeed.

So, what I expect from Professor Tu's paper is a different kind of understanding of creativity. It is helpful to know how our ancestors have attempted to understand and to co-operate with nature in preserving their life and in continuing to give new life. However, as to whether their view is compatible to modern physics, or whether our modern science is only a continuation of the cosmic view of our ancestors, this question is not yet answered. I guess Professor Tu perhaps agrees with me on this matter.

Commentary 4

A Comment on the Paper of Tu Weiming

Chloë Starr

Tu Wei-ming's wide-ranging paper moves from cosmogony to science, modern spirituality, Gaian theories of the equilibrium of nature, and appropriate moral responses to heaven's creativity. It raises questions of the links between humanity and heaven, the naming of heaven/God, and the relationship between religious and scientific paradigms. In this brief response, I want to focus on two interrelated questions tangential to the paper: how Tu's 'Heaven' relates to the Christian 'God,' and how the two traditions of Confucianism and Christianity have conceived of speaking of this Heaven/God.

Tu presents a very brief overview of traditional Chinese philosophical views of Heaven (pp 4-6), concentrating on particular anthropomorphic aspects. It is worth pausing to consider this question of what Heaven is, and look at some of its functions. Although direct comparisons between Christian and Confucian conceptions create a rather naïve methodology, there are times when it is worth drawing attention to implied or assumed differences. If we take Mencius alone, it is clear that there are a great variety of understandings of the term *tian*, and ambiguity as to its referents. Heaven has a geophysical aspect as sky, the place where rain is made (1a/6; 2a/2); it is something that humans fear (1b/3) and a being/force which humans can delight by their right action; it is the creator of humankind (1b/3, *Shujing*); the entity that grants success, disaster, and bestows honour (1b/10, 14). Heaven governs human fate and human action, both good and bad (1b/16; 4a/7); it appoints officers and has a will for human-kind, determining the peace of the Empire (2b/13). Heaven alone is great (3a/4); it does not speak, but reveals itself through acts and deeds (5a/5); The mandate of Heaven is not immutable (4a/8, *Shijing*), and Heaven many be involved in interaction or bargaining with humans, especially rulers, but is not bound by their requests (5a/5). Heaven sees in the eyes of its people and hears in the ears of its people (5a/6). Some of these attributes have parallels in the Christian God, some do not.

Tu's reading of a Confucian Heaven seems to be limited to our earth or universe only, whereas the Christian God is not consubstantial with Heaven, but rather, as Tu acknowledges, radically ontologically separate, as the Creator of heaven and of the heavens (in the New Testament the Greek term is more frequently plural). The intimate link between Heaven and earth as both entity and linguistic compound is less obvious in the Christian case, where God is understood as much more than Heaven. Although a similar confusion between the heavens as dwelling place of God and as created by God permeates common Christian discourse, the closest parallel to the heaven-earth binary is significantly found in the figure of Jesus, the one who unites heaven and earth.

For Tu, an anthropomorphic or anthropocentric Heaven entails the assumption that the whole dynamic of creation took place for the sake of the human, which he labels "untenable". Although in the second Hebrew creation account in Genesis there is no assumption that the earth was created for humans, but rather that man was some form of afterthought. What separates humanity from the rest of creation in Christian understanding, and places it in a unique relationship with the Creator, is the fact that this Creator of heaven and earth chose to become human and experience life on earth as a human being. The doctrine of incarnation cuts through any anthropocentric account of creation.

The question of Big Bang speculation that Tu raises is interesting to the Christian theist as to the physicist, but has little bearing on faith: God is outside of time and the creator of all matter that began in time. Tu's speculations on Big Bang and Heaven as an evolutionary process and on forms of life on other planets might benefit from more grounding in science to avoid remaining mere speculation; there are places in the paper where the divisions between scientific ponderings and philosophy are not clear. It is not obvious, for example, why the life-generating, on-going process of creation, with an immanent involvement of qi, is "not conducive to mechanistic and theistic explanations." The point is moot because Tu appears to suggest that the Hebrew/Christian account of creation does not allow for continuing development, as science and common-sense hold. Yet there is nothing in the biblical account to suggest an end-point to all of God's creative work (a day of rest suggests, after all, a resumption afterwards); nor is it obvious that the Holy Spirit may not parallel aspects of qi as a life-generating force.

A substantive point of Tu's paper is the tension between a human discourse on Heaven and the reality of Heaven as an entity beyond human conception; the paradox of an anthropological reading of heaven and a cosmic one. For Tu, this poses insuperable problems, but ones which are re-cast by the notion of humanity as co-creators with Heaven in cosmic processes. Although the notion of co-creation has some parallels in Christian understandings of the role of humans as stewards of God's creation, the guiding motifs in Christian thought have been governed by submission to a God whose will and purpose is sovereign and to be sought (contra the discussion on p. 9 whereby humans becoming partners through knowing their own natures and thus Heaven's nature). This cannot be reduced, however, to "mere creatures passively submitting to an absolutely incomprehensible power," (p.147) for the Christian any more than the Confucian. Christian theologians have long discussed the problem of integrity in discourse of that which is beyond human knowledge. Rowan Williams, in commenting on human attempts to discuss a moral universe, argues that such human attempts can be seen as strategies for responding to the world's complexity. Religious and theological integrity is possible "as and when discourse about God declines the attempt to take God's point of view (i.e. a 'total perspective')."[1] Liturgy, for example, is one means of surmounting the problem of discussing the ineffable; in addressing God in worship, the language itself ascribes value to God; it does not control the meaning of the words used.

Whereas Tu brings new insight to early texts, which themselves are surprisingly lacking in sustained reflection on the nature of language relating to the divine and the cosmos, there is a significant stream of early Christian thought that had addressed the question of the incomprehensibility and ineffability of the deity. The paradox of an all-too-human heaven (where Tu questions: can there only be a heaven where there are humans?) is met for these writers by a response which posits the 'darkness' of God, which captures God only in the negative, the unknown. From the early Syrian Pseudo-Denys the Areopagite to Anselm and Aquinas, the question of what we may know of God and how we speak of the unknowable held a strong pull on early and medieval thought. As Maximus the Confessor writes, 'God is communicable in what he imparts to us, but he is not communicable in the incommunicability of his essence.' The Flemish mystic Jan van Ruusbroec reiterates:

> The incomprehensible nature of God transcends all creatures
> in heaven and on earth, for everything that a creature can
> comprehend is creaturely; because God is above all creatures
> and is both within and without them, every created concept
> is too narrow to comprehend him. If a creature were to com-
> prehend, understand, and experience God, he would have to
> be drawn beyond himself into God and so comprehend God
> with God. Whoever, then, might wish to know what God is
> and to inquire into this would be doing something forbidden
> and would go mad. (*Spiritual Espousals* I.3.A).

Earlier Christian philosophers had held that language used of God may not be taken in the same sense as that used of other beings, or may warp the usual sense. As Anselm, who builds up from careful reason deriving from the earthly world a picture of the Supreme Being, writes:

> But how shall we meet the truth ... that the supreme Being,
> is so above and beyond every other nature that, whenever
> any statement is made concerning it in words which are also
> applicable to other natures, the sense of these words in this
> case is by no means that in which they are applied to other
> natures. (*Monologion* LXV).

For the Christian theologian, this is true of human language, and true at a deeper metaphysical sense: 'how can objects so different as the creative and the created being be expressed by one Word' Anselm questions. In a sustained discussion on language, in Chapters 65 and 66 of the *Monologion*, Anselm addresses the question of how the supreme being may be discussed at all, if ineffable, and charts the breakdown of language used of God. Words used in a common sense are 'alien' to the supreme Being, and lead to the paradox that something and nothing can be said of God: 'in some sort' can truth be discovered, and 'in some sort' nothing proved regarding it. We can capture the likeness of God in human language, but not God: 'we express and see it through another; we do not express it, and do not see it by virtue of its own proper nature;' it can be 'intimated' through a likeness, as what is seen in a mirror or told in a riddle, but not revealed (LXV).

For a scholar such as Thomas Aquinas, again musing on God and Heaven, knowledge of creatures enables us to use words to refer to God, even if these words cannot fully express God. Two main problems arise in speaking of God: his essence is beyond what we can know of him, and the expressions we use signify in a way appropriate to material creatures, not heavenly beings. Since we know in a composite and temporal way, we can understand and speak of eternity only in our temporal manner. Words, for Aquinas, can be used to speak of God, but 'fail to represent adequately what he is.' To those who contest that we cannot use words at all to speak of God (concrete nouns are excluded because God is simple; abstract nouns because they do not signify a subsistent thing; verbs and particles because they imply time; pronouns because they are relational terms), Aquinas replies that words are signs for thought, and refer indirectly to things through thoughts. Knowledge of creatures enables us to use words to refer to God, even if these words cannot fully express God. Language is twice removed in God's case, since it refers to creatures, and since words themselves are only signs. Creatures resemble God, but fail to reproduce perfectly the form of the cause, so 'good' and 'wise' may signify something of God, but they signify imperfectly, as creatures represent God imperfectly. All words used metaphorically of God apply primarily to creatures and only secondarily to God, signifying merely a parallel, whereas for other words, non-metaphoric words may be used primarily of God and only derivatively of creatures.

The relationship between language and scripture is a key component of Christian discussions of God and Heaven – as of all that may only be known through revelation. Scripture is an affirmatory mode of writing: it presumes that God can be spoken of, but by its modes it also conceals, and causes the reader to go beyond its surface words and symbols. In his long treatise on the Divine Names, the sixth-century Pseudo-Denys avers that any incongruity of celestial imagery serves to remind humans that these are merely representations of the divine, and the more unlikely the metaphors the better, since the most suitable terms belong to the way of negation, and terms for the divine 'completely at variance' are so far removed as to transcend all materiality. In Denys' own writings, symbolic language is used to speak of this God beyond words: the whole of the Divine Names can be read as a treatise on the interpretation of language. The unknowability and inexpressibility of God runs as a leitmotiv throughout: 'since the unknowing of what is beyond being is above and beyond speech, mind or being itself, one should ascribe to it an understanding beyond being,' he writes. God is beyond thought and beyond language, and therefore not contained in or expressed through Scripture. How can we speak of the Divine Names at all, asks Pseudo-Denys, if the transcendent surpasses all discourse and all knowledge? That he does, at some length, is reason enough to contest an absolute apophaticism. The words of scripture may be used as a base (an affirming but ultimately distorted picture of God) from which to be lifted up towards the One who is beyond the words. Beyond the cataphatic optimism of written scripture lies the apophatic realms of spiritual epiphany, and it is this 'beyond' that governs an appropriation of scripture, and our grasp of God (or, heaven).

Christian speaking about God is in this tradition limited firstly by what we can know of the mysterious divine, and by the inherent limitations of human language. Such early Christian 'mystical' texts produce one considered response to Tu's paradox of an overly-anthropomorphic Heaven, yet present a challenge to the co-creator anthropocosmic vision.

NOTE

1 Rowan Williams, *On Christian Theology* (Oxford: Blackwell, 2000), 6.

A Comment on the Paper of Tu Weiming

Christopher Hancock

Professor Tu Weiming's paper connects classical Confucian cosmological reflection and contemporary cosmology and ecology. He understands the interconnectedness of all cosmic reality, in its plenitudinous self-generating and life-generating processive fullness, in which all life – including humanity – finds its creative place and fulfillment. Central to his rhetorical argument is the claim that humans should understand their relationship to heaven in terms of "co-creating' 'anthropocosmic interrelatedness", with all the aesthetic, moral, and ecological implications that follow from this. As he writes, "We are entrusted, individually and communally, with the duty to realize through self-cultivation both our aesthetic ability to appreciate the wonderful presentation of Heaven's resourcefulness and our moral power to actively continue Heaven's great work". Heaven's creativity in humanity's 'conscious and unconscious endeavors' is, for Professor Tu, demonstrated in 'the preservation of the cumulative traditions of literature, history, philosophy, arts, and the elaborate constructions of economic, political, social and cultural institutions'.

Professor Tu has a high view both of humanity's calling and its competency. As he writes again, "We are capable of educating ourselves to become worthy partners of the cosmic process. We are empowered to apprehend Heaven through our self-knowledge. As Mencius avowed, if we can realize the full measure of heart-and-mind, we will know our nature; if we know our nature, we will know Heaven." The stress is on human "self-effort", and on humanity's ultimate ability, however hard the way, to "carry Heaven's Way in the world".

Eschewing both an anthropocentric depiction of Heaven (which is inconsistent with humanity's contingency in both "Big Bang" and "steady state" cosmologies) and an anthropomorphic cosmology that "only superficially grasps Heaven's all-embracing fullness", Professor Tu argues that humanity best understands and fulfils itself as "embedded" in the web of life on planet Earth "while simultaneously attending to the significance of our radical distinctiveness as a form of life" (quoting Gordon Kaufman, op. cit., p. 153). In other words, as a mandate for a wise ecological equilibrium, and the co-existent flourishing of humans and Planet Earth, humanity must grasp the depth of its co-creating/co-dependent relationship to the world/Heaven. As he concludes, "For the Confucians, an essential reason for humans to act rationally, responsibly, and humanely is their faith in the delicate equilibrium of their microcosm. By emulating the macrocosm of Earth and Heaven, they try to make their self-organizing system adapt to new challenges by maintaining its stability, resilience, and balance."

Contemporary Western Christian theology has sought to address many of the concerns that are either implicit or explicit in Professor Tu's paper. Some Christian theologians have been stung by secularist claims that a mis-reading of human 'dominion' over creation in Genesis 1 and 2 has encouraged prolonged ecological irresponsibility. They have sought to make clear humanity's flawed governance of the world, the Bible's strong ecological mandate and celebration of the created order, and the essential relationship that exists between God, the natural world and the human creature. Other theologians have gone further and either presented God and the created world as inhabiting one ontological domain (monistic panentheism), or presented 'God' in terms of cosmic process (viz. as less a static impassible 'Being' and more a dynamic, passible 'Becoming'), who participates in - even as - the natural world and human life (hence divinizing humanity, or naturalizing 'God'). Classical patristic traditions contain data to assist contemporary Christian theology find ways of reducing the bifurcation of God and Creation, whilst preserving their distinction: Alexandrine incarnational theologies, for example, stress the active incorporation of the created world in the salvific work of Jesus Christ. But the tendency towards Platonic dualism is still strong. Biblical language and imagery, which address the relationship between God and the world in Jesus Christ, can at times seem to be irreducibly dualistic, viz. 'entry', 'coming', 'above' and 'below', even 'the world' (understood as the fallen condition of humanity caused and maintained by human sin), create a sense of "otherness" between God and the World, which the incarnation of the Son both expresses and addresses.

Twentieth century theology has found in the image of the "Cosmic Christ" of Colossians 1 and Ephesians 1 a basis to engage with the kind of holistic vision of reality Professor Tu's paper reflects. Colossians 1: 15-21, in particular, provides a valuable christological perspective on Christian cosmologies. Here the visible man Jesus Christ (so recently crucified by the Romans) is remarkably described as "the image of the invisible God, the first born of all creation" (v15): that is, the one who perfectly represents both God on earth, and creation in perfection. "By him all things were created", verse 16 declares, "things in heaven and on earth, visible and invisible, whether thrones or powers or rulers or authorities; all things were created by him and for him". Here Jesus Christ is both architect and end of "all things". Crucially, verse 17 adds, "He is before all things, and in him all things hold together". The Platonic principle of rationality, the Logos, is here personified in the life and work of Jesus Christ, the cosmic Lord in and over all. Twentieth century theologians from William Temple to Teilhard de Chardin have found in the image of "the cosmic Christ" a dynamic person and a coherent ethical and ontological principle through which to engage with the vitality, (seeming) randomness, pain and pointlessness of the human condition and the natural world. In a person, and not in an arbitrary power, natural process, or philosophical principle, the world and human life find their ultimate goal and supreme point of meaning and coherence. Existential reality, in all its fearfulness, finitude and fragility, finds here questions to address and answers to consider.

Classical Christian theology faced by an anthropocosmic Confucianism must surely welcome its dynamic appeal to humanity's moral obligations and 'co-creating' energy. However, in owning a set of canonical texts that provide coherence and continuity, it processes human perception through the lens of biblical identity and listens for divine wisdom through these texts and human engagement with them. In doing this, it calls "Heaven" by a personal name (Jesus Christ). It admits human culpability and flawedness apart from God's grace-filled, forgiveness through the saving death of Jesus Christ on the wooden cross of Calvary. It resists surrendering "otherness" to God's ways, however compelling human virtue and pressing contemporary optimism. It seeks to engage with the reality of individual, institutional, trans-national, and global "evil" expressed in human actions, corporate failure, individual tragedies and natural disasters. It does not accept the humanist's claim that self-improvement is a sufficient resource, or ground of appeal, to better the human condition, being wary of human self-deception and mindful of human pride. No, the theo-logic of classical Christian theology sees humanity's role in creation as derivative of the "work of Christ" and dependent upon it. It sees Planet Earth not as a self-subsistent source of self-generating life, but a created order sustained by divine providence and ordered by the immanent, mysterious will of an active God. It sees the 'end' of all things as consummation in and through Jesus Christ, when the historical order will give place definitively to the 'new heaven and the new earth', which is God's eternal purpose.

Chapter 7

Globalization, Christianity and Confucianism: On Strangification and Generosity to the Other

Vincent Shen

GLOBALIZATION, STRANGIFICATION AND GENEROSITY TO THE OTHER

China, together with other countries in the world, is now facing the challenge of globalization, understood basically as a process of deterritorialization or cross-bordering, involving all humankind on the globe as a whole, and this is happening now in every domain of human activities: health care, technology, environment, economics, politics, education, culture, religion... etc. "Deterritorialization" here should be understood in a broader sense as a process of crossing borders, or going beyond oneself to the other. I'll argue in this paper that globalization is the present historical stage of realizing the unceasing process of human strangification and a further invitation to human generosity to the other.

Institutionally speaking, the process of globalization starts with modernity, but goes beyond it. Modernity has produced, on the economic level, the ever-extending market; and on the political level, the Nation-States and their sovereignty. Beyond that, post-modernity is now producing, on its negative side, the de-constructional critique of modernity's principles: subjectivity, representations and rationality; and, on its positive side, the global information society. In the process of globalization we see on the one hand the extension of market economy into global market, the global politics playing beyond the limit of nation-state and the concept of sovereignty, and finally the global culture in contrast and in dialectic with self-awakening local cultures.

Taking all these into account, I would define globalization as "A historical process of deterritorialization or cross-bordering, by which human desire, human universalizability and interconnectedness are to be realized on the planet as a whole, and to be concretized now as global free market, transnational political order and cultural glocalism."

Since globalization is a process that concerns human kind as a whole, it should have some foundation in the nature of human being. Philosophically speaking, it should be based in human desire to go always beyond and its nature longing for universality or better, universalizability. Globalization as a technological, economical and cultural process, should be seen as the material implementation of human nature's universalizing dynamism of always going beyond. For us humans as a historical being there should be no universality pure and simple but only process of universalization in time. This is to say "universality" is only an abstract ideal existing in an ever-retreating horizon.

The real historical process is unceasingly going beyond and towards higher levels of universalizability.

Anthropologically speaking, this could be traced back to the moment when a human being picked up the first chopping stone and came to use utensil or instrument. In this way, human being went beyond the determinism of physical nature and established thereby a free relationship with the material world. Since then human being stepped into the stage of hominization. But, *homo faber*, though beyond the determination of the material world in using them as instruments, still depended on them, and therefore not totally human. When human beings were able to communicate with others through language, a system of signs collecting human experiences and revealing intelligibility of things in communication with others, they started to exist on a new level of universalizability. Moreover, when human beings came to engage themselves in disinterested activities, such as playing, sacrificing and artistic creativities… there emerged higher levels of freedom, even to the point of fusion with things and people. Just imagine human beings got easily tired after a whole day's labor, but they would continue day and night dancing, playing and engaging in ritual activity of sacrifice without any boredom or fatigue. This shows human beings seemed to be more human in these free playful and creative activities.

Therefore, *homo loquutus* and *homo ludens* are more human, more universalizable and therefore more humanized than merely hominized. Born together with humanization, there is the universalizable dynamism in human nature that came to the scene of human historical process. Probably this is why philosophers East and West in the axial age, which happened between the 8th and the 2nd Centuries BCE, in the time of philosophical breakthrough, would understand reason as the most essential function of human mind. In ancient Greek philosophy, human being was defined as "to on logon exon", later translated into Latin as "animal rationale", the proper function of which was *theoria*, which produced knowledge for knowledge's own sake, in looking for the theoretically universalizable. In ancient China, with the emergence of Confucianism and Daoism, the concern was more with the impartial or the universal in human praxis, that is, the practically universalizable.

But it is clear that having the idea and tendency of universalizablility is not yet the process of globalization. This needs the whole technological, institutional and historical development through modern times to implement the universalizable in form of gloablaization, even if that which has been implemented is merely part of the universalizable. Globalization concerns the globe or the earth all as a whole, though still in fact but a tiny star in the immense universe. The day when we're ready not only for a global ethics, but also a universalizable ethics in term of the universe, we human would be qualified then to go beyond the global era to enter into the universal era.

Now we should consider this: globalization brings with it the contrast with localization, unity in contrast with diversification. This is a moment of human history that people in the word feel so close to each other on the one hand, and so vulnerable and susceptible of conflicts of any kind on the other.

Now it is the critical historical moment of opening toward the other instead of keeping within one's self-enclosure. In responding to today's urgent situation full of conflicts created by self-enclosure of different parts such as different disciplines, economic interests, cultures, political and religious groups, etc., we humans should be more concerned with each other and the possibility of mutual enrichment. In order to overcome antagonism by appealing to effective dialogue, I have proposed in recent years "strangification"[1] and "language appropriation" as viable strategies. The term "strangification," a neologism that might appear strange in English, yet is much more understandable in Chinese—waitui 外推, means etymologically the act of going outside of oneself to the other, or going outside of one's familiarity to strangeness, to the strangers. This act presupposes the appropriation of language by which we learn to express our ideas or values in languages understandable to others. In their turn, "strangification" and "language appropriation" presuppose an original generosity toward the other, without limiting oneself to the claim of reciprocity, quite often presupposed in social relationship and ethical golden rules. Three approaches could be put into practice:

First, linguistic strangification. If one discourse/value or cultural expression/ religious belief can be translated into discourse/value/cultural expression/religious belief understandable to another scientific, cultural or religious community, then it has a larger or universalizable validity. Otherwise, its validity is limited only to its own world and reflection must be made on the limit of one's own discourse/value or expression/belief.

Second, pragmatic strangification. If one discourse/value or expression/belief can be drawn out from its original social and pragmatic context and be put into other social and pragmatic context and is still valid, this means it is more universalizable and has larger validity than merely limited to its own context of origin. Otherwise, reflection must be made on one's discourse/ value or expression/belief to see why it's limited only to one's own social and pragmatic context.

Third, ontological strangification. A discourse/ value or expression/ belief, when universalizable by a detour of experiencing Reality Itself, for example, a direct experience with Reality itself, such as other people, Nature, or even the Ultimate Reality, would be very helpful for mutual understanding among different scientific micro-worlds (disciplines or research programs), cultural worlds, and religious worlds.

The original generosity implied in this act of going outside of oneself should be seen as the condition sine qua non of all situation of reciprocal relationship. Philosophically speaking, before we can establish a sort of reciprocity, emphasized for example in Marcel Mauss' *Essai sur le don* as the principle of human society, there must be previously a generous act of going outside of oneself to the other, so that there can be established accordingly a relation of reciprocity. If in the classical world, golden rules are so much emphasized and reciprocity was seen as the basic principle of sociability, now in the postmodern world and in the world of globalization, we need a principle more than that of reciprocity. The new principles for society and ethics that we are looking for should base themselves on original generosity and strangification as the act of going outside of oneself to the other. By "the other", I understand other people, Nature and the Ultimate Other such as God in all monotheistic religions, the Dao in Daoism, Buddha or Śūnyata in Buddhism…etc.

CHRISTIANITY, A RELIGION OF GENEROSITY AND STRANGIFICATION

According to my understanding, Christianity has brought with it a message for the original generosity and strangification to the other. Like Buddhism, Christianity is a religion of strangification par excellence.[2] By Christianity I mean those religious doctrines and institutional organizations, such as the Catholic, Protestant, Orthodox…etc., based on their faith of Jesus Christ. This spirit of generosity to the other not only exists in it doctrine, but also in its historical impetus of expansion.

On the level of theology, the Christian doctrine that God has created the world could be seen as God's generosity, God's originally generous act of producing creatures out of his infinitely powerful and immensely abundant creativity. Therefore the emergence of various forms of existence in the universe and their successive evolution are supposed in Christianity to be produced by this original act of generosity and successive acts of transformation. In the first version of Genesis, to what He has created, God says, "it was good"[3]. The ontology of goodness is therefore the outcome of divine generosity. After creation, God lives also in the universe by the laws of nature that not only regulate all creatures' movement and life but also bring them to go outside of themselves, to better perfection, to the emergence of higher forms of being. Human being, created in the image of God[4], according to his inner nature and dynamism, should also go beyond him/herself for better perfection, in the mean while, because of his/her free will, he is also able to choose to stay in his/her self-enclosure in the imagined subjectivity, without caring about his/her relation with others, and bound miserably to the selfish-enclosure, that is what actually meant by original sin. The incarnation of Christ is an act of generosity, that God becomes human and takes the form of human body, and sacrifices his own life for the benefit of human beings and the whole world. Redemption should be understood in the sense of being saved from one's finite self-enclosure and open again to the other, both horizontally to other people and Nature, and vertically to the Ultimate Other, God. Christ, being the core to the faith of all forms of Christianity, serves as the paradigm of strangification and generosity, that all human kind and all being in the universe should go outside of their finite self-enclosure and go to the other, so as to return eventually to the infinite perfection.

This Christian generosity and strangification to the other are also founded in Christian doctrine of human nature, in the human as Imago Dei and therefore the goodness of human nature. There has been a misunderstanding among Christians and Confucians based on the stereotyped contrast of original sin in Christianity with the original human goodness in Confucianism. In fact the theology of Imago Dei would tell some essential similarity between them.

It is true that for some theologians the original sin represents the original darkness in human nature inherited from Adam and Eve after they acted against the prohibitive rule of God. But, if we take into account the Biblical context in which the narrative of fall appears, we'd better interpret it as a fall of human nature originally created by God as good. The narrative in the Genesis shows human nature as originally created good, given the ontology of goodness and theology of Imago Dei. First, the environment of human existence is constituted by all things which, after each created by God, were proclaimed by Him as good. This is the ontological foundation from which human beings emerge. Second, human beings are created by God according to his Image. "God created man in the image of himself, in the image of God he created him, male and female he created them."[5] Since God is the Supreme Good, his likeness should also be good, not evil. Third, human beings are created with cognitive ability and free will and thereby responsible for their own action. These capacities are the transcendental foundation of human moral good and evil.

The so called "evil" or "fall" happens when human beings abused their free will and interrupted arrogantly his relation with the Ultimate Other, God, relation which was represented by a covenant or agreed rule of action. By this interruption of relation, human beings were enclosed in his own subjectivity, cutting himself from his relation with God. Right after this interruption, human beings began to suffer. Evil and suffering were then the consequences of the fall of human nature as Imago Dei and the refusal of one's relation with God.

Here is something comparable with Confucianism. In Christianity, human nature, created in Image of God, is originally good, but in the actual exercise of his/her free will, human being could choose to be self-enclosed, to the point of denying good relationship with God and others, and falls thereby. In Confucianism, Mencius asserts that human nature is transcendentally good because of the four sprouts, whereas the naturalist Confucian Xunzi would say that human nature is evil. Contextually speaking, in the Xin Er Chapter, Xunzi's position is to be understood as saying that human being is born with desires, which, if without education and cultivation, will develop into individual's conflict and violence against each other, and thereby create disorder. Evil is understood as social and political disorder rather than as the darkness of human soul. But, in chapter 38 of the Laozi, it was shown the degeneration process from *ren* (humaneness) to *yi* (rightness) and *li* (propriety), because of human negligence and forgetfulness of the Dao and *de*.[6] Altogether, these philosophical reflections show us a more complete image of the originally good human nature with its actual process of degeneration or falling.

For Christians, human beings are born with free will by which he can make free decision and are thereby responsible for their actions. Because of his free will, human beings could also indulge in their own subjectivity and seclude themselves from all others, even to the point of rejecting God. By this we understand the Christian doctrine of hell. The so-called "hell" is in fact the state of existence of absolute self-enclosure, in which individual refuses God and cuts himself totally from all relation with the other, and in totally excluding itself from God and others, excludes himself also from his own possibility of perfection, his salvation. That is where human beings suffer the most. According to the *Catéchisme de l'église catholique*, "C'est cette état d'auto-exclusion définitive de la communion avec Dieu et avec les bienheureux qu'on désigne par le mot 'enfer'". [7] (The word "hell" indicates this definitive state of self-exclusion from the communion with God and with the blessed.) But even if man would arrogantly exclude himself from God, the love of God is infinitely immense so that such a state of existence could not refuse the penetration of God's love. St. Augustine, who sustained most strongly the doctrine of Hell, said that, "Even if I were in Hell You would be there for if I go down into hell, Thou art there also." [8] These words of St. Augustine's suggest to me God's love would penetrate also into hell. I tend to think that, even if human beings could refuse God arrogantly, as finite beings, their refusal of God, no matter how arrogant it is, is still a finite refusal and therefore there will always be possibilities of penetration by God's infinite love. The generosity of God's love will never abandon any being whatsoever.

If God himself is love and generosity, God's act of creation is the act of strangification and generosity in its absolute originality and initiative; human nature, as Imago Dei, is invited to act also as generously as possible in the unceasing process of strangification.

A GIFT FROM THE WEST: CHRISTIANITY'S STRANGIFICATION TO CHINA

In its historical dynamism of expansion, Christianity is also a religion of strangification par excellence. The fact that Christianity has extended from the Sea of Galileo to the whole Judea, then to Rome and Greece, to Europe and Africa, to Asian and China and the whole world, could be seen also as an unceasing act of strangification and religious generosity. This is the essence in the complex history of Christianity that has entered into diverse civilizations and cultures in the world, become one of their internal dynamic factors and again pushed them to go out side of themselves and beyond. In short, Christianity is a religion of strangification and incarnation: it has incarnated in divers forms of spiritual and material civilizations and then urged them each in its own way to go beyond itself to the other, eventually to the Ultimate Other. As I suppose, the message that Christianity has brought to the Confucian China, message still urging us today, is purely and simply this generosity to the other by way of strangification, in a way that makes us Chinese people more balanced in the dynamic contrast of immanence and transcendence, love and justice, meaningful construction and further strangification.

Christianity came to China, first in form of Nestorianism, in the glorious days of the Tang Dynasty. Nestorian priest Alopen, bringing with him Christian scriptures, entered the City of Chang An in 635AD, welcome by

Fang Xuanling the Chinese prime minister and was placed in the royal court to translate his scriptures, then received by the Emperor Taizong in his royal office. This should be the most favorable condition all later Christian missionaries would be much envious of. Nestorianism had enjoyed quite a flourishing period till it was hit by the 846 A.D.'s persecution of Buddhism by Emperor Wuzong, when the Nestorians suffered and missionaries were expelled from China. Nevertheless, the translated scriptures such as the *Messiah Sutra, On One God*, and others, were in fact the first introduction of Monotheism into China, for good or for bad, and therefore their importance should not be neglected in the intellectual and religious history of China.[9]

The second phase of Christianity in China began with Matteo Ricci's arrival in China in 1583. He brought with him Christianity together with European science and philosophy. This has indeed open up a most remarkable page in the history of cultural interaction between China and the West. For better understanding philosophy East and West[10], it should be noted that in works such as Matteo Ricci's *Tianzhu shiyi* (The True Meaning of the Lord of Heaven), Francisco Furdato's *Mingli Tan* (Investigation of Names and Principles), and Julius Aleni's *Xixuefan* (Introduction to Western Sciences)…etc., we find names and ideas of Western philosophers such as Socrates, Plato, Aristotle, St. Augustine, St. Bernard, St. Thomas…etc., who could be seen therefore as the first names of Western philosophers known by Chinese people. Aristotle was the first among all Western philosophers to be introduced and translated, or better, reinterpreted, into Chinese. In fact, systematic introduction of Christian interpretation of Aristotle's works was one of Ricci and his colleagues' missionary projects in China, supposed by them to be a country of philosophers or one run by philosophers.[11]

According to Rev. Fang Hao, four Aristotelian books in the form of commentaries by Jesuits' of Coimbra College, were "translated" into Chinese in the late Ming period. They were the *Mingli tan*, the *Huanyou Quan*, the *Lingyan lishao*, and Alphonsus Vagnoni's *Xiu Shen Xi Xue*[12]. But, when I check them with the *Commentarii Collegii Conimbricensis Societatis Jesu*[13], I discover that they were not "translations" at all. In fact, three of them were in freely abridged texts rewritten for the Chinese the Christian interpretations of Aristotelian works based on Aristotle's discourses in *De Categoriae, De Caelo*, and *De Anima* as well as their commentaries by Coimbra College. As a fact, the *Mingli tan* was signed as *yiyi* (translated as to meaning) by Francisco Furdato and *daci* (expressed in literary Chinese) by Li Zhizao[14]; the same case with the *Huanyou quan*, which was based on the Coimbra commentary on Aristotle's *De Coelo*. The *Lingyan lishao*, based on the Coimbra commentary on Aristotle's *De Anima* also with much free abridgment, was signed as "orally narrated" by Franciscus Sambiasci and transcribed into literary Chinese by Xu Guanqi. Besides, Alphonsus Vagnoni's work titled *Xiu Shen Xi Xue* was a Chinese syllabus of Aristotelian ethics, not only a mere translation.

By further check with the *Commentarii Collegii Conimbricensis Societatis Jesu*, we should add to the list the *Suida* (Dialogue on Sleeping) by Francescus Sambiasci, which contains texts that is in fact a Chinese rewriting in form of dialogue, not to say "translation," of Aristotle's *De Somno et Vigilia* and *De Somniis*. Part of *De Somno et Vigilia* and *De Divinatione per Somnium* could also be found in Aleni's *Xingxue cushu*, always based on their Coimbra commentaries but with more Chinese references[15]. Also, the *Kongji gezhi* (Investigation of Heavenly Phenomena), signed as *zhuan* (authored) by Alphonsus Vagnoni, contains in fact, in its first volume, part of Coimbra's commentary on Aristotle's *De Generatione et Corruptione*, especially that on four elements, and in its second volume, a lot of materials from Aristotle's *Meteorology*, based on the Coimbra's commentary of it in the *Parva Naturalia*. The basic idea in their enterprise of translation is the "harmonious synthesis" of Western philosophy with Chinese wisdom. As Julius Aleni's in his *Xixuefan* (Introduction to Western Sciences) says,

> We who travel from as far as ninety thousands li are willing to translate into Chinese all the previous mentioned treatises. We will be able to finish translating them by using more than ten some years, so that those in their younger days with good talent start to learn them progressively with their innocent heart...in order that the sciences of sages in the Eastern sea and Western sea will be able to meet in one thread leading to harmonious synthesis.[16]

Besides this intention to meet Western philosophy with Chinese philosophy, the most admired (by Chinese intellectuals) contribution of Jesuits to Chinese culture was their introduction of Western science and technology: astronomy, geometry and mathematics, logic, phonetics, cartography, clockworks... etc., just to mention a few. Jesuits' introduction of Western mathematics, logic and scientific method had influenced upon the scientific method of philological studies in the Qianjia school(乾嘉學派), inspired the Yan-Li school(顏李學派) towards more pragmatic way of learning(such as organizing their school into fours halls of learning: classics and history, literary matters, military craft, and practical arts), also influenced the development of philosophy, philology, investigation by evidence and other method of learning in Qing Dynasty.

The third phase of Christianity in China started in mid 19th century, in which the most important feature is the establishment of deferent levels of educational institutions, especially institutions of higher education such as colleges and universities, first by the Protestants then by the Catholics. More advanced Western science and technology have been introduced to China. But, unfortunately, with their inextricable ties with Western colonial powers, Christian churches has been misunderstood, and even became the target of anti-Christian movement because of their ambiguous relation with the imperialist aggressive acts that hurt Chinese collective subjectivity. Short of space, I'll not indulge myself in more detailed historical discussions here.

Now Western science and technology have become one of the inner dynamic factors of modern Chinese culture, and for this, we should be grateful to Christianity's effort in bringing Western science and technology into China. Both sciences and techniques brought to China by the Jesuits in the 16th and 17th Centuries, and more modern science and technology introduced later and more recently, have helped to develop scientific rationality in China. They develop in a way to develop Chinese instrumental rationality and material civilization. Therefore, even if they have contributed a new cultural dynamism to China, yet if staying merely on the level of instrumental rationality and material civilization, without any further philosophical reflections, they could not be shown, on the ethical and spiritual levels, as generosity towards the other (I mean the other as other people and as Nature), and eventually as openness to the Ultimate Other.

It has been more than thirteen centuries since Alopen appeared in the City of Chang An, or at least more than four centuries since Matteo Ricci's arrival at Zhaoqing, unfortunately Christianity has not become one of the major constitutive elements in Chinese culture. Christianity itself might be responsible of not having made it clear its true message in the context of Chinese culture. On the other hand, Chinese culture under the dominant influence of Confucianism, though compatible with Christianity, nevertheless might have something inherent in it that limited itself to grasp that truly Christian spirit. The invitation to further strangification and generosity to the other in the era of globalization may be a good historical occasion for both sides to a deeper mutual understanding.

CONFUCIAN SHU AND GENEROSITY TO OTHER

Any historical process and social institution, no matter what they are, should always be lived existentially and ethically with meaningfulness by human beings. This is also the case with the process of globalization, which, developed by today's communication technology and implemented on economic, political and cultural levels, is bringing humankind into more and more systematic networks. This situation of living in networks existentially exemplifies the ontology of dynamic relationship affirmed since long by classical Confucianism. The Confucian concept of *ren* denotes somehow the interconnectedness between human being and all things existing in the universe (Heaven and earth). Because of *ren*, human beings can be affected by and respond to one another, and by the act of *shu*, they can enlarge their existence to larger realms of existence from oneself to the other, to family, to social community, to the state, to all under heaven, now interpreted by the term "globalization." The networks of this dynamic relationship cannot be said to exist in form of substance, neither can't they be said not to exist, as nothingness. They're always there, dynamically developing, not only on the ontological level, but also on the ethical level.

Basically, Confucianism will be able to contribute to this process of globalization by its way of life as a process of ethical extension, especially by Confucian virtues and values such as *ren* (humanness), *shu*(altruism), *yi*(righteousness), *zhi*(wisdom), *cheng*(sincerity), *xin*(faithfulness)...etc. In the networks developed by globalization, human beings, if they want to keep to the dignity of their life as human, should always deal with each other with sincerity and especially with the virtue of *shu*.

Going outside of oneself and generosity to the other are supposed to be the most needed virtues in the process of globalization. In Confucianism, *shu* could be seen as such a basic virtue. Although quite often translated as "altruism"[17], or "putting oneself in other's place"[18], or even as "using oneself as a measure to gauge others"[19] or empathy(a psychological interpretation insufficient today when our life is mediated now by symbolic languages and technical objects), it's best understood and interpreted now in term of strangi-fication, in the sense that "he who practice *shu* knows how to strangify"(shu zhe shan tui) and "extend from oneself to the other"(tui ji ji ren). In the Ana-lects, not much was said about *shu*, though it was told by Confucius himself to be the expression to act upon till the end of one's life.

> When Zigong asked, "Is there one expression that can be acted upon till the end of one's days?" The master replied, "There is *shu*怒: do not impose on others what you yourself do not want"[20]

Here *shu* was understood in the spirit of the negative version of gold-en rule, "do not impose on others what you yourself do not want". The same negative golden rule was repeated by Confucius when answering Zhonggong's question about *ren*.[21] From this repetition we can see a very close relationship between *ren* and shu, given the fact that they have the same definition. On the other hand, a positive version golden rule was given as answer to the question about the concept of *ren*(humanity), asked by Zigong, "A man of humanity, wishing to establish his own character, also establishes others, wishing to be prominent himself, also helps others."[22]

As we can see, both negative and positive versions of golden rules are, in Confucian terms, based on a reciprocal basis as to the relation between self and other. With *shu*, one extends one's existence to larger and larger circles. It is the act of going always beyond oneself to the other, from self to family, from family to community, from community to the state, and from the state to all under heaven. This is the act of "extending or strangifying from oneself to the other"(tui ji ji ren). A Confucian existence is an ever-expanding life based on self-cultivation. In this process, authenticity and perfection of self are in priority over dependence on others. That's why Confucius emphasized learn-ing for perfecting oneself. In the following sayings emphasis was put more on the side of self-perfection or self-preparation than on others.[23]

So it seems that self-cultivation and self-perfection is more on the part of individual, while harmonious relation with others should be achieved in the social context. The Confucian way of life is extension of one's exis-tence in the context of larger and larger circles of life basing on the perfection of one's self. Even if self-cultivation is in priority over others in the order of moral perfection, strangification or *shu* is always necessary in the order of ethical and political implementation. That's why Mencius would say, "Hence one who extends his bounty can bring peace to the Four Seas; one who does not cannot bring peace even to his own family. There is just one thing in which the ancients greatly surpassed others, and that is the way they extended what they did."[24]

In Confucianism, the tension between self and other is to be solved in reference to golden rules, both negative and positive, based ultimately on the principle of reciprocity. In this sense, we can say that, in the Confucian world, in which human behaviors have to be regulated by li, even the act of going outside oneself to the other launched by *shu*, and the original generosity it implied, have to be regulated by reciprocity.

The principle of reciprocity becomes a guiding principle of social and political philosophy in the Great Learning, where it is called the principle of measuring square (*Jiejuzhidao*絜矩之道). The text reads first a positive version of the principle to be followed by a negative version of it. They are put in the context where it is explained the extension from governing the state to making peace within all under heaven. The positive version reads,

> What is meant by saying that the peace of the world depends on the order of the state is: When the ruler treats the elders with respect, then the people will be aroused towards fil-ial piety. When the ruler treats the aged with respect, then the people will be aroused towards brotherly respect. When the ruler treats compassionately the young and the helpless, then the common people will not follow the opposite course. Therefore the ruler has a principle with which, as with a measuring square, he may regulate his conduct.[25]

The major point here is the governance by *ren*(humanity): when the ruler governs his people by respect and humanity, people will respond with peace and harmony, in form of filial piety, brotherly respect and submissive-ness. The positive reciprocity is here expressed in terms of the filial piety, brotherly respect and compassionate for the young and the helpless...etc., initiated by political leader. On the other hand, there is also the negative ver-sion of the measure of square:

> What a man dislike in his superiors, let him not show it in dealing with his inferiors. What he dislikes in those in front of him, let him not show it in preceding those who are be-hind; what he dislikes in those behind him, let him not show it in following those in front of him; what he dislikes in those on the right, let him not apply it to those on the left; and what he dislikes in those on the left, let him not apply it to those on the right. This is the principle of the measuring square.[26]

As it is clear, the reciprocity here is enlarged analogically from one side to the opposite side: from superior to inferior, from inferior to superior; from right to left, from left to right; from front to behind, from behind to front, and thereby forming a cubic relationship, not merely a square, of reciprocity, though always taken in a negative sense. Within this cubic structure of reciprocal relationship, more attention have been paid to the horizontal, that is, from right to left, from left to right; from front to behind, from behind to front, than the vertical relation between superior and inferior, mentioned only once. Nevertheless, the concept of "extended reciprocity" plays a major role in this largest extension of human relation—from the state to all under heaven.

CONFUCIAN GENEROSITY TO THE OTHER

Now, how about Confucian virtue of generosity? I agree with Aristotle that generosity could be understood as liberality as well as magnanimity[27]. When we look for Confucian virtue of generosity in the sense of liberality or generosity as to the giving or sharing of one's material goods, we might first think of Zilu. When assisting Confucius with Yan Hui, asked by Confucius as to what they would like most to do, Zilu said, "I would like to share my horses and carriages, my clothing and furs, with my friend, and if they damage them, to bear them no ill will."[28] This shows Zilu has a virtue of liberality. Even if it concerns sharing and not unconditional gift, nevertheless it expresses his non-possessiveness and generosity in sharing with others as friends. Zilu didn't say "share with any other in general," but "share with my friends," who were equal one with another and reciprocal in being good to each other. So it seems that Zilu cherished more friendship than material goods.

But Zilu's generosity in terms of liberality regarding material goods, and his ambition to govern well a state of thousand chariots, were not highly evaluated under Confucius eyes, in comparison with another's. When Zilu, Zengzi, Ranyou and Gong Xihua were asked by Confucius about how would they do if someone did recognize their true selves, among all the answers, Confucius would say only "I'm with Zengxi."—Confucius was more in praise of Zengxi's free life style in union with Heaven and earth: "At the end of spring, with the spring clothes having already been finished, I would like, says Zengxi, in the company of five or six young men or six or seven children, to cleanse ourselves in the Yi River, to revel in the cool breezes at the Altar for Rain, and then return home singing."[29]

From this we understand Confucius put emphasis on the existential feeling as a whole and the spiritual horizon that comes closer to the rhythm of nature. This shows the cosmic breath of Confucius' mind in the sense of magnanimity. In general Confucius would emphasize generosity that is genuine, and blame the false liberality. That's probably the meaning of Confucius' blame of Wei Shengao in saying "Who said that Wei Shengao is upright? When someone begged vinegar from him, he in turn begged it from his neighbors and then presented it to the person who has asked him for it."[30]

Indeed, Confucius mind was so great, that his virtue of generosity is not limited to liberality, but much closer to what Aristotle said as "magnanimity." On the one hand, Confucius did not care much about the gain or lose in material goods, his spiritual horizon was much loftier than any desire for fortune and position, as shown when he said, "To eat coarse food, drink plain water, and pillow oneself on a bent arm—there is pleasure to be found in these things. But wealth and position gained through inappropriate means—these are to me like floating clouds."[31] Confucius' own ambition was much higher, which, according to his own words, was "to bring peace and contentment to the aged, to share relationship of trust and confidence with my friends, and to love and protect the young."[32] Which means the existential comfort of all people at all ages, as demanded by the universalization of the virtue of humanness.

We should point out here that Confucius understood generosity mostly in the sense of reciprocity. He said, when answering to Zizhang's question about *ren*, "One who can practice five things wherever he may be is a man of humanity…Earnestness, liberality, truthfulness, diligence, and generosity." Among the five virtues, *kuan*(liberality) and *hui*(generosity) are related to generosity, when all five are related to reciprocal virtues, as Confucius himself explained, "If one is earnest, one will not be treated with disrespect; If one is liberal, one will win the heart of all, If one is trustful, one will be trusted. If one is diligent, one will be successful. And if one is generous, one will be able to enjoy the service of others."[33] Note that Confucius said all these in the context of consequences, that you'll not be treated with disrespect, you will win the heart of all, you will be trusted, you will be successful, you will be able to enjoy the service of others etc. Which means Confucius considered moral matters also from the consequentialist, not only from the intentionalist, point of view. Liberality and generosity in Confucian sense, as to the consequences they invite, still stand on reciprocity.

I understand Confucian virtues in two senses, "relational virtues" defined as harmonization of relationship; and "aptitudinal virtue" defined as excellence in one's natural ability. Reciprocity is the basis on which was built Confucian relational virtues and social relationship in general. It is clear that all relational virtues refer to others and response from others, relation always measured by reciprocity. This is much clearer when we come to relational virtues in the five relationships, consisting always in their harmonization, whether it concerns relation between husband and wife, or parents and children, or brothers and sisters, or friends and lovers, or individual and society. These are not to be seen merely as biological or social relationship, more than that, they are to be realized as ethically meaningful relationship. The meaning of virtue such as piety, fidelity, scurrility, royalty…etc., could be interpreted differently according to change of time, but its essence as the harmonization of relationship stays always valid.

The process of harmonization of relationship should be a process of enlargement from reciprocity to universalizability. Reciprocity is essential for human relationship according to Confucianism. But the good human relationship comes to its fulfillment when enlarged from reciprocity to universalizability. This might be in Confucius's mind, when asked by Zilu concerning how an exemplary person behaves, he answered first by the cultivation of oneself for one's dignity, then cultivation of oneself for the happiness of other's, finally cultivation of oneself for the happiness of all people. From reciprocity to universalizability, this means human being should transcend the limit of special relationship to universalizable relationship, even to the point of seeing all people within four seas as brothers. With ren, one can treat other fellowmen, despite their difference in family, profession, company, race and nation, with a universalizable love. With *shu*, one can go out side of one's self through language appropriation and strangify from one's self to the other, till all under heaven. This is the way by which Confucianism enlarges the harmonization of human relationship, the fully unfolding of which is the process of formation of virtuous life, not merely a life of observing stagnant rules of obligation.

Ideally speaking, there must be such a dynamism inside Confucianism to strangify, to universalize, to extend to all under heaven. But historically speaking, Confucianism itself didn't take initiative to expand itself to all under heaven to the extent of including the Western world in the past, like Christians Alopen in the 7th century and Matteo Ricci in the 16th century, who took a generous initiative to come to China despite the difficult and dangerous long distance trip. It was also Matteo Ricci and other Jesuits who had taken the initiative to introduce Confucianism to Europe. The lesson of this historical fact should allow us Confucians to rethink the limit of reciprocity and understand that, without the original generosity to take the first step, there would be no reciprocity in Confucian sense.

CONCLUSIONS

China is now starting a new historical moment in which she will play a more influential role as a big country, not only economically and politically, but also culturally and spiritually. China will be able to play this role if she understands and practices the spirit of strangification and the virtue of generosity. Here China has something to learn from the true spirit of Christianity, and not to indulge in looking only to the negative sides of Christianity in the past in a self-defensive manner.

From the point view of interaction between self and other, Western civilization has been, since the 16th Century, the other of Chinese culture. From the beginning of this complicated history of China's interaction with the West, there was already the involvement of Christianity, serving as one of the deep structural constituents of Western civilization. For it or against it, one should understand it in depth. Even Nietzsche's radical attitude of anti-Christ and his claim of "God is Dead" were deeply rooted in his understanding of Christianity as background of his life experience.

Fundamentally speaking, modernity could be characterized by the principle of subjectivity, culture of representation, rationality and domination. The historical complexity in which Christian missionary came to China, inextricably connected with European colonial expansion in the spirit of modernity under the pretext of civilizing other, has made Christian missionary misunderstood as serving as religious instrument of European imperialism. Nevertheless, those Christian missionaries, bringing generously with them European science, philosophy, Christianity, charity and educational networks to China despite long and dangerous voyages, should be seen as representing an act of generosity. Not to mention that Christianity has its long history before the dawn of modernity. The primitive Christians lived as a community of agape (unselfish love) that emphasized a life of devotion and generosity to the other. Unselfish love and generosity to the other are indeed the true spirit of Christianity, always urging Christians and others to take a generous initiative before any reciprocity. This is something that Confucianism and Daoism didn't do in the past. The *Liji* (Book of Rites) might have synthesized the Confucian minds, all in emphasizing the reciprocity of li,[34] it says, "I have heard [in accordance with *li*] that scholars come to learn; I have not heard of [the master] go to teach", though the emphasis was put on the value of truth and dignity of master, unfortunately the original generosity was quite often forgotten.[35]

Let me conclude. From philosophical point of view, the process of globalization should be seen as a historical process of realizing the ever-universalizing human nature going beyond boarders of any kind. The dynamism behind this is the universalizability and perfectibility of human intelligence and desire, developed since humankind's humanization with language and culture, and further developed in a self-aware manner after the philosophical breakthrough. In modernity, human being has been searching for the resource in his own subjectivity and the rational construction of this world by way of representations. But now, in entering the process of globalization, we need a new ethics fundamentally based on the generosity to the other through unceasing strangification. Without globalization, it would not be possible for human universalizability to be realized on a higher and global level. Globalization itself should pay respect to and bring its resources from different cultural traditions. It should be an invitation, not an imposition. In this context, Confucian concept of *shu* and virtue of generosity will still be a resource of inspiration, even if they have some limit as to their emphasis on reciprocity and need further development as to find a deeper layer of resources for an original generosity. It's particularly on this point that Confucianism could learn from Christianity. All things considered, if we human beings are not ready for further strangification and greater generosity to the other, we will not be ready, not even worthy, of a real globalization, not to mention entering into a higher form of universalization in terms of the universe.

NOTES

1 The idea of strangification was first proposed by F. Wallner, University of Vienna, as an epistemological strategy for interdisciplinary research. This concept was later developed by myself to the domains of intercultural interaction and religious dialogue.

2 Concerning the strangification in Buddhism, see Vincent Shen, "Appropriation of the Other and Transformation of Consciousness into Wisdom, Some Philosophical Reflections on Chinese Buddhism", in *Dao: A Journal of Comparative Philosophy*, December 2003, Vol. III, No. 1, pp.43-62

3 *The New Jerusalem Bible*, (London: Darton, Longman and Todd Ltd., 1990), p.5

4 Ibid., p.5

5 *Genesis*, 1:27, in *The Jerusalem Bible, The Old Testament*, p.16

6 "Therefore, when *Dao* is lost, there comes *de*(creative power). When *de* is lost, there comes *ren* (humaneness). When *ren* is lost, there comes *yi* (rightness). When *yi* is lost, there comes *li* (propriety)." Laozi, *Daodejing*, Ch. 38.

7 *Catechisme de l'église catholique,*(Paris: Mame/Plon, 1992), p.271

8 St. Augustine, *Confessions*, translated by R.S. Pine-Coffin,(London: Penguin Classics, 1961), p. 4.

9 If we check the effort of strangification by the Nestorians in China, as to linguistic strangification, the Nestorians had not well appropriated Chinese language, the earlier translations were either misleading or coarse that would not invite Chinese religious faith, such as the term Jesus was translated as yishu(移鼠), a moving mouse, Maria as moyan(末艷), the least fair, John as ruohun(若昏), the seemingly confused...etc., not only without any aesthetic sense of letter, but also provocative of sense of disdain. Later, Nestorian translation over appropriated Daoist and Buddhist terms, such as using Buddha, Dao, Marvelous Dao, to translate God, which, not only misinterpreted the Christian message, but also made itself indistinguishable from Buddhism or Daoism. The fact that the Nestorian texts such as the *Messiah Sutra, On Trinity*, and the Nestorian Inscription were included in the Buddhist Canon is an evidence that at least it was perceived as something closely related Buddhism. As to Pragmatic strangification, even if Nestorians had made effort to adapt to Confucian ethics such as loyalty to political leaders and filial piety, as evidenced by the Messiah Sutra saying that "The most important three things: The first to serve God, the second to serve Emperor, the third to serve parents."(一種先事天尊，第二事聖上，第三事父母) But it could not avoid being politically used and abused by Tang's policy and could not survived the political persecution after 845 A.D., if not in form of Christian Daoist, as evidenced by some archeological evidences and some texts such as Lu Dongbin's *Complete Works* in which we find some chants are in fact Christina prayers. As to the ontological strangification, the mixture with Daoist terms such as Dao, Marvellous Dao, wu(non-being), Xuan, Original non-being... etc, was misleading in confusing the Christian Ultimate Reality with that of Daoists. This confusion not only unhelpful in religious dialogue, it could be misleading also in its own self-understanding.

10 For me this challenge from the West started a new period in Chinese Philosophy. I have divided the history of Chinese philosophy into four major periods: First, the pre-Qin and early Han period (6th to 1st Centuries

BCE), in which were emerged and developed Confucianism, Daoism, Mohism, Legalism, School of Names etc. Second, the late Han and Weijin, Sui-Tang period(1st century CE to 10th Century), with the introduction of Indian Buddhism and the development of divers schools of Chinese Mahayana Buddhism such as Sanlun School, Weishi School, Tiantai School, Huayan School, Chan Buddhism etc. Third, the emergence and development of Neo-Confucianism from early Song to late Ming/early Qing (11th to 16th century). Fourth, the period of facing the challenge of and integrating with Western philosophy, after the introduction of Western science, philosophy and Christianity by Matteo Ricci and other Christian missionaries (since late 16th century to the present). I believe this periodization can, among others, render justice to Ricci, his Jesuits' colleagues and early Chinese Christians' contribution to Chinese philosophy.

11 On the level of ethics, the Christian ethics of Matteo Ricci and his followers emphasized ascetic values, quite similar to Buddhism and Neo-Confucianism of that time. Neo Confucianism replaced pre-Qin Confucianism's creative and harmonious attitude towards human feeling and desire with a dualistic and repressive world vision, such as "discard human desire and conserve heavenly principle" Both Neo-Confucians and Christians understood a "repressive concept of virtue", rather than a "creative concept of virtue", which, for Aristotle, means mainly the excellence of one's natural abilities; and, for classical Confucianism, means mainly harmonization of human relationships. The Christian ethics could be seen in the *Qi Ke* (七克On Overcoming Seven Capital Sins), by Didacus de Pantoja (龐迪我). "Virtue" was considered there as the overcoming of seven capital sins: humbleness as overcoming pride, benevolence as overcoming jealousy, generosity as overcoming misery, patience as overcoming anger, simplicity or frugality as overcoming gluttonousness, chasteness as overcoming lust, and diligence as overcoming laziness. Under their influence, Christian Chinese intellectuals also understood virtue in its repressive concept. For example, Chen Liancai wrote in his prefaced to *Qi Ke*, "By using the method of keeping oneself on guard and in dread (jiesheng konju 戒慎恐懼) one could lead one's human nature endowed by heaven so as to follow law of heaven. This is the true learning of our Confucians. Yet being afraid of ordinary people not knowing what is heaven and see it merely as the surface of the sky, they say for the reason of expediency that "Heaven is in my own mind/heart." Thereafter the scholars would go further to understand "my mind/heart is heaven" and run wild and uncultivated, shaking off all rules all in believing that truth is on my side and I should enjoy my happy freedom, then they become thereby a base person without any scruple. How could this be the teaching of Duke of Zhou and Confucius?"(Li Zhizhao, editor, *Tianxue Cuhan*(天學初函), Vol.2, Taipei: Students Bookstore, 1985, pp.704-705, My English translation) This remark shows a repressive idea of virtue by focusing on the method of keeping oneself on guard and in dread, in the sense of Christian checking one's conscience; on the other hand, it proposed a crucial critique of Neo-Confucianism's too humanistic understanding of human heart as heaven, which absolutized hu-

man heart and encourage self-content and self-enclosure of subjectivity by radically affirming that "all men on the street are already sages." This debate between Christian Confucians and Neo-Confucians is still going on today, where the main point is to say that even human can be in union with heaven, still human heart is not Heaven Itself.

12 Fang. Hao, *Li Zhizao Yanjiou*李之藻研究 (Taipei: Taiwan Commercial Press, 1966), p.103

13 I appreciate the Thomas Fisher Rare Book Library, University of Toronto, to have allowed me the access to the precious *Commentarii Collegii Conimbricensis Societatis Jesu* it possesses.

14 *Mingli tan* should have been based on the *Commentarii Collegii Conimbricensis Societatis Jesu:In Universam Dialecticam Aristotelis Atagiritae*, Nunc Primum in Germania in lucem editi. Coloniae Agrippinae, Apud Bernardum Gualtherium, 1611. It is also not a translation in exact sense. Some comparisons on this part has been done by Robert Wardy in the second chapter of his *Aristotle in China*, (Cambridge: Cambridge University Press, 2000). Apart from the published volumes of the *De Categoriae*, there still have other translated volumes yet unpublished because of lack of financial support as well as positive response from Chinese readers, such as *De Interpretatione*, *De Syllogismo*(Analytica Priora) and *De Demonstratione*(Analytica posteriora).

15 *Commentarii Collegii Conimbricensis Societatis Jesu in Libros qui Parva Naturalia appelantur,* 19-36, 36-48, 48-54

16 Li Zhizhao, ed., *Tianxue Cuhan*, Vol.1, (Taipei: Students Bookstore, 1985), p.59, My English translation.

17 W.T. Chan, *A Source Book in Chinese Philosophy*, (Princeton: Princeton University Press. 1963), p.44

18 R. Ames and H. Rosemont, translators. *The Analects of Confucius, A Philosophical Translation.* (New York; Ballantine Books, 1998), p.92

19 D.C. Lau, translator. 1970, *Mencius*, (New York: Penguin Books. 1970), p.74

20 *Analects* 15:24; R. Ames and H Rosemont, *A Philosophical Translation.* p.189

21 *Analects* 12:2, R. Ames and H Rosemont, p. 153

22 *Analects.* 6: 28; W.T.Chan, *Source Book*, p.31

23 For example: "Don't worry about not being recognized by others; worry about not having any reason for them to recognize you."(*Analects* 14:30, R. Ames and H. Rosemont, p.179) "Exemplary persons are distressed by their own lack of ability, not by the failure of others to acknowledge him."(*Analects* 15.19, R.Ames and H. Rosemont, p.188) "Exemplary persons (*junzi*) make demands on themselves, while petty persons make demands on others."(*Analects* 15.21, R. Ames and H. Rosemont, p. 189)

24 *Mencius* 1: 7, D.C.Lau's translation, p. 57

25 W.T.Chan, *Source Book*, p. 92

26 Ibid., p. 92

27 Aristotle, Nicomachean Ethics, 1123b1-30, in Complete Works of Aristotle, Vol.2, Princeton, Princeton University Press, p.1773

28 *Analects* 5.26, R. Ames and H. Rosemont, p 102

29 *Analects* 11:26, R.Ames and H. Rosemont, p. 150

30 *Analects* 5.24, R.Ames and H. Rosemont, p. 101

31 *Analects* 7:16, R.Ames and H. Rosemont, p. 114

32 *Analects* 5:26, R.Ames and H. Rosemont, p. 102

33 *Analects* 17:6, W.T.Chan, *Source Book*, pp. 46-47

34 "What the rules of propriety values is that reciprocity. If I give a gift and nothing comes in return, that is contrary to propriety; if the thing come to me and I give nothing in return, that also is contrary to propriety." *Li Chi, Book of Rites*, 1885, Part I, trans. by James Legge, reprint by Kissinger Publishing, p.65

35 The sentence in the *Liji* "In the highest [antiquity] they prized simply conferring good", right before the secondary reciprocity, may be talking about this original generosity that is quite often forgotten. Ibid., p.65

The Element of Equality in the Global Era:
A Comment on the Paper of Vincent Shen

Li Chenyang

Professor Shen has presented us with an enlightening paper. Based on his understanding of the historical process as "unceasingly going beyond and towards higher levels of universalizability," Shen argues powerfully that "globalization is the present historical stage of realizing the unceasing process of human strangification and a further invitation to human generosity to the other."

There are three key concepts in this paper. The first concept is strangification. It is articulated by Professor Shen in three ways. First, linguistic strangification. This refers to the translatability of one discourse/value or cultural expression/ religious belief into discourse/value/cultural expression/religious belief understandable to another scientific, cultural or religious community. Second, pragmatic strangification. This refers to the applicability of one discourse/value or expression/belief in other social and pragmatic contexts. Third, ontological strangification. This refers to the universalizability of a discourse/value or expression/belief "by a detour of experiencing Reality Itself, for example, a direct experience with Reality itself, such as other people, Nature, or even the Ultimate Reality" (p.182). The second key concept in Shen's paper is generosity. It is to be understood as liberality as well as magnanimity. Liberality is the act of freely or openly sharing resources with others. Magnanimity is loftiness of spirit enabling one to bear trouble calmly, to disdain meanness and pettiness, and to display a noble liberality. The third key concept is reciprocity. Reciprocity means mutually benefiting. It is the Latin expression of "Quid pro quo," which means "something for something," or an equal exchange or substitution. Reciprocity is exemplified by the American expression "You scratch my back, and I'll scratch yours." Understood this way, reciprocity is not a noble virtue. Thus it is understandable that, among these three concepts, Professor Shen advocates strangification and generosity; he does not consider reciprocity, as manifested in the Confucian idea of "*shu*," a high virtue, and indeed he does not think of it as an adequate principle for our global age.

I find two things particularly interesting in his paper. The first is his development of the concept of "strangification" or "waitui 外推," which means "the act of going outside of oneself to the other, or going outside of one's familiarity to strangeness, to the strangers." (It is unfortunate that "strangification" at the first glance does not give us the kind of positive meaning that it implies, perhaps because people are customarily wary of anything associated with "strange." But let us have faith that this neologism will gain its own life in our philosophical discourse.) This concept, like Tu Weiming's "anthropocosmic approach," Habermas's "communicative action," and Charles Taylor's "self in the moral space," is an important tool for us to understand the contemporary age and to act toward the building of a good world. If Shen's concept of strangification receives the kind of attention it deserves, it will play an influential role in our philosophical discourse of globalization. The second striking point of Shen's paper is his generous assessment of Christianity's contribution to the process of strangification and his critical reflection of Confucianism in this regard. This is particularly admirable from a scholar who is manifestly Confucian. Shen's paper, I take it, is itself an exemplar of strangification.

I have some questions, however, about strangification, generosity, and reciprocity. Their relationships are indicated in the paper as Shen writes that "strangification and language appropriation presuppose an original generosity toward the other" , that "the original generosity…should be seen as the condition sine qua non of all situations of reciprocal relationship", and that "without the original generosity to take the first step, there would be no reciprocity in Confucian sense". According to these passages, both strangification and reciprocity presuppose "original generosity." My first question is on the very meaning of "original generosity." At one place, Shen suggests that it means "the act of going outside of oneself to the other." He writes, "The original generosity [is] implied in this act of going outside of oneself… Philosophically speaking, before we can establish a sort of reciprocity, emphasized for example in Marcel Mauss' *Essai sur le don* as the principle of human society, there must be previously a generous act of going outside of oneself to the other, so that there can be established accordingly a relation of reciprocity. "

Shen's use of "original" as a qualifier of "generosity" suggests that "original generosity" is not just "generosity," it may be a sort of primordial generosity. However, I would think it is a sort of generosity nevertheless; otherwise it would not have been labeled as generosity. If that is the case, I am not sure "the act of going outside of oneself to the other" qualifies as generosity at all. "The act of going outside of oneself to the other" can be a generous one, e.g., when I approach you to offer help. It certainly can also be an ungenerous one, e.g., when I approach you for your sacrifice on my behalf.

Second, does reciprocity presupposes generosity? It seems to me, while generosity can be a good motivation for strangification, reciprocity does not have to presuppose generosity. For example, Thomas Hobbes's social contract is based on reciprocity, but not on generosity at all. Indeed, it is precisely based on selfishness, the opposite of generosity.

My third question is whether generosity should be taken as a fundamental principle of human conduct in the global age. Reciprocity, as limited as it is, at least is based on some kind of equality. In reciprocity, we treat one another as equals. A reciprocal relationship is an equal relationship in which no one can claim superior status. Generosity, on the other hand, does not presuppose equality. Understood as liberality and magnanimity, generosity implies a sense of loftiness, a sense of being in a superior position (though it does not have to be arrogant). Generosity is undoubtedly a good virtue, but one wonders if it is appropriate to take it as basis for the "new principles for society and ethics" of our global age. If the global era is a pluralist era, in which equality is a fundamental ideal, then justice or humanity based on human equality may serve better as a basis for new principles for society and ethics than generosity. Even though the more the merrier, virtues nevertheless are "supererogatory" in an age of human rights, whereas principles are bottom lines. A good principle for a better society should not be based on a supererogatory quality.

In conclusion, I would like to come back to Professor Shen's central concept of strangification. I understand strangification as based on equality. Because I take you as equal, I cannot force you to engage in dialogue with me in my language alone. If I want to make myself understandable to you, I need to strangify my discourse into your language. If I want to make my ideals universally 'practice-able', I cannot force you to practice it in my social context; I need to strangify my ideals into your social context. In this sense, strangification is the minimum reasonable approach to globalization, as it is directly opposed to hegemony. Furthermore, on the basis of strangification, we can go above and beyond to be generous toward others. Although one can be generous without strangification, generosity is better served on the basis of strangification, because strangification is based on equality, which in turn is the most important moral ideal in a pluralistic global age. For all these reasons, strangification should be taken as the fundamental approach or principle of social and ethical behavior of our global age. Professor Shen is to be congratulated for his timely articulation of this extremely valuable concept for us.

A Comment on the Paper of Vincent Shen

Chloë Starr

Vincent Shen's paper is itself an example of globalisation: written by a non-native speaker of English, perhaps even translated from a second language, with the attendant tessellation of linguistic and cultural contexts that the processes of globalisation entail. The paper presents an interesting thesis, examining the contributions, past and potential, of both Christianity and Confucianism to globalisation through their common aim of 'going beyond' the individual to the Other in acts of generosity and selflessness. It is good to have underlined again recent trends towards a more positive re-evaluation of the historic contribution of Christian mission to the Chinese nation in so many arenas (healthcare, education, and even to areas such as language reform, as Yuan Jin's work in Shanghai is now demonstrating). Shen's section on aspects of generosity within Confucianism also presents a useful overview of the terms involved in the debate, and of the differences between reciprocity and generosity.

In bringing together globalization with a religious going-beyond, as in any linkage between disparate academic discourses, caution needs to be exercised. Globalisation, and glocalisation, to which Shen also refers, are terms whose sense has been developed largely by economists and management theorists. Globalisation relates primarily to the dynamics of economies, and only secondarily to cultural exchange. It is not usually seen as quite so amenable, for example, to Confucian virtues as Shen proposes. Since papers and conferences on glocalism proliferated following the First Glocal Forum in Rome in 2002, the debate on globalisation has been furthered by a recognition of the simultaneous processes of globalisation and localisation in the world, and by the need to seek better balances between global forces and local needs. Although Shen notes glocalism (i.e. a two-way, tempering process), a sense of checks, balances and breaks on globalisation is underplayed in the paper, which seems to present globalisation as an upwards, unidirectional movement.

The question of terminology is raised throughout Shen's paper. I was hoping for greater discussion of some of the terms he uses; an early explanation of the phrase "the global culture", for example, may have helped elucidate his perspective for the reader. The title to Shen's paper refers to his concept of strangification, which he admits may sound odd to the English speaker. One of the reasons for this sounding odd, however, is that strangification should mean "a making strange," an estranging or making-foreign, rather than, as Shen uses the term, the act of going outside of oneself to the other. Shen suggests that the concept presupposes the acquisition of language, but it would seem that such acts of going beyond oneself readily transcend language and do not suppose the separation out of one's own values from those of the other before the act can be performed. Likewise, Shen's use of universal, and particularly "universalizability" renders opaque, rather than clarifies, the discussion. It is not entirely clear how globalisation is necessarily linked to a desire for all to be applicable to all: again, the distinction may hinge on how benign one assumes globalisation to be. A slight shift in definition takes place when Shen moves on to discuss a universalisable ethics in terms of the universe itself.

Shen presents a substantial discussion of sin and free will. The discussion of sin as 'self-enclosure' is insightful, but it is arguable whether in the Christian case sin can be limited to self-enclosure, being linked to a wilful, conscious wrong-doing, or transgression of God-given laws. Self-enclosure as sin is a derived, rather than biblical, image.

Some other specific points of note:

- To say that Xunzi would say that human nature was evil is an oversimplification of a much-argued debate between heaven-given nature and human artifice (as D.C. Lau demonstrated so admirably back in 1953, "Theories of Human Nature in Mencius and Shyuntzyy," *Bulletin of School of Oriental and African Studies* Vol 15: 541-565), as a footnote could have reminded us.

- The process of globalisation, as defined by the parameters Shen sets, long predated modernity, and the present increase of speed in globalisation is firmly rooted, one could argue, in the post-modern rather than modern era. Interlinkages between Shen's three types of strangification might also be made more explicit: the third case, ontological strangification, for example, seems to require the first (linguistic strangification) for its mediation.

- Shen's rich paper, which itself goes beyond the self-enclosures of academic disciplines that he so denigrates, is marred, for this reader, by a tendency to prescriptive rather than neutral discourse. Why should the critique of modernity be the 'negative side' of post-modernity? Twice, misunderstandings of Christianity in China are described as unfortunate, as in the phrase "unfortunately Christianity has not become one of the major constitutive elements in Chinese culture". This is scarcely a universal viewpoint. The engagement Shen suggests between Confucianism and globalization is likewise rather value-laden: humans within global networks "should always deal with each other with sincerity," we are advised. If the forces of globalisation are truly as beneficial and inclusive as Shen's paper implies, then the need for such moralising should fade along with the self-enclosure that difference and diversity seem to concede.

Chapter 8

The Goodness of Human Nature and Original Sin: A Point of Convergence in Chinese and Western Cultures

Zhao Dunhua

When someone sees my title, which suggests the comparison between two different views of human nature, they may object that the Christian dogma of original sin was given through the revelation in the Bible, whereas the Confucian theory of the goodness of human nature was founded upon human reason. The two therefore cannot be compared since there is no connection between divine revelation and human reason. To this I reply that the comparison is not my innovation. Quite a few Western scholars have drawn particular attention to a comparison of this kind, which can be seen in such works as *The Sixth Volume of the True Meaning of Heavenly Doctrines (Tianxue Shiyi)* by Matteo Ricci, the *Prolegomena of Mencius' Work* by James Legge, *Chinese Religion* by Max Weber, and most recently, *China and the Christian Impact: A Conflict of Culture* by Jacques Gernet. All of these writers, except for Ricci, emphasize the irreconcilable conflict between the doctrine of original sin and the theory of the goodness of human nature. It is worthwhile noting that there has been a contrary trend amongst Western scholars, especially amongst the thinkers of the Enlightenment in the 18th century who adopted to a certain extent the Confucian view of the goodness of human nature in its encounter with the Christian notion of original sin. In spite of the differences in standpoint and orientation, both parties generally agreed on the divergence of the Christian and Confucian views on human nature. This paper will express a disagreement with this prevalent assumption, pointing out, as its sub-title suggests, the convergence of these two different views on human nature.

From the very beginning, I would like to acknowledge that I do not deny the divergence in question. If it is true that nothing but the reflection of different nations on their own nature can show most clearly the cultural difference between them, then the Confucian and Christian viewpoints on human nature certainly manifest, in a concentrated manner, the divergence between Chinese and Western culture. The key point is, however, that this divergence has appeared to many scholars as a diametrical opposition and total incompatibility. For example, Max Weber wrote,

> Completely absent in Confucian ethics was any tension between nature and deity, between ethical demand and human short-coming, consciousness of sin and need for salvation, conduct on earth and compensation in the beyond, religious duty and socio-political reality.[1]

James Legge wrote,

> Mencius' doctrine of human nature was defective in as much
> as even his ideal does not cover the whole field of duty.
> ...That he never indicates any wish to penetrate fu-
> turity, and ascertain what comes after death, that he never
> indicates any consciousness of human weakness, nor moves
> his mind Godward, longing for more light: these are things
> which exhibit strongly the contrast between the mind of the
> East and the West. His self-sufficiency is his great fault. To
> know oneself is commonly supposed to be an important step
> to humility, but it is not so with him.[2]

It seems to me that both these conclusions are a little hasty. I often
feel that, perhaps, assertions of this kind have been derived from over general-
ized and superficial impressions and have led to popular yet naive opinions.
The philosophical ideas and argumentation involved in this question have
constantly been ignored or underestimated. If we compare the distinctions
and clarifications, arguments and inferences, explanations and interpretations
made by Chinese and Western philosophers concerning these two kinds of
view of human nature, we can reveal the similarity in mentality and moral
consciousness beneath the appearance of Chinese and Western cultural divergence. On the basis of this line of reasoning, I shall attempt to demonstrate
that the doctrine of original sin and the theory of goodness of human nature
are:

    a. Logically non-contradictory;
    b. Theoretically complementary; and
    c. Practically play a similar moral role.

LOGICALLY NON-CONTRADICTORY

Logically, the theory of the goodness of human nature contradicts the
theory of the evil of human nature. This contradiction was given expression
in the historical controversy between Mencius and Xunzi . However, when
Mencius spoke of human nature he was not referring to the same notion that
Xunzi discussed. The former refers to the moral essence of human beings, that
is to say, the four origins of humanity and rightness, namely, the feeling of
commiseration as the origin of humanity, the feeling of shame and dislike in
relation to rightness, the feeling of reverence and respect as that of propriety,
and the feeling of right and wrong as that of wisdom.[3] Xunzi referred human
nature to the natural instincts, that is, to the sensuous desires originating in
the organs of the body.[4] Mencius did not deny these instincts and desires,
but made a further distinction between nature and fate. Sensuous instincts
and desires are people's fate, in the sense that they are always present, determined and unavoidable; moral essence, on the other hand, is what is natural to

people in the sense that it awaits realization. Their failure to realize it would result in its absence or even complete loss. Mencius, who was concerned with the realization of human moral nature, comments that a gentleman attributes instincts to fate but not to human nature and moral essence to human nature but not to fate.[5] Mencius' distinction between fate and nature is decisive in resolving the apparent contradiction between his theory of the goodness of human nature and Xunzi's theory of the evil of human nature.

Some traditional Chinese philosophers disagreed with the theory of the goodness of human nature either individually or collectively. Yang Xiong (53-18BC), from the perspective of the individual, spoke of the mixture of good and evil in human nature. Dong Zhongshu (179-104BC) and Han Yu (768-824AD), from the perspective of the collective, spoke of the three degrees of human nature, that is to say, the high degree of pure good, the middle degree of the mixture of good with evil, and the low degree of complete evil. Generally speaking, the mainstream of Confucianism is to endorse Mencius' theory of the goodness of human nature but incorporating in it the above views of Yang Xiong and Dong Zhongshu, even compromising it with the above mentioned view of Xunzi on evil nature.

Most Confucians considered that good and evil are not opposed at the same level. Good, they argued, is fundamentally metaphysical. This is the level to which human moral nature belongs. Evil, on the other hand, is related to the corporeal and as such, physical or physiological. This is the level to which human sensuous elements belong. For example, Li-Ao (772-841) differentiated between nature and feeling, saying that "nothing in nature is not good" (性無不善), and "feeling is illusionary and wicked" (情則妄邪).[6] The Confucian rationalist Zhu Xi(1130-1200), like his predecessors, distinguished between heavenly nature (天命之性) and material nature (氣質之性). According to his interpretation, the good nature that Mencius spoke of refers to original nature which can be equated with heavenly Reason, while material nature is derivative due to the fact that any human characteristic is formed together with something corporeal, yet still made out of heavenly reason. The mixed or hierarchal nature of good and evil as proposed by other Confucians is thus assigned to the derivative position of characteristic nature.[7] His teacher, Hu Hong (1106-1161) put it clearly, "good" is the lofty term for praise, to which no evil can be opposed (性善不與惡對).

I conclude from the above that no theory of human nature in traditional Chinese thought, in the final analysis, is really in conflict with Mencius' theory of the goodness of human nature.

I will now look at the doctrine of original sin. This doctrine can by no means be reduced to the simplistic assertion that people are by nature evil, especially, morally evil. On the level of moral metaphysics, Christian theologians shared with Confucians the view that all nature, in so far as it is created by God, is fundamentally good. Human nature in particular is good since people were made according to the image of God. Augustine explained moral evil in terms of aversion (or, more precisely, perversion) of true nature. Evil is not, properly speaking, a nature and consequently has no real existence; it is only the privation of existence. He thus denied the evil of human nature in the ontological sense of the term.[8]

According to some theologians, even after the fall, when human nature had become corrupted it had not completely lost the goodness God created in human beings. In philosophical and theological terms, the unchangeable goodness of human nature consists either in freedom of will, and/or in the truthfulness of reason (ratio), and/or in the innocence of conscience (*synderesis*). Thomas Aquinas, for example, wrote, "what is natural to man was neither taken away nor added to him by sins" and "since human nature is not so completely corrupted by sin as to be totally lacking in natural goodness, it is possible for him in the state of corrupted nature to do some particular good things by virtue of his nature."[9]

Admittedly, almost all theologians have insisted that the goodness of human nature is so weak in its corrupted state that human beings are incapable of saving themselves; hence, they need grace. Generally speaking, the Christian view on human nature holds that it is a mixture of good and evil (as did the Confucian Yang Xiong). Nevertheless, Christian theologians did not spend as much time, as Confucians did, on clarifying the level, distinction and inter-relationship between good and evil in human nature. The doctrine of original sin often appears ambiguous on the question whether human nature is good or evil. This is probably a partial reason why the struggle of the Catholic Church with Pelagianism on the issue of freedom of will in the Middle Ages became so entangled that, even the orthodox position could not extricate itself from the accusation of semi-Peligianism by Martin Luther. Even so, the ambiguous view on the mixture of good and evil implied in the notion of original sin, in the final analysis, in no way contradicts the clear view on the level and distinction of good and evil of the theory of the goodness of human nature.

THEORETICALLY COMPLEMENTARY

The pre-condition of sin is free will. This should be judged as one of the most important contributions of Christianity to ethics. One of the general principles of ethics is that a person is responsible only for what he or she freely chooses. Thus, if there were no free choice there would be no moral responsibility.

The Christian doctrine of original sin speaks of the will in terms of capacity to make free choices, but it also stresses that the will is not equally free to choose between good and evil. Otherwise, the will would be as perplexed as Buridan's ass which was unable to decide which haystack it should turn to eat. There is a tendency inherent in free choice to choose good over evil. According to Augustine, the hierarchy of nature was created in such a way that the lower should obey the higher. Since desire is a faculty lower than reason, the will naturally tends to choose reason, to which desire subordinates itself. Yet, in the dispute with Pelagianism, he stressed that human beings have lost free will and are in need of Grace to recover it. Anselm of Canterbury amended this with his own doctrine of free choice. He insisted that the capacity for free choice can never be lost no matter what the condition. What was lost after the fall was the actual tendency towards good.[10] Thomas Aquinas accepted the Aristotelian notion of prudent reason as the deliberative decision in the procedure of choosing good ends and means. He defined will as "rational volition".[11] Later, Martin Luther attacked the scholastic doctrine of freedom of will, but he did not, as he is unjustly accused of, give up the notion of the freedom of the individual. He declared in a well-known statement, "A Christian is a perfectly free lord of all, subject to none, A Christian is a perfectly dutiful servant of all, subject to all."[12]

In summary, the doctrine of original sin does not content itself with the natural tendency towards good, but emphasizes the difficulty of choosing good and avoiding evil in the state of human corruption. In this way, it intensifies the Christian duty before God, and cultivates the personal consciousness of moral responsibility. Basically, Christianity provides both exterior and interior incentives to morality. The exterior factor is the divine imperative. The interior factor is freedom of will in choosing between good and evil.

Confucian ethics, on the other hand, regards moral prescripts and actions as the autonomous realization of a human nature that is intrinsically good. Confucius said, "seeking for humanity and then gain it" (求仁而得仁) and "I wish humanity, and then it reaches to me."(吾欲仁，斯仁至矣。)[13] Mencius' theory of the goodness of human nature, as has been seen, aims at the a priori origin of morality. All of these entail the notion of the autonomy of morality. Confucians always insisted that ethical norms flow from the heart of people and follow the principle of heaven. As such, they are based on autonomous self-restraint and not determined by heteronymous imperatives.

Confucians assigned to sages the status of law-givers. Sages formulated moral rules in accordance with the Heavenly principle. Confucius and Mencius seemed to stress natural inclination rather than artificial formulation. Confucius said, "Establish what I want for myself, then establish it for man. Achieve what I want for myself, then achieve it for man. To be able to judge of others in analogy to what is close to me, this can be said as the rightness of humanity."[14] Mencius said, "The ancients who did not make big mistakes is good at extending what he did for himself."[15]

More importantly, the universal validity and applicability of the moral law were explained by the common good nature shared by sages and ordinary people. In Mencius words, "sages and I belong to the same species", "Emperor Shun is a man, I am a man, too", and hence, "Everybody can become Emperor Yao and Emperor Shun".[16]

From what has been stated above, it follows that the theory of the goodness of human nature is the foundation of the Confucian idea of the autonomy of morality. This idea was weakened, even ignored in history in circumstances in which Confucian ethics and doctrine of Heart were, used by political rulers as coercive codes and rules. The doctrine of Heart, as presented by Lu Jouyuan (1139-1193)and Wang Yangming (1472-1528), made a great effort to revive the Confucian notion of autonomy. Its ideas include the original heart of humanity and justice, the moral practice as reaching one's own conscience, the natural flowing of original heart, against sophisticated rites and contrived decorum. The historical significance of those ideas can be evaluated on the basis of the relation of the theory of the goodness of human nature to the autonomy of morality.

The above analysis reveals the possibility that Confucianism and Christianity can complement each other. The God of Christianity is an absolute law-giver. His transcendence and the unbridgeable gap between God and humans make it difficult for Christian prescripts to be autonomous. Some theologians, for example, Thomas Aquinas, often appealed to the Stoic notion of natural law to defend moral autonomy. Nevertheless, the autonomous acceptance of natural law can hardly avoid the negative effect of original sin within the framework of religious faith. The Christian theory of natural law is not as successful as that of the Stoics, nor is it as coherent as that of the Confucians.

The Confucian theory of the goodness of human nature, on the other hand, attributed the failure to realize the good nature to unnatural or pervasive conditions and accidental ignorance. This often resulted in decrease in moral enthusiasm and a reduction in the sense of responsibility. In circumstances, unfavorable to moral practice, the theory of the goodness of human nature could be misused to ease the rigorous conflict between good and evil, and often failed to provide sufficient incentive for good to overcome evil. Due to the lack of moral incentive, the autonomy of morality remained, throughout most of Chinese history, for the majority of ordinary people, only an unrealized ideal.

I thus venture to suggest that the Confucian idea of moral autonomy be complemented with the Christian incentive to moral choice, in order to develop the advantages, as well as to avoid the disadvantages, of both parties.

PRACTICALLY PLAYING A SIMILAR MORAL ROLE

Both the theory of the goodness of human nature and the doctrine of original sin stressed the necessity of perfecting human nature and urged people to meet some moral demands. Both Confucian and Christian ethical demands can be classified into two kinds: to purify one's own mind, and to commit oneself to a social career.

The goodness of human nature, as Confucians affirmed, is an innate predisposition that is realized in practice. They also acknowledged that this predisposition can be hindered, averted, weakened, even destroyed by various social factors and by people themselves. Confucianism emphatically teaches self-cultivation. The Confucians of the Song Dynasty adopted from the ancient maxim that "the human heart is endangered, the rational heart is to be refined and unified, keep the middle way", in order to encourage themselves to overcome dangerous desires and to develop Heavenly reason in one's heart. Confucianism is also committed to a social ethics. It is well known that its teachings consisted in assigning social duties to individuals according to their particular status. Confucian self-cultivation is a preparation for moral action on a large scale. The eight items in the book "Great Learning" are: investigation of things, extension of knowledge, being sincere in will, rectifying mind, self-cultivation, regulating one's family, governing the state, bringing about peace all over the world. For the superior man, these cover completely the whole domain of moral demands, from the personal to the social, from interior to exterior.

Max Weber regarded Confucianism as a totally secular ethics. Its objective was, he believed, to accommodate people to this world. He contrasted it with the active attitude of the Puritans towards the transformation of this world in accordance with the ideal of the world beyond. I am convinced, however, that Confucian ethics was characterized by a combination of secular and holy values. Needless to say, Confucianism played an active role in Chinese society. It did not merely seek a passive accommodation with this world. When the actual state of affairs was contrary to the Confucian ideal, the Chinese gentleman, in accordance with the dictates of the Confucian ideal, sought to rectify bad habits, amend the unhealthy mind, and improve social conditions. The Confucian ideal for society and the world is not revolutionary, yet it does not lack a progressive or evolutionary outlook.

In contrast to Confucianism, early Christianity was not actively engaged in social and political activities. For many Christians the primary concern was with the salvation of their individual souls. The prevailing mode of the early monastic system was influenced by St. Paul's notion of sin, which stressed spiritual struggle against sin. He said: "I myself, subject to God's law as a rational being, am yet, in my unspiritual nature, a slave to the law of sin" (Romans 7:25). Admittedly, the ascetic and mystical exercises undertaken for personal salvation did not preclude a commitment to social welfare on the part of the early monasteries and churches. During the period when the Church was the dominant power, it often intervened in political and other social matters. It is also true, no doubt, as Weber pointed out, that in the history of Christianity, Protestants, especially, puritans, were the most active in economic, political and scientific endeavors. However, in my opinion, the difference between Confucianism and Puritanism lies in the aspect of transformation and not, as Weber assumed, in the attitude towards this world.

NOTES

1 Max Weber, *The Religion of China*, trans. by H.H. Gerth, Free Press, 1951, p.214.

2 James Legge, *Prolegomena of Mencius' Work*, in *Chinese Classics*, vol. 2, Clarendon Press, Oxford, 1895, p.26.

3 The word yi (义) was translated as righteousness. I prefer to translate it as rightness.

4 Mencius Books, 6A:6.

5 Hsun Tzu, "On Nature", in *A Source Book in Chinese Philosophy*, transl. by Wing-Tsit chan, Princeton University Press, 1963, p.116.

6 Mencius Books, 7B:24.

7 Li Ao, "The Recovery of Nature", cf. *A Source Book in Chinese Philosophy*, pp.456-8.

8 *The Complete Work of Chu His*, 62-66, in *A Source Book in Chinese Philosophy*, pp.623-5.

9 Augustine, *On Free Will*, ii, 19.

10 Thomas Aquinas, *Summa Theologia*, I, i, 98, 2.

11 "Freedom of Chioce", I, in *Anselm of Canterbury*, ed. by J. Hopkins and H. Richardson, vol, II, Edwin Mellen, Toronto, 1976, pp.105-6

12 *Summa Theologia*, I, ii, 6, 2.

13 *Luther Works*, (Weimar edition), 7:21.1ff.

14 Analects,7:14, 29.

15 Analects, 6:28.

16 Mencius Books, 1A:7.

17 Ibid., 6A:7, 6B:2.

Comments on the Papers of
Tu Weiming, Vincent Shen and Zhao Dunhua:
From a Historian's Point of View

Daniel H. Bays

The topic of this session, 'Dialogue between Confucianism and Christianity,' could be approached from many different angles, including those of linguistic analysis or translation, debates between representatives of believers or adherents on both sides, social scientific methods of sociologists or anthropologists, and of course philosophy, as we have here today. I am a historian thrown in among all you philosophers, and I am struck by the tendency towards large generalization and linguistic creativity in all of these papers—especially Prof. Tu Wei-ming's marvelous creation of the term "anthropocosmic." Actually the term works all right in the context in which he explains the concepts behind it; but it was nevertheless new to me. And another surprise to me was Prof. Vincent Shen's word "strangification," which I realize he has used before, and apparently is not new to philosophers, but it was to me, a simple historian.

Historians for the most part look with suspicion on large general statements, and even with suspicion on large entities or subjects of discussion and analysis—like Confucianism and Christianity. Our tendencies are to look for the incomplete, the exception to the dominant pattern, the varieties of explanations that might be adduced to explain something that has happened in the past. We are usually hesitant to explain causation without noting countervailing trends or cases that don't fit the template we're creating. Sometimes we get taken up by case studies and concrete examples and neglect the larger picture.

So as a historian, what I would instinctively do as a first step with this Confucianism-Christianity issue and the dialogue or interaction or linkage between them is to look for historical patterns, concrete cases of individuals or groups who tried to identify with both sides, and how they did it. In other words, to look at cases of self-consciously "Confucian Christians" or "Christian Confucians," people or groups reasonably familiar with the essentials of both, and who tried to *be* both. The next step would be to consider the authenticity and outcomes of their attempts, including the previous debates among historians over some of these people and the success or failure of their attempt to be both Confucian and Christian.[1]

A quick look through my own library reveals a number of Chinese Confucians who seem to have considered themselves to be still fully Confucians even after they converted to Christianity and were baptized. Of course there are the oft-cited 'three pillars' of the church in late Ming, who, Willard Peterson claims, among other reasons which varied, all converted because they "found in [Christianity] a moral discipline based upon an external ...force."[2] (And to "fortify traditional values" that were eroding). And David Mungello convincingly (to me, at least) describes the late 17th century Hangzhou Christian leader, Zhang Xingyao, as being an authentic Christian and still a full-fledged Confucian.[3]

Let's move on to the 19th and 20th centuries. The first important Protestant convert, Liang Fa, who converted before 1820, was not highly educated but very sincere in his Confucian values and ethics, and distressed that he did not have the power to live up to these ethical demands. In the "moral monotheism" of Protestant Christianity, i.e. the moral seriousness of monotheism, as well as in the concept of the power of the Holy Spirit, Liang Fa (according to Richard Bohr) found the means by which to live up to, or to believe he was capable of living up to, his Confucian ethical standards.[4] There are other cases of self-conceived Confucian Christians in the 19th century, although interestingly some foreign missionaries in these decades did not believe that the two were compatible. Some of the most virulent opposition to missionaries from the 1860s to 1900 was clearly led by die-hard Confucians, leading some missionaries to despair of the Confucian elite ever abating its opposition to Christianity.[5] And yet the most celebrated convert of the theologically conservative China Inland Mission of Hudson Taylor in the entire 19th century was "Pastor Hsi" (Xi Shengmo, Xi the demon-queller) of Shanxi province, who as portrayed in the missionary literature remained staunchly loyal to his Confucian identity even as he took on the identity of Christian and pastor.[6]

In the early 20th century, in the last years of the Qing dynasty, a significant part of an entire generation of young people well educated in the traditional Confucian-centered fashion was confronted with the abolition of the clearly obsolete examination system in 1905, and then with the final death throes of the dynasty. These young Confucian-trained scholars, born from the late 1880s to the mid-1990s, during the few years just before and just after the 1911 Revolution and the establishment of the new Republic, converted to Christianity in striking numbers in comparison with previous generations of Confucians-in-training. But on the whole they remained discernibly "Confucian" as well. Philip West's fine book on Yenching University, which has stood the test of time magnificently almost 30 years after publication, contains trenchant capsule biographies of the five major Chinese activists in the Life Fellowship (Sheng-ming she).[7] These, all members of the school of religion at Yenching, were Liu Tingfang (T. T. Lew, 1891-1947); Wu Leichuan (1870-1944), a degree holder and a *hanlin* scholar in the late Qing; Xu Baoqian (1892-1944), whose conversion created in him a self-consciously Confucian identity underlying the new Christian identity; Zhao Zichen (1888-1979), China's foremost theologian of the 20th century; and Hong Ye (William Hung, 1893-1980), perhaps the best scholar of the lot, who repeatedly averred that he was both Confucian and Christian.[8]

Therefore, from my vantage point as a historian it is clear that some, perhaps many, modern Chinese intellectuals have considered themselves both

Confucian and Christian. Surely this indicates successful dialogue—unless these people were deluded, and we can show that they really weren't Confucians—or Christians—after all.

Confucianism and Christianity both were targets of many attacks in recent decades, from the May 4th movement to mass campaigns which erupted periodically during the years of the People's Republic of China after 1949. Christianity was routinely reviled for cultural aggression against China, and Confucianism has been seen as responsible for China's perceived backwardness, social class divisions, gender inequities, and unwillingness to give up tradition for "progress." In the early 1970s Lin Biao was posthumously proven rotten to the core by associating him with Confucius. Despite these 20th-century traumas, Christianity has survived very well. I'm not so sure about Confucianism. How many Chinese in the PRC today identify themselves as *ru*, "Confucian" (in values, ethics, behavior, child-rearing techniques, any aspect of life)? I don't know more than a handful of possibles, and perhaps there are almost none. What an irony for "dialogue" between two systems of thought and belief to end because there are no more Confucians with whom to dialogue. Perhaps what remains of Confucianism is contained in the hybrid entity "Confucian Christian," or "Christian Confucian."

NOTES

1 Not surprisingly, I have in mind here the extensive debates over the claims of Jacques Gernet, *China and the Christian Impact: A Conflict of Cultures* (1985), that Christianity and Confucianism were utterly incompatible.

2 "Why did they become Christians?..." in Ronan and Oh, eds., *East Meets West, the Jesuits in China, 1582-1773* (1988)

3 *The Forgotten Christians of Hangzhou* (1994).

4 "Liang Fa's Quest for Moral Power," in S. Barnett and J.K. Fairbank, eds., *Christianity in China: Early Protestant Missionary Writings* (1985).

5 Note from 1877 or 1890 big meeting record, or one of Griffith John's diatribes.

6 The CIM printed and reprinted this book for decades. Mrs Howard Taylor, *Pastor Hsi, Confucian Scholar and Christian* (first publ. 1900, 20th ed. revised, 1949).

7 *Yenching University and Sino-Western Relations, 1916-1952* (1976).

8 Ibid., ch. 3. An excellent book on Hong Ye, partially based on extensive interviews with him during the last two years of his life, is Susan Chan Egan, *A Latterday Confucian: Reminiscences of William Hung (1893-1980)* (1987).

Commentary 2

Comments on the Papers of
Tu Weiming, Vincent Shen and Zhao Dunhua:
From a Theological Point of View

Evyn Adams

Tu Weiming

From the basic presuppositions of Confucianism as explained by Tu Weiming it becomes clear that the basis of Confucianism is an "anthropocosmic" view of the world or the cosmos. Philosophically this is an inference or an a priori drawn from nature; religiously it is an initial assumption of faith in the order of things.[1] There is no myth or story of creation but an assumption of the eternal cycle of yin and yang of nature or heaven; time always was and will always continue. Hence the revelation that comes to Confucius is from the natural world.

Comparing this with Christianity we note some major differences. God (or Heaven) is the creator of the cosmos. Christians believe that God created the world *ex nihilo*, out of nothing, e.g. God minus the cosmos is still God. Along with nature, time was created, so Christianity has a linear definition of history. There is a beginning, there is a mid-point that reveals its meaning (Christ, the Cross and the Resurrection) and there will be an end, which will usher in a new Creation. The revelation that comes to the .Christians is from God and is mediated by Scripture with an historical focal point in Christ.

Vincent Shen

Another name for this theme from the Christian standpoint is "Concern for the world and its peoples". The concern of God (His *Pathos*), the search for a people in the Old Testament, the Prophet's cry for this concern (Prophetic *Pathos*) and the concern of Jesus in his passion, the ending of the New Testament in the concern of the revelation of John, all speak to this world wide view. The ethos of this concern however is not just generosity or recognition of the rights of the "other", but the salvation of the "other". The making of a holy people is the final motivation.

Confucius too, was concerned about the morality of the man who was aware of the nature of things. The Confucian sage merges into a saint, a holy person. So the difference is found in the means of transformation of character. But Vincent Shen's point that Confucianism must become global is well-taken.

Zhao Dunhua

The interpretation of the meaning of original sin varies in Christianity according to the standpoint of the school of theology doing the examining. Reformed Theology, Luther, Calvin and the Reformed Theologians follow Augustine's statements to the point where Grace and God's Concern are unilaterally applied in the salvation theory, leaving little or no space for man's initiative.

However, Catholic Theology, the Theology of the Church of England, Wesleyan Theology and Eastern Orthodoxy adopt a more moderate stance in which there is a synergism of the work of Man and God in salvation as their theological basis. Added to this is the ongoing activity of the Holy Spirit. John Wesley restated this position clearly when he termed it "Prevenient Grace", or the ongoing activity of the Holy Spirit within each individual person.It is true the John Wesley saw that the moral aspect of the Image of God was destroyed, but the natural and political aspects still remained. He maintained that the Holy Spirit along with the Evangelical announcement of God's Grace and Forgiveness worked in man's heart and soul to bring about repentance.

Hence salvation is the restoration of the Image of God in man, in making him righteous and holy.Therefore, the mediating position in Christian Theology fits more directly into Professor Zhao's thesis than does Reformed Theology. Semi-Pelagianism and the prevenient work of the Holy Spirit fit more closely with the Confucian understanding of human nature.

NOTE

1 See Rodney L. Taylor: "Religious Dimensions of Confucianism" SUNY Press, 1990.

Part III

Dialogue between

Islamic and Western Civilizations

Chapter 9

Advances and Deadlocks of the Dialogue of Philosophy in an Era of Globalization

Seyyed Mohammed Khamenei

'In the Name of God, the Compassionate, the Merciful'

DIALOGUE AND COMPARISON

From a philosophical point of view, one of the specific features of human beings is their ability to dialog with each other and exchange their ideas. Such acts are not limited to philosophers or philosophy; however, there is always a philosophy behind them. According to Socrates, reality can be obtained through a correct definition of concepts and words. Dialog not only help to clarify the intentions of the two sides, but also leads to numerous social effects and consequences. This is because the resulting agreements can be used to remove the fallacies and contradictions and avoid violent conflicts and confrontations, which are typically beastly. It is crystal clear that in this way, peace and comfort could be established at all levels of life, even at an international level. As Rumi, the Iranian poet, says, when personal desires and intentions are put away, everybody attains peace of mind.

Here, we can conclude that the purpose of having dialog is to remove disagreements and reconcile differences. Therefore, when we speak of dialog in the era of globalization at an international level, we are not referring to discussing diplomacy, short-term policies, or economic demands and achievements. Rather, we are referring to dialog among various cultures, philosophies, and civilizations to develop a safe world and establish a just and peaceful system of government. This purpose can be obtained only when cultures and philosophies are ready to have such dialog.

In order to study the context of this dialog, the perspective of a united world, and the role of a dialog among eastern and western philosophies in this regard, it is necessary to cast a glance at past and present philosophies and the principles and purposes of eastern and western schools of thought. According to the studies done by some researchers working in the field of philosophy, the cradle of this field of science and its place of growth was a region between Iran and the subcontinent of India. They also maintain that philosophy traveled from this place to Ionia, Byzantium, southern Italy, and Mediterranean islands and shores. It was developed in Greece in the time of Thales and Pythagoras and journeyed to Iskandariyyah, Northern Africa, and Northern Saudi Arabia Peninsula in later times. After a halt, with the rise of Islam it went to the present Iraq. In the second Islamic century (the 8th Christian century), a great number of books written on philosophy and other sciences were translated from the Syriac and Greek languages into Arabic. It did not take long before philosophy reached its culmination in the works of such Iranian thinkers and geniuses as Farabi and Ibn Sina. They increased the number of philosophical issues threefold.[1] With the transfer of Islam to Spain, philosophy, Islamic gnosis, and other sciences traveled to that country, too. Following this, a number of prominent scientists appeared in that land and some important libraries were opened in its cities, including Toledo.

Upon the Christian domination of Spain, according to the Pope's order, all the scientific, philosophical, and law books of Muslims were translated into Latin. The priests of that time taught and discussed these books in the schools affiliated with the Roman church. It did not take long before philosophers such as Albert and Thomas Aquinas continued the tradition of Scholastic philosophy as a branch of Islamic philosophy in Europe. In the Renaissance period and after the French revolution, the major social constitutions in Europe underwent certain changes. Due to their detest for religious authorities, people left the churches and turned their backs even on Scholastic philosophy. The official enmity of the church with sciences made some scholars and scientists such as Galileo and Bacon stand against it. Descartes was the first western philosopher who based philosophy on a series of new principles. In fact, the modern period of philosophy and philosophical thought started at that time.

Nevertheless, western philosophy did not comply with Descartes completely. Rather, since his ideas and thoughts represented a raw and vulnerable philosophy in comparison to Islamic philosophy, each of the thinkers followed a different way after his demise. In England, Hobbes and Frances Bacon, and, after them, John Locke and Hume founded practical and theoretical philosophy on the basis of the senses, the negation of dogmatism, and a denial of spirituality. In contrast to the current stream of thought in England and France, Kant, the German philosopher, based his philosophy on Idealism. Later, some other thinkers such as Hegel, Fichte, and Schelling followed his philosophy, creating a few changes in it.

In the 19th and 20th centuries, the existing philosophical thought in Europe and North America was transformed, and a number of philosophical schools such as Existentialism, Phenomenology, analytic philosophy, linguistic philosophy, and pragmatism came upon the scene. After a short while, the star of such schools set in the west and the thinkers of this region shifted their attention to hermeneutics.

At the same time that western philosophy was fast branching out in a chaotic patter, every once in a while one of the philosophers of the West founded an independent school in his own name and dismissed others' ideas. Islamic and Chinese philosophies experienced a different process of development. It enjoyed stability and continuity, and followed a 'linear', perfectional, and conjunctive system. For instance, four centuries ago, a number of apparently opposed Islamic schools of thought such as Peripatetic philosophy, Illuminationism, and gnosis were combined with each other by the prominent Iranian philosopher, Mulla Sadra, and formed the body of a unitary school of thought called 'the Transcendent Philosophy'. Following this, philosophy experienced a rapid and outstanding process of growth and development and its waves touched the shores of other countries. It is now the right place to cast an analytic and comparative glance at the present eastern and western philosophies of the world and compare their basic principles with each other.

AN ANALYTIC VIEW OF DIFFERENT SCHOOLS OF PHILOSOPHY

As we know, each philosophy is founded on a series of basic principles. On the whole, except for a few pseudo-gnostic schools of thought or those following Thomas Aquinas, post-Renaissance western philosophy is based on a few principles,-- the most important of which include materialism, sensualism, the centrality of man, and relativity of ethics. We can see the traces of these principles among English philosophers from Hobbes, John Locke, and Hume to Russell and Wittgenstein; in such German philosophers as Kant, Hegel, Fichte, Schelling, Nietzsche, Schopenhauer; in 20th century Christian philosophers; and in French thinkers from Descartes to Sartre, Foucault, Ricco, and Derrida. The journey of European philosophy to America was not very fruitful and resulted in the addition of such new principles as pragmatism, utilitarianism, and literalism to philosophy.

The above schools rely on their personal benefits (short-term), and are heedless of man's inner and spiritual needs and happiness; they play with ethics and deprive man's true rights and dignity of their real meaning. One of the distinctive features of most western philosophies is their being occupied with abstract issues and taking no heed of the real man living in the present human society. By this man, we mean a person who enjoys external reality, has to be helped for his happiness and welfare and protected against injustice, and should be given advice about how to defend his rights. The main purpose of Islamic and other eastern philosophies, as well as the most important mission of all prophets and sages, is to help this man.

There are certain principles in Islamic and eastern philosophies which are completely in contrast to western principles. Islamic philosophy and the Chinese and Indian philosophies (eastern schools) are mainly based on realism and belief in the two worlds of sense and reality beyond the senses. They also believe in the absoluteness of the established ethical principles, the Almighty God, and the relation between the earth and the world above in the heavens.

Differences in principles are also reflected in the purposes, features, and functions of philosophies. This is exactly similar to how the chemical characteristics of elements determine the possibility or impossibility of their synthesis with each other. As mentioned before, eastern and Islamic philosophies are fundamentally different from the common philosophies followed by politicians and programmers in the West. Such a difference in principles affects their applications as well and, as we can see, the western societies and cultures allow individualism, heedlessness to moral values and principles, materialism and love of wealth, free sexual relations as is seen in animals, and great violence in so-called civilized environments. Western values, which are the offsprings of western philosophies and cultures, are in harsh contrast to Islamic and eastern values. This is the very reason why we can never agree on a common criterion for a dialog among philosophies and cultures. That is also why such a dialog is almost impossible. It is also likely that one side gives up its own culture, historical traditions, and national and religious values to the advantage of the other.

The purposes are also inconsistent in eastern and western philosophies and cultures. This is because the western culture does not much believe in spirituality and views everything in the light of materiality and dependence on the present. It demands everything for itself and seeks material pleasures. Such purposes affect the western man's social, political, economic, and cultural behavior and promote his selfishness and love of power. As mentioned above, the purposes in Islamic and eastern gnosis and philosophy are totally different from those in the western world. In Islamic thought, the purpose of knowing philosophy or wisdom is to develop a correct and all-inclusive world-view, and, as a result, devise a good program for a safe world which guarantees happiness, security, and comfort even in the world after death.

In Chinese philosophies, for example, in those of Buddha, Laotze, and Confucius, some programs are suggested for true happiness and welfare in individual and social life. In Islamic and eastern philosophy, 'ethics' has some absolute and universal criteria and is not relative. Here, material affairs and sense phenomena are considered a part of the reality rather than all of it. All the related religions preach that human beings should do as they would want others to do to them. In such religions, the worldly life is related to the heavens and God Who has created man and loves him. They maintain that man is not the center of the world; rather, he depends on it.

In the Islamic and eastern philosophies, extreme individualism is prohibited and people are encouraged to philanthropy and altruism. Such schools have had some great achievements and trained a number of distinguished figures in different periods. In fact, they are the origin of some great civilizations to which the West owes a great debt. However, western philosophies have never been able to create any characters, civilizations, or societies like the ones created by Islamic and eastern philosophies. In contrast, the present corrupt western thought is the outcome of the western philosophies developed by modernism. Moreover, the winds of its tornado have also endangered and corrupted other healthy and secure societies.

In addition to the essential differences between eastern and western philosophies, there are some other problems hindering the dialog, and they are as follows:

(1) The prerequisite for having a dialog is to begin from a common point and follow some shared goals. Nevertheless, the present western philosophies are so incoherent and scattered that none can be introduced as the representative of another. In other words, no western philosophy can be considered as the spokesperson for these many contrasting schools. Besides,

apart from their ideological roots, there are no common points among them to be considered as the center of their philosophical discussions or dialogs.

(2) Islamic and eastern philosophies, each in its own way, are ready for dialog and listening to the ideas of the other side. For example, the Holy Qur'an praises those believers "who hear advice and follow the best thereof. Such are those whom Allah guideth, and such are men of understanding." (Chapter Zumar: verses 17 and 18)

However, those who publicize globalization and advocate the related philosophies, in spite of some verbal and diplomatic ceremonies, do not view themselves as one side of the dialog. Rather, they maintain that they are higher than others and should play the role of an administrator, supervisor, and even judge of the dialog. They insist on the truth of the following dogma: "Not philosophies, but just one philosophy, and not cultures, but just one culture!" In this case, there remains no chance for Islamic and eastern philosophies to attain any success in having a dialog with the West.

(3) Globalization is, in fact, a philosophy that the West introduces in its own favor and on the basis of the philosophy of utilitarianism and pragmatism, in which there is no place for love, philanthropy, and humanism. The West is after globalization in order to secure its political purposes and establish its strategy of hegemony, rather than to provide people with happiness and safety. Eastern nations have no share in this process. However, Islamic and eastern philosophies represent universal thoughts that, in addition to introducing the world from a philosophical point of view, work in favor of the entire humanity. From a political and social point of view, they wish happiness and prosperity for all, without having one or some nations dominating others. They are for true and sincere peace and freedom rather than for hypocritical ones.

For instance, in the light of Islamic mysticism, thinkers try to publicize altruism and humanism. The Iranian poet, Saadi, says in this regard, "I love the whole world; since it belongs to Him". However, such a doctrine is absent in western philosophies, particularly in the theory of globalization.

NATURE OF GLOBALIZATION

It is now necessary to have a look at the nature of globalization and its historical background and purposes and to examine the possibility of a dialog among various philosophies and the different views in this regard in the world of today. The phenomenon of globalization (which the Judeo-Christian West publicizes) is often introduced merely in terms of its economic or commercial dimensions. Nevertheless, a major part of this phenomenon pertains to the globalization of a single culture (the western one) and a single philosophy and weakening the political, legal, traditional, cultural, and even linguistic borderlines. The western theoretician, Fukuyama, refers to it as 'the end of history', and Huntington stipulates that this phenomenon will arise as a result of the confrontations of cultures and civilizations, and, consequently, that American culture will be dominant and globalized.

This doctrine has a historical record in Europe. It started with the Westphalia peace treaty and encouraged European countries to attack other nations in other continents in order to put an end to civil wars in Europe and the wars between Christian governments. Thereafter, the road was paved for exploitation and colonialization of Asian and African nations.

The purpose of the church in doing so was the globalization of Christianity along with looting the natural resources of Asia and Africa. It also intended to found a hegemony of Christian Europe over the world under the pretext of modernism and civilizing the backward nations. Nowadays, the above policy is employed on the basis of the previous experience and another thesis inspired by a racist religion. It also follows some other political-religious purposes as well. Some of the Presidents of the United States of America have advocated this policy under various pretenses such as defending the human rights, establishing democracy, fighting terrorism, and the like.

Following the disintegration of the ex-Soviet Union, the Western imperialism has always followed the policy of monopolizing political and economical power and establishing a single universal system whose body consists of capitalism and liberalism (the legacy of the 19th century) and whose soul consists of the present western culture (in more exact terms, the degenerated American culture). This pole intends to break the 19th century European hegemony as old and reactionary, to destroy it, and to take control of its economy.

The designers of this policy refute any philosophy that theorizes against this thesis. In other words, they maintain that, due to the development of means of communication, the world has become smaller (and insist on calling it a small village). Thus there is no choice but to have only one leader, one culture, and one philosophy in the world and have all its people think in the same way. Globalization has started with employing uniform laws and principles in commerce; however, the words of western authorities and politicians indicate that the purpose of this policy is to establish uniformity in other areas as well, even in such fields as culture and religion. They also purport to destroy everything which is against the western logic in this regard under the pretext of its being an obstacle in the path towards globalization.

They emphasize that cultures should be integrated in the globalization era so that a unitary and borderless culture is born. In so doing, all dissenting cultures and religions have to be either destroyed or totally isolated and individualized. Following this, governments having an ideology or, in the legal sense of the term, 'independent governments', must be disarmed (i.e. be deprived of their independence) and turned into parts of a common and universal government, follow a single system, and advocate a single culture and philosophy. Moreover, all cultures, the internal affairs of all countries, and international relations must be controlled by a central government that is naturally at work in the United States of America.

They claim that this controlling system is based on a number of 'scientific and cybernetic principles'. This centralized government can make cultures and impose its favorite culture and philosophy on the world. This is because according to such principles, one who wishes to obtain political power must first obtain cultural power. It is said that an "ideological majority is more important than parliamentary majority". If this universal culture is the very commonplace and semi-wild western culture, it will result in man's humiliation and deprivation of his spiritual dignity. And if it is philosophy itself that thinks about nothing but animal desires, violence, and dominance over others and is based on Machiavellian, materialistic, and utilitarian principles, only God knows what will happen to the future of the world and civilizations with thousands of years of history that have tried to raise man and make him distinct from animals.

Considering the above-mentioned points, we should examine the perspective of a dialog between Islamic and eastern philosophies, on the one hand, and western philosophy, on the other hand, from an academic point of view. We should also see whether it is theoretically possible to have such a dialog or not. Still a related question is: considering the huge distance, which is referred to as 'the great gap' in the present political literature, between the East and the West and their cultures and philosophies, are we justified in predicting that all the people working in this regard will finally face a deadlock?

The myth and utopia of globalization is against eastern philosophies, traditions, and values both theoretically and practically and aims at obtaining cultural and political hegemony over others. Thus one might doubt the chances for having a successful dialog between the philosophies of these two sides. Moreover, he might ask if there any way beyond the possible deadlocks in this dialog.

CONCLUSION

If we view the issue of globalization and the dialogue between eastern and western philosophies in the era of globalization, the only (wise) way to break the related deadlocks seems to be a dialogue based on a number of strict principles securing the happiness and prosperity of all humanity in a world in which dominance of one nation over others is totally refuted.

The proximity of eastern philosophies to each other, the theoretical unity of Islamic and Chinese schools of thought, and devising some common practical programs for reviving human rights and establishing true peace and justice in the world in the light of a universal policy could brighten the horizons of hope for all people. According to Lorenz, "A butterfly stirring the air today in Beijing can transform storm systems next month in New York." It is hoped that the efforts to arrange dialog among different philosophies and cultures in a safe context will result in many positive effects in a world that is considered small. May the efforts consolidate the bases of peace and justice in the world. May the sun rise in the East as always.

NOTE

1 It is said that the problems were originally 200 in number but were increased to 700 by Iranian philosophers.

Chapter 10

Is a Dialogue between
Western and Islamic Civilizations Possible?

Marietta Stepanyants

It might sound strange that I question the possibility of the dialogue between the two civilizations at the time when there is so much talk around about the significance of that dialogue. It is true that the most respectable international organizations, like the UNO, the governments of the states, the prominent public spokesmen everywhere speak about the dialogue between civilizations. Yet, let us be frank, little has been achieved to eliminate tension, hostility and aggressiveness. Wars and terrorist actions are increasing in number. It is quite legitimate then to ask the above question, keeping in mind that we talk about the dialogue in the context of a new world situation - in the time of globalization.

There are certainly those who will answer to the question negatively. Some of them "respond" by actions: launching wars and terrorist attacks. These are those who not only disbelieve in dialogues, but strongly resist the latter due to different reasons (mostly, quite selfishly political and economic). The only way to prevent that dangerous development is to oppose it by really strong pressure on behalf of the widest public opinion. It is here that the role and responsibility of the intellectuals are of the greatest importance.

Unfortunately, even among the enlightened minds there are disbelievers in the possibility and fruitfulness of the dialogue. At the Ninths East-West Philosophers' Conference in Honolulu one of the most respected and prominent philosophers admitted that he doubted the usefulness of intercultural dialogues about which there is so much fuss. Cultural plurality, to his view, will become as useless as differences in currencies since the process of cultural hybridization would result eventually in the unification of all cultures in one.

Unanimity does not exist even in the ranks of those who formally accept the dialogue of cultures. They greatly differ in the understanding of its final purposes. To a few the dialogue should be aimed at the creation of one (their own) civilization dominant over the others by "convincing" the latter of its superiority. Some claim "the European *mission civilisatrice*" eventually will make the rest of the world "see the advantage of a democratic way of life". Others, like Francis Fukuyama, declare "the end of history because there is only one system that will continue to dominate world politics, that of the liberal-democratic West". He is sure that time is on the side of modernity, and "sees no lack of the US will to prevail"[1].

The strongest opposition to the above mentioned claims comes from the side the Muslim world. The resistance comes from many sides: from those who are in power or fight for it, from masses who suffer from social injustice, from religious fanatics, etc. The Muslims not only resist, they often make their own claims for the dominance. In recent years one can notice drastic changes in the mood of the Muslim academic community which has been driven in the above mentioned direction. The prominent professor of philosophy at Cairo University, Hassan Hanafi, states:

> Islam appears as the only savior of the World. It is the foun-
> dation of a new world order. It offers a solution of the actual
> world crisis in the East as well as in the West. Islamic Umma
> is ready for it. It is the best Umma which ever existed on
> Earth. It is still the guardian of principles and the custodian
> of universal values.... Islam is the final revealed religion,
> the accomplished prophecy and the perfect model of life[2]

The confrontation between the West and the Muslim world has become so strong that it makes some lose hope in the fruitfulness of any dialogue. "It seems to me, - admits Richard Rorty, - that the idea of a dialogue
with Islam is pointless. There was no dialogue between the philosophers and
the Vatican in the eighteenth century, and there is not going to be one between
the mullahs of the Islamic world and the democratic West"[3]. I know there are
many who are ready to join this highly respected American philosopher in
his rather desperate conclusion, many, at least, among the intellectuals in my
own country. In my view, that desperation results from a number of causes,
including insufficient knowledge of a culture, measuring the latter by one's
own world-views and moral standards. Heidegger was right in saying that
the global encounter or dialogues today typically are not conducted between
cultural partners, but rather on the basis of a linguistic and conceptual framework supplied entirely by Western (or European) civilization. He called it the
"complete Europeanization [Westernization] of the earth and humankind".
     It is true that the acknowledgment of particular cultures logically
leads to making borders between that which is your own and that of the other.
Yet, there is nothing wrong in the procedure of such differentiation if it does
not end in constructing a border similar to the Berlin wall aimed to exclude
any contacts, or even more any interaction between those who are behind the
different sides of the border. In Charles Taylor's words, the accentuation of
the borders without the acknowledgment of interconnection is fraught with
a danger to stifle in us an ability to respond to the deepest and the strongest
human aspirations.[4]
     Among the frontiers established by people between themselves the
most insurmountable and impregnable seem to be those which are building
up in minds and hearts, and which originate not so much from rational considerations as from a blind belief. The latter is most unshakable when it is
religious. History has demonstrated that too often frontiers were established
in order to segregate the adherents of different religious confessions. However, paradoxically that kind of division contradicts the very assignment of

religion: to bring man close to God, and consequently, to unite people with each other. Pointing to this very function of religion, and particularly of a monotheistic creed, an outstanding Russian philosopher, Vladimir Solovyov, affirmed: "The unity of God logically demands the unity of humanity"[5].

As a matter of fact, the Holy Scriptures clearly presupposes the unity of humanity: `Is it not written "My house shall be called a house of prayer for all the nations? "' (Mark, 11:17, see also: Isa, 56:7). In the same spirit the Koran says: "It is He Who created you from a single person" (VII: 189), and "Mankind was but one nation, but differed (later)" (X: 19).

Nevertheless one might find in the Holy Scriptures a number of passages where it seems that intolerance, enmity and even violence towards the people outside one's own confession are justified. How one can explain the existence of such contradictory statements in the Holy Books? An atheist will easily respond to the question by considering religion to be created by man, and thus to be subjected to human passions, vile motives, rivalry and the fight for power. For a believer there is no way for the Lord to contradict Himself, since God is perfect, He is Absolute. Thus, what looks like contradictions in the Scriptures is explained as resulting from human misunderstanding of the true meaning of the Divine Word.

For centuries those very "contradictions" of the Holy Scriptures have been used for moral justification of hostility and even aggression towards heterodoxies. Intolerance to those behind the frontiers, who are segregated as "the others", is particularly dangerous when it is sanctified by the Divine authority. Then aggression and violence are presented as actions approved by God being aimed to bring the victory of the Good over the Evil. Thus St. Augustine's warnings are ignored: "Do not fight evil as if it were something that arose totally outside of you".

Is peaceful coexistence between people of different religious creeds at all possible? I believe the answer could be positive if there is a wish and a will to give up confrontation and to start dialogue. At what should religious dialogue be aimed; what could one expect from it? Sometimes dialogue is carried on in anticipation of a synthesis. However the latter is rarely achieved. A certain kind of syncretism might take place only as a result of long coexistence and interaction of traditions when they function on the same or at least neighboring territories. (That is, for example, how the Sikh Religion emerged in India).

More often what is called synthesis, happens to be in fact something else. For example, there have been efforts to ward a bring Christian-Muslim synthesis in the XIX-XX centuries. However, the economic and political inequality of the Muslim side has excluded a genuine synthesis. The economic superiority of the Christian world prompted the presentation of the Christian values as higher and more corresponding to the modern demands than those of Islam. Hence, "synthesis" has happened to be nothing but a superficial adjustment of the Islamic values to those of Western-Christianity. Such an imposed "synthesis" is in the long run rejected as a forced transplantation of an alien model in the "body" of Muslim culture.

Equally doubtful is the effectiveness of the ecumenical form of synthesis, in particular aimed to unite all religious creeds in a new world faith. That is how synthesis is conceived by the adherents of the Baha faith established by Baha'a'llah (1817-1892). The Bahai community counts about 3 million believers inhabiting all the continents and represents 2100 ethnic groups. The Baha faith is certainly cosmopolitan. Its leaders, like Shogi Effendi, consider that the process of the formation of sovereign national states has come to the end. The mature world should give up the fetish of national sovereignty and accept the unity of the humanity by establishing the new world order: "The Earth is but one country and mankind its citizens". Bahai preaching appeals to those who sincerely wish to overcome race, ethnic, class, religious hostility. However it is not clear how that New World Order could be achieved. The Bahai orientation to establish the New Order once and forever, to maintain it by the World State, etc. is fraught with the threat of totalitarianism.

There is also another approach to religious dialogue - a mystical one. In this case, the unity of all the religions is sought through a discovery of the perennial core. It is considered that the differences in beliefs, rituals, institutional forms which seem to be important in everyday experience fade away when we see and affirm the timeless and infinite reality that is no longer broken or differentiated into various forms. In the perennial philosophy infinite reality is compared with light: when light passes through a prism, one can see the various shades of blue, yellow, green, and red; however, no one of these colors, which are like the different cultural forms of religion, is light itself.

As there are different levels of reality (terrestrial, intermediate-psychic, celestial and infinite) there are four levels of selfhood: body, mind, soul, and spirit. The developing, ever changing religious traditions have a common core. The differences of ethical claims and the different evaluations of the life expressed in the physical world, psychic experiences, and theological expressions disappear and become one in a limitless, wholly transcendent pure consciousness, or infinite self. The purpose of the dialogue is to bring forth a deeper apprehension of the spirit, the inner identity of all religions.

The mystical approach is used by the advocates of "the perennial philosophy" like Seyid Hossein Nasr, Frithjof Schuon and Huston Smith. To those who do not share their views, still it would be difficult not to acknowledge that the mystical approach could be helpful in carrying on dialogue, in reducing confrontations based on the differences concerning theological, ethical, etc. problems. That might be an explanation why the mystical approach is rejected strongly by fanatic fundamentalists, while it is referred to by those who would like to put the end to the communal fights and tension.

In direct contrast to the mystical approach stands a dialogue carried on rational grounds by the comparativists who look at confessional differences as complementary alternatives that never could be fully eliminated. The only effective way out then is to concentrate attention on certain notions, categories, trying to grasp the logic of their emergence and formulation (for example, on the understanding of Good and Evil, on life and death, on salvation, on perfection, on salvation, etc.)

None of the participants of the dialogue has a right to claim that the fundamental principle of his/her religion (say, the Divine Trinity of the Christianity, or the finality of Muhammad's prophesy in Islam) is of universal value, and consequently should be acknowledged by everybody. Those who are engaged in the dialogue are expected to be ready to look critically at their own religious traditions and their practices, while at the same time to wish to understand the convictions and beliefs of the others. The comparative dialogue is mostly carried on by academics. It is quite effective though not free from its own shortcomings. It is criticized for being too relativist, for ignoring the transcendental Reality, and for rationalization of religious experience which never could be grasped by reason.

Still the comparative approach attracts by its orientation on creative understanding of religious cultures as such. It permits one to put to other cultures the questions which they never ask from themselves, and in this way to discover some new meaning. Every culture maintains its identity, while by "opening" themselves to each other they are mutually enriched.

Any kind of interreligious dialogue could be effective only if it is based on the acknowledgement of the equality of all sides participating in it and on mutual respect. Nor should anybody claim superiority of his/her belief and on that premise to judge what is right and what is wrong in somebody's actions. Even if it is not accepted that the law is to be administered on the secular foundations of the democratic procedures, and one insists on the rule of the Law of God, it is to be remembered that the most important attributes or names of the Lord have been Just and Merciful. "The Lord is gracious and merciful; slow to anger and abounding in steadfast love. The Lord is good to all, and his compassion is over all that He has made" (Psalms 145: 8-9). Likewise the opening *sura* of the Koran says: "...Praise be to Allah, Lord of the Worlds, the Beneficent, the Merciful, Owner of the Day of Judgment..."

Holy Scriptures prescribe to the believers to follow God's way by being merciful and avoiding violence. In fact, teachings of Christianity and of Islam, for example, consider human life to be sacred, since it is a Divine gift. The Bible recalls the saying "If a man is burdened with the blood of another, let him be a fugitive until death, let no one help him" (From the proverbs of Solomon 28:17) or "He shall judge between the nations, and shall decide for many peoples, and they shall beat their swords into plowshares, and their spears into pruning hooks. Nation shall not lift up sword against nation neither shall they learn war any more" (Isa 2:3-4).

One does not find in the Koran the same direct and clear protection of a human life. The critics of Islam would insist on the contrary, by referring to the Koran, on the justification of vengeance: "O ye who believe! The law of equality is prescribed to you in case of murder: the free for the free, the slave for the slave, the woman for the woman"(II: 178).[6] However this injunction could be understood otherwise. In fact, many Muslim interpreters insist on a quite different reading of that prescription. The Great Sheikh Ibn

Arabi in his "Gems of Wisdom" (Fusus al-Hikam) explains Koranic instruction for vengeance as the proof of God's condemnation of killing as such and
His wish to defend humanity from violence by prescribing strong punishment
for the latter (chapter 18). In fact, the Koran says: "The recompense for an
injury is an injury equal thereto (in degree): but if a person forgives and makes
reconciliation, his reward is due from God; for (God) loveth not those who do
wrong" (XLII: 40).

The critics of Islam also refer to the practice of jihad - holy war carried on by the Muslims - as a proof of the aggressive character of Muhammad's teaching. However, one should be really careful with such conclusions.
First, it should be pointed out that the Koran strongly condemns the killing
of a believer: "If a man kills a believer intentionally, his recompense is hell,
to abide therein (for ever): and the wrath and the curse of God are upon him,
and a dreadful penalty is prepared for him" (IV: 93). If killing of a believer
happens by mistake, it is also condemned and a certain kind of compensation
is to be paid to the family of the deceased.

The believers include not only the Muslims but also the people of
all the Scriptures: "Those who believe (in the Koran), those who follow the
Jewish (scriptures), and the Sabians and the Christians, - any who believe in
God and the Last Day, and work righteousness, - on them shall be no fear, nor
shall they grieve" (V: 72).

The Koran warns its adherents not to follow the advice of those who
want them to take actions of punishment without proper considerations: "Yet
they ask thee to hasten on the Punishment! But God will not fail in His promise. Verily a Day in the sight of thy Lord is like a thousand years of your reck-
oning" (XXII: 47). God expects from a believer to be restrained and avoid
aggression. In fact, jihad is prescribed as a *defensive* act: "But fight them not
at the Sacred Mosque, unless they (first) fight you there; but if they fight you,
slay them. Such is the reward of those who suppress faith" (II: 191), or "Let
there be no hostility except to those who practice oppression" (II: 193). All
the *ayats* from the Koran which call for the Holy War would be misinterpreted
if they are taken out of the general context of the history of Mohammed and
first years of the life of the Muslim community. One is always to remember in
what particular historic situation prophet Muhammad made his statements.

In case hostility and fight are inevitable, Koran calls Muslims to follow a set of rules of warfare concerning prisoners, women and children, elder-
ly people, etc. It is said in a number of *ayats*: "Fight for the cause of God those
who fight you, but do not transgress limits; for God loves not transgressors"(II:
190). It is quite significant that Islamic teaching prescribes peace-making as
an honorable art and duty: "And if they incline to peace, incline thou also to
it, and trust in Allah" (VIII: 62).

Among the names or attributes of Allah the most important are Just
and Merciful. Hence the Koran too calls the believers: " Be foremost in seeking forgiveness" (57: 21); "Race towards forgiveness from your Lord" (3:
133); "Restrain anger and pardon men" (3: 134); "Forgive, even when angry"
(42: 37); "Let evil be rewarded with evil. But he that forgives and seeks rec-

oncilement shall be rewarded by God. He does not love wrongdoers." (42: 40).

It will be no exaggeration to affirm that all the religious teachings give preference to achieving victory of the Good over the Evil through non-violent ways. It is true though that the believers instead too often have resorted to force. In all the times, among all the peoples there have existed the two opposite parties: a party of war and a party of peace. Stressing the aggressive sides of the historical experience or interpreting the Scriptures as justifications for aggressiveness one consciously or unconsciously takes the side of the parties of war. Would it not be wiser to share with the people like Mahatma Gandhi their beliefs: that non-violence is the law of our species, while violence is the law of animals; hence that the dignity of man requires obedience to a higher law -- to the strength of the spirit, that the only hope for the suffering world is the specific and direct way of nonviolence; and that "the Allah of Islam is the same as the God of the Christians and the Ishvara of the Hindus. Living faith in this God means equal respect for all religions. It would be the height of intolerance - and intolerance is a species of violence - to believe that your religion is superior to other religions" ("Harijan", 14 May 1938).

Non-violence might not triumph in the near future. Its progress is extremely slow; the voices of the champions of non-violence may not be heard by many in the tumult and shouting of today. But it will have to be heard and understood some time or other if this world is to survive in any civilized form.

The acknowledgment of a specific, cultural particularly might create premises for respect towards "the other," and hence promote a dialogue. However, very often it results in the opposite in producing antagonistic consequences. That happens when the specific is interpreted not as value neutral, but rather as a proof of the superiority of one culture over the other, which has an exclusive possession of the Truth. In this way act the so-called Islamic fundamentalists, from one side, and those Westerners who are inclined towards arrogant and hostile attitude against anything associated with Islam.

The understanding of the causes which had brought cultural differences allows one to eliminate the obstacles on the way to dialogue. The latter is possible only if the common features are disclosed. People can not be absolutely different in everything. If they differ in one way, they are definitely the same in other ways. Daya Krishna, a distinguished Indian philosopher, justly points out: "... if philosophy is an enterprise of the human reason, it is bound to show similarities across cultures to some extent and, similarly, as a human enterprise it is bound to be concerned with what man, in a particular culture, regards as *summum bonum* for mankind"[7].

Not only abstract confirmation of commonness, but the discovery of concrete forms of its manifestation in two cultures which look alien to each other, that is, the cultures of the West and of the Muslim world, could prepare a new generation, fortunately, less burdened with stereotypes than the older people, to join the dialogue and carry it out successfully.

Here are a few points to which special attention should be given.

(1) There is a commonality in the very genesis of the cultures of the West and of the Muslim world.

In the minds of ordinary people as well as in the rhetoric of many politicians the West is exclusively identified with the Christian civilization. Yet, Western civilization was formed under the impact of a complex set of factors. The most important of them are: the heritage of Greece and Rome, the Judea-Christian legacy, and the culture of "modernity" which in its turn was mostly influenced by the Renaissance, Reformation and Enlightenment.[8]

Similarly, Islamic civilization is an "amalgam" originating from the pre-Islamic legacy, the Islamic traditions, and Judeo-Christian and ancient Greek influences. To the above mentioned usually accepted components should be added the impact of Zoroastrianism.

(2) The religious constituent of the two civilizations is stamped by a major likeness: Christianity and Islam are monotheistic teachings. The name given to God is not as important as the belief that He is the only One.

The first among the five "pillars" (*arkan*) of Islam, which is basically the foundation of the others, is *shahada*. Whoever confesses in public: "I testify that there is no deity save God and that Muhammad is the messenger of God" has accepted Islam. It is worth noting that this very point of likeness between Christianity and Islam was specially emphasized in the Declaration of the Second Vatican Council "Concerning the Attitude of the Church to Non-Christian Religions". It says: "The Church respects the Muslims, who worship the One God".

The second part of the *shahada* is no less significant. In keeping with various Koranic verses, the Muslims accept all the prophets who taught before Muhammad, from Adam through the patriarchs, Moses, and Jesus up to Muhammad - the last messenger ("the seal of the prophecy"). Though the Koran does not recognize Jesus' divine status, yet it refers to him as being "the Nearest to God" (Sura 3, ayat 45) and having an angelic nature.

It is also remarkable that there is a single woman's name mentioned in the Koran. It is the Virgin Mary, who according to Islamic tradition is one of the four best women who ever lived on earth.

(3) The Christian and Islamic civilizations have known similar phenomena, like atomism, notions of emanation, mysticism, etc.

Those who are engaged in the dialogue are expected to be ready to look critically at their own religious traditions and their practices, while at the same time to wish to understand the convictions and beliefs of the others.

Most preferable is the dialogue carried on as a never ending process, the dialogue which is aimed at continuing the development of an openness and sensitivity for respectful understanding of the particularity of the others' position, on communicating one's own value system or faith, and on learning from others for mutual benefit in living in a global community.

In conclusion I would add that today we have a real chance to answer positively to the question in the title of this paper. There is the perspective which has been opened recently by those changes which take place in the Muslim world and which some call post-Islamism. The onset of a "post-Islamist" turn took place after the end of the war between Iran and Iraq (1988), the death of Ayatollah Khomeini (1989), and the launching of the programme of post-war reconstruction under president Rafsanjani in Iran. Iran's post-Islamist experience has also contributed to an ideological shift among some Islamist movements (such as the Tunisian Al-Da`wa Islamic Party led by Rashed Channoushi), to the split in the Lebanese Hizbullah, to the emergence of Al-Wasat Party in Egypt as an alternative to both militant Islamists and the Muslim Brothers, to the inclusive policy and practices of Islamic parties in Turkey (Rifah, Virtue, and Justice and Development Parties), to the emergence in Saudi Arabia of an "Islamo-liberal" trend. Each displays some diverse versions of post-Islamism.

Post-Islamism is a conscious attempt to conceptualize and strategize the modalities of transcending Islamism in the social, political, and intellectual domains. As Asef Bayat - the Academic Director of ISIM and the ISIM Chair on Islam and the Modern World at Leiden University, points out: "Yet, post-Islamism is neither anti-Islamic, un-Islamic, nor is it secular. Rather ... it wants to marry Islam with individual choice and freedom, with democracy and modernity, to achieve what some have termed an 'alternative modernity'"[9].

It is quite unfortunate that these changes are not seen or are ignored by many in the West. To those who have not yet realized the vital need for dialogue between civilizations and cultures I might cite the words of the foremost Iranian and Islamic political philosopher and theologian, Abdolkarim Soroush:

"The world of ideas is a world of dialogue".
"Religious knowledge is a variety of human knowledge, subject to change, contraction, and expansion".
"Truths everywhere are compatible; no truth clashes with any other truth. They are all the inhabitants of the same mansion and stars of the same constellation. One truth in one corner of the world has to be harmonious and compatible with all truths elsewhere, or else it is not a truth"[10].

NOTES

1 F. Fukuyama, "The West Has Won: Radical Islam Can't Beat Democracy and Capitalism," http://www/guardian.co.uk

2 Hassan Hanafi, *Islam in the Modern World*. In two volumes. Vol. 2 (Cairo, 1995), p. 21.

3 Richard Rorty and Gianni Vatimo, *The Future of Religion* (Columbia University Press, 2004), pp. 72-73.

4 Charles Taylor, *Sources of the Self: The Making of Modern Identity* (Cambridge, MA: Harvard University Press, 1989), p. 520.

5 Vladimir Solovyev, *Muhammad* (St. Petersburg, 1902), p. 28 (in Russian).

6 The Christian Holy Book is not free of revenge motives as well,

though vengeance in it is expected to be administered by God. The Lord is called by a believer to revenge in the most sever way: "Arise, O Lord! Deliver me, O my God! For thou dost smite all my enemies on the cheek, thou dost break the teeth of the wicked"(Psalms, 5:7); "Arise, O Lord, in thy anger, lift thyself up against the fury of my enemies"(7:6). The same kind of prayer can be found in many other psalms.

7 Daya Krishna, *Comparative Philosophy: What It Is and What It Ought to Be: Interpreting Across Boundaries, New Essays in Comparative Philosophy*, G.J. Larson and E. Deutsch, eds. (Princeton: Princeton University Press, 1988), p. 71.

8 Fred Dallmayr, *Dialogue among Civilizations: Some Exemplary Voices* (Palgrave Macmillan: N.Y., 2002), pp. 24-25.

9 Asef Bayat. "What is Post-Islamism?" *ISIM Review*, 16 (Autumn 2005), p. 5.

10 Abdolkarim Soroush, *Reason, Freedom & Democracy in Islam, Essential Writings of `Abdolkarim Soroush* (Oxford, 2000), pp. 13, 16, 21.

Similarities between Christianity and Islamism: A Comment on the Paper of Marietta Stepanyants

Mel Stewart

Formal and informal exchanges between Western scholars and those representing Islamic cultures may not only help build cultural bridges, but establish friendships and contribute to greater mutual understanding in an ever-shrinking world. Hence the relevance of the main objective of this Forum and the one that preceded it, "The Harmony and Prosperity of Civilizations."

Because of the time constraint, I have chosen to comment on only one point made in Professor Marietta Stepanyants' (Russian Academy of Science) paper, "Is the Dialogue Between Western and Islamic Civilizations Possible?" Noting the influence of Christianity upon Western culture, Professor Stepanyants rightly points out that "The religious constituents of the two civilizations is stamped by a major likeness: Christianity and Islam are monotheistic." On that point, I would like to expand, and on various other convergences, and moreover suggest briefly ways in which these convergences might be salutary to further friendly discourse and discovery. Focusing only upon differences can be counterproductive to the objective of peace and harmony of rival religious groups. But collaborative practices of inquiry into points of analogy and similarity could lead to greater mutual understanding and harmony between or among cultural groups in which we find these religious orientations so inextrically interwoven.

Let me offer an initial list of what might count as points of significant similarity, and suggest ways they might generate further more careful examination, which could, in turn, generate an appreciation of various commonalities, and a greater tolerance toward and appreciation of differences.

Points of Similarity

First, as has been noted by Professor Stepanyants, both are monotheistic. Differences in divine names are typically, and perhaps rightly flagged,[1] but both faith orientations hold that God is metaphysically one. Christians hold to an ontological Trinity that the Qur'an clearly and emphatically denies. So while there is an ontological difference as to nature, there is an agreement that God is one. The first of five pillars, all of which are obligatory for an obedient Islamic believer, is the Witness or *Shahada*: "I witness that there is no God but Allah, I witness that Muhammad is His Messenger." That singularity finds its counterpart in the Hebrew-Christian tradition,[2] clearly revealed in the Old and New Testaments and to one degree or another reflected in Christian discourse through the centuries.

Second, both religions give a very high place to the authority of their respective scriptural canons. Islamic believers, like Christians, hold that the word from God is eternal. The Islamic believer claims that this eternal word, the Qur'an, the Mother of the Book is equivalent to the Word of God who made Arabic in the Replica of the Book. Analogously for the Christian, Jesus is equivalent to the Word of God made human.[3]

Third, Allah like the Christian God is viewed as compassionate, omnipotent, omniscient, and sovereign Creator. Each of the Suras, from I, The Opening, to Sura CXIV Men (114), begins with, "In the Name of God, the Merciful, the Compassionate."[4] Time and again Allah is described as omnipotent (Sura II, 19, "The Cow,") and omniscient (Sura II, 27), and He is depicted as Creator, Sura II, 19. God and his attributes is the first part of the *Iman*, or Faith. Regarding the latter attribute, the God of the Hebrew/Christian faith is described in Genesis 1:1 as the Creator of all that exists besides Himself, thus "Bereshiyth bara Elohiym eth hashamayim, ve-eth ha aretz" ("In the beginning, God created the heavens and the earth"). That the Hebrew-Christian God is compassionate, omnipotent and omniscient can be clearly seen not only in the Scriptures but passim in the literature of the tradition through the centuries.

One brief expansion on God as Creator might be viewed as suggestive of a possible collaborative venture. I have in mind the reflective thought process Al-Ghazali went through during a period of spiritual crisis as it is described by Eric Ormsby.[5] It is recorded that during this period, Al-Ghazali observed that while the world could be conceived as being other than it is, it couldn't be conceived as being better than it is, as Aquinas thought. His next observation is of greater interest to the point expanded briefly here, namely the reflection that though the actual world is "unsurpassibly excellent", it is not to be viewed as the "best-of-all-possible worlds." That is because of a further insightful point advanced by Al-Ghazali, namely, that God creates out of divine wisdom, and so the excellence envisioned, or the variant, best-of-all-possible notion must be parsed in terms of this wisdom. While the detailed semantics are different, I make a similar point with regard to the best-of-all-possible worlds notion in the context of a discourse on evil and this world in my *The Greater-Good Defence: An Essay on the Rationality of Faith*.[6] There I argue that although there are no logical upper limits to the best-of-all-possible worlds notion, conceivably, there might be a best-of-all-possible worlds *type* with regard to some purpose P, and value V, both of which (P and V) might be viewed as reflective of, or as issuing from, divine wisdom. While further development is a temptation here, it is not suited to the limitations of the assigned task.

Fourth, the prophetic role is not only an essential element in their respective teachings, but interestingly both Moses and Jesus appear on the list of revered prophets for Islamic followers. They add Muhammad believing that he alone enjoys a final and superior authority.

Fifth, both religious orientations hold to a life after death and to rewards for the faithful and punishment for the wicked.

Sixth, both affirm the need for prayer as a way of communicating with God. Hence there is a mutual emphasis upon the mystical as expressive of the reality of divine-human encounters.

Seventh, both affirm that God is the source of salvation for humanity. And while the respective natures of salvation are very different, the source is the same, Allah/God.

Eighth, both share a common concern regarding the corruptive influence of the world. It is probably fair to say that the Muslim perceives himself and herself as far more aggressive in avoiding this corruption than is his/her counterpart.

Ninth, both hold that the divine is transcendent, and so the mystery regarding God is mutually affirmed.

Finally, both affirm that if faith in God/Allah is genuine, then this faith will issue in a changed life marked by good works.

There are other important intersections, such as the high estimation of Mary, the Mother of Jesus. Time does not allow for further expansion here. Such practices of inquiry as the study of similarities and differences, may be truth - conducive, and may promote better mutual and self understandings. What has been noted along the way, passim, is that since there are similarities, and so intersections, drawing attention to these common features might generate more finely-tuned and accurate doctrinal accounts. Dialogue, perhaps at times in an apologetic mode, between religiously diverse groups sharing common elements may assist in more accurate formulation of belief.

Thus a mutual study of points of intersection along with their finely-tuned differences can bring scholars and believers together in friendly and mutually productive discourse, and this in turn can be a means to promot good will and harmony among those of different faiths. But over and above this, the collaborations might not only promote mutual understanding and greater appreciation of common elements, but such engagements have the potential of mutually prompting deeper inquiries into points of doctrine which might thereby offer a clearer understanding of one's own system of beliefs. Moreover, such practices of inquiry might prove to be truth-conducive regarding claims made as to the nature of God, and in such cases this could result in bringing people closer to Allah/God in terms of understanding the divine Other, thereby also satisfying His desire to be close to the creature. And if believers from both traditions are drawn to Him, this will likely enhance and expand friendships.

Practices of inquiry into comparative religious beliefs can be viewed as having the potential of leading to better self-understandings, mutual understandings, practices of devotion and worship for those of the respective religious persuasions. But such practices might also prove to be truth-conducive, as scholar-believers representative of these traditions devote their time and energy to working together with those whose objective is to discover truth about the Creator of this world. There is little doubt that this could and likely would result in a greater harmony and prosperity of the cultures/civilizations in which these religious orientations are variously instantiated.

NOTES

1 The *Qur'an* for example, lists ninety-nine names each counting as revelational faces of Allah, see David Burrell, "Al Ghazali as Philosophical Theologian," see Chapter 10 below.

2 In Exodus 3:14, God is speaking to Moses and says, "I am [that] I am," signaling his singular divine ultimacy. Words in brackets added.

3 I am indebted to David Burrell for this comparative equivalence picture.

4 The Islamic believer would no doubt prefer the word *Allah* for *God*. Here I am following he reference which uses the word *God*.

5 I am indebted to David Burrell for the account of Al-Ghazali's views on the sort of creation an omnipotent, omniscient and all-good Allah would bring about. See his article, "Al Ghazali as Philosophical Theologian."

6 See (London: Macmillan/New York: St. Martin's Press, 1993), pp. 57-65. An unpublished manuscript, "The Best-of-All-Possible Worlds Argument," contains a more fully detailed discourse on this.

Commentary 2

A Comment on the Paper of Marietta Stepanyants

Miikka Ruokanen

I thank very much Dr. Stepanyants for her detailed, profound and thought-provoking paper. She puts forward many views I can easily agree with. For instance, all religions should prefer "achieving victory of the Good over the Evil through non-violent ways". Any healthy religion should be in service of life, not against it. Her remarks on the similarities of the concept of God as "the Just and the Merciful" in Abrahamic religions (Judaism, Christianity and Islam) are promising.

Furthermore, as Dr. Stepanyants also claims, religions should foster the unity of humankind, and in this way make contributions to peace, justice and the development of the global human community. I also agree with her [negatively] critical remarks on the "complete Westernization of the earth and humankind". In regard to religious dialogue this means that encounter between various religions has taken place too much in terms of Western academic discourse.

In one fundamental methodological sense I cannot agree with Dr. Stepanyants. She seems to propose some kind of modern pluralist paradigm as a proper method of religious dialogue. She says that "none of the participants of the dialogue has a right to claim that the fundamental principle of his/her religion is of universal value". Or: "Neither should anybody claim superiority of his/her belief and on that premise to judge what is right and what is wrong in somebody's actions." She also employs the metaphor often used now by fashionable Christian pluralist theologians: Infinite reality is compared with light which passes through a prism. Each religion should see itself as one colour of the prism, as one aspect of the totality of the truth. No religion has the full truth; religious truths are partial; therefore religions are complementary to each other.

Several critical remarks have been raised against the pluralist paradigm of religious dialogue. First, the doctrinal, philosophical, ritual, cultural, historical, etc., embodiments of various religions seem to be so different from each other that it is impossible to look for a common unifying factor or "inner identity" of all religions. Stepanyants seems to prefer a "mystical" approach to religions to a rational "comparativist" method.

Second, and even more importantly, by definition religious faith means a total commitment to something that a person regards as the truth; thus "truth-pluralism" is a negation of authentic religious faith! Religion is something that explains the ultimate mysteries of existence which cannot be answered by science: Why does the universe exist? Why do I exist? What is the fate of the universe? What is my personal fate? What is death? What is the value of life? What is true happiness? Etc.

In spite of its Westernism, I like the definition of religion by Peterson, Hasker, Reichenbach and Basinger: "Religion is constituted by a set of beliefs, actions and emotions, both personal and corporate, organized around the concept of an ultimate reality." This definition is broad enough to include all kinds of religions, covering the rational, psychological, ritual, moral, personal and social aspects of religion. Being broad, it also is specific enough to state the most important function of religion as something around the "ultimate reality", leaving open a closer definition of the content of that reality.

I understand that trying to achieve agreement or unity on the essence of religion or religion proper is an unrealistic and even an unnecessary goal for religious dialogue. It is enough trying to understand more authentically and more deeply other believers' views concerning the ultimate questions. An increase in mutual understanding and tolerance are high enough goals. The real progress of religious dialogue could, instead, take place in the field of ethics or morality, including social ethics. I basically agree with Hans Küng and his programme for the "Global Ethic". There are features of moral principles common to all major religions of the world, such as the Golden Rule. Of course, in different religions moral systems have varying religious motivations. But it seems that the practical consequences for moral rules are similar enough so that we can have a meaningful dialogue. There exists a common ground for trying to achieve common ethical rules and moral practices.

In order to have meaningful progress in religious dialogue, the real committed believers of each religion - not just academic observers and outsiders - should actively engage in this kind of a dialogue! We could say that only committed believers can understand the real inner nature of his/ her religion. And only the true believers really represent their religious communities. Only this kind of a participation of the real representatives of living religious communities can make some impact on the true progress of mutual understanding and tolerance between various religions and their followers.

Coming from a Western Christian background, I feel ashamed that one of the greatest threats to humankind in our days is the tension between the three monotheistic Abrahamic religions. How is it possible that the God who indeed is the Just and the Merciful can be followed in such conflicting ways? Or is it that the good intentions of the religions are being perverted by the social, cultural and political contexts of those religions? In that case it would mean that the religions do not have inner power to improve the societies where they exist, but they themselves fall victims to non-religious factors or are misused for political purposes. We have many examples of this kind of adulteration of Christianity in the history of Europe. There is a great need for a self-critical evaluation of everyone's own religious tradition, as Dr. Stepanyants correctly presumes.

Chapter 11

Al-Ghazali as Philosophical Theologian

David Burrell

The effect of the book of "Faith in divine Unity and Trust in divine Providence" ["Kitab al-tawhid wa'l-tawakkul"] of the *Ihya' `Ulum al-Din* [*Revivifying Religious Sciences*], together with "al-iqtisad al-i`ttiqad" ["Preserving the Faith"], is to qualify al-Ghazali as a Muslim theologian in the full medieval meaning of that term, and not merely in the descriptive sense extended to include any thinker adept at *kalam*, or the dialectical defense of faith. That is, Ghazali was intent on using human reason, as he found it elaborated in Ibn Sina and others, not merely to defend the faith but to lead the Muslim faithful to a deeper penetration of the mysteries of their revealed religion--the central mystery being the free creation of the universe by the one God.[1] The works of the philosophers themselves were not always helpful to him in their native state, so he had to set out first to purify them of their pretensions to offer an access to truth independent of, and superior to, that of divine revelation,--the Qur'an. Hence his need to understand them thoroughly, embodied in the work entitled "The Intentions of the Philosophers [Maqasid al-falasifa]," itself conceived as an extended introduction (and hence also published as the Muqaddima al-Tahafut) to his "Deconstruction of the Philosophers [Tahafut al-falasifa]."[2] The negative tone of this latter work, together with its detailed refutation by Averroes [Ibn Rushd: Tahafut al-Tahdfut], has left the impression that Ghazali should never be ranked with "the philosophers" but always left with "the theologians" as a defender of *kalam* orthodoxy in the face of reasonable inquiry. It is precisely that stereotype which this book challenges, and so can offer Ghazali's own assistance to deconstruct the historical image which he helped to create for himself. It will involve challenging Averroes's self-styled role as the pretended paragon of philosophy, and concentrate on Ghazali's intent, leaving an assessment of his success to the reader.

The "Book of Faith in Divine Unity" [tawhid] and "Trust in Divine Providence" [tawakkul]" is Book 35 in Ghazali's masterwork, the *Ihya' `Ulum al-Din*. The French summary of this magnum opus, "Revivification des sciences religieuses," reminds us how forceful is the key term taken from the fourth form of the Arabic verb [*ihya*], probably best rendered in English as "Putting Life Back into Religious Learning."[1] For that would convey Ghazali's intent, as well as his assessment of the state of such learning in his time. He is intent upon a clear understanding of matters religious, yet one which continues to give primacy to practice: faith is rooted in trust and must needs be expressed in a life of trust. The pretensions of the philosophers to understand the mysteries of the heavens and the earth and all that is between them [15:85], proceeding by conceptual argument alone, must be exposed as just that--pretension, in the face of the central assertion that the universe was freely created by the one sovereign God. Yet reason, which they are so intent to elaborate, will prove to be an indispensable tool in directing our minds and our hearts to understand how to think and how to live as a consequence of that signal truth.

Such is Ghazali's intent. It is displayed in the structure of his *Ihya'* as well as in the pattern adopted for his treatise expounding the ninety-nine canonical "names" of God, where he devotes an extensive introduction to explaining the human practice of naming and how it might be understood in relation to the names which God has given Himself in the Qur'an.[4] It turns out that the only way to extend the limits of human knowledge of such divine things is by "adorning oneself" with the meaning of the names, so the commentary on each name begins with semantics and closes with a counsel: how one might oneself become more like God so presented. This pattern will become the master strategy of the *Ihya'* as well, where the entire gamut of Muslim life--beliefs together with practices--is laid out in a way which displays the importance of both knowledge and state [of being], that is, of understanding together with practice. Readers familiar with Aquinas will marvel at the way in which Ghazali's master plan aligns with that thinker's insistence that theology is at once a speculative and a practical mode of knowing.[2]

It is fair to say that the "Kitab al-Tawhid wa' l-Tawakkul" plays an axial role among the other books in the *Ihya'*. For *tawhid*, or "faith in divine unity," sounds the distinctive note of Islam which grounds everything Muslims believe in the *shahada*: "There is no god but God." Islamic reflection on tawhid is reminiscent of rabbinic commentary on divine unity as evidenced in the *shema*: "Hear, O Israel, the Lord our God, the Lord is One" (Deuteronomy 6:4). It is hardly at issue that God be one rather than many; it points instead directly to the injunction against idolatry: all Israelites know thereby that they must orient their entire lives to God--through the Torah, to be sure--and nowhere else. So a philosophical argument culminating in the assertion that God is one would hardly interest the rabbis, nor would it Ghazali. Its conclusion may be true enough, but what is at issue is not the unity itself, but the implications of the community's faith in divine unity. Yet that cannot be a blind faith, so what is being asserted is that everything comes from God and that "there is no agent but God."

In cataloguing degrees of assent to this *shahada*, Ghazali notes: "The third kind [of believer] professes faith in divine unity in the sense that he sees but a single agent, since truth is revealed to him as it is in itself; and he only sees in reality a single agent, since reality has revealed itself to him as it is in itself because he has set his heart on deter-mining to comprehend the word 'reality' [*haqiqa*]--and this stage belongs to lay folk as well as theologians" (11).[3] He sketches out the two-part structure of the book by way of showing how *tawakkul*--trust in divine providence--is grounded in an articulate *tawhid*, as practice is anchored in faith, or state [of being] in knowledge. In so doing, he is even more insistent: this first part

will consist in showing you that there is no agent but God the

Most High: of all that exists in creation-sustenance given or withheld, life or death, riches or poverty, and everything else that can be named, the sole one who initiated and originated it all is God Most High. And when this has been made clear to you, you will not see anything else, so that your fear will be of Him, your hope in Him, your trust in Him, and your security with Him, for He is the sole agent without any other. Everything else is in His service, for not even the smallest atom in the worlds of heaven and earth is independent of Him for its movement. If the gates of mystical insight were opened to you, this would be clear to you with a clarity more perfect than ordinary vision (15-16).

These last words are telling, and signal Ghazali's "method" in the first section elaborating faith in divine unity. There is no attempt to show how everything-that-is is of God; that would be beyond the capacity of our intellect to grasp. And should we try, we would invariably end up articulating something like Ibn Sina's emanation scheme, modeled on logical inference and amounting to a twin denial of divine and of human freedom.[6] Indeed, when Ghazali tries to articulate what he attributes to mystical insight, it sounds uncannily like Ibn Sina, though he begins with a characteristic verse from the Qur'an:

'We did not create heaven and earth and what lies between them in jest; we did not create them but in truth' [44:38-39]. Now all that is between heaven and earth comes forth in a necessary order that is true and consequent, and it is inconceivable that it be otherwise than the way it comes forth, according to this order which exists. For a consequent only follows because it awaits its condition; for a conditioned before a condition would be absurd, and absurdity cannot be ascribed to the being of-an object of divine omnipotence. So knowledge [can be said to] follow upon sperm only if one supplies the condition of a living thing, and the will which comes after knowledge [can be said to] follow upon sperm only if the condition of knowledge be supplied as well. All of this offers a way of necessity and the order of truth. There is no room for play or chance in any of this; everything has its rationale and order. Understanding this is difficult... (40).

So he will offer images to move us away from a literal acceptance of the Avicenna-like scheme, for in such matters human reason can at best offer models; yet neither mode of apperception is privileged for Ghazali, in contrast to "the philosophers," notably Averroes. The images offered by the Qur'an, however, will certainly take precedence.

But what about human freedom? Have we not exalted God's sovereign freedom, as the only agent there is, to the inevitable detriment of human initiative? It certainly appears that the intent of Ghazali's images is to take us by the hand and lead us on, in hopes that we

> may come to under-stand the emanation of things so or-dained [*muqaddarat*] from the eternal omnipotence, even though the omnipotent One is eternal and the things ordained [mqgdurat] temporal. But this [train of thought] knocks on another door, to another world of the worlds of unveiling. So let us leave all that, since our aim is to offer counsel regarding the way to faith in divine unity in practice: that the true agent is One, that He is the subject of our fear and our hope, and the One in whom we trust and depend (41-42).

These gnomic words will be somewhat clarified in the text itself, but he also wants to show us that the test of our understanding of divine unity will not come by way of clever philosophical schemes but through a life of trust [*tawakkul*], in which concerted practice will bring each of us personally to the threshold of the only understanding possible here, that of "unveiling."[8] Yet some clarifications can be made; reason can offer some therapeutic hints to attenuate the apparent scandal.

He introduces a typically Muslim objection:

> How can there be any common ground between faith in divine unity and the *sharia* [religious law]? For the meaning of faith in divine unity is that there is no god but God Most High, and the meaning of the law lies in establishing the actions proper to human beings [as servants of God]. And if human beings are agents, how is it that God Most High is an agent? Or if God Most High is an agent, how is a human being an agent? There is no way of understanding 'acting' as between these two agents. In response, I would say: indeed, there can be no understanding when there is but one meaning for 'agent.' But if it had two meanings, then the term comprehended could be attributed to each of them without contradiction, as when it is said that the emir killed someone, and also said that the executioner killed him; in one sense, the emir is the killer and in another sense, the executioner. Similarly, a human being is an agent in one sense, and God--Great and Glorious--is an agent in another. The sense in which God Most High is agent is that He is the originator[9] of existing things [*al-mukhtari' al-mawjud*], while the sense in which a human being is an agent is that he is the locus [*mahal*] in which power is created after will has been created, and that after knowledge had been created, so that power depends on will, and movement is linked to power, as

a conditioned to its condition.⁴ But depending on the power of God is like the dependence of effect on cause, and of the originated on the originator. So every thing which depends on a power in such a way as it is the locus of the power is called 'agent' in a manner which ex-presses that fact of its dependence, much as the executioner can be called 'killer' and the emir a killer, since the killing depends on the power of both of them, yet in different respects. In that way both of them are called 'killer', and similarly, the things ordained [maqrurat] depend on two powers (43).

He goes on to note how the Qur'an often attributes agency to God as well as to creatures, showing that revelation acknowledges and exploits the inherently analogous character of agency as exhibited in the multiple uses of the term 'agent'. This small clue offers the best way of presenting Ghazali's intent and his strategy to contemporary readers. What he wanted to do was to help believers to recognize that theirs is a unique perspective on the universe: each thing is related in its very existence to the one from whom it freely comes. (As Aquinas will put it: "the very existence of creatures is to-be-related to their creator" [ST 1.45.3].) Yet since we cannot articulate this founding and sustaining relationship conceptually, for to do so would trespass on divine freedom, we can only display our understanding by the way we live our life: trusting in the One who so sustains us.

To the recurring objection that all this amounts to *jabr* [coercion] on the part of God, he replies:

This has to do with the divine decree [*qadar*],⁵ intimations of which we saw with respect to the faith in divine unity which brings about the state of trust in divine providence, and is only perfected by faith in the benevolence and wisdom [of God]. And if faith in divine unity brings about insight into the effects of causes, abundant faith in benevolence is what brings about confidence in the effects of the causes, and the state of trust in divine providence will only be perfected, as I shall relate, by confidence in the trustworthy One [*wakil*] and tranquillity of heart towards the benevolent oversight of the [divine] sponsor. For this faith is indeed an exalted chapter in the chapters of faith, and the stories about it from the path of those experiencing the unveiling go on at length.... He enhanced knowledge, wisdom, and reason in a great number of [Sufi sheikhs], and then unveiled for them the effects of things [al-'awaqil al-amur], apprising them of the secrets of the intelligible world, teaching them the subtleties of speech and the hidden springs of punishment, to the point where they were thus informed regarding what is good or evil, useful or harmful (47-48).

This summary offers a springboard to part two of the book, which relates one Sufi story after another, while judiciously selecting them and weaving them into a pattern that allows persons to discriminate in making subtle decisions regarding the way they lead their lives aware of God's benevolent care, exhibiting the sorts of choices they make in typical situations. If Ghazali closes the first part with what looks like a backward-looking conceptual reminder, he opens the way to an entirely different mode of consideration in part two:

> Indeed, all this happens according to a necessary and true order, according to what is appropriate as it is appropriate, and in the measure proper to it; nor is anything more fitting, more perfect, and more attractive within the realm of possibility.[12] For if something were to exist and remind one of the sheer omnipotence [of God] and not of the good things accomplished by His action, that would utterly contradict [God's] generosity, and be an in-justice contrary to the Just One.[13] And if God were not omnipotent, He would be impotent, thereby contradicting the nature of divinity (48-49).

Yet omnipotence cannot be the last word; generosity is a more operative one, for it modifies God's omnipotence in the direction of a benevolent creator. The upshot of *tawhid*, then, must be the believer's profound conviction "of the unalterable justice and excellence of things as they are ..., of the 'perfect rightness of the actual'."[6]

Eric Ormsby sees this conviction as the upshot of the ten years of seclusion and prayer following Ghazali's spiritual crisis. By "the actual" he means what God has de-creed, itself the product and reflection of divine wisdom. And by asserting the primacy of the actual over the possible, Ghazali shows himself a true theologian. Contingency, for philosophers, tends to focus on the logical fact that "whatever exists could always be other than it is." Yet while it may be "logically correct and permissible to affirm that our world could be different than it is, it is not theologically correct and permissible,-- indeed, it is impious--to assert that our world could be better than it is. The world in all its circumstances remains unimpeachably right and just, and it is unsurpassably excellent."[7] Yet the excellence in question is not one which we can assess independently of the fact that it is the product of divine wisdom, so Ghazali is not asserting that ours is the "best of all possible worlds," as though there were a set of such worlds "each of which might be ranked in terms of some intrinsic excellence." Such an assertion would quite miss the point of Ghazali's quest: to find ways of expressing that relation of creator to creatures which quite resists formulation. The deconstructive moment had been his rejection of the emanation scheme; the constructive task is taken up in this twin discourse on faith in divine unity and trust in divine providence, but especially in this second part where practice will allow us to traverse domains which speculative reason cannot otherwise map.

What sort of a practice is *tawakkul*: trust in divine providence? It entails accepting whatever happens as part of the inscrutable decree of a just and merciful God. Yet such an action cannot be reduced to mere resignation, and so caricatured as "Islamic fatalism." It rather entails aligning oneself with things as they really are: in Ghazali's terms, with the truth that there is no agent but God Most High. This requires effort since we cannot formulate the relationship between this single divine agent and the other agents which we know, and also because our ordinary perspective on things is not a true one: human society lives under the sign of *jahiliyya* or pervasive ignorance. Yet this effort cannot be solely intellectual; that is, I cannot learn "the truth" in such a way as to align myself with it, in the time-honored fashion in which speculative reason is supposed to illuminate practical judgment. For the all-important relationship resists formulation. Nevertheless, by trying our best to act according to the conviction that the divine decree expresses the truth in events as they unfold, we can allow ourselves to be shown how things truly lie. So faith [*tawhid*] and practice [*tawakkul*] are reciprocal; neither is foundational. The understanding we can have is that of one journeying in faith, a salik, the name which Sufis characteristically appropriated for themselves.

There are stages of trust in divine providence, to be sure, which Ghazali catalogues as (1) the heart's relying on the trustworthy One [*wakil*] alone, (2) a trust like that of a child in its mother, where the focus is less on the trust involved than on the person's orientation to the one in whom they trust; and (3) the notorious likeness of a corpse in the hands of its washers, where the relevant point is that such trust moves one quite beyond petition of any sort. Yet the operative factor is present already in the initial stage, which is not surpassed but only deepened by subsequent stages: trusting in the One alone. The formula for faith here is the *hadith*: "There is no might and power but in God," which Ghazali shows to be equivalent to the Qur'anic *shahadah*: There is no god but God, thereby reminding us that the *hadith* does not enjoin us to trust in power or might, as attributes distinct from God, but in God alone. It is in this context that he selects stories of Sufi sheikhs, offering them as examples to help point us towards developing specific skills of trusting: habits of responding to different situations in such a way that one learns by acting how things are truly ordered, the truth of the decree. The principle operative throughout is that a policy of complete renunciation of means [*asbab*] is contrary to divine wisdom, the *sunna Allah*, but those who journey in faith will be cognizant that there are different kinds of means, as they become aware of hidden as well as manifest ones.

The situations which he canvasses begin with the daily question of sustenance: should one seek it by working for it, or ought one wait for it to come to him or her? At issue here is a practice of some Sufis to sequester themselves in a mosque in prayer while relying on the generosity of the faithful, as well as more dramatic adventures of journeying into the desert without provisions. Ghazali notes with approval that when the illustrious al-Hawwas undertook such journeys, he never left home without four items: a pot, a rope, scissors, and a needle and thread. For while he was convinced that

God would provide for him on his journey, he realized that, according to the *sunna* of Allah, water would not be found on the surface of the desert (hence the pot and the rope), and should his sole tunic rip he would not be likely to run across a tailor (hence the scissors, needle and thread: "lest his nakedness be exposed"[76]). He also notes that judiciousness in such matters will differ considerably whether one be a single person or a householder. Other situations which involve a judicious practice of trust in divine providence include saving, repelling injury or resisting danger, our response to theft of our property, and the manner in which we relate to illness: ought one or may one simply dispense with all treatment? May we conceal the fact that we are ill from those who care for us, or must we disclose it? Here especially he strives for a sane "middle way": dispensing with treatment cannot be said always to be the "better way" for those who trust in God's providence.

The bevy of stories which Ghazali mines offer living examples of the attitude proper to one who firmly believes in divine unity, namely, a total trust in God's providential care. He uses them to offer one object lesson after another of a way to take esoteric Sufi lore and allow it to inspire one's practice, as in the following:

> Should you say that it has been said of certain ones that a lion put his paws on their shoulders without their being agitated, I would respond: It is said about certain ones that they ride lions and make them subservient, but there is no need to deceive yourselves about that station.[16] For even if it were authentic in itself, it would hardly be healthy to imitate a path which one learns about from someone else. That station is marked by an abundance of miracles and is certainly not a condition for trusting in God; it is rather replete with secrets which cannot be divined by those who have not attained it. You might also say: What are the signs by which I could know that I had attained it? I would respond: One who attains it does not need to look for signs. However, one of the signs of that station does in fact precede it: that a dog become subject to you, a dog which is always with you, indeed inside your skin, named Anger [or Resentment]. [Normally] it does not stop biting you and biting others. But if this dog becomes subservient to you, to the extent that when it becomes agitated and irritated it will be subject to you instantaneously, then your standing will be enhanced to the point where a lion, the very king of beasts, will be subject to you. It is more appropriate that the dog in your house be subject to you than a dog in the desert; but it is even more appropriate that the dog inside your skin be subject to you than the dog in your house. For if the dog within is not subject to you, how can you hope to make the dog outside subject to you (115)?

So there is a school whereby we learn how to respond to what happens in such a way that we are shown how things are truly ordered. This school will involve learning from others who are more practiced in responding rightly; Ghazali's judicious use of stories is intended to intimate the Sufi practice of master/disciple wherein the novice is helped to discern how to act. Philosophy is no longer identified as a higher wisdom; speculative reason is wholly subject to practical reason, but that is simply the inevitable implication of replacing the emanation scheme with an intentional creator! [17] So the challenge of understanding the relation of the free creator to the universe becomes the task of rightly responding to events as they happen, in such a way that the true ordering of things, the divine decree, can be made manifest in one's actions-as-responses. Ghazali expresses this relationship between speculative and practical reason by noting that we need to call upon both knowledge and state [of being] in guiding our actions according to a wholehearted trust in God. What he wishes to convey by those terms in tandem is an awareness of the very structure of the book itself: when put into practice, the knowledge which faith in divine unity brings can lead one to a habitual capacity to align one's otherwise errant responses to situation after situation according to that faith. In short, what Ghazali terms a state, relying here on a Sufi anthropology, would be more familiar to western readers as Aristotle's stable "second nature" of virtue.

It is tied, however, not to the Hellenic paradigm of "the magnanimous man" but to a Quranic faith. This is also evident in his treatise on the names of God, for it is the ninety-nine names culled from the Qur'an, names by which God reveals the many "faces" of the divine, which offer a composite picture for human perfection. If we take names to identify attributes, then the book can be read in two distinct, yet related, ways: as a condensed summary of Islamic theology and as offering a revealed counterpart to Aristotle's Ethics. Perhaps enough has been said so far to begin to make my case for Ghazali as an Islamic theologian, in the non-native and not merely descriptive sense of that term. If he tends to resort to mystical insight in places where philosophers would prefer conceptual schemes, one ought to acknowledge that he is also gesturing thereby that certain domains quite outstrip human conceptualizing. Yet more significant, however, is that everything he says about practice can be carried out quite independently of such "mystical insight," as indeed it must be for the vast majority of faithful.

NOTES

1 G.-H. Bousquet (Analyse et Index) (Paris: Max Besson, 1955).

2 *Summa Theologiae* 1.1.4: "Sacred doctrine takes over both [speculative and practical] functions, in this being like the single knowledge whereby God knows himself and the things he makes" (cf. *Summa Theologiae* 1.14.5).

3 All numbers in brackets in this paper refer to the page numbers of *al-Ghazali on Faith in divine unity and trust in Divine providence* [Kitab al-

tawhid wa'l-tawakkul] Louisville KY: Fons Vitae, 2001), ed. and translated by David Burrell.

4 See Al-Ghazali: *The Ninety-nine Beautiful Names of God,* tr. David Burrell and Nzazih Daher (Cambridge: Islamic Texts Society, 1992),

5 William Chittick proposes that we render *qadar* as "the measuring out," and with respect to human understanding, the "mystery of the measuring out"-see *Faith and Practice in Islam* (Albany: State University of New York Press, 1992) 21, 189, 213.

6 For a sketch of that model, see my *Knowing the Unknowable God* (Notre Dame IN: University of Notre Dame Press, 1986)

Comments on the Papers of
Marietta Stepanyants and David Burrell

William C. Chittick

Marietta Stepanyants

Professor Stepanyants speaks with the voice of a sensitive observer of the contemporary situation. She takes into account both the conflicting claims of contending ideologies and a variety of proposed approaches for bringing peace and harmony to the world. Along the way she shows a deep sympathy for the goals of traditional Islamic religiosity and much insight into its compatibility with various dimensions of the Christian tradition. She does not, however, attempt to capture the voice of Islamic philosophy.

Nor does Professor Stepanyants offer us any suggestions as to how we should define "civilization" in the context of civilizational dialogue. She seems to assume that the conflicting ideological claims so loudly voiced in the contemporary world are legitimate expressions of two different "civilizations," whatever the word may mean. She all but ignores Heidegger's dictum, which she so aptly quotes in her discussion: Cultural encounters are nowadays carried out not by equals, but on the basis of "a linguistic and conceptual framework supplied entirely by Western civilization." Her only attempts to bring in the views of contemporary Muslim "philosophers" illustrate Heidegger's point. She refers first to Hassan Hanafi, who is quoted in ideological mode as trumpeting the superiority of "Islam" over the West and the rest; and second to Abdolkarim Soroush, a former ideologue of the Islamic revolution of Iran who has now set himself up as the voice of an enlightened Islam. Both of these spokesmen for Islamic "philosophy" pose the discussion in a conceptual framework supplied by Western civilization, certainly not by traditional Islamic thought. The Algerian/French philosopher Mohammad Arkoun has summed up the position of such contemporary purveyors of a new and improved Islam in these terms:

> [They present us with] the triumph of a social imaginary that is termed "Islamic" but that in fact sacralizes an irreversible operation of political, economic, social, and cultural secularization. . . . [Islam has been turned into] an instrument of disguising behaviors, institutions, and cultural and scientific activities inspired by the very Western model that has been ideologically rejected. [1]

David Burrell

Professor Burrell provides a welcome counterpoint to Professor Ste-panyants. He looks at al-Ghazali, one of the greatest philosophers of Islamic history, and analyzes his approach to the theoretical and practical dimensions of living a life of wisdom (*hikma*), which was the goal of the philosophical and Sufi traditions in Islam. He tells us implicitly that any philosophical dialogue among Muslim and Western civilizations needs to find adequate spokesmen on the Islamic side. Non-Muslims as well as most modern-day Muslims are generally ignorant of Islamic philosophy and perhaps unaware that the current conversation among civilizations is in fact a monologue, carried out entirely by those who speak for political and social programs invented by the modern West, whatever the nationality of the speakers may be.

If Islamic philosophy is to be part of this discussion, the participants need to be aware of the principles that underlie it. To speak of any civiliza-tion, we need to understand the concept of human nature and human good that inspired its founders and guided its unfolding. It would be difficult to find another thinker as representative of the Islamic consensus over history as al-Ghazali. Like all pre-modern Muslim thinkers, al-Ghazali defines the human ideal in terms of the divine. To be truly human is to live in harmony with the divine nature. Burrell puts it in more philosophical terms: Living up to human nature means "aligning oneself with things as they really are." This means that the goal of life is to become, as he says, "more like God." For a civilization to be Islamic, it must provide a model of human nature rooted in Islamic principles (Koran, *Hadith*) and it must point to a praxis that allows this model to become actualized in individuals and society. To begin by speaking of "human rights" and other such buzz-words of contemporary political discourse is to put the cart before the horse. The rights of God and the rights of our own immortal souls must be taken into account before we can turn our attention to the structures, institutions, and laws that will supposedly guarantee civil rights.

We need to have a sense of Western history and not forget that the current "civilizational" dialogue is rooted in ideology, by which I mean socio-political programs built on analyses of human nature that are claimed to be rational and scientific. Such programs were unknown in pre-modern times. They owe their genesis to the Enlightenment and the Scientific Revolution, which effectively stripped all earlier forms of human discourse of their cogni-tive content. Talk of "God"—not to mention the Tao or the Buddha-nature—was relegated to the realm of poetry if not superstition. With science and a totally new understanding of human nature, there was no longer any need for "myths." But it was precisely these myths that were the foundation of all seri-ous engagement with the fundamentals of the universe and human destiny in pre-modern times. Moreover, these same myths still animate the worldview of countless human beings today.

Any discussion of "civilization" in the context of Islam must begin by taking seriously the fundamental premises of Islam, that is, unity (*tawhid*), prophecy, and the return to God. These premises declare that Ultimate Reality (God) is one, that Ultimate Reality Itself discloses the Way, and that all things will return to the Ultimate Reality from which they came. The Way is the path that human beings need to follow in order to bring themselves into conformity with Ultimate Reality and to prepare themselves for the meeting with that Reality after death. God discloses the Way by sending messengers, whom Muslims typically call "prophets"; Chinese Muslims long ago recognized that the word was synonymous with "sage" (*sheng*).

In the chapter discussed by Professor Burrell, al-Ghazali summarizes the practical and moral implications of Islam's three premises as *tawakkul* or "trust." Trust is to acknowledge the first premise, Unity or *tawhid*, not simply by giving it lip-service, but by conforming oneself to it externally and internally, that is, in activity, morality, attitudes, and understanding. It is not simply to acknowledge the rooting of all things in the True, the Good, and the Beautiful, it is actually to become true, good, and beautiful through the purity of one's heart and understanding.

People can conform themselves to the Ultimate Reality because they were created in the image of the Ultimate Reality. Only such conformity allows the achievement of human perfection. In other words, to live up to our own human nature, we must undertake to become embodiments of the harmony of heaven and earth. This understanding of what it means to be human was central to the philosophical and spiritual traditions of Islam down to modern times. Only recently has it been replaced by the ideological claims of Muslims mirroring the corresponding claims of Western triumphalism.

In the traditional Islamic view of things, the ideal human society is one in which people strive to follow the divine model "to the extent of human capacity," as the philosophers liked to put it. The first prerequisite here is to understand the nature of Ultimate Reality and what It demands of us, and then to set out to achieve the perfection of the human state. This is precisely what al-Ghazali is talking about in terms of *tawhid* and *tawakkul*.

Genuine Islamic philosophy is nothing if not a quest for wisdom, a term that was defined as knowing things as they truly are and acting in perfect conformity with what one knows. By definition, the quest for wisdom was always intensely personal. Where can we find wisdom if not in our own hearts? The wisdom of the sages can certainly act as a model, but their wisdom is not my wisdom or your wisdom. The goal is to be wise oneself.

This goal of becoming wise was often called *tahqiq* or "realization." The Arabic word means to actualize *haqq*, and *haqq* is one of the most important terms in the Islamic vocabulary. It means truth, right, real, and reality. Its primary designation is the Real, that is, God himself, the Supreme Reality. Second, the word *haqq* designates heaven, earth, and the myriad things as the manifestations of the truly Real. Everything in the universe, inasmuch as it manifests the Supreme Principle, is itself *haqq*—real, right, true, appropriate, and worthy.

Among all the ten thousand things, only human beings have the ability to upset the balance of heaven and earth by deviating from the *haqq*. Thus, in the human context, *haqq* also means duty and responsibility. It designates right and appropriate activity in each situation. To be fully human, one must act in accordance with the will of the Supreme Lord in order to help achieve the harmony of heaven and earth, the harmony of society, and the harmony of one's own soul. The path of wisdom, then, was the path of "realization," *tahqiq*, actualizing *haqq*. It demanded knowing the Supreme Real and Its manifestations in the universe and in the soul, and, on the basis of one's right knowledge, acting rightly, truly, and properly.

If a discussion is to take place between Islamic and Western (or Chinese, or Indian) civilization, and if that discussion aspires to be a philosophical dialogue rather than ideological, it must first come to an agreement on human nature. Yet, the "civilization" spawned by the Enlightenment spurns first principles and insists on being "scientific," which means that Supreme Reality and the humanly divine image have been effectively tossed in the dustbin. This, I think, is why Professor Stepanyants speaks of Christianity and the principles it holds in common with Islam, since modern Western civilization has long since abandoned those principles. There is plenty of commonality in the Muslim and Christian understanding of first things, but Christian thinking and Christian claims to have a true understanding of human nature have ceased to have any real effect on the way in which Western institutions and societies develop. Moreover, on the Islamic side, the principles of Islam are also being marginalized, though not nearly to the degree that has happened in Western Christianity.

If we are to have a civilizational dialogue, we need to go back to first principles and investigate our points of agreement and disagreement. We need to recover a definition of "civilization" that can be shared by the great historical traditions. We need to remember that the monologue that goes on today in the name of civilizational dialogue is the fruit of the domination of the principles of the Enlightenment over modern structures of thought. As long as the presuppositions of the Enlightenment are taken for granted by participants, then, as Heidegger said, the "linguistic and conceptual framework" will be "supplied entirely by Western civilization."

The presuppositions of the Enlightenment are in many ways symbolized by Descartes, who spoke for the annulment of the divine image in human nature. The result was a profound bifurcation of the human substance and a deep split between fact and value, between object and subject, between human beings and their cosmic matrix. In the great civilizations, the realization of wisdom was always considered the source of virtuous activity, because wisdom could only be achieved by unifying the true, the beautiful, and the good and by recognizing that all true knowledge makes moral and spiritual demands on us. In contrast, the scientific rationality invented by the Enlightenment has focused on achieving control and domination over the physical realm and has relegated all values—not to speak of virtue—to the realm of personal opinion and feelings.

The effect of the Enlightenment was to eliminate the transcendent dimension of reality and to leave human subjectivity as the lord of all. Some thinkers may have given lip-service to God, but always as an appendage of human feeling and human needs. In fact, the post-Enlightenment world has had "no need for that hypothesis," so God was considered dead and irrelevant, or, at best, a psychological sop for the feeble-minded. Eventually, science—that is, empirical knowledge limited to the physical realm and devoid of wisdom—reigned supreme, and it still reigns supreme. By eliminating the unitary and unifying wisdom that was the goal of human understanding in pre-modern civilizations, the Enlightenment led the West to develop a science and a technology that have made a mockery of its wonderful ideals—liberty, equality, fraternity, and so on. In fact we have lived for the past 150 years in the most brutal, vicious, violent, bloodthirsty, and inhuman world that history has ever known.

Islam and the other great traditional civilizations, if they hold true to their principles, want to ask some pointed questions before they start talking about what should be done to bring peace and harmony to the world. How can we speak of human rights and dignity if we do not know what human beings are? How can we know what human beings are if we do not situate ourselves in the total spectrum of reality, which includes transcendent dimensions infinitely more vast than the "reality" acknowledged by post-Enlightenment thinking?

Any civilizational dialogue that does not recognize how far the modern world has departed from wisdom and true understanding of human nature will only be a discussion among like-minded people, all striving to accomplish their own narrow interests. A real civilizational dialogue must focus on bringing back to life the various dimensions of each civilization that explain the true nature of the human substance and its fundamental, ontological rooting in Beauty, Truth, and the Good. The goal should be to help us understand what it means to be human. First we must understand who we are and why we are here. Then we can ask if "development" and "progress" are in truth "necessities of our time."

NOTE

1 *Rethinking Islam*, translated by Robert D. Lee (Boulder: Westview Press, 1994), p. 13.

Chapter 12

Islam and Christianity in the Social Context of China

Wang Jianping

There is very little publication on the subjects of the relationship between Islam and Christianity in the Chinese social context and of how to understand these two religions in the contemporary society of China. If a comparative study with the two religions is to be made and understood an analysis concerning the two religious doctrines for their similarity and dissimilarity should be undertaken. As a scholar of Islamic studies for long time I only took the course of Christianity studies only when I was a post-graduate student long time ago. So it is a challenge to me to deliver a lecture on this themes and I have to venture on the basis of past textual research.

SIMILARITY AND DISSIMILARITY BETWEEN THE TWO RELIGIONS

First let me introduce the similarity of the two religions. Both Islam and Christianity belong to the monotheism of the Abrahamic religious tradition. Both religions originated in the Middle East. They have a close relation with Jerusalem since Christianity and Judaism find their original sources in Jerusalem, which Islam regards it as one of its most holy places.

Second, the two religions were born in the cradle of Semitic culture and both were under the influence of Judaism.

Third, although the names for God in Christianity and Allah in Islam are different, actually their contents are the same: both have subscribed to the tenets of monotheism, and their God is the one Lord of the world, the Creator and the highest supreme being. In spite of their different names, for both religions God covers the same content in theological ontology.

Lastly, in the sphere of the religious doctrines Islam and Christianity have many similar conceptions, for example, Lord, angels, sacred writings, prophet, paradise, hell, the last day's judgment, Resurrection and the next life. The theological discourse and ideals of both are very close and similar. Islam recognizes Jesus as prophet and the Bible to be a holy book bearing God's words. Many stories in the Quran actually are taken from the Old and New Testaments. For example, the Genesis, the creation of the earth and the universe in seven days, the garden of Eden, Adam and Eve, the virgin-birth of Jesus by Maria, the Holy Mother, and so on. Of course, some names and titles given by the two religions are slightly different. For instance, Jesus in the Bible is pronounced as Ersa in the Chinese version of the Quran, Adam as Adan, Eva as Haowa, Abraham as Ibraham, Maria as Maieryan, Paradise in Christianity as Heavenly Garden (tianyuan), and Hell as Firey Hell, and so on. All these changes show that Islam wants to keep its own identity and independence after it was founded in the seventh century.

Surely, some differences between Islam and Christianity are grave. First, Islam strongly opposes the theory of Trinity in Christianity. Islam considers that the sole Lord or Creator of the world should not be taken anthropomorphically and cannot be compared to man or material things. Islam definitely does not accept the theory of the Father, Son and Holy Spirit. It holds that God cannot be have the imagination and attributes of man; more directly it says that God could not have a son as does man.

Second, Islam is adamantly against the theory that Jesus died in the manner of a Crucifixion. Islam thinks that Jesus died in a natural way after persecution instead of by crucifixion on the cross. When Jesus was resurrected his body was intact and bore no marks of having been nailed through his limbs.

Third, the greatest different is that Islam regards Mohammed as the last or "Seal of the Prophets". There is no prophet after him. The prophets before him such as Adam, Abraham, Mose, Jesus etc, are all recognized by Islam in their status as prophet. The reason why Islam regards Mohammed as the final Prophet is that the Jews and Christians had distorted the holy scriptures; only Mohammed follows the way laid out by the previous prophets in a most comprehensive and complete form, therefore, Islam is the only true religion.

Both Christians and Muslims accuse each other of distorting the holy scriptures and misinterpreting the creed. Christianity denounced Islam as a heresy, and declared that Mohammed was not a "Seal of the Prophets" since he distorted the doctrine of Christianity. Christians blamed Islam for having a violent nature, and launching holy wars, "one hand holding the Quran, one hand holding a sword". They charged that Muslims treated women unequally since women's status was very low in the Muslim society which practiced polygamy, thinking that a man could have four wives according to the Quran.

In another way, Islam charges Christianity with bearing responsibility for the moral decline in the Christian society because the Western society is full of indecent culture, sexual liberty, a high rate of divoice, materialism, hedonism, individualism, violence and pornography in film and television, alcoholism, homosexual practice and freedom of abortion, etc. Also Islam cannot accept the modernization and democratization imposed by the Western world.

Finally, the two religions are different in their cultural customs. The founding zone of Islam closely related with the desert environment of the Arabian Peninsula, so Muslims do not eat pork, blood or deceased cattle. Muslims do not eat beef or lamb if the oxen and sheep are slaughtered without chanting the formulation in the Islamic textbook. Muslim do not consume the meat of the beasts with violent nature. Muslims are prohibited from drinking alcohol. The Quran instructs women on wearing a proper costumes or suitable Islamic garment. Besides that in the aspects of sculpture and painting, movies and the fine arts orthodox Islam due to their opposition to idolatry, does not advocate nude or other human figures. In contrast, Christianity has no such restrictions and prohibitions.

Because of the difference in their doctrines the two religions had great hostilities and confrontations in history. For example, both sides were involved in a war for more than one hundred years for command over the holy city Jerusalem. The Christian Popes launched eight crusaders against the Islamic world. After the capitalist industrial revolution in Europe, the Western powers established many colonies in their world expansion and gunship policy. In this drive the Islamic world was the first zone of colonization. In the heartland of the Islamic world, i.e., in the Western Asia and the northern African many countries and regions fell under colonial control. Countries such as Britain and France dug the Siez Canal and controlled it. Britain occupied the South Asian Sub-continent. Netherlands occupied Indonesia. France colonized North and West Africa. The Western powers waged war against the Ottoman and Persian Empires. Thus for a long time there were many confrontations and great tension between the two religions or in their names.

However, in the beginning of the Islamic imperial period the Arabs invaded and occupied the lands of the Christian world. For example, the East Roman Empire or the Byzantine Empire. Muslims occupied the Mediterranean Sea, the Satin Island, Southern Italy and Sisal Island. The most serious was that Muslims crossed the Jablotuo Strainght and invaded Spain where they established an Islamic dynasty and ruled for nearly eight hundred years. Only at the end of the 15th century did the Spanish expel Muslims from the Iberian Peninsular.

Thus the two religions were always in the competition and confrontation during the flow of history.

THE ENTRANCE OF THE TWO RELIGIONS INTO CHINA AND THE CHARACTER OF THEIR MISSIONARY WORK

Both religions came to China in the 7th century or in the period of the Tang Dynasty. The date of the Christian entrance was a little earlier than that of Islam. The coming of Christianity to China is known from the inscription of "the Monument of the Nestorian Church Spreading from the Roman Empire". The Nestorian Group (advocating Gnostic theory and the separation of God from man) was a Christian heresy, and was persecuted by the Pope in the Roman Empire and later by Eastern Orthodoxy. It spread from Syria and was called Jing Religion. Islam came to China following that event.

The Nestorian Group spread into Changan and Shaaxi. This region became the window for Islam's entrance into China a little later. Of course, due to the commercial links with Arabs Islam also came to Hangzhou, Guangzhou and Quanzhou (Zayton). In these areas the Muslim merchants set up foreign enclaves. The entrance of Islam into China was mainly through the channels of the commercial connection between China and Arab, diplomatic exchanges and military aid. It was known that the rebellion by Warlords An and Shi caused the Tang Dynasty to lose Luoyang, the Eastern Capital and

Changan, the Western Capital. Almost half land of the country was controlled by the rebel forces so that China was in great internal turmoil. Emperor Xuanzong had to abdicate his power to his son and sacrifice his favored concubine to appease his military troops which already showed their strong discontent of the policy of the emperor.

At that time most of the land of the Tang Empire was lost to the rebel forces, and the Tang Royal court asked the help of the Arab Empire. At the invitation of the Chinese emperor the Abbassid Dynasty sent three thousand Muslim soldiers, mostly Arab and Persian. They included Turkish and Uighur soldiers, but the main body of this troop was composed of Muslims. This event was recorded by Chinese chronicle and its authenticity is without doubt. These Muslim soldiers cooperated with Chinese troops in the fighting. By their joint efforts the rebel forces led by An Lushan and Shi Siming were defeated and the two capitals and the occupied land were recovered. After the military campaigns were completed, the Tang Emperor granted land and houses to these Muslim soldiers for their military contribution. So the Muslim soldiers settled down in China and the Muslim Hui community in Lotus Lake District of Xi'an can trace its history to that time. These Muslim soldiers inter-married with Chinese women in Shaaxi and formed today's Hui communities. Therefore, several mosques in Xi'an are regarded as the mosques with long history. At least two of these mosques were thought by local Muslims as have been built in the Tang Dynasty.

Thus unlike the way of the Christian missionaries from Europe Islam's coming to China was through commercial trade, diplomatic exchanges, military cooperation and intermarriage with Chinese women, etc. Because the Muslim soldiers and merchants including Arabs and Persians were assigned land or purchased land they were well-off and with the practice of polygamy their population grew rapidly. Their descendants basically inherited their family tradition and cultural customs, and they continually believed in Islam. In Inland China Islam mainly developed through the Hui groups by the expansion of their families and clans. Hence, the development of Islam was achieved by the natural growth of the clan population, expansion of the foreign communities, influxes of population, economic exchange, migration, etc.

In the period of the Mongol or Yuan Dynasty in Chinese history the Mongols first conquered Western Asia; then they turned back to launch the Eastern Expedition, conquered the South Song Dynasty and established the Yuan Dynasty. In the Western Expedition the Mongols captured many Muslims as prisoners of war and recruited them into the Muslim Army of Western Asia. The Mongol rulers put all people into four categories of which the Mongols were the first rank and the noblest class; the second class was Semu people regarded as the various ethnic groups from Central Asia and the Western Asia. Many of them took positions as minister, premier and local officials, military commander and tax officials. They included also many soldiers and merchants, etc., of which many were Muslim. The third class was the Northern Han Chinese, because they yielded to the Mongols earlier as the latter conquered China. The last class was the Southern Han Chinese since they resisted the invasion of the Mongols severely and surrendered at the last minute.

The Semu people worked as officials or as soldiers stationed all over China to safeguard the territory of the Mongol Empire. There was a saying that the Huihui or Muslims lived all over China. This manifests that the phenomena of Muslims widely spreading in China was already established. These Muslims did not do missionary work, for example, Sayyid al-Ajall Shams al-Din Umar, whose name means in Arabic: the glorious offspring of the Prophet, the Sun of Religion (Islam), was the governor of Yunnan Province. He came from Bukhara of Central Asia and although he was the provincial governor he did not undertake a policy of Islamization. Rather he continued to establish Confucian education, build Confucian Temples, formulate the administrative system of prefecture and county. Thus, he carried off the Sinolization policy and finally integrated Yunnan into Inland China both culturally and politically.

In contrast, the development of Christianity in China was discontinuous or disrupted at times, unlike Islam in China which developed in a continuous manner. For instance, the Nestorian Church from the Roman Empire came to China in the Tang Dynasty but disappeared later on. According to archeological discoveries, many Nestorian churches became the temples of Taoism and Buddhism in later generations. Another possibility is that the Nestorians merged into Islam.

In the Ming Dynasty, France and Spain introduced the Catholic Church into China; the missionaries put their emphasis on the upper class. Matteo Ricci, a well-known Italian missionary, and his colleagues even took official positions in the Royal court of the Ming Empire. At first, the relationship between the missionaries and the imperial officials was good, and the missionaries played a bridging role of cultural communication. But in the reign of emperor Kangxi of the Qing Dynasty, the development of the indigenous Christian force in China faced the crucial issue of whether or not to accept the ancestor-worship of Chinese traditional culture? The Holy Roman See (the Vatican) and the Pope strongly opposed ancestor worship, since they held that it conflicted with the basic tenet of Christianity. Also there were clashes with the established authority of Pope. Therefore, the Roman Pope dispelled ancestor worship from the creed and practices of the Catholic Church in China. This action offended the Emperor Kangxi since the Qing imperial ruling was based on the Confucianism philosophical principles and codes of ethics that the subjects should obey the monarch, as the son obeys the father, and the wife obeys the husband. Before that emperor Kangxi had a very unconfortable relationship with the missionaries; even his teacher was missionary. Therefore, emperor Kangxi issued an order to expel all foreign missionaries. Christianity in China fell to the lowest level (ebb) since the reign of Kangxi and even disappeared in many areas.

In the Opium War the Qing empire was defeated and had to sign an agreement opening the door or ports to commercial trade. One of the articles gave the right of the missionaries to enter China to teach Christianity. Thereafter, Western missionaries came to China in large number. Thus the spread of Christianity in Modern China was realized mainly through the expansion of the Western powers, or backed by the colonization or gun-power policy. It was a natural extension of the elite culture. From this point of view the missionary methods between Christianity and Islam differed.

The two religions differed also in the means of teaching religious doctrines in China. Christianity confronted and clashed with China's central government in history, therefore its missionary work was blocked at certain times. Later on Western colonialism enforced an open door in China backed by military forces, and cowed the Chinese rulers into accepting Western values and convictions. As early as the reign of Qianlong Emperor the diplomats from Western countries refused to prostrate in front of Chinese emperor in their diplomatic mission, which event caused a quarrel in diplomatic interchange. The Chinese rulers compromised over the entrance of a large number of Christian missionaries into China which embodied the expansion of their strong cultural force. Therefore, Western Christianity always maintained a very tense relationship with the Qing rulers. In later times there took place the Boxing Movement, expelling foreigners, killing missionaries, etc., events. With the failure of the Reform in 1898, and the Western supporting of Emperor Guangxu and his reform policy, Empress Dowager (Cixi) targeted Western missionaries as scapegoats in order to cover the conflicts in the empire and the discontent of the people. The massacre to the foreigners in the Boxer Movement led to an invasion by the eight Western powers, so that the Qing government had to yield to the West, make peace and sign humiliating conventions. Meanwhile the imperial government suppressed the Boxer movement cruelly. The Western missionaries gained victory in their encounter with the Qing Empire through reliance on force.

However, Islam kept a low profile and did not actively pursue the Han Chinese to believe in its religion. Therefore, the Muslims had few clashes with non-Muslims over the issue of faith in Chinese society, and Muslim missionary work took the form of peaceful conversion. Of course, many confrontations between the Hui Muslims and Han Chinese did take place in China, however, such conflicts occurred mainly due to the ethnic hatred and to the issues of resources including those of land, water, mining and trade, and did not deeply involve clashes over religious doctrines. In short Islam and Christianity as two religions had very different situations in the social context of China.

THE INFLUENCE OF THE TWO RELIGIONS UPON CHINESE CULTURE

In short, the introduction of Islam into China was limited by ethnicity and racial boundaries. For instance, in the period of the Tang and the Song Dynasty Islam was confined to the foreign communities, and its influence did not go beyond those enclaves. In Hongzhou at that time a very strange thing happened that a couple of foreign Muslims held a wedding party, their

Han Chinese neighbors were so curious that they climbed over the roof of the chamber of the Muslim new couple to see the wedding ceremony in the house. The people on the roof were so many that the roof could not bear the heavy burden and crashed. A happy event became a tragedy. The bride and bridegroom and the Muslim guests invited to the wedding party were killed in the crash.

In addition, the Confucian Han intellectuals composed an ironic poem to bother these foreign Muslims, describing their strange names such as Alwa Al-Din, Mahmad. Their physical feature looked very strange, i.e., big nose, curly hair and cat-like eyes. Also the poem criticized their strange living customs. All in all, the Han Chinese laughed at them in an ironic way and felt happy at the troubles suffered by Muslims.

We see from this point of view that the contacts between Muslims and the Han Chinese were not so good. If a Han Chinese married a Muslim, the precondition was that the Han accept or convert to Islam. If a Han Chinese woman married a Muslim she would easily accept the Islamic faith held by the husband due to the low social status of women in China. The man or husband dominated in the family, as did his faith in this regard. On this question the Confucian society was the same as the Islamic society. Therefore, if the Han woman or a woman from another ethnic minorities married a Muslim man the precondition was that she must convert to Islam or at least accept the Islamic cultural traditions or living customs as her life style. If a Han Chinese man married into a Muslim family he also must convert to Islam.

Generally speaking, the influence of Islam over the Han Chinese culture or Confucian culture was not so significant. In the fields of astrology, medicine, handcraft, some technology and cooking Islam impacted upon Chinese society to some extents, but it was only confined in the imperial court and among the people of the upper class, or limited to neighborhoods where Muslims were located. In the modern Chinese society the influence of Islam over Han Chinese culture could not match that of Christianity.

However, Christianity was far different. After its missionaries came to China the foreign Christian churches established schools, hospitals, kindergartens, printing houses, relief centers, and they published newspapers, magazines and sponsored charitable activities. Although Christianity had a difficult relationship with the authorities, they emphasized work among the ordinary people, thus they achieved great influence over Chinese society. Of course, as is well known that the missionaries did not only bring the religious faith but also introduced Western science and technology, an advanced educational system, the value and concepts of democracy and beneficial, universal love. Hence, we should evaluate this period of history properly and objectively. We should not simply brand the missionaries as "dogs of the Western imperialism's cultural invasion". It must be pointed out factually that the missionary charity organizations helped the suffering and dying people with relief works when the Yellow River was flooding severely. It was the missionaries who protected the ordinary people in the occupied land and exposed to the media of the savage slaughter when the Japanese invading army committed the massacre and rape of Nanjing. It is the missionaries who provided medical treatment for the wounded and injured in the hospitals set up by church and sheltered those who lost their home as the civil war broke out and the warlords fought each other in the NorthWest China. In the early part of the 20th century more than 20 percent of the Western missionaries were medical doctors or related with the medical profession. They contributed greatly to the Chinese civilians and ordinary people with their medical treatment and the improvement of the health condition. Such an important role played by them could not be taken away from history.

HISTORY OF THE CO-EXISTENCE OF THE TWO RELIGIONS

In the Middle Ages Islam and Christianity were always in ferocious conflict. This was especially true against the background of the struggles for Jerusalem between the Crusaders and the Muslim soldiers. Since modern society the long expedition and colonialism expansion in Egypt and the Islamic world launched by Napoleon and European powers cannot erase the historical wounds left by the rivalry between the Islamic and Christian worlds. After the Second World War, the independent movement and the wars in the Muslim countries against the colonial invasion made the relationship between Islam and Christianity worse and more difficult.

However in China, since the two religions belong to minority groups and do not belong to the religious mainstream, the relationship between them is generally on good terms and one of peace. In the time of the Tang Dynasty when the two religions were introduced there was no animosity between the two; actually there was no substantial contact and communication between them. Both religions came to China as guests and guest cultures.

In the Yuan Empire although "the Muslims were scattered in all parts of China", the two religions followed their own doctrines and practiced their own rituals. The Mongols who held power in that period mainly believed in Shamanism and Buddhism. Especially Gengis Khan, Monge Khan and Khublay Khan took a positive attitude toward religions, were tolerant of various religions and treated them on an equal footing. In such circumstances each religious tradition acted in its own way and chose its own direction, therefore they did not collide with one another. In spite of small skirmishes these conflicts did not reach the level of lack of compromise or tension. Once Christians said something bitter against Muslims in front of Monge Khan and wanted to make trouble in the relation between the Mongols and the Muslims, but they failed in this.

Khublay Khan once organized various religious groups for debates on the respective religious doctrine in the royal palace, in which Christianity and Islam stated their own religious creeds and defended their own religious tenets. In such debates both Christians and Muslims competed with each other to convince the Mongol rulers that their religion was absolutely correct. The winner usually depended on his oral capability or debating skill. For example, for the argument to make the emperor and officials think its religion correct, and the argument needed strong logical power and touching force, etc. However, whatever religion succeeded in winning, the Emperor of the Yuan Dynasty did not take a stand on its side. He was tolerant of all religions and treated all equally; he did not set any official religion. In this the faiths of the Royal family were a good example. Some members of the royal family believed in Christianity, some believed in Islam, more members in Shamanism, Buddhism. The worship of natural forces and totems prevailed among the nomadic tribes in the steppes.

But in the Yuan Dynasty an unpleasant thing happened when Christianity and Islam were hostile to one another. The Pope sent an envoy to the Mongol court to persuade the Mongols to attack the Arab Muslims in order to revenge the loss of the Crusaders' eastern expedition. At that time, in his small circle the emperor of the Yuan Dynasty sometimes held that the teaching of Christianity was reasonable, but Khublay Khan had some personal unhappiness with Muslims.

Once Khublay Khan invited Muslim officials to attend an official dinner. But the Muslim officials did not consume pork, or lamb and beef if the cow and sheep were slaughtered by non-Muslims. Therefore, as these many dishes were served, the Muslim officials did not touch the food even with chop-sticks, which made the emperor lose face. Therefore, Khublay Khan deeply hated Muslims. Meanwhile the Mongols and Muslims had different ways to slaughter cows and sheep. The Muslims adopted the method of cutthroat, since Muslims did not drink blood, they must discard the blood. However, the Mongols had a way of hanging the animals so as to kill or slaughter them without cutting through their throat. Hence the blood remained in the bodies of cattle. Due to the unpleasant event between the Khoblay Khan and the Muslims, the emperor issued an order that in China the killing of cattle must follow the way of the Mongols so that Muslims had no meat to consume.

The power struggle within the Yuan imperial court was usually a factional clash between the Muslim and Han groups. Sometimes, this power struggle would involve some Christians, but only in individual cases. In the period of the Ming and Qing dynasties, both Muslims and Christians took positions in the imperial governments and in spite of their different faiths they showed loyalty to the emperors. Since the Song Dynasty all the calendars were composed or edited by the Muslims invited from the Central Asia and Persia until the Ming Dynasty. These calendars were entitled as "Huihui Calendars". In the Royal court Catholic medical doctors provided Western medicines to treat the patients and these worked more quickly than the Chinese medicines. Some Muslims worked in the royal palace, for example in "the Translation Bureau" or "Tongwen Hall", engaged as diplomatic, imperial envoys and interpreters. These had been no bloodsheds between the two religions. In the Ming and Qing dynasties, no large-scale confrontation took place between Christianity and Islam. Because the two religions were outside of the mainstream of China culture and small groups of people there was no fundamental conflict between their interests, while both had some conflicts with the mainstream national Han and Confucian cultures.

In the Qing Dynasty there occurred several large-scale Hui uprisings which were severely suppressed. For instance, in Yunnan, the kingdom of lead, copper, zinc and tin, there were many incidents of fighting over the mining ores between the Han and the Hui Muslims. In NorthWest China there were incidents of fighting over water resources and land. If the local governmental officials mishandled the cases or showed bias, it could lead to bloodshed between the Hans and the Hui Muslims. If the administrative work was so bad and officials so corrupted, the mediation of the Hui-Han conflict could be wrong and biased so that there would be no fairness in the legal suits. In some cases the Hui Muslims held that the local officials favored the Han and discriminated against the Hui. As the Hui Muslims were a very determined people with a capability for mobilization, if some law-case was not handled very well ethnic conflicts could occur. Even mutual massacres and large-scale bloodshed could break out between different ethnic groups.

In the Reigns of Xianfeng and Tongzhi in the Qing Dynasty at the time of the Taiping and Nian Armed rebellions, social tension were high. The policy of discrimination against the Muslims and the historical hatred which remained till that time due to the mishandling of ethnic conflicts brought about a Muslim resistance movement in the NorthWest and SouthWest China. The uprisings were suppressed by the imperial troops led by Zuo Zongtang and other imperial officials. Millions of Muslims were killed in ethnic cleansing. In NorthWest China and Yunnan the Muslim population dropped so drastically that the economic regions prosperous in the past turned into ruins with no people or signs of life. In the reign of Daoguang the Hui Muslim population of one million decreased to under 100,000 after the suppression of the Hui uprising. A similar situation took place in Shaaxi Province where of 500 Muslim Hui villages in the 500 square li in Qing Valley according to the monument inscription, after the Hui uprising that population was found only in Xi'an city whose total residents were less than 50,000.

Christianity received good treatment after the Opium War since the Western Powers were in a strong position and on the offense, and the missionaries were protected by them. Except for a few individual incidents of bloodshed Christianity developed rapidly in this period. This was conducive to the hatred of the Boxer Movement against the missionaries and the later humiliation of Christianity.

In the Republic of China led by Sun Yanshan, the new regime carried out the policy of religious equality and raised the slogan of "Republic for Five Nationalities". The five nationalities were Man, Han, Mongol, Hui and Tibetan. The government first raised minorities such as Muslims to an equal level with the Han in Chinese society. In the time of the Republic led by Jiang Jieshi, he married Madam Song Meilin as the First Lady and converted to Christianity. Moreover, his Republic government was based on the Western Alliance led by Britain and America. Christianity then had much closer relations with the government and had rapid growth in Chinese society.

But the Muslim population had decreased after Islam suffered suppression by the Qing Empire, so it entered a stage of recovery and revival in the Republic. While Christians received good treatment in society, Muslims were not so lucky. In NorthWest China especially the ethnic tension was sometimes high and bloodshed often broke out. In Inland China a series of the incidents of insult to Islam happened. For example, some articles in newspapers and magazines misinterpreted the custom of Muslims abstinence from pork, even insulted them groundlessly. Therefore, the Muslims held demonstrations and smashed the publishing house of the newspaper. In such incidents Muslims in China particularly the Hui manifested solidity and coherence. Such coherence caused fear in Han Chinese people, and the emergence of bias and stereotypes increased the chances of skirmishes and group fighting between the Hui and the Han.

During the 1920s to the 1940s the Western missionaries taught Christian doctrine in the regions in the NorthWest and Northern China inhabited by Muslims; they wanted to spread the good news to the Muslim peoples in order to convert Muslims to Christianity. The China Inland Missionary Church established by the Western organized "Friends of Moslems" agency especially targeted the Hui Muslims in NorthWest and Inland China as a strategy to try to let them join the rank of Christians. Missionaries such as Samuel Zwemer, Isaac Mason, Claude Pickens, Carter Holton, Martin Taylor personally went to Qinghai, Gansu, Ningxia, Shaaxi and Sichuan, etc., to teach Christianity among the Muslim communities. They distributed the Bible and Pamphlets in Arabic and even published magazines to promote their missionary work. They also did fieldwork and social studies, even some academic research to understand the Muslim ethnic minorities and their customs and life style. Although they made great efforts in missionary propaganda, they had very little success and made almost no progress. This was due to the fact that the basis of the Muslim religious tradition and Islamic culture in China was not so shallow as imagined by the missionaries; in contrast it was profound with a long history. Besides, Islam in China was so closely related with the ethnic characteristics and the ethnic culture that the Muslims could not give up their tradition and accept the new faith. Although the Western missionaries taught Christianity and did propaganda work to transmit Jesus' teaching, Muslims in China did not expel them and did not treat them rudely. Everywhere the missionaries went they received hospitality and friendship from the Muslims in China. Some were very touched that the missionaries discussed in Arabic with Akhonds the doctrines and theological theory. In the cultural atmosphere where the cultures of Confucianism, Buddhism, Taoism dominated, the relationship of the Muslim and the Christian minorities was considerably harmonious and friendly, with mutual respect for each other.

THE RELATIONSHIP AND CONTEXT OF THE TWO RELIGIONS IN CONTEMPORARY CHINA

Besides the Hui Muslims China has many other Islamic nationalities. For example, there are the Urghur, Khazak, Kirkiz, Uziberk, Salar, Tatar, Tajiksand, Dongxiang and Bao'an. These ten Muslim nationalities are minorities in China. In the 1950s, the People Republic of China had a program to distinguish and promote their participation; it carried out a policy of preferential treatment of ethnic minorities which continues today. A member of an ethnic minority, more easily find entrance to a university in the national examination. Some ethnic minorities benefit from special policies, e.g., they enjoy a particular welfare system, a special family planning policy which is less restrictive than for the Han. Some ethnic groups do not implement the population control program. Apart from these, some beneficial programs are formulated for the welfare of Muslims. For example, the living subsides for Muslims are a little higher than for Han Chinese. In the period of the Three Years' Natural Disaster (1959-1962) the government provided a little more meat and cooking oil to Muslims than to Han Chinese. Many units and enterprises give Muslims or ethnic minority persons more chances to become cadre, professional promotion, apartments, and awards for work. In addition, the state government agencies such as People's Congress, the Political Consultation Committee, the Nationality Affairs of State Council, the Department of the United Front of Central Committee of CCP, the State Bureau of Religious Affairs, the Ministry of Civil Administration of State Council, and the Islamic Association of China have been assigned many Muslim cadres and ethnic minority cadres take leading positions. China has set up national autonomous regions, prefecture, counties, townships and rural villages where a certain proportion of ethnic minority cadres must be guaranteed. For example, the Hui Muslim population in Ningxia Hui Autonomous Region are only one third of the total population of the region, but the proportion of the Hui cadres actually is higher than those of other ethnic groups. Therefore, the government has policies and programs which greatly favor Muslim peoples. They pay much attention to the ethnic minority groups particularly to Muslim minorities.

These policies are implemented in religious affairs and hence are conducive to a differentiation in treatment between Islam and Christianity. It is well known that in the 1950s China regarded the Western powers such as USA as the fundamental enemy and Christians as related with imperialist invasion policies. The New China not only expelled all foreign missionaries from the country, but also established the Christian Three-Self Patriotic Committee. In the period when the Extreme Leftist Hard-liners took power the government totally severed relations of the Chinese Church with all abroad. Especially due to the Cold War between China and USA, the two countries were in a tense encounter and China considered Christianity as a hostile force. Having been connected with the Western imperialism. Under the heavy pressure of the Extreme Leftist Hard-line, particularly during the Cultural Revolution, Christians in China suffered more persecution and restriction than did Muslims and Buddhists.

The fate of Islam in China was a little different from others during that time. This is due to the fact that Islam is a religion believed by ethnic minorities and that, before China returned to the United Nations in 1971, the UN Assembly voted annually on whether the seat of China in the UN should belong to Taiwan or the Mainland. Therefore, the votes of the Middle Eastern countries and of the Muslim countries were very crucial for Mainland's return to the UN. In order to have a good image and also to win the support from the Islamic countries, the policy of Chinese government toward Islam has been considerably favorable. For instance, after the New China was founded, there was no diplomatic tie between China and Saudi Arabia, but since the early 1950s the New China initially sent an Islamic pilgrimage delegation to Mecca in Saudi Arabia to participate in the Haji pilgrimage every year. Meanwhile the delegation also visited Egypt, Syria, Jordan, Iraq, Yemen and Pakistan and other Islamic countries on good will missions. During the 1960s and the 1970s China wanted to be the leader of the Third World between the two Superpowers: USA and the Soviet Union. For example, China supported the Palestine National Liberation Movement, and Pakistan on the issue of Kashmir in the India-Pakistan confrontation. After 1979 China supported the Mujahaddin's to fight against the Soviet Union's invasion to Afghanistan. All these efforts by China showed that it wanted to make friends or improve the relation with the Third World. When the governments of those Islamic countries sent their delegates or leaders to visit China, they brought copies of the Quran to Muslims and mosques in China. On this the Chinese government kept silent. Since the 1990s with the increasing reliance on the petroleum in the Middle East, China cannot risk harming the relationship with the Arabic and Islamic countries or do gravely wrong in its policy toward the Islam and toward Muslim minorities in China.

However, the attitude toward Christianity is different. It is not allowed to transport copies of the Bible into China, and they are confiscated by the Customs Office. Of course, many copies of the Quran were brought by the state leaders of the Islamic countries who visited China, and the Chinese government had to accept this fact. The government treated its Muslims in the same way as the funds poured into China from the foreign countries to help Muslims repair or rebuild mosques. China permits the Muslims and mosques to accept the aid from the oversea religious organizations and groups. During Communism's New China, because Muslim nationalities are minorities, and there are the requirements of diplomatic relations uniting the Third World, the situation of Islam was better than Christianity, especially before China opened its door to the outside and initiated its reform policy. The example in the Cultural Revolution was very remarkable: while all Christian churches were closed down, a few mosques in Beijing, Shanghai and Urumqi were still open to the public although most of mosques also were forced to close down. Especially where diplomatic officials from the embassies of the Third World Muslim countries needed prayer services, these mosques were open for them by Foreign Affairs and maintained officially. However, Christianity had no such luck. Because Islam is seen in terms of ethnic minorities that potentially impact foreign affairs and relationships with the Third World, the situation of Islam is generally better than that of Christianity.

After China opened its door and launched its reform and market policy, both religions have had great development. Many Han Chinese students choose Europe and America for their oversea studies, while the Muslim students choose the Middle East countries, such as Egypt, Saudi Arabia, Kuwait, the United Arab Emirate and Iran studies overseas. Some of them also select Malaysia, Pakistan and Indonesia for higher or religious education. In NorthWest China and SouthWest China, Muslims take advantage of the reform and open door policy; they have established many Chinese-Arabic schools in which the young Muslims can study Arabic and Islam. In Xinjiang Islam receives more favored treatment than Christianity. Of course, there are some ethnic separatists among the Uighur people. Toward these the Chinese government takes a firm stand. Concerning public security departments, Christianity has the problem of underground churches, especially the Catholic Church. Islam has no such problem.

Currently the terrorists who attacked the USA in the event of 9/11 were identified as "Muslims". After 911 America launched the counter-terrorist war. It made wars against the Taliban Government in Afghanistan and Iraq ruled by the Sadam regime. Therefore, the relationship between the Arabic world and the West becomes tense once again. Before 9/11 some people in the West had negative feeling against Muslims and Islamic culture, which even led to hatred and some skirmishes. After 9/11 such contradiction and conflict between two cultures related with their religious faiths have become much more tense and conflicts often occur.

Such tension of course impacts the sentiments and thinking of the 20 millions Muslims in China. After the event of 9/11, some Hui Muslims wore T Shirts with the portrait of Ben Laden in Lanzhou and Tianjin. Some Hui Muslims privately admitted that Ben Laden did a heroic terrorist deed in attacking the World Trade Center. As the American air-force raided Afghanistan ruled by the Taliban, the Hui Muslims in Hebei, Tianjin and Henan appealed to the local governments to organize a volunteer army to go to Afghanistan to fight for the Taliban regime. When America invaded Iraq the Muslims in China donated funds and other materials to the Iraqi people. The Akhonds denounced the American invasion in a sermon in the mosque. Some Muslims even burned in effigy President Bush and American flags in a mosque. Chinese Muslims hold that in the deep confrontation of Arab and Israel the USA supports Israel and is very hostile to Islam and Muslims. The Islamic world also feels the invasion of the Western culture, i.e., Coco Cola, MacDonald fast food, movies from Hollywood, the coming of Western value and concepts, sexual liberty, homosexuality and abortion. The Islamic world blames Western culture and its hegemonic policy for their own social problems. It is said that the Western Church wanted to send Chinese Christians to the Islamic countries in the Middle East as missionaries. To do that could impact the relationship between China and the Arabic countries.

Before 9/11 event there were armed conflicts related to religion between Islam and Christianity. For example, in the war in Bosnia and Herzegovina there was large-scale bloodshed among Muslims, Catholics and Eastern Orthodox. In the war of Kosovo there was bloodshed between Solvinians in Eastern Orthodox and Albanian Muslim. There is war in Somali; the war in Chechnya between Russia inspired by Eastern Orthodox and Chechnyan Muslims inspired by Islam over Chechnyan independence; and war between the Catholics and the Muslims in the Southern Philippine. More serious is the war between Christians and Muslims in Indonesia where many people have died and many villages became ruins. In Sudan there is a civil war between the Muslims in North and Christians in South, as also in Nigeria there are conflicts between Islam and other religions, and within Judaism in Israel, Hinduism in India, and Buddhism in Thailand.

The impact of these international events upon the Muslims in China is appearant. It has stirred the hatred of Muslims in China to the hegemonic policy of America and Western powers. Talking with Chinese Muslims in a mosque one finds strong discontent toward the hegemonic action of USA, and anger toward the American invasion of Afghanistan and Iraq. On the other hand, the compacted Muslim communities in China complain of aggressive missionary work by Western missionaries. For instance, in Xinjiang Christianity has developed rapidly during last ten or more years. Not a few foreign missionaries, including some from South Korea, Han Christian missionaries from Inland China, and Henan Christians have gone to Xinjiang as missionaries. Some Eastern Orthodox missionaries have entered Xinjiang from Russians, Kazakhstan and Kyrgyzstan.

The Chinese government cracks down on the separatists and terrorists in Xinjiang. When a bomb exploded on a bus near Xidan in Beijing on March 8, 1997, ordinary Chinese are alarmed, and hold that all this terrorism is done by the separatists in Xinjiang. Because of the pressure of public opinion which relates Islam to terrorism, people have strongly biased and stereotypical prejudice toward Muslims. In this circumstance some individual Muslims joined the rank of the Eastern Orthodox in order to avoid of suspicion as separatists. Therefore, the issue of converting Muslims to other religions, reported to the local bureaus of the ethnic and religious affairs for registration, may cause nervousness regarding conversion to other religions, and lead to tension among the cadres. This is because the converted Muslims could face punishment within the Islamic community and their safety could not be guaranteed. For example, conversion brings a death sentence in Saudi Arabia and in Arabic countries politics is integrated with religion. In addition, the conversion of Muslims to Christianity could lead to a protest movement in the Islamic world.

Therefore, there has been some displeasure between Christianity and Islam in Xinjiang. For the government the overwhelming task is stability. The Muslim people belong to ethnic minorities, and surely the government favors Islam. As a result, the Department of the United Front of the Xinjiang Communist Party and the Nationality and Religious Committee issued a document which prohibits teaching Christianity among the Muslims in Xinjiang. If anyone breaks this regulation he will be punished by law. Therefore, the state government used administrative means to interfere with religious affairs in order to avoid Christian missionaries causing bloodshed. For Christians such a regulation is not fair. Thus, counter-terrorism worldwide after 9/11 is conducive of continuing tension between Christianity and Islam. China is no exception from such an impact and influence.

Because Christianity has a dominant position and teaches its doctrine everywhere, even its missionary work penetrates Muslim areas. In view of the fact that individual Muslims convert the Christianity some Muslim scholars in China call on Islam and Muslims seriously to consider the fact of the Christian missionary. They want to make great efforts to enlighten Islamic culture and Islamic tradition in this regard. They also prefer to do missionary as do Christians in order to increase the influence of Islam and its religious capacity.

If we look closely at the characteristics of Islam and Christianity in contemporary Chinese social context again we find a strange and complicated phenomenon: although Islam is favored in policy and given much attention, its public opinion and social influence are at a disadvantage, and it is often misunderstood by non-Muslims whose bias against Islam is growing. However, although Christianity has not received favored treatment as has Islam, its image among the people and in society is steadily good and its influence growing. This can be seen from Christmas celebration, Christmas card exchange and the Valentine Day; such Christian cultural events have become very popular in China in recent years.

Today we emphasize the dialogue between the different civilizations; this is needed in China too. It strengthens the force of peace and reduces confrontation. However, generally speaking, due to the fact that Christianity and Islam are the religions believed by the minority groups and exist in the mainstream cultural system of the communist atheism, there should be no fundamental conflict and conflict of interest between these two great religions. Generally they co-exist peacefully, and follow their own ways. Despite the two sometimes having tensions, these are on the margins. Also due to the circumstance of an atheist ideology dominating society, the contradiction of the two religions will not develop into a large-scale confrontation. From this point of view and given historical lessons, it is likely impossible that the two great religions could conflict severely in the Chinese social context. Hence, in many aspects both Christianity and Islam could understand and sympathize with each other side by side. The relationship between them could be good, rather than so tense as between the Western and the Islamic worlds. Certainly, the living customs of Islam could clash with those of the Han Chinese the issue of pork is the most notable example. The Yangxin incident occurred in December, 2000; the Zhongmou Incident in Henan happened in October, 2004. Both reflect a certain conflict between the Hui Muslims and the Han Chinese.

Therefore, it is likely impossible that a large-scale bloody conflict take place between Christianity and Islam in the Chinese social context. Whether or not it will happen in the future depends on the various elements involving government policy, law enforcement and the human environment across China.

Chapter 13

Islam and the West:
Clash in Dialogue or Dialogue in Clash

Gholamreza Aavani

In the name of God
The infinitely Good, the infinitely Merciful

True understanding and harmony can be achieved through dialogue; peace and harmony are themselves the fruits of such meaningful dialogue. But if we ask why dialogue is possible at all, a presumable answer might be that it is possible because man has been endowed with the luminous "logos", the most exalted and praiseworthy of the Divine gifts. Man is the highest manifestation of this logos, which he can moreover share with other human beings. This by itself justifies gathering together to remove collisions, conflicts, confrontations, splits and misunderstandings through dialogue.

One might object that dialogue is taking place within the context of philosophy, which is itself the self-disclosure of reason in the course of history. But how is dialogue possible within the matrix of religion, there being such a diversity, differentiation, nay even opposition between religions? We might answer by saying that the founders of religions such as Lao-Tze, Confucius, Buddha, Moses, Jesus or Muhammad were the most perfect embodiments of the Divine Logos, being the first locus of manifestation of Divine Intelligence. Hence the dialogue is even more feasible within the context of religions, provided that we have sure access to the inner logic of their enlightened and Divine logos.

Task of talking about "The Dialogue between Islamic and Western Civilizations: The religious and secular perspectives," rather difficult, give the state of affairs going on in the world around us, filled with strife, conflicts and tribulations. But in order to offer a tentative solution I should first try to give a rather short historical account concerning the encounter of the East and the West in the pre-Islamic era and then will proceed to an analysis of the confrontations between Islam and the West, both in the Christian and the Modern eras. After having delineated the nature of Islam as a world religion and what associates and sets it apart from the other world religions, I will take into consideration the confrontation of Islam with the Modern West and whether there is possibility for a fruitful and meaningful dialogue in the future.

THE EASTERN QUESTION

I take this title to signify not what the historians refer to in the context of the long-standing rivalries and hostilities between Europe and the Ottoman Empire, but in its wider context of the cultural, military and political liaison between the Western hemisphere (Europe and recently the United States) and the East (Near and Middle East in particular). Of particular significance are the military expeditions between ancient Persia and Greece and the conquest of the latter by the Achamenid King Xerxes which made Asia Minor and Greek Satraps or provinces of the Achamenid Empire. This Persian conquest was later revenged by the Macedonian Emperor Alexander who not only conquered Egypt , but also was able to annex Syria, Asia Minor, the Persian Empire and India. Had he not been hampered by his own generals due to exhaustion, he might have intended to go as far as China. But what is of particular significance for us here is that both the Persian and Greek expansions were more of a military nature and scarcely had a deep impact on the cultural and intellectual life of the subjugated countries. The sole exception was Hellenistic culture which the successors of Alexander were able to establish in Alexandria, which was to have a pervasive influence first in Christian and then in Islamic civilizations. This expansionism was more territorial and geographical than cultural and intellectual in nature. That is why with the subversion of the political dominion of the ruler or the dynasty in question, the hegemony and domination of the aggressive power would immediately come to an end. We do not perceive any clear trace of a mutual and persistent cultural exchange or a continuous intellectual dialogue between these cultures.

The same is *mutatis mutandis* true about the Arascid and Sassanid Empires, on the one hand, and the Roman Empire, on the other, which for centuries were engaged in futile and corrosive battles over certain adjacent provinces. Again this quest for supremacy and domination was more political than cultural in nature. There might be some exceptions which however did not prove the rule, such as the seeking refuge of the seven Athenian philosophers in the court of the Sassanid king Anushirvan after the closure of Plato's Academy by the edict of the Roman emperor Justinianus in 529 ACE or the migration of the Nestorians to the Sassanid Empire after being persecuted by the Monophysite majority.

Moreover the Roman Empire wielded supreme command and coercive authoritarian rule over the vast regions in North Africa and the Near East such as Syria, Iraq, Palestine and the Asia minor to such an extent that their inhabitants were not treated as free Roman citizens, but were regarded as bondsmen, vassals and serfs. It was first Christianity and then Islam which were to liberate them from this debasing bondage and serfdom.

But the matter is quite different when we come to Islam and Christianity which was destined by God to become the religion of the West. Before proceeding to the confrontation between Christianity and Islam, some general remarks about the nature of religions in general and Christianity and Islam are in order. Notwithstanding all their external differences religions have many things in common which makes them much akin in spirit, function and essence. All religions believe in some supernatural trans-phenomenal reality which they variously call by different names such as Yahweh, Allah, Brahman, Ti'en, or by other names and appellations. In some religions the impersonal deity is beyond any names, epithets and descriptions and hence cannot be named and designated by qualities and determinations. Moreover all religions make a distinction between the Absolute and the relative, between the Atma and the Maya, between the creator and creatures, between the phenomenal and a supra-phenomenal order. All religions in addition, place emphasis on the primacy of the Divine order and its priority in the rank of causality. In the traditional religious universe, everything emanates from the Divine and consequently is permeated by its perfume. Religions unanimously agree that this mundane and terrestrial existence is not the terminus or the blind dead-end; in other words death is not the end of human destiny but is the beginning of an everlasting life. There depending on one's meritorious or vicious acts one is doomed to either eternal bliss or abiding and perpetual damnation: hence the significance of the idea of salvation in all religions. In the practical sphere all religions emphasize the practice of virtues and shunning all kind of vice. The idea of cardinal sins plays a crucial role in all religions and their enumeration is more or less the same in all religions.

Cosmology, moreover, in all traditional religions has a spiritual significance and is not confined to quantitative aspects as in modern science, but is rather qualitative and symbolic in nature. The world is seen not only in its "horizontal" or "latitudinal", but also in its "vertical" and "longitudinal" aspect too, which comprises other supernal and spiritual domains whether angelic or demonic, subtle or luminous. The world and everything in it, symbolically alludes to its everlasting archetype. Everything in the universe, is in the terminology of the Christian sages of the Middle Ages a *Vestigio Dei* or in the phraseology of Muslim sages the signs (*Ayat*) of God. In the expression of the great sages of China, all on earth is a reflection of realities in Heaven (*Ti'en*) without which it would not be conceivable. Everything by virtue of its existence, its essential form and the peculiar qualities it manifests, is divine. The universe, in virtue of being a manifestation of the principle and due to the presence of the transcendent principle immanently in the manifestation, is sacred by nature because the sacred by definition is nothing but that which embodies in itself such Divine presence. Hence the ancients regarded the world as a holy temple or a place of worship, worthy of utmost respect; its profanation would be considered as a shameful and outrageous sacrilege. Of utmost significance for the traditional religious man is our planet earth which is his abode in this world and the habitation of his body after death. The traditional man, while being down-to-earth in his realism, was well aware of his restrictions, limitations, and the precariousness and the ephemeral character of his existence on this globe.

In this traditional religious world-view, man played a significant role. He functioned as an intermediary between Heaven and Earth. He acted as a pontiff or the vicegerent of God on earth. The guru, the saint, the sage, the avatar, the perfect man were considered the consummation of the spiritual hierarchy and as a divine microcosm manifesting all the perfect attributes of the Divinity. He was considered by some sages even to be the macrocosm and the *raison d'etre* of the existence of the universe.

ISLAM AND CHRISTIANITY

What we sketched above is meant to indicate that world religions are so close in their quintessential doctrine. They are as if the prismatic refractions of a single source of light or the manifestations of a unique reality. That is why some contemporary metaphysicians such as Frithhof Schuon, René Guenon, Ananda Coomeraswamy and Seyyed Hossein Nasr have propounded the theory of the Transcendent unity of religions. They argue that religions like the radii of a circle converge toward the centre (substance) and diverge toward the periphery and the circumference (in their outward form and external accidents). Karl Jaspers, the famous contemporary German philosopher has spoken of the so-called Axial Age, i.e. the era extending from the eighth to the second centuries B.C. in which not only the great founders of religion and the authors of sacred scriptures such as Lao-Tze, Confucius, Chuang zu in China; the writers of Upanishads, Mahabharta and Shakyamuni Buddha in India, Zoroaster in Persia, and the Jewish prophets such as Isaiah, Elias, Jeremiah, Joshua and Daniel lived. This axial Age also includes paradoxically enough the great sages-philosophers of Greece such as Empedocles, Parmenides, Heraclitus and Plato. What is interesting in Jasper's scheme is that the perennial philosophy of Plato and the pre-Socratics rubs shoulders with the *religio perennis* of the Eastern prophets. This might explain why the Greek philosophy has been so much absorbed into the Abrahamic religions such as Judaism, Christianity and Islam.

Going back to Christianity and Islam, we might say that these two religions being the true scions of the Abrahamic tradition, have more in common than what we find between Islam and the Eastern religions. It is even stated in the Holy Quran that the Christians are closest in spiritual kinship to Muslims when compared with other religions. Nonetheless there are certain morphological differences between Islam and Christianity which might be briefly summarized here.

(1) Islam is the religion of pure monotheism and while it accepts the immaculate birth of Christ and considers him to be the logos or the word of God (*Kalimat-ullah*) it does not accept his Divinity and hence does not accept the doctrine of Trinity.

(2) Islam and Christianity are not autochthonous religions belonging to a particular race, tribe or nation, but are universal by nature. But whereas Christianity accepts the authenticity of the Jewish prophets and patriarchs, being at best indifferent to other religions, Islam accepts the authenticity of all Divine religions Abrahamic or otherwise. The creation of man without his ultimate guidance and salvation would have been futile. That is why God has chosen the best men in every community to lead men to ultimate truth and moral perfection. According to one tradition attributed to the Holy Prophet there have been one hundred and twenty four thousand prophets and Messengers chosen by God to fulfill this Divine mission. According to the Holy Quran there is no abrogation of Divine religions and it is the duty and obligation of Islam to protect and preserve all of them. It is the function of Islam

to fulfill and accomplish the promise of God in all religions. That is why the second article of Islamic faith is belief in the institution of prophecy as a universal phenomenon and the believers are commanded to believe in the veracity of all previous messengers and sacred books. But paradoxically whereas belief in all Divine messengers and holy books is obligatory for all Muslims, Islam has not been accorded an equal status by other religions, especially by Judaism and Christianity.

(3) Islam makes a clear distinction between man as such and the collective man and considers these two realities about man profoundly linked together. No man can be born without a family and moreover no man can achieve happiness and perfection without the virtues associated with the communal life. So there are individual, filial and collective virtues (such as charity, love of neighbor, paying alms for the poor as Holy war) which have a deep spiritual value, perhaps the highest of these collective and communal virtues is justice. After disbelief there is no vice and error higher than injustice. According to a saying of the Holy prophet, a kingdom can survive through disbelief, but never through injustice. According to another saying: heaven and the earth were established through justice. For a sovereign, moreover, one hour of justice is deemed worthier than seventy years of worship. So an ideal community is one in which justice reigns supreme in the individual, in the family and in the community.

Two phases in the encounter of Islam and the West are worthy of note; the Christian phase and the modern secular phase. The first phase can be characterized as "dialogue in clash", because the two civilizations of Christendom and Islam were both religious, belonged both to the Abrahamic tradition, and shared almost the same ideals. The second phase comprises the confrontation of Islam with the modern West which is secular and mundane by nature and hence is incompatible with the core spiritual teachings of religions, whether Abrahimic or non- Abrahimic in general and the last revealed religion, i.e. Islam, in particular. Hence there is the possibility that any dialogue might end in a clash insofar as the West is persistent in adhering to such a secular outlook.

ISLAM AND THE CHRISTIAN WEST

As said earlier Islam as the last religion recognizes the veracity and the authenticity of all revealed religions and the prophet of Islam as the seal of prophecy has attested to the Divine origin of all messengers before him whether their name is mentioned in the Holy Quran or not. The followers of other religions are called the People of the Book (*ahl-al-Kitāb*) and are allowed to follow their religion, practice their own religious rites and enact their sacred law in the Islamic community. Muslims are obliged to respect them and let them be free in the practice of their religion. It is incumbent on the Caliph or the ruler of the Islamic community to protect them and vouchsafe their security and integrity as a minority group. They are not to be enlisted in the military service and instead have to pay a certain annual tax to the treasury. For this reason the Islamic community at large has shown the utmost degree of moderation and tolerance towards other religions, unprecedented in the annals of history.

Unlike other religions there has scarcely been persecution of non-Muslims in the Islamic lands. Muslims are not allowed to combat the people of the Book unless they first enkindle the fuel of war and enter into combat with Muslims. There are strict injunctions regarding the people of the Book in the Holy Quran and in the practice of the Holy prophet which have been emulated and observed by Muslims throughout the ages. This is particularly true of Christians who have been well commended in the Quran. There is a historical report that when the prophet of Islam saw the icon of Jesus and Mary, he reverently touched it, kissed it and wept profusely. When the name of any prophet or Messenger of God is mentioned by Muslims it is immediately followed by the salutary phrase "Peace and benedictions of God be upon him". In modern constitutions of most Islamic countries, parliamentary representation for religious minorities has been well provided.

But the same does not hold with regard to Christians vis-à-vis Islam, which they envisaged as a deviation and an aberration of Judeo-Christian tradition. Instead of turning their left cheeks, they got entangled in a "just war" (*bellum justum*) against the infidel barbarians and heretics and the popes promised salvation to those who died while fighting the infidels. Clerics and the laity alike were summoned to take part in this holy enterprise. It was thus that the so-called crusades came into being, especially when in 1095 the pope Urban II envisaged an armed pilgrimage to the East to liberate the Holy land and especially Jerusalem . We are not going to expatiate here on the history of the crusades. But suffice it to say that they went on intermittently for two hundred years, in which four crusades were fought between Muslims and Christians and in May 1291 the fall of Jerusalem. This holy City was to remain in the hands of Muslims ever since, except for the last few decades.

Nonetheless, there was a vast amount of cultural exchange between the Muslim and Christian civilizations which is without precedent in the chronicles of the dialogue between civilizations. The Syriac Christians, for instance, were very instrumental in translating the Greek scientific and philosophical texts into Arabic. Alexandria, as mentioned before, played a major role in the transmission of Greek philosophy and science to Christian and Islamic civilizations and was the cradle of Jewish and Christian theology. There flourished also other great centers of learning, mostly Christian Greek and Syriac which were quite influential in transmitting the Greek *Padeia* to the Muslims. Among these centers one can mention the school of Antioch founded in 270 A.D. where the philosophy of Plato together with Christian theology was taught; the school of Edessa (or al-Ruha, the modern city of Urfa, east of the upper Euphrates) founded in 363 A.D., where Greek philosophy including the texts of Aristotle with the commentaries of Alexander were taught in Greek and Syriac and where the Old Testament was for the first time translated into Syriac; Nisibis (near the upper Tigris, northwest of Mosul); Resain (Ra's al-'ayn or Theosiodopolis); Kinnesrin (Qinnasrīn); the latter two being cloisters; Emessa (Hums) and Baalbak (Heliopolis); the city of Harran, a short distance south of Edessa, which was primarily a locality of star-worshippers, probably heirs of the ancient Chaldean and Babylonian astronomy.

When in 489, Emperor Xenon closed down the school of Edessa due to its Nestorian proclivities, its scholars and teachers took refuge in the school of Nisibis which was under the Sassanid protection and some of them went to teach in the university of Jundishapur in southern Persia which was one of the great centers of science, especially medicine. Later they were to emigrate to the newly-founded city of Baghdad. Jundishapur probably was the host of the seven philosophers who had fled to Persia after the closure of the Athenian school by Emperor Justinian in 529. This city, with its burgeoning academy, its great and well-equipped hospital and its enormous library came to function as the medium of exchange between the cultures of Persia, Greece , Rome, Syria and India.

Christians again, primarily Nestorians and then Jacobites assisted immensely in the majestic translation movement of the Greek philosophical texts into Arabic, already started in the late first and early second centuries A.H., but which reached its culmination when Mansūr the Abbasid built the city of Baghdad, which was to become the capital of the Abbasids and was to supersede Athens and Alexandria as the metropolis of culture and civilization for many centuries to come. The Abbasid caliph Ma'mūn established a great centre for translation called the House of Wisdom (Bayt al-Hikmah) in 917 A.H. (839 A.D.) under the supervision and headship of the Christian Nestorian Yuhanna ibn Masuyah, where immediately a host of very competent scholars and translators assembled. Ma'mūn sent a considerable number of emissaries to the great centers of Greek learning in Iraq, Syria and Byzantium and to the Christian monasteries to collect the best extant Greek manuscripts, which after being collated and edited, were translated and revised by eminent scholars who had been trained in Alexandria and Byzantium. We do not have time nor space to mention all the names of the translators here. But suffice it to mention here that this movement, later to be headed by the illustrious Hunayn Ibn Ishaq and his son Ishaq Ibn Hunayn, was to continue for about a century and a half, in which all the major Greek works in science and philosophy together with the major commentaries were translated into Arabic. To cite an example, all the works of Aristotle, with the possible exception of politics of which no trace has been found so far, together with the commentaries of Theophrastus, Alexander Aphrodisias, Themestius and Simplicius were translated into Arabic. Even some spurious works such as the *Book of Theology* (Kitab al-Rububiyyah) (an epitome of the *Enneads* of Plotinus), *Liber de Pomis, Liber de bonitatis purae* (Kitab al-Khayr al mahd) which were in fact neo-Platonic writings were attributed to Aristotle. Similar translations were also made in various scientific disciplines such as optics, mechanics, astronomy, geometry, arithmetic, and others. This tremendous translation enterprise was enough to set in motion and cause a great intellectual upheaval with few precedents in the annals of cultural history. For many centuries Islamic civilization was to bear the torch of knowledge and intellectual and spiritual enlightenment.

In the wake of this epoch-making movement there emerged a vast literature in all fields of knowledge. Some of the translators were the first to write commentaries or to compile books in the related subjects. In the field of philosophy (which in the object of my special concern) there appeared a host of very distinguished philosopher-sages such as al-Kindi Farabi, Avicenna, (Ibn Sina), Ghazzali, Shahrastani, 'Amiri, Nasir-ad-Din Tusi, Suhrawardi (the founder of the school of Illumination and Mulla Sadra (the founder of the school of Transcendent philosophy). It is interesting to note that such great philosophers as Farabi, Avicenna and Averroes could write a whole range of commentaries on the works of Aristotle or philosophize on the basis of the peripatetic philosophy without knowing any Greek. This was due to the fact that there were so many good translations and often several of them for a single work, that they could reason out and resolve very abstruse questions.

A parallel translation movement and as colossal and epoch-making as the previous was the one initiated in Spain. When in 1085 A.D. the city of Toledo, the great centre of Islamic learning collapsed and fell into Christian hands, Christian bishops came into possession of very great libraries, including the library of the great Mosque of Toledo, whose site is still visited by tourists. The Catalan Ramon (Raymond), bishop of Toledo, promoted the translation movement. Fortunately we have the names of some translators in the city of Toledo: Gerard of Cremona, Dominic Gundissalinus, John of Spain (Johannes Hispanus), Avendehut (probable Ibn Davoud, a Jewish name), Alfred Sarashel (Alfredus Anglicus), Solomon the Jew, Hermannus Alemannus, William of Luna and Michael Scotus. The works of Aristotle, Farabi , Avicenna, Ghazzali (called alghazal by the Latins), Qusta bin Luqa (Constabulinus) Alexander Aphrodisias, Al-Kindi and others were translated from Arabic into Hebrew and Latin.

To mention but one significant instance, nearly all the works of Averroes were translated from Arabic into Latin. This eminent Muslim philosopher known as "the Commentator" by the medievals, and placed in Purgatory by Dante had written three kinds of commentaries nearly on all the works of Aristotle: the short (*talkhis*), the middle (*awsat*) and great or large commentaries (*sharh Kabir*), the latter being lemmata or section-by section quotations and commentaries on the works of Aristotle. When these commentaries were translated into Latin the medieval teachers had the complete works of Aristotle translated from Arabic. Another conspicuous instance is the translation of Avicenna's magnum opus al-Shifa (*"Sufficientia"*), recently edited and published as Avicenna Latinus in more than ten volumes. We are not going to produce here the details of this intellectual movement but it is enough to mention that they provided the text books for the newly founded universities in England, France, Italy and elsewhere. When the art of printing was invented by Gutenberg, the Latin version of Avicenna's *Canon* (al-qanūn) in medicine was the second book after the Bible to go into print and within ten years it was reprinted many times. The translation of these scientific and philosophical works into Latin created the third phase in Medieval philosophy, called "scholasticism". What is important for our argument here is that the philosophical and scientific ideas of the Muslim philosopher-sage-scientists were well accepted by the great sage-saints of Christianity and they were incorporated into the mainstream of Christian philosophy. The most distinguished philosopher of the scholastic period, Thomas Aquinas, in his *Summa Contra Gentiles*, mentions Avicenna, more than any other philosopher, including Aristotle. The Franciscan philosopher-scientist, Roger Bacon, called Avicenna the "prince of physicians and philosophers". The Latin West, which knew about Aristotle only through Boethius' translation and commentary of the *Posterior Analytics* was to rediscover him in his amplitude through Muslim philosophers.

THE MODERN PERIOD

While in Islam and Christianity the norm was the saint (*wali*) and the sage (*hakim*), and this was the main reason for a fruitful intellectual and cultural dialogue between Islam and the Christian West, in modernity, that is, in the post-Renaissance period, they (i.e. the saint and the sage) are put aside and marginalized from the ordinary life of the modern society. There emerges, at an accelerating rate a sort of secularism, verging towards skepticism and nihilism, which alienates the West from the Eastern tradition and religions, especially Islam. We do not deny that there have been great philosophers and scientists in modern times from Descartes to Wittgenstein, but most of them are secular in spirit, and increasingly far off from the great sages of the East and pre-Modern European philosophers such as Plato, St. Augustine and St. Thomas Aquinas. I cannot go far in elaborating this point here but I can summarize my argument by underlining briefly the following points which characterize the modern outlook and are diametrically opposed to the traditional religious viewpoint.

(1) Humanism. In the modern outlook "man is the measure of all things" in the Protagorean sense, but in the traditional religious view, to quote the words of Plato in the *Protagoreas*, "God is the measure of everything" or as he says in the *Timaeus*, God is the first, the last and the middle of all things. For the traditional religious man, God is manifest in everything and for a moment, he cannot conceive of himself or of the world without God. This God-consciousness, or in other words, 'Consciousness of the Principle', permeates his entire being. Modernity is based on the marginalization and forgetfulness of the principle, which itself is a corollary of humanism and secularism.

(2) Subjectivism. Another characteristic of modernism which is more or less observed in almost all modern philosophy, is what can be called Subjectivism which is in a sense the self-engrossedness of the human subject within itself without reference to the Divine Subjectivity. From the traditional perspective, one cannot separate one's determined self from the Self, or one's determined and phenomenal ego from the Absolute Ego, the Atma, in Indian terminology, of which it is a faint reflection. The self-absorption of the human ego or subject in itself hinders its absorption in the true Self, so that the phenomenal self plays the function of the Absolute. Subjectivism, being a self-plunging of the subject in itself, deters one from an objective consider-

ation and contemplation of the subject itself. Eastern sages have tackled the problem of the human ego and Subjectivity quite differently.

(3) Reductionism. Another feature of modernism is what we can term "Reductionism," which reduces reality to one of its phenomenal aspects. This is characterized by "reality is nothing but...""; this gives the one aspect of the phenomenal and the relative a noumenal and absolute status. Reality is nothing but history (historicism), economy (economism), matter (materialism), Spirit (idealism), nothing but what modern science tells us (positivism) and so on. Modernity lacks the synoptic view (in the Platonic sense) which regards all phenomena as many facets and reflections of one reality.

(4) The modern conception of science. For the Christian sages *scientia* (the etymological root for the modern science) was the lowest degree of knowledge in the hierarchy. Higher than the *scientia* in the vertical scale, were *disciplina*, and the *sapientia*, the latter being considered as the absolute knowledge considering the prime questions about reality. Now modern science appropriates to itself the prerogative of being absolute knowledge at the expense of the ulterior kinds, especially sapiential knowledge. In addition there has been an epistemological metamorphosis in the very conception of science. For Aristotle, Avicenna, and St. Thomas Aquinas, *scientia* (or the knowledge of the physical things) was theoretical and speculative in nature. It was, for example concerned with the formal, final, efficient and material causality. The form of a thing or its *eidos* (coming from the infinitive *idein*, i.e., to know and to see) was its knowable essence, and the hylomorphic theory taught that no matter was without form or that being is inextricably interwoven with knowing. By reducing material substance to pure extension (*res extensa*) Descartes denigrated the formal, efficient and final causality. The mathematization of science was construed as a kind of blind mechanism which without being philosophically analyzed came to explain away everything.

Unlike the Greek episteme, modern science is not concerned at all with the why (*dioti*) and the whatness (*ti esti*) of things, but tells us how things operate: according to what mathematical formula such and such a body moves. Rather than being a knowing-why, modern science is a sort of know-how for the subjugation and exploitation of nature.

(5) Profanation of man and nature. According to the traditional worldview man, due to his theomorphic nature and in his function as a vicegerent and pontiff of God on earth, had a sacred and sacerdotal function which he has been robbed of in modern civilization. He has been forsaken, lone and forlorn in a desolate wilderness. Traditional man also considered nature to be sacred and an object of contemplation .Nature has been more and more desacrelized, profaned and polluted by modern science and technology. Blasphemous exploitation of nature and the consideration of its resources in a few decades has been one of the greatest achievements of modern science.

(6) Neo-slavery and colonialism. Traditional man in addition to seeing man and the universe under the aegis of Divine agency deems all human beings equal in the sight of God. Moreover, everything gets its intrinsic right and value in relation to God. Modern man functioning as a demigod has tried

to subjugate other human beings to the status of slaves. The Islamic world has suffered tremendously from such exploitative ruthless and oppressive measures dictated by the West. The West has coercively colonized about a dozen Islamic countries in the last two or three centuries, something which a modern Muslim can never accept. It is important that these issues and grievances be addressed.

Chapter 14

Islam as Perceived from the West: Secular and Religious Views

George F. McLean

INTRODUCTION

In the general context of "Dialogue between Islamic and Western Civilizations: The Religious and Secular Perspectives" I shall study Islam as perceived from the West. Indeed, in 1991 when studying in Cairo, I was asked to speak at the al-Azhar on exactly this topic. Today the issue is increasingly urgent and of the highest importance. The news is not all good.

But for balance and especially here I would like to precede addressing the topic directly by noting the balancing, general council of the Holy Prophet, namely the importance of going in search of wisdom even to China.

I remember reading in Cairo two main reasons given for the importance of this in our day. One by a French Islamic author was cultural and psychological; I can only propose it for your qualified evaluation. It is that the Asian temperament values harmony over competition, and hence the future of Islam lies in the ability here in Asia to draw out the message of justice and peaceful progress that is basic to the Qu'ran. Another French author came to the same conclusion but by a cultural-historical route. He wrote that, for historical reasons being continually engaged with the West, Islam in West Asia took on an excessively competitive and/or defensive view of itself. This was not favorable to unfolding the full riches of the heritage of its sacred book and he too looked to the East for a more exemplary understanding of the message of the Prophet.

It is, at any rate, my deep and continuing conviction, especially today in defense against the flattening[1] and secularizing effect of an imperial Western culture, that Islam and all faiths need to find fellowship with the great and deeply religious philosophies of the East lest they be overwhelmed by the aggressive secularism of the West. We must remember that there is not only the West, but the East and the South as well, and that the latter are natively supportive of Islam's religiously-based culture.

To appreciate this, however, it will be essential to see the monotheisms of the religions of the Book not as contradictions, but as progressive developments of the pervasive and unifying sense of the great religions of the East. In this light philosophers and theologians may prove more important than the geopolitical or military strategists in building our common global future.

Turning now directly to our theme, I have news both bad and good regarding Islam as perceived from the West. Addressed in secular geo-political terms the news tends to be bad, but less perduring; seen philosophically and religiously the view is good, and hopefully more lasting. I will speak to them in that order, with the former serving to introduce the latter.

THE SECULAR GEO-POLITICAL VIEW FROM THE WEST: THE BAD NEWS

To understand the bad news I would suggest looking at two areas: cultural and ideological.

(1) *Cultural Blindness*. Unfortunately, the first thing to be said about this is that our situation is one of early emergence from a basic ignorance. Perception, in some contrast to knowledge, is always from the point of view of the perceiver and in this sense the perception from the West has always been Eurocentric. Marshall Hodgson in his classic, *The Venture of Islam*,[2] noted the need to recenter the view of history from Europe, which after Rome was but a set of crude and petty kingdoms, to the great Islamic realm extending from the Nile to the Oxus. Otherwise world history is bound to be perceived through glasses which distort.

Moreover, till this new millennium Islam remained the field of study for a small and relatively esoteric band of orientalists. Thus, the present sudden intense interest in Islam is a largely amateur field in which wildly divergent interpretations are guided more by prejudice and opportunism than by reality. What is more, as the pragmatic reasons advanced for military adventurism in West and Central Asia were progressively shown to be unfounded and the perdurance and intensity of the resistance grew, there evolved first a deep sense of bewilderment. This was followed by fear before what was unintelligible to the materialist utilitarian mind, which led in sequence to increasing alienation and antipathy. Where at first for fear of a religious war notable care was taken to avoid interpretations which touched upon Islam as a religiously-based culture, with time this care disappeared and negative references to Islam became more overt.

Finally, this misconception is intensified systematically by the very difference in the history of the two regions. The political history of the West has come to be told in terms of the British "Magna Carta", the French "Rights of Man" and the American "Bill of Rights." It is one of progressive projection and defense of individual freedom. Islam's self-understanding is quite different. As man is vice-gerent of God, it is submission and fidelity, rather than self-assertion against all forms of authority, that is the key understanding of freedom. Hence, the Western view does not find in the East the emphasis on "freedom from" which it considers essential to the human dignity and welfare. As it struggles to relate freedom and fidelity, its attempts to promote "liberation from" take the form of attacks on Islam. Words and meanings bear opposite content and Eastern and Western cultures blindly collide.

(2) *Liberal Democratic Theory*. All of this is sharpened by Western political theory. Here the evolution of the rhetoric with which the invasion of Iraq was justified in the American Press and to the United Nations is in-

dicative. "Weapons of mass destruction" was succeeded by "need for regime change," then "liberation of women" and finally the need to establish democracy and freedom across the region. All this was abbreviated to the establishment of "liberal democracy" based on individual freedom.

It is especially indicative for our concern, namely, "Islam as perceived from the West," that liberal democracy has come to be expressed almost interchangeably as "secular democracy". Many see this secularity as essential to Western liberal democratic theory. The present prime political theoretician, the late John Rawls, proposed in his *Theories of Justice and Political Liberalism*³ that religion and all integrating or synthetic views need to be removed behind a "veil of ignorance" in order to create an open public space in which all ideas could equally compete. The model, of course, is that of the free market in individualistic Western capitalism in which all compete equally and thereby set the (economic) value of material goods. As political theory this places man over God and money over man. Thus the blind hand of the market is proposed as the requisite condition in order for political discourse to be authentic.

U.S. military action points to a second cultural interpretation only recently openly stated, namely, that Islam is perceived as a violent religion. Therefore it said that Islam needed to be suppressed or at least marginalized from public life in the name of peace. (Of course, in this context it goes without saying that enigmatically the key here is not Islam itself, which is a religion of peace, but the very effort to suppress Islam, or 'marginalize' Islam, which evokes ever stronger reaction.)

This has been radicalized not only by lack of understanding of religion from without, but by blind fundamentalisms within the great religions East and West. In turn, it is compounded by the failure effectively to correct such excesses by these religions. Their primary tasks now more than ever is to assure a proper interpretation of their foundational religious texts: Torah, Bible and Koran.

(3) *Neo-Conservative Ideology.* Convergent with this is another strain of political interpretation, namely, the neo-conservative political theory, especially of Leo Strauss, a professor of political science at the University of Chicago. Strauss relates back to Moses Maimonides' work on writing in a time of persecution. His theory distinguishes notably two readings of Plato's *Republic*. One is overt and written in terms of the good, of virtue and of responsible human freedom. These are the words of Socrates and the overt sense of Plato's text. However, considering human freedom and its adhesion to the good to be too unstable a basis for the order needed for the political life of a complex world, the Straussian interpretation reads in an opposite manner. It considers Plato's personal position to have been hidden in the text and expressed in a covert manner in the words not of Socrates, but of Thracymicus, for whom peace comes only from power harshly applied. That, he said, is the whole reality of justice. Similarly in Sophocles' *Antigone*, it is the tyrant, Creon, who states the real art of statecraft.

From this follows the present neo-conservative rationale that peace in our global world cannot be based upon free agreement of cultures and peoples in negotiations according to a "road map," but rather requires a hegemonic power which levels, subjugates and integrates all peoples in its unipolar economic and political order.

(4) *Overall Assessment.* My sense is that, while the fighting is still intense, Islam has prevailed. For all the effort expended and to be expended, what is gone from Iraq is the secular Baath Party, now succeeded by the beginnings of a government led by religiously oriented Shiite parties. Meanwhile, the vast U.S. armed forces now equal in expenditures that of all of the rest of the world combined. Yet it is trapped in an occupation which drains its men and equipment and renders it powerless as a credible threat elsewhere in the world. Its very size generates its weakness, and attracts as well a near universal and debilitating hatred of its hegemony.

A longer view of history may conclude that the two opponents in the cold war, as the culmination of modernity and hence of modernity itself, were defeated by Islam – the U.S.S.R. in Afghanistan and the U.S. in Iraq. This was due not to physical force, but to religious and cultural conviction. Indeed it is not inconceivable that Islam may free the West from its secular fundamentalism if it can teach the hard lesson that in the end the human heart is ruled not by economic and military power – no matter how great, they can only enslave – but by the spirit which frees. This is the lesson needed for a global age. The deeper truth remains: "Blessed are the meek, for they shall possess the land!"

THE INTER-RELIGIOUS AND PHILOSOPHICAL VIEW FROM THE WEST: THE GOOD NEWS

(1) *Human Subjectivity.* For well over a millennium both East and West have been on the same holy campaign, namely to conquer the world for God. For Moslems this meant for Islam; for Christians it meant for Christ. The result was a pincer movement of Islam on Europe coming from the West through Spain to Tours in France, and from the East through Constantinople across the Balkans to the gates of Vienna. Geopolitically the crusades are perceived in the West as defensive thrusts against Islam perceived as a mortal enemy. Could this ever change?

Probably in the terms in which the relationship was then understood no change could be expected. Each was an object for the other, each was different, each claimed to be the true path to the unique God to whom each was and must remain totally dedicated. Could new modes of understanding be developed which would enable the scriptures and truths of the faiths to be understood more richly and lived jointly?

Such a development would recognize both God's transcendence as beyond any ability of the human mind, and at the same time the human ability to image this infinite love in multiple ways. Indeed, it must be diversely imaged in multiple religious modes if the many peoples with their differences are each to respond to God with a full heart.

This redirects our attention from the more surface and horizontal economic, political and military jostling to the deeper grounding of culture in religion. It is from here that must begin the work of healing and of constructing a new global order in which all can live in fidelity with freedom and dignity. I see this as already underway, and like a new tooth, its emergence as the basic reason why the old order of contrast and conflict, no matter how much coercive force it can muster, can no longer perdure.

In philosophy, the opening of this great change lies in recognition of the dimension of subjectivity or interior self-awareness. 2500 years ago in a decisive response to the political chaos of the time, Socrates sought out stable guides for human behavior. Plato articulated these virtues as ideas above humankind which, like the stars in the sky could provide guide posts by which to navigate life. This was a decisive choice for the West, namely, to think in terms of objects, things outside of and over against (*ob-ject*) human consciousness. This was true in both Islamic and Christian circles in the Middle Ages, but was radicalized in the rationalist reduction of all to scientific reason which characterized modern times.

It could be expected that once this proved inadequate because insensitive to the emergent human self-awareness and sense of freedom or self-determination, an approach would be found which could value this power of human consciousness and bring it out into the light (the etymology of *phenomen-ology*). Then human alienation built by exclusive and exclusionary consideration of others – other persons, other cultures, other religions – would begin to crumble.

This emergence of human self-awareness can be traced philosophically through Wittgenstein,[4] Husserl, and Heidegger.[5] By the mid 20th century it had shifted the emphasis from essences and structures to existence and creative freedom. Something truly new was in the air. In response Pope John XXIII called the Second Vatican Council – something done on the average of only once every 400 years – to assess this development and its implication for the deeper, and ultimately religious, level of human life.

(2) *The Second Vatican Council.* A work by Mahmut Aydin, *Modern Western Christian Theological Understandings of Muslims Since the Second Vatican Council,*[6] assesses the impact of the Council for the Western perception of Islamic culture. Two things stand out. First there was a recognition of deep human freedom, even and perhaps especially with regard to religion. The document on religious liberty, which recognized the right of conscience to, and in, religious affairs was written principally by John Courtney Murray, an American Jesuit. I was with him in Rome at the very moment it was being decided whether to advance this document for final consideration and approval in the Council's last session. He acknowledged that an adequate supporting theology had not yet been developed – which work remains as a mandate for all. But he said that from the experience of modern life it was obvious that the freedom of conscience with regard to religion had to be acknowledged. Note: this was not a matter deduced by reason; it was a new awareness of the importance of what was emerging in the interior of the human consciousness, in the

hearts and minds of the people of the time. It consituted a new recognition that human subjectivity had to be factored in, along with objectivity.

A second and corresponding step was taken in the document, significantly entitled *Nostra Aetate* ('Our Age'), which was the main concern of the work of Mahmut Aydin. The challenge is the definitive commitment of each people to God's revelation and to the path this opens for them. This can blind our eyes to the superabundance of the divine, and hence to the multiplicity of the paths he has given the different peoples to come to Him in their different climes and cultures, histories and languages. The authenticity of these multiple paths is due less to their deficiency, for God always gives us a way that is sufficient, but first of all to the way the divine surpasses all things human. Moreover, the religious paths which God gives to diverse peoples and which they elaborate through their many ages and places must be multiple if they are to be appropriate for all dispersed and disparate peoples to relate to the one infinite God.

The step of the Second Vatican Council in this regard was to move beyond what had been the classical ecclesiastical principle "outside the Church there is no salvation" ("extra ecclesia nulla salus"), and to recognize that indeed peoples who have not acknowledged Christ or Muhammad, or even heard of them, were in God's loving providence and care.

It was a decisive step, even earth-shaking, for it opened the way for the West to look at Islam now no longer as an enemy or even as a competitor, but as another dimension of God's providence for the salvation of humankind.

(3) *The Theologians*. But Aydin did not stop there. As Courtney Murray acknowledged, in his document on religious liberty this step was taken without a developed theology or even a set of practical guidelines to implement this new vision of the relationship between the faiths. Hence Aydin writes the history of the attempt over the following decades to develop a set of norms and guidelines for this cooperation. It is a history of "two steps forward and one step back." The Catholic Church in its Second Vatican Council took the decisive step and led the way. The largely Protestant World Council of Churches at first followed with its own series of steps, forward and back. More recently, it has advanced further than the Vatican in the recognition of other religions as ways of salvation.

This is not bad, as it is due to the deep concern of the Vatican that the theology or truth of Christ not be attenuated or watered down in the process. Typically it proceeds slowly and allows insight to be gained, matured and applied, rather than in haste that might lose any of the ultimately precious content of the faith.

Where in Islam the question would be what is the status of Muhammad and the Koran, in Christianity the question for the theologians concerns is the nature of Christ and hence the character of belief in his regard. In order to understand how the different faiths converge and can live together some theologians would focus on the interior effects of religion in the human heart and see similarity there, but ignore the issue of the divinity of Christ.[7] Others would retain both as a matter of faith, but shift attention from Christ to God.[8]

Aydin is suspicious of both, for he rightly sees any attenuation by Christians of the centrality of Christ as suggesting a parallel attenuation of the Moslem appreciation of the unique role of the Prophet of Islam. Rightly, this forewarns him that attenuation of the faith is not the way to understanding its content or its role in the world. Hence, while some would look with impatience at the Vatican as slowing down the process, this would seem intended not to impede the process, but to insist that it be done well in order that the fullness of the faiths of human kind be preserved and promoted.

(4) *The Philosophers.* We await then the development of appropriate philosophical and theological tools to enable us to proceed in full fidelity to ever more rich appreciation of our faiths and of their interrelation. The history of these disciplines shows that such advances can take ages. In fact, such ages are delineated less by the details unveiled, than by the development of new modes of human awareness which enable whole new ways of understanding.

Moreover, we not only enjoy the riches which the achievement yields, but suffer in the delay and especially at the points of transition and change. We can cooperate, however, in elaborating and assembling such philosophical resources as the following, which are notably Platonic in character.

The first is drawn from Nicholas of Cusa who was the papal legate to Istanbul in the years following its coming under Ottoman sovereignty. His suggestion was to think in terms of this human world not as an assemblage of essentially limited and multiple realities, but in terms of the one absolute Being and of the whole of his work of creation, i.e., to think not analytically in terms of the separate beings we encounter one by one, but synthetically in terms of the whole. In this context each limited reality, including each faith is a partial manifestation, but a partial manifestation of the whole itself and ultimately of the divine One. Thinking in these terms, each particular reality is related to all the others, each of which complements and fulfills it. The other is a special manifestation of the whole which I strive to image and manifest as fully as possible. Thinking thus in terms of the whole others pertain to one's very nature or definition.

In this light the great religious are not competitors, but are in fact essentially dependent on each other in accomplishing their own task of revealing God in our time. The awareness that each needs the other is beginning to be lived, for example, as Christians take up Buddhist mediation in order to live more fully conscious of the deep riches of their own faith.

The second is the recognition of analogy in the use of language. Cornelio Fabro[9] refers to this as the language of participation, which is precisely the manifestation (Plato would call it the imaging – mimesis) of the one by each of the many.

There is similarity in difference between multiple religions as each properly realizes its religious life in its own way. Technically, this has been termed an analogy of proper proportionality. That is the existence of A is realized according to the essence of A in a manner not identical or equal, but proportional to the way the existence of B is realized in a manner proportionate to the essence of B (existence of A: essence of A : : existence of B : essence of B). In this manner the religion of Islam as lived according to (:) the nature of Islam is not identical but proportionate (::) to the way the Christian religion is lived according to (:) its own Christian nature. Neither is in any part the same as the other; neither can be replaced by the other. The similarity lies rather in each realizing itself as fully as possible.

Here, however, we are talking not about self-made human cultures, but about religions which are first of all the creative and salvific work of God, the one creator whose formal effect is precisely the existence of each. This entails as well what is technically termed analogy of attribution, according to which each is denominated as a religion precisely in terms of its relation to the One creator of all existence (the way food and scalpel are termed healthy as supporting the health that is found only in the living body). Each is properly religious by an analogy of attribution according as each explicitly expresses that each person is from the one creator and toward the one goal of all.

The third is hermeneutic with regard to religions, namely, whether the combination of the deep immersion in, and commitment to, one's cultural tradition thereby traps one in insuperable opposition to the interests and strivings of those in other traditions. Can we overcome such opposition? Indeed can the commitments we have to our own cultural tradition become a means for other peoples to look into their own traditions? If so, this would provide the key to effective cooperation between religious and cultures.

It should be understood that cultural traditions will be multiple according to the historical grouping of people, the diverse circumstances in which they shape their lives and the specific challenges to which they respond and in so doing ever more profoundly shape themselves. More foundationally they reflect the specific mode in which God chooses to speak to his peoples and the message he conveys through his prophets to help peoples find their way on their pilgrimages.

Contemporary attention to the person enables us to be more conscious of the distinctive formative pattern of our proper culture and its religious foundations. This can enable us to appreciate it as uniquely different and among others. However, being situated among one's own people and hearing the same stories told in the same way, one's appreciation of the rich content of one's tradition could remain limited.

The way to break out of this limitation of the human condition is to encounter other peoples with other experiences in order to check one's bearings. This is not to copy the other or to graft alien elements onto one's culture. It is rather to be stimulated by the experience of others and thus enabled to go more deeply into one's own cultural heritage and sacred books. Here the aim is to draw out meaning which had always been there in the Infinite ground of my culture, but which thus far had not been sounded.

Rather than abandoning or lessening allegiance to one's cultural tradition this is a higher fidelity thereto. It is built on the conviction that my tradition as grounded in the infinite divine is richer than I or my people have thus far been able to sound, that it has more to say to me, and hence that I need to be open to new dimensions of its meaning.

This is the special opportunity of our time of globalization, communication, and mutual interaction. Rather than looking upon the other as a threat, communication with other cultures as they plumb their own religious tradition can enable one to draw more fully upon one's own. This enables one to cooperate with others in the development of „their own cultures from the resources of their own religious tradition. In this way all religious cultures are promoted each in their unique character. This is more than a dialogue between differences; it is cooperation in developing distinct but convergent pathways for the coming millennium.

IMPLICATIONS FOR LIVING TOGETHER IN
A MULTI-CULTURAL AND MULTI-RELIGIOUS WORLD

A basic present threat, as seen above, lies in liberalism's assumption of total autocracy for the individual, which neo-liberalism and neo-conservatism direct to the selfish pursuit of power and profit. Liberation from these perduring fascinations requires a new horizon which enables one to control and shape these pursuits. Such an horizon must transcend our material reality and situate this in a broaden and more integrating context of human and social goods and spiritual purposes. This is the religious context which makes human freedom possible and hence restores to human subjects the initiative to shape their cultures. As religiously based these cultures in turn have a number of characteristics essential to our times.

First, each culture is unique and hence diverse from all others. As a culture is created by the free self-determination of a people it is unique to that people, and like each act of freedom it is their responsibility; it could be done by no other. That is, each culture is the distinctive manner in which a specific people realizes its life or *esse* according to its own formative decisions and commitments, for which that people alone is responsible.

Cultures then are truly unique inasmuch as each people realizes its life or being, not as an univocous instances of the same specific type, but in its own existentially proper manner. Cultures are shaped over time not only by their circumstances, but even more by the freedom of peoples in making their own decisions and commitments. It is crucial to human freedom then, indeed it is essence, that the cultural uniqueness of each people not be compromised, but rather maximized. There must be no cultural dismissal of human creativity, no lobotomy of peoples in search of a common or universal least-common-denominator. The real challenge now is rather to be able to live fully our unique and distinctive identities in this newly global context.

Second, similarity in the diversity between cultures. This lies paradoxically in the effort of each people to live its own proper culture in its own way. Where before philosophers spoke of an abstract, universal and univocal nature (e.g., rational animal), now it is possible to take account from within also of the long exercise of freedom by a people in their concrete circumstances. The nature according to which we live is not a generic freedom, but the actual cumulative freedom that has constituted our culture as the pattern in terms of which we see, judge and act. Similarity in these existential terms cultures are realized not by diminishing or compromising their distinctive identities or cultures, but in living them to the full.

Third, complementarity between cultures. The unity here is one of complementarity between diverse cultures. As each acts according to its nature, all reflect in their own way the One divine source and goal which is unlimited, infinite and hence unique. In Plato's terms all else are its limited effects, participations or images. But if each is a limited yet unique manifestation of the One, they must in turn be complementary one to the other.

Fourth, convergence of cultures. This relationship must moreover be one of convergence. Living is a matter not of theory, but of teleology. As noted above, all are not only from the One by the efficient causality of the creator, but also are a pursuit of that One as goal and Omega: each culture, in pursuing its own unique and limited perfection, pursues more ultimately the one, infinite good or perfection which it imitates. Thus all cultures are convergent in that each in its own distinctive manner tends toward the same infinite divine perfection. This dynamic pursuit of perfection is the way Iqbal contrasted the more theoretical, detached and distant work of philosophy to religion, which he pictured as active, engaged and uniting one with another.

> The aspiration of religion soars higher than that of philosophy. Philosophy is an intellectual view of things; and as such, does not care to go beyond a concept which can reduce all the rich variety of experience to a system. It sees reality from a distance as it were. Religion seeks a closer contact with Reality. The one is theory; the other is living experience, association, intimacy. In order to achieve this intimacy thought must rise higher than itself, and find its fulfillment in an attitude of mind which religion describes as prayer – one of the last words on the lips of the Prophet of Islam.[10]

> Metaphysics is displaced by psychology, and religious life develops the ambition to come into direct contact with the ultimate reality. It is here that religion becomes a matter of personal assimilation of life and power; and the individual achieves a free personality, not by releasing himself from the fetters of the law, but by discovering the ultimate source of the law within the depths of his own consciousness.[11]

A first implication of the recognition of culture as the cumulative and creative freedom of a people is that all structures for living together must avoid domination or suppression of this freedom in others, any reduction of the other to either a clone or a client. Rather, to recognize that others are fellow free and creative humans; all are pilgrims on the path of development as peace and justice. This is the search for ever more full participation in the ultimately divine truth, goodness and beauty. This entails three cautions regarding things to be avoided, while revealing three principles for progress and three conclusions.

It cautions against human hubris, that is:

- a pseudo-generosity, based on the supposition that what one people has worked out should be imposed upon all others;
- a pseudo-stability, which for a limited time can come from over-whelming power ruthlessly applied;
- a pseudo-peace, that comes from suppression as practiced in the so-called *realpolitik*.

Instead, for living together it is necessary to recognize three basic and ultimately religious principles: namely

- that all are created equal and therefore free by the One God
- and hence that peace lies in the mutual pursuit of human fulfill-ment;
- that the human person is essentially relational as reflecting its one divine source and goal
- and hence that our futures are so bound together as to require mu-tual recognition, respect and cooperation; and
- that peace can be had only from the free pursuit of human har-mony
- and hence, especially in our global age, "blessed are the peacemak-ers, for they shall possess the land."

From this we can draw the following conclusions for life in a multi-cultural and multi-religious world:

- that an understanding that transcends human egoism, along with skills for responding to, and cooperating with, other cultures must supplant ideological aggression;
- that the only real safeguard is not closure upon one's own protec-tion, but openness of heart to the existential concerns of others and to the cultures they have struggled to create as their acceptance of God's gift of being; and
- that the true *realpolitik* is that imaged by Isaias, namely, that which sees all peoples each on their own pilgrimage and all convergent on the one holy mountain where God will be All in all.

Hence the hope and task of this new century is that, as we approach the Divine center, and in so doing draw closer to one another, we will be able to appreciate as hymns the cultures and religions of other peoples, raise our voices together, and unite in a great symphony of praise and hence of peace.

NOTES

1 Thomas L. Freeman, *The World is Flat: A Brief History of the 20ᵗʰ Century* (New York: Farrar, Straus and Giroux, 2005).

2 Marshall G. S. Hodgson, *The Venture of Islam: Conscience and History in a World Civilization* (Chicago: University of Chicago Press, 1974).

3 John Rawls, *A Theory of Justice* (Cambridge, Mass.: Belknap Press of Harvard University Press, 1999); *Political liberalism* (New York: Columbia University Press, c1993).

4 Ludwig Wittgenstein, *Philosophical investigations*, translated by G.E.M. Anscombe (Oxford, UK ; Malden, Mass. : Blackwell, c1997).

5 Martin Heidegger, *Being and Time*, translated by John Macquarrie & Edward Robinson (San Francisco, Calif.: Harper, San Francisco, c1962).

6 (Washington, D.C.: The Council for Research in Values and Philosophy, 2003).

7 John Hick, "Religious Pluralism and Absolute Claims," in Leroy S. Rouner, ed. *Religious Pluralism* (Notre Dame: University of Notre Dame Press, 1985), pp. 193-213.

8 Paul Knitter, "World Religions and the Finality of Christ," in R.W. Rousseau, ed., *Christianity and Islam: The Struggling Dialogue* (Scranton: Ridge Row Press, 1985), pp. 202-221.

9 Cornelio Fabro, *Participation et causalité selon S. Thomas d'Aquin.* Préface de L. De Raeymaeker (Louvain, Publications universitaires de Louvain, 1961).

10 Iqbal, *Reconstruction of Religions*, ed. M. Saeed Sheikh (Lahore, Pakistan: Iqbal Academy and Institute of Islamic Culture, 1984), p. 143.

11 *Ibid.*, pp. 48-49.

Contributors

Carine Defoort is associate Professor of Sinology at Louvain University, Blijde Inkomststraat 21, 3000 Leuven, Belgium. E-mail: carine.defoort@arts.kuleuven.be

Cheng Chung-Ying is Professor of the Department of Philosophy, University of Hawaii at Manoa, and Honourable President of the International Association of Chinese Philosophy, Manoa, Honolulu, Hawaii 96822, USA. E-mail: ccheng@hawaii.edu

Chenyang Li is Professor and Chair of the Department of Philosophy at Central Washington University, 400 East University Way, Ellensburg, WA 98926, USA. E-mail: lic@cwu.edu

Chloe Starr is Lecturer of Queen's College at Cambridge University, 3 College Farm Cottages, Garford, Abingdon, UK. E-mail:cfstarr@gmai.com; cfsll@cam.ac.uk

Christopher D. Hancock is the Director of the Institute of Christianity in China at Oxford, Oxfordshire OX13 5PF, UK. E-mail: chancock@btinternet.com

Daniel H. Bays is Professor of History and the Director of the Asian Studies Program at Calvin College, Garnd Rapids, MI49546-4402, USA. E-mail: dbays@calvin.edu

David Burrell is the Hesburgh Professor in Philosophy and Theology at the University of Notre Dame, 327 Malloy Hall, Notre Dame IN 46556, USA. E-mail: Burrell.1@nd.edu

Evyn M. Adams is Emeritus Professor of the Department of Religious Studies at the University of Hawaii at Hilo, and the President of International Leadership Group, 21 Crest Haven Drive, Belleville, Illinois, 62221, USA. E-mail: evyna@maf.net

George F. McLean is Emeritus Professor at the Catholic University of America and the Director of the Council for Research in Values and Philosophy, P. O. Box 26, USA. E-mail: mclean@cua.edu

Gholam-Reza Aavani is Professor and Director of the Iranian Institute of Philosophy, No. 6 Arakelian St., Neufelloushato St., Vali-asr Ave., Tehran, Iran. E-mail:banki@irip.org; aavani@irip.ir; academy@irip.ir

Jeu-Jenq Yuann is associate Professor of the Department of Philosophy at Taiwan University, no.106, 4-1, Roosevelt Road, Taipei, Taiwan, ROC. E-mail: jjyuann@ntu.edu.tw

Jiyuan Yu is Professor of Department of Philosophy at the State University of New York at Buffalo, Buffalo, NY 14260-4150, USA. E-mail: acgcyu@yahoo.com

Kelly James Clark is Professor of the Department of Philosophy, at Calvin College, 353 Hiemenga Hall, Grand Rapids, MI 49546, USA. E-mail: kclark@calvin.edu

Marietta Stepaniants is the Director of the Center for Oriental Phi-losophies' Studies, Institute of Philosophy, Russian Academy of Sciences, 14 Volhonka Street, Moscow, 119 992 Russia. E-mail: mstepani@iph.ras.ru

Mel Stewart is Emeritus Professor at Bethel University/Capella University, USA, and visiting professor at Wuhan University, China.

Miikka Ruokanen is Professor of Dogmatics (Systematic Theology) at the University of Helsinki, Finland and a visiting Professor at Nanjing Seminary, 17 Datongying Xiang, Nanjing, China. E-mail: miikka.ruokanen@ helsinki.fi

Roger T. Ames is Professor of the Department of Philosophy at the University of Hawaii, and Director of the East and West Center of Philosophy, 2530 Dole Street, Honolulu, HI 96822, USA. E-mail: rtames@hawaii.edu

Sasaki Chikara is Professor of the Department of History and Philos-ophy of Science, Graduate School of Arts and Science, University of Tokyo, 3-8-1, Komaba, Meguro-ku, Tokyo 153-8902, Japan. E-mail: ch-sasaki@msi. biglobe.ne.jp

Sayyid Muhammad Khamenei is the Director of the International Institute of Mulla Sadra and a professor of the Islamic Philosophy Research Institute, Building No. 12, Imam Khomeini Complex, Resalat Highway, P. O. Box 15875-6919, Tehran, Iran. E-mail: Mullasadra@dpimail.net

Tang Yijie is Professor of the Department of Philosophy and the Director of the Center for the Complete Literature of Confucianism, Peking University, Beijing, 100871, China. E-mail: office@phil.pku.edu.cn

Tran Van Doan is Professor of the Department of Philosophy at Tai-wan University, no.106, 4-1, Roosevelt Road, Taipei, Taiwan, ROC. E-mail: tran@ntu.edu.tw

Tu Weiming is the Director and Professor of the Harvard-Yenching Institute at Harvard University, 2 Divinity Ave, Cambridge, MA 02138-2020, USA. E-mail: wtu@fas.harvard.edu

Vincent Shen is the Lee Chair Professor in Chinese Thought and Cul-ture at the University of Toronto, 130 St. George Street, Room 14209, Toronto ON, Canada M5S 3H1. E-mail: vincent.shen@utoronto.ca

Wang Jianping is Professor of the Department of Philosophy at Shanghai Normal University, 100 Guilin Road, Shanghai, 200234, China. E-mail: wujingdong@citiznet

William C. Chittick is Professor of the Department of Asian and Asian-American Studies at Stony Brook University, 7 Fowler Lane, Mt. Si-nai, NY11766, USA. E-mail: William.chittick@Stonybrook.edu

Zhao Dunhua is Professor and Chair of both the Department of Phi-losophy and the Department of Religious Studies at Peking University, Bei-jing, 100871, China. E-mail: zhaodh@phil.pku.edu.cn

Index

Heidegger 23, 29, 45, 104, 115, 118, 121, 242, 267, 270
He Lin 103
Hempel 146, 150
Hermeneutics 16, 34, 38, 52, 108, 124
High God 85, 176
Hinduism 25, 29, 287
History vii, 13-17, 20, 23-24, 26, 33-34, 36-38, 44, 52, 55, 57, 74, 79, 104-105,
       108-109, 115-117, 127, 129, 132-135, 140, 142-144, 167, 172, 183-186, 195,
       200, 204-206, 212-214, 229-231, 241, 246, 256, 268, 271, 275-276, 278-280,
       283, 291, 296-297, 300
Hobbes 124-125, 220
Holmes 155
Holy Spirit 158, 190, 234, 274
Hominization 200
Horn 108
Huang Zunxian 33
Humaneness 90, 97, 99
Humanism 20, 24, 26, 30, 75, 77, 127, 167, 178, 299
Humanity ix, 18, 20, 26, 61, 63-65, 68, 76, 104, 121, 127, 129, 139, 165, 168-169,
       181, 186, 189, 190, 195-197, 208-209, 211, 221, 226, 229, 243-244, 246, 253
Humanization 200, 213
Human nature iv, x, 18-19, 62-63, 76, 165, 168, 171, 199, 200, 202-204, 213, 215,
       224-230, 268-271
Hume 124, 125
Hursthouse 77
Hu Shih 103, 108
Husserl 45, 115, 118, 120-121, 131-132

I

Ibn Arabi 245
Ibn Sina 124, 259, 298
Idealism 34, 44, 52, 54, 104, 124, 131, 300
Ideology ix-x, 15, 16, 20, 23-24, 103-104, 106-107, 111, 113, 128, 268, 288
Illuminationism 124
Imago Dei 186
Immanence 67, 70, 204
Individualism 24-25, 125-126, 274
Injustice 111, 125, 242, 295
Integrity 53, 190, 295
Intention 29, 75, 82, 206
Ionia 123
Isaiah 175-176, 177, 294
Iskandariyyah 123
Islam v, x, 13, 19, 20, 123-124, 175, 242-251, 255, 258, 266-271, 273-288, 291-
       292, 294-296, 299
Islamism v, viii, x, 248-251
Ivanhoe xii, 98, 101

THE COUNCIL FOR RESEARCH IN VALUES AND PHILOSOPHY

PURPOSE

Today there is urgent need to attend to the nature and dignity of the person, to the quality of human life, to the purpose and goal of the physical transformation of our environment, and to the relation of all this to the development of social and political life. This, in turn, requires philosophic clarification of the base upon which freedom is exercised, that is, of the values which provide stability and guidance to one's decisions.

Such studies must be able to reach deeply into one's culture and that of other parts of the world as mutually reinforcing and enriching in order to uncover the roots of the dignity of persons and of their societies. They must be able to identify the conceptual forms in terms of which modern industrial and technological developments are structured and how these impact upon human self-understanding. Above all, they must be able to bring these elements together in the creative understanding essential for setting our goals and determining our modes of interaction. In the present complex global circumstances this is a condition for growing together with trust and justice, honest dedication and mutual concern.

The Council for Studies in Values and Philosophy (RVP) unites scholars who share these concerns and are interested in the application thereto of existing capabilities in the field of philosophy and other disciplines. Its work is to identify areas in which study is needed, the intellectual resources which can be brought to bear thereupon, and the means for publication and interchange of the work from the various regions of the world. In bringing these together its goal is scientific discovery and publication which contributes to the present promotion of humankind.

In sum, our times present both the need and the opportunity for deeper and ever more progressive understanding of the person and of the foundations of social life. The development of such understanding is the goal of the RVP.

PROJECTS

A set of related research efforts is currently in process:

1. *Cultural Heritage and Contemporary Change: Philosophical Foundations for Social Life.* Focused, mutually coordinated research teams in university centers prepare volumes as part of an integrated philosophic search for self-understanding differentiated by culture and civilization. These evolve more adequate understandings of the person in society and look to the cultural heritage of each for the resources to respond to the challenges of its own specific contemporary transformation.

2. *Seminars on Culture and Contemporary Issues.* This series of 10 week crosscultural and interdisciplinary seminars is coordinated by the RVP in Washington.

3. *Joint-Colloquia* with Institutes of Philosophy of the National Academies of Science, university philosophy departments, and societies. Underway since 1976 in Eastern Europe and, since 1987, in China, these concern the person in contemporary society.

4. *Foundations of Moral Education and Character Development.* A study in values and education which unites philosophers, psychologists, social scientists and scholars in education in the elaboration of ways of enriching the moral content of education and character development. This work has been underway since 1980.

The personnel for these projects consists of established scholars willing to contribute their time and research as part of their professional commitment to life in contemporary society. For resources to implement this work the Council, as 501 C3 a non-profit organization incorporated in the District of Colombia, looks to various private foundations, public programs and enterprises.

PUBLICATIONS ON CULTURAL HERITAGE AND CONTEMPORARY CHANGE

Series I. Culture and Values
Series II. Africa
Series IIA. Islam
Series III. Asia
Series IV. W. Europe and North America
Series IVA. Central and Eastern Europe
Series V. Latin America
Series VI. Foundations of Moral Education
Series VII. Seminars on Culture and Values

****

Series I. Culture and Values

I.1 *Research on Culture and Values: Intersection of Universities, Churches and Nations.* George F. McLean, ed. ISBN 0819173533 (paper); 081917352-5 (cloth).

I.2 *The Knowledge of Values: A Methodological Introduction to the Study of Values;* A. Lopez Quintas, ed. ISBN 081917419x (paper); 0819174181 (cloth).

I.3 *Reading Philosophy for the XXIst Century.* George F. McLean, ed. ISBN 0819174157 (paper); 0819174149 (cloth).

I.4 *Relations Between Cultures.* John A. Kromkowski, ed. ISBN 1565180089 (paper); 1565180097 (cloth).

I.5 *Urbanization and Values.* John A. Kromkowski, ed. ISBN 1565180100 (paper); 1565180119 (cloth).

I.6 *The Place of the Person in Social Life.* Paul Peachey and John A. Kromkowski, eds. ISBN 1565180127 (paper); 156518013-5 (cloth).

I.7 *Abrahamic Faiths, Ethnicity and Ethnic Conflicts.* Paul Peachey, George F. McLean and John A. Kromkowski, eds. ISBN 1565181042 (paper).

I.8 *Ancient Western Philosophy: The Hellenic Emergence.* George F. McLean and Patrick J. Aspell, eds. ISBN 156518100X (paper).

I.9 *Medieval Western Philosophy: The European Emergence.* Patrick J. Aspell, ed. ISBN 1565180941 (paper).

I.10 *The Ethical Implications of Unity and the Divine in Nicholas of Cusa.* David L. De Leonardis. ISBN 1565181123 (paper).

I.11 *Ethics at the Crossroads: 1.Normative Ethics and Objective Reason.* George F. McLean, ed. ISBN 1565180224 (paper).

I.12 *Ethics at the Crossroads: 2.Personalist Ethics and Human Subjectivity.* George F. McLean, ed. ISBN 1565180240 (paper).

I.13 *The Emancipative Theory of Jürgen Habermas and Metaphysics.* Robert Badillo. ISBN 1565180429 (paper); 1565180437 (cloth).

I.14 *The Deficient Cause of Moral Evil According to Thomas Aquinas.* Edward Cook. ISBN 1565180704 (paper).

I.15 *Human Love: Its Meaning and Scope, a Phenomenology of Gift and Encounter.* Alfonso Lopez Quintas. ISBN 1565180747 (paper).

I.16 *Civil Society and Social Reconstruction.* George F. McLean, ed. ISBN 1565180860 (paper).

I.17 *Ways to God, Personal and Social at the Turn of Millennia: The Iqbal Lecture,*

Lahore. George F. McLean. ISBN 1565181239 (paper).
I.18 *The Role of the Sublime in Kant's Moral Metaphysics.* John R. Goodreau. ISBN 1565181247 (paper).
I.19 *Philosophical Challenges and Opportunities of Globalization.* Oliva Blanchette, Tomonobu Imamichi and George F. McLean, eds. ISBN 1565181298 (paper).
I.20 *Faith, Reason and Philosophy: Lectures at The al-Azhar, Qom, Tehran, Lahore and Beijing; Appendix: The Encyclical Letter: Fides et Ratio.* George F. McLean. ISBN 156518130 (paper).
I.21 *Religion and the Relation between Civilizations: Lectures on Cooperation between Islamic and Christian Cultures in a Global Horizon.* George F. McLean. ISBN 1565181522 (paper).
I.22 *Freedom, Cultural Traditions and Progress: Philosophy in Civil Society and Nation Building, Tashkent Lectures, 1999.* George F. McLean. ISBN 1565181514 (paper).
I.23 *Ecology of Knowledge.* Jerzy A. Wojciechowski. ISBN 1565181581 (paper).
I.24 *God and the Challenge of Evil: A Critical Examination of Some Serious Objections to the Good and Omnipotent God.* John L. Yardan. ISBN 1565181603 (paper).
I.25 *Reason, Rationality and Reasonableness, Vietnamese Philosophical Studies, I.* Tran Van Doan. ISBN 1565181662 (paper).
I.26 *The Culture of Citizenship: Inventing Postmodern Civic Culture.* Thomas Bridges. ISBN 1565181689 (paper).
I.27 *The Historicity of Understanding and the Problem of Relativism in Gadamer's Philosophical Hermeneutics.* Osman Bilen. ISBN 1565181670 (paper).
I.28 *Speaking of God.* Carlo Huber. ISBN 1565181697 (paper).
I.29 *Persons, Peoples and Cultures in a Global Age: Metaphysical Bases for Peace between Civilizations.* George F. McLean. ISBN 1565181875 (paper).
I.30 *Hermeneutics, Tradition and Contemporary Change: Lectures In Chennai/ Madras, India.* George F. McLean. ISBN 1565181883 (paper).
I.31 *Husserl and Stein.* Richard Feist and William Sweet, eds. ISBN 1565181948 (paper).
I.32 *Paul Hanly Furfey's Quest for a Good Society.* Bronislaw Misztal, Francesco Villa, and Eric Sean Williams, eds. ISBN 1565182278 (paper).
I.33 *Three Theories of Society.* Paul Hanly Furfey. ISBN 978-1565182288 (paper).
I.34 *Building Peace In Civil Society: An Autobiographical Report from a Believers' Church.* Paul Peachey. ISBN 978-1565182325 (paper).

Series II. Africa

II.1 *Person and Community: Ghanaian Philosophical Studies: I.* Kwasi Wiredu and Kwame Gyeke, eds. ISBN 1565180046 (paper); 1565180054 (cloth).
II.2 *The Foundations of Social Life: Ugandan Philosophical Studies: I.* A.T. Dalfovo, ed. ISBN 1565180062 (paper); 156518007-0 (cloth).
II.3 *Identity and Change in Nigeria: Nigerian Philosophical Studies, I.* Theophilus Okere, ed. ISBN 1565180682 (paper).
II.4 *Social Reconstruction in Africa: Ugandan Philosophical studies, II.* E. Wamala, A.R. Byaruhanga, A.T. Dalfovo, J.K.Kigongo, S.A.Mwanahewa and G.Tusabe, eds. ISBN 1565181182 (paper).
II.5 *Ghana: Changing Values/Chaning Technologies: Ghanaian Philosophical Studies, II.* Helen Lauer, ed. ISBN 1565181441 (paper).
II.6 *Sameness and Difference: Problems and Potentials in South African Civil Society: South African Philosophical Studies, I.* James R.Cochrane and Bastienne Klein, eds. ISBN 1565181557 (paper).
II.7 *Protest and Engagement: Philosophy after Apartheid at an Historically Black South African University: South African Philosophical Studies, II.* Patrick Giddy, ed. ISBN 1565181638 (paper).

II.8 *Ethics, Human Rights and Development in Africa: Ugandan Philosophical Studies, III.* A.T. Dalfovo, J.K. Kigongo, J. Kisekka, G. Tusabe, E. Wamala, R. Munyonyo, A.B. Rukooko, A.B.T. Byaruhanga-akiiki, M. Mawa, eds. ISBN 1565181727 (paper).

II.9 *Beyond Cultures: Perceiving a Common Humanity: Ghanian Philosophical Studies, III.* Kwame Gyekye ISBN 156518193X (paper).

II.10 *Social and Religious Concerns of East African: A Wajibu Anthology: Kenyan Philosophical Studies, I.* Gerald J. Wanjohi and G. Wakuraya Wanjohi, eds. ISBN 1565182219 (paper).

II.11 *The Idea of an African University: The Nigerian Experience: Nigerian Philosophical Studies, II.* Joseph Kenny, ed. ISBN 978-1565182301 (paper).

II.12 *The Struggles after the Struggles: Zimbabwean Philosophical Study, I.* David Kaulemu, ed. ISBN 9781565182318 (paper).

Series IIA. Islam

IIA.1 *Islam and the Political Order.* Muhammad Saïd al-Ashmawy. ISBN   ISBN 156518047X (paper); 156518046-1 (cloth).

IIA.2 *Al-Ghazali Deliverance from Error and Mystical Union with the Almighty: Al-munqidh Min Al-dalil.* Critical edition of English translation with introduction by Muhammad Abulaylah and Nurshif Abdul-Rahim Rifat; Introduction and notes by George F. McLean. ISBN 1565181530 (Arabic-English edition, paper), ISBN 1565180828 (Arabic edition, paper), ISBN 156518081X (English edition, paper)

IIA.3 *Philosophy in Pakistan.* Naeem Ahmad, ed. ISBN 1565181085 (paper).

IIA.4 *The Authenticity of the Text in Hermeneutics.* Seyed Musa Dibadj. ISBN 1565181174 (paper).

IIA.5 *Interpretation and the Problem of the Intention of the Author: H.-G.Gadamer vs E.D.Hirsch.* Burhanettin Tatar. ISBN 156518121 (paper).

IIA.6 *Ways to God, Personal and Social at the Turn of Millennia: The Iqbal Lecture, Lahore.* George F. McLean. ISBN 1565181239 (paper).

IIA.7 *Faith, Reason and Philosophy: Lectures at The al-Azhar, Qom, Tehran, Lahore and Beijing; Appendix: The Encyclical Letter: Fides et Ratio.* George F. McLean. ISBN 1565181301 (paper).

IIA.8 *Islamic and Christian Cultures: Conflict or Dialogue: Bulgarian Philosophical Studies, III.* Plament Makariev, ed. ISBN 156518162X (paper).

IIA.9 *Values of Islamic Culture and the Experience of History, Russian Philosophical Studies, I.* Nur Kirabaev, Yuriy Pochta, eds. ISBN 1565181336 (paper).

IIA.10 *Christian-Islamic Preambles of Faith.* Joseph Kenny. ISBN 1565181387 (paper).

IIA.11 *The Historicity of Understanding and the Problem of Relativism in Gadamer's Philosophical Hermeneutics.* Osman Bilen. ISBN 1565181670 (paper).

IIA.12 *Religion and the Relation between Civilizations: Lectures on Cooperation between Islamic and Christian Cultures in a Global Horizon.* George F. McLean. ISBN 1565181522 (paper).

IIA.13 *Modern Western Christian Theological Understandings of Muslims since the Second Vatican Council.* Mahmut Aydin. ISBN 1565181719 (paper).

IIA.14 *Philosophy of the Muslim World; Authors and Principal Themes.* Joseph Kenny. ISBN 1565181794 (paper).

IIA.15 *Islam and Its Quest for Peace: Jihad, Justice and Education.* Mustafa Köylü. ISBN 1565181808 (paper).

IIA.16 *Islamic Thought on the Existence of God: Contributions and Contrasts with Contemporary Western Philosophy of Religion.* Cafer S. Yaran. ISBN 1565181921 (paper).

IIA.17 *Hermeneutics, Faith, and Relations between Cultures: Lectures in Qom, Iran.* George F. McLean. ISBN 1565181913 (paper).

IIA.18 *Change and Essence: Dialectical Relations between Change and Continuity in the Turkish Intellectual Tradition.* Sinasi Gunduz and Cafer S. Yaran, eds. ISBN 1565182227 (paper).

Series III.Asia

III.1 *Man and Nature: Chinese Philosophical Studies, I.* Tang Yi-jie, Li Zhen, eds. ISBN 0819174130 (paper); 0819174122 (cloth).
III.2 *Chinese Foundations for Moral Education and Character Development: Chinese Philosophical Studies, II.* Tran van Doan, ed. ISBN 1565180321 (paper); 156518033X (cloth).
III.3 *Confucianism, Buddhism, Taoism, Christianity and Chinese Culture: Chinese Philosophical Studies, III.* Tang Yijie. ISBN 1565180348 (paper); 156518035-6 (cloth).
III.4 *Morality, Metaphysics and Chinese Culture (Metaphysics, Culture and Morality, I).* Vincent Shen and Tran van Doan, eds. ISBN 1565180275 (paper); 156518026-7 (cloth).
III.5 *Tradition, Harmony and Transcendence.* George F. McLean. ISBN 1565180313 (paper); 156518030-5 (cloth).
III.6 *Psychology, Phenomenology and Chinese Philosophy: Chinese Philosophical Studies, VI.* Vincent Shen, Richard Knowles and Tran Van Doan, eds. ISBN 1565180453 (paper); 1565180445 (cloth).
III.7 *Values in Philippine Culture and Education: Philippine Philosophical Studies, I.* Manuel B. Dy, Jr., ed. ISBN 1565180412 (paper); 156518040-2 (cloth).
III.7A *The Human Person and Society: Chinese Philosophical Studies, VIIA.* Zhu Dasheng, Jin Xiping and George F. McLean, eds. ISBN 1565180887.
III.8 *The Filipino Mind: Philippine Philosophical Studies II.* Leonardo N. Mercado. ISBN 156518064X (paper); 156518063-1 (cloth).
III.9 *Philosophy of Science and Education: Chinese Philosophical Studies IX.* Vincent Shen and Tran Van Doan, eds. ISBN 1565180763 (paper); 156518075-5 (cloth).
III.10 *Chinese Cultural Traditions and Modernization: Chinese Philosophical Studies, X.* Wang Miaoyang, Yu Xuanmeng and George F. McLean, eds. ISBN 1565180682 (paper).
III.11 *The Humanization of Technology and Chinese Culture: Chinese Philosophical Studies XI.* Tomonobu Imamichi, Wang Miaoyang and Liu Fangtong, eds. ISBN 1565181166 (paper).
III.12 *Beyond Modernization: Chinese Roots of Global Awareness: Chinese Philosophical Studies, XII.* Wang Miaoyang, Yu Xuanmeng and George F. McLean, eds. ISBN 1565180909 (paper).
III.13 *Philosophy and Modernization in China: Chinese Philosophical Studies XIII.* Liu Fangtong, Huang Songjie and George F. McLean, eds. ISBN 1565180666 (paper).
III.14 *Economic Ethics and Chinese Culture: Chinese Philosophical Studies, XIV.* Yu Xuanmeng, Lu Xiaohe, Liu Fangtong, Zhang Rulun and Georges Enderle, eds. ISBN 1565180925 (paper).
III.15 *Civil Society in a Chinese Context: Chinese Philosophical Studies XV.* Wang Miaoyang, Yu Xuanmeng and Manuel B. Dy, eds. ISBN 1565180844 (paper).
III.16 *The Bases of Values in a Time of Change: Chinese and Western: Chinese Philosophical Studies, XVI.* Kirti Bunchua, Liu Fangtong, Yu Xuanmeng, Yu Wujin, eds. ISBN 156518114X (paper).
III.17 *Dialogue between Christian Philosophy and Chinese Culture: Philosophical Perspectives for the Third Millennium: Chinese Philosophical Studies, XVII.* Paschal Ting, Marian Kao and Bernard Li, eds. ISBN 1565181735 (paper).
III.18 *The Poverty of Ideological Education: Chinese Philosophical Studies, XVIII.* Tran Van Doan. ISBN 1565181646 (paper).
III.19 *God and the Discovery of Man: Classical and Contemporary Approaches: Lectures in Wuhan, China.* George F. McLean. ISBN 1565181891 (paper).
III.20 *Cultural Impact on International Relations: Chinese Philosophical Studies,*

XX. Yu Xintian, ed. ISBN 156518176X (paper).

III.21 *Cultural Factors in International Relations: Chinese Philosophical Studies, XXI.* Yu Xintian, ed. ISBN 1565182049 (paper).

III.22 *Wisdom in China and the West: Chinese Philosophical Studies, XXII.* Vincent Shen and Willard Oxtoby †. ISBN 1565182057 (paper)

III.23 *China's Contemporary Philosophical Journey: Western Philosophy and Marxism ChineseP hilosophical Studies: Chinese Philosophical Studies, XXIII.* Liu Fangtong. ISBN 1565182065 (paper).

III.24 *Shanghai : Its Urbanization and Culture: Chinese Philosophical Studies, XXIV.* Yu Xuanmeng and He Xirong, eds. ISBN 1565182073 (paper).

III.25 *Dialogues of Philosophies, Religions and Civilizations in the Era of Globalization: Chinese Philosophical Studies, XXV.* Zhao Dunhua, ed. ISBN 978-1-56518-243-1 (paper).

IIIB.1 *Authentic Human Destiny: The Paths of Shankara and Heidegger: Indian Philosophical Studies, I.* Vensus A. George. ISBN 1565181190 (paper).

IIIB.2 *The Experience of Being as Goal of Human Existence: The Heideggerian Approach: Indian Philosophical Studies, II.* Vensus A. George. ISBN 156518145X (paper).

IIIB.3 *Religious Dialogue as Hermeneutics: Bede Griffiths's Advaitic Approach: Indian Philosophical Studies, III.* Kuruvilla Pandikattu. ISBN 1565181395 (paper).

IIIB.4 *Self-Realization [Brahmaanubhava]: The Advaitic Perspective of Shankara: Indian Philosophical Studies, IV.* Vensus A. George. ISBN 1565181549 (paper).

IIIB.5 *Gandhi: The Meaning of Mahatma for the Millennium: Indian Philosophical Studies, V.* Kuruvilla Pandikattu, ed. ISBN 1565181565 (paper).

IIIB.6 *Civil Society in Indian Cultures: Indian Philosophical Studies, VI.* Asha Mukherjee, Sabujkali Sen (Mitra) and K. Bagchi, eds. ISBN 1565181573 (paper).

IIIB.7 *Hermeneutics, Tradition and Contemporary Change: Lectures In Chennai/ Madras, India.* George F. McLean. ISBN 1565181883 (paper).

IIIB.8 *Plenitude and Participation: The Life of God in Man: Lectures in Chennai/ Madras, India.* George F. McLean. ISBN 1565181999 (paper).

IIIB.9 *Sufism and Bhakti, a Comparative Study.* Md. Sirajul Islam. ISBN 1565181980 (paper).

IIIB.10 *Reasons for Hope: Its Nature, Role and Future.* Kuruvilla Pandikattu, ed. ISBN 156518 2162 (paper).

IIB.11 *Lifeworlds and Ethics: Studies in Several Keys.* Margaret Chatterjee. ISBN 9781565182332 (paper).

IIIC.1 *Spiritual Values and Social Progress: Uzbekistan Philosophical Studies, I.* Said Shermukhamedov and Victoriya Levinskaya, eds. ISBN 1565181433 (paper).

IIIC.2 *Kazakhstan: Cultural Inheritance and Social Transformation: Kazakh Philosophical Studies, I.* Abdumalik Nysanbayev. ISBN 1565182022 (paper).

IIIC.3 *Social Memory and Contemporaneity: Kyrgyz Philosophical Studies, I.* Gulnara A. Bakieva. ISBN 9781565182349 (paper).

IIID.1 *Reason, Rationality and Reasonableness: Vietnamese Philosophical Studies, I.* Tran Van Doan. ISBN 1565181662 (paper).

IIID.2 *Hermeneutics for a Global Age: Lectures in Shanghai and Hanoi.* George F. McLean. ISBN 1565181905 (paper).

IIID.3 *Cultural Traditions and Contemporary Challenges in Southeast Asia.* Warayuth Sriwarakuel, Manuel B.Dy, J.Haryatmoko, Nguyen Trong Chuan, and Chhay Yiheang, eds. ISBN 1565182138 (paper).

IIID.4 *Filipino Cultural Traits: Claro R.Ceniza Lectures.* Rolando M. Gripaldo, ed. ISBN 1565182251 (paper).

IIID.5 *The History of Buddhism in Vietnam.* Chief editor: Nguyen Tai Thu; Authors: Dinh Minh Chi, Ly Kim Hoa, Ha thuc Minh, Ha Van Tan, Nguyen Tai Thu. ISBN 1565180984 (paper).

Series IV.Western Europe and North America

IV.1 *Italy in Transition: The Long Road from the First to the Second Republic: The Edmund D. Pellegrino Lectures.* Paolo Janni, ed. ISBN 1565181204 (paper).

IV.2 *Italy and The European Monetary Union: The Edmund D. Pellegrino Lectures.* Paolo Janni, ed. ISBN 156518128X (paper).

IV.3 *Italy at the Millennium: Economy, Politics, Literature and Journalism: The Edmund D. Pellegrino Lectures.* Paolo Janni, ed. ISBN 1565181581 (paper).

IV.4 *Speaking of God.* Carlo Huber. ISBN 1565181697 (paper).

IV.5 *The Essence of Italian Culture and the Challenge of a Global Age.* Paulo Janni and George F. McLean, eds. ISBB 1565181778 (paper).

IV.6 *Italic Identity in Pluralistic Contexts: Toward the Development of Intercultural Competencies.* Piero Bassetti and Paolo Janni, eds. ISBN 1565181441 (paper).

Series IVA. Central and Eastern Europe

IVA.1 *The Philosophy of Person: Solidarity and Cultural Creativity: Polish Philosophical Studies, I.* A. Tischner, J.M. Zycinski, eds. ISBN 1565180496 (paper); 156518048-8 (cloth).

IVA.2 *Public and Private Social Inventions in Modern Societies: Polish Philosophical Studies, II.* L. Dyczewski, P. Peachey, J.A. Kromkowski, eds. ISBN.paper 1565180518 (paper); 156518050X (cloth).

IVA.3 *Traditions and Present Problems of Czech Political Culture: Czechoslovak Philosophical Studies, I.* M. Bednár and M. Vejraka, eds. ISBN 1565180577 (paper); 156518056-9 (cloth).

IVA.4 *Czech Philosophy in the XXth Century: Czech Philosophical Studies, II.* Lubomír Nový and Jirí Gabriel, eds. ISBN 1565180291 (paper); 156518028-3 (cloth).

IVA.5 *Language, Values and the Slovak Nation: Slovak Philosophical Studies, I.* Tibor Pichler and Jana Gašparíková, eds. ISBN 1565180372 (paper); 156518036-4 (cloth).

IVA.6 *Morality and Public Life in a Time of Change: Bulgarian Philosophical Studies, I.* V. Prodanov and M. Stoyanova, eds. ISBN 1565180550 (paper); 1565180542 (cloth).

IVA.7 *Knowledge and Morality: Georgian Philosophical Studies, I.* N.V. Chavchavadze, G. Nodia and P. Peachey, eds. ISBN 1565180534 (paper); 1565180526 (cloth).

IVA.8 *Cultural Heritage and Social Change: Lithuanian Philosophical Studies, I.* Bronius Kuzmickas and Aleksandr Dobrynin, eds. ISBN 1565180399 (paper); 1565180380 (cloth).

IVA.9 *National, Cultural and Ethnic Identities: Harmony beyond Conflict: Czech Philosophical Studies, IV.* Jaroslav Hroch, David Hollan, George F. McLean, eds. ISBN 1565181131 (paper).

IVA.10 *Models of Identities in Postcommunist Societies: Yugoslav Philosophical Studies, I.* Zagorka Golubovic and George F. McLean, eds. ISBN 1565181211 (paper).

IVA.11 *Interests and Values: The Spirit of Venture in a Time of Change: Slovak Philosophical Studies, II.* Tibor Pichler and Jana Gasparikova, eds. ISBN 1565181255 (paper).

IVA.12 *Creating Democratic Societies: Values and Norms: Bulgarian Philosophical Studies, II.* Plamen Makariev, Andrew M.Blasko and Asen Davidov, eds. ISBN 156518131X (paper).

IVA.13 *Values of Islamic Culture and the Experience of History: Russian Philosophical Studies, I.* Nur Kirabaev and Yuriy Pochta, eds. ISBN 1565181336 (paper).

IVA.14 *Values and Education in Romania Today: Romanian Philosophical Studies,* Marin Calin and Magdalena Dumitrana, eds. ISBN 1565181344 (paper).

IVA.15 *Between Words and Reality, Studies on the Politics of Recognition and the Changes of Regime in Contemporary Romania.* Victor Neumann. ISBN 1565181611 (paper).

IVA.16 *Culture and Freedom: Romanian Philosophical Studies, III.* Marin Aiftinca, ed. ISBN 1565181360 (paper).

IVA.17 *Lithuanian Philosophy: Persons and Ideas Lithuanian Philosophical Studies, II.* Jurate Baranova, ed. ISBN 1565181379 (paper).

IVA.18 *Human Dignity: Values and Justice: Czech Philosophical Studies, III.* Miloslav Bednar, ed. ISBN 1565181409 (paper).

IVA.19 *Values in the Polish Cultural Tradition: Polish Philosophical Studies, III.* Leon Dyczewski, ed. ISBN 1565181425 (paper).

IVA.20 *Liberalization and Transformation of Morality in Post-communist Countries: Polish Philosophical Studies, IV.* Tadeusz Buksinski. ISBN 1565181786 (paper).

IVA.21 *Islamic and Christian Cultures: Conflict or Dialogue: Bulgarian Philosophical Studies, III.* Plament Makariev, ed. ISBN 156518162X (paper).

IVA.22 *Moral, Legal and Political Values in Romanian Culture: Romanian Philosophical Studies, IV.* Mihaela Czobor-Lupp and J. Stefan Lupp, eds. ISBN 1565181700 (paper).

IVA.23 *Social Philosophy: Paradigm of Contemporary Thinking: Lithuanian Philosophical Studies, III.* Jurate Morkuniene. ISBN 1565182030 (paper).

IVA.24 *Romania: Cultural Identity and Education for Civil Society.* Magdalena Dumitrana, ed. ISBN 156518209X (paper).

IVA.25 *Polish Axiology: the 20th Century and Beyond: Polish Philosophical Studies, V.* Stanislaw Jedynak, ed. ISBN 1565181417 (paper).

IVA.26 *Contemporary Philosophical Discourse in Lithuania: Lithuanian Philosophical Studies, IV.* Jurate Baranova, ed. ISBN 156518-2154 (paper).

IVA.27 *Eastern Europe and the Challenges of Globalization: Polish Philosophical Studies, VI.* Tadeusz Buksinski and Dariusz Dobrzanski, ed. ISBN 1565182189 (paper).

IVA.28 *Church, State, and Society in Eastern Europe: Hungarian Philosophical Studies, I.* Miklós Tomka. ISBN 156518226X (paper).

IVA.29 *Politics, Ethics, and the Challenges to Democracy in 'New Independent States'.* Tinatin Bochorishvili, William Sweet, Daniel Ahern, eds. ISBN 9781565182240 (paper).

IVA.30 *Comparative Ethics in a Global Age.* Marietta T. Stepanyants, eds. ISBN 978-1565182356 (paper).

IVA.31 *Lithuanian Identity and Values: Lithuanian Philosophical Studies, V.* Aida Savicka, eds. ISBN 9781565182367 (paper).

IVA.32 *The Challenge of Our Hope: Christian Faith in Dialogue: Polish Philosophical Studies, VII.* Waclaw Hryniewicz. ISBN 9781565182370 (paper).

IVA.33 *Diversity and Dialogue: Culture and Values in the Age of Globalization: Essays in Honour of Professor George F. McLean.* Andrew Blasko and Plamen Makariev, eds. ISBN 9781565182387 (paper).

IVA.34 *Civil Society, Pluralism and Universalism: Polish Philosophical Studies, VIII.* Eugeniusz Gorski. ISBN 9781565182417 (paper).

Series V. Latin America

V.1 *The Social Context and Values: Perspectives of the Americas.* O. Pegoraro, ed. ISBN 081917355X (paper); 0819173541 (cloth).

V.2 *Culture, Human Rights and Peace in Central America.* Raul Molina and Timothy Ready, eds. ISBN 0819173576 (paper); 0-8191-7356-8 (cloth).

V.3 *El Cristianismo Aymara: Inculturacion o Culturizacion?* Luis Jolicoeur. ISBN 1565181042.

V.4 *Love as theFoundation of Moral Education and Character Development.* Luis Ugalde, Nicolas Barros and George F. McLean, eds. ISBN 1565180801.

V.5 *Human Rights, Solidarity and Subsidiarity: Essays towards a Social Ontology.*

Carlos E.A. Maldonado ISBN 1565181107.

Series VI. Foundations of Moral Education

VI.1 *Philosophical Foundations for Moral Education and Character Development: Act and Agent.* G. McLean and F. Ellrod, eds. ISBN 156518001-1 (cloth) (paper); ISBN 1565180003.
VI.2 *Psychological Foundations for Moral Education and Character Development: An Integrated Theory of Moral Development.* R. Knowles, ed. ISBN 156518002X (paper); 156518003-8 (cloth).
VI.3 *Character Development in Schools and Beyond.* Kevin Ryan and Thomas Lickona, eds. ISBN 1565180593 (paper); 156518058-5 (cloth).
VI.4 *The Social Context and Values: Perspectives of the Americas.* O. Pegoraro, ed. ISBN 081917355X (paper); 0819173541 (cloth).
VI.5 *Chinese Foundations for Moral Education and Character Development.* Tran van Doan, ed. ISBN 1565180321 (paper); 156518033 (cloth).
VI.6 *Love as the Foundation of Moral Education and Character Development.* Luis Ugalde, Nicolas Barros and George F. McLean, eds. ISBN 1565180801.

Series VII. Seminars on Culture and Values

VII.1 *The Social Context and Values: Perspectives of the Americas.* O. Pegoraro, ed. ISBN 081917355X (paper); 0819173541 (cloth).
VII.2 *Culture, Human Rights and Peace in Central America.* Raul Molina and Timothy Ready, eds. ISBN 0819173576 (paper); 0819173568 (cloth).
VII.3 *Relations Between Cultures.* John A. Kromkowski, ed. ISBN 1565180089 (paper); 1565180097 (cloth).
VII.4 *Moral Imagination and Character Development: Volume I, The Imagination.* George F. McLean and John A. Kromkowski, eds. ISBN 1565181743 (paper).
VII.5 *Moral Imagination and Character Development: Volume II, Moral Imagination in Personal Formation and Character Development.* George F. McLean and Richard Knowles, eds. ISBN 1565181816 (paper).
VII.6 *Moral Imagination and Character Development: Volume III, Imagination in Religion and Social Life.* George F. McLean and John K. White, eds. ISBN 1565181824 (paper).
VII.7 *Hermeneutics and Inculturation.* George F. McLean, Antonio Gallo, Robert Magliola, eds. ISBN 1565181840 (paper).
VII.8 *Culture, Evangelization, and Dialogue.* Antonio Gallo and Robert Magliola, eds. ISBN 1565181832 (paper).
VII.9 *The Place of the Person in Social Life.* Paul Peachey and John A. Kromkowski, eds. ISBN 1565180127 (paper); 156518013-5 (cloth).
VII.10 *Urbanization and Values.* John A. Kromkowski, ed. ISBN 1565180100 (paper); 1565180119 (cloth).
VII.11 *Freedom and Choice in a Democracy, Volume I: Meanings of Freedom.* Robert Magliola and John Farrelly, eds. ISBN 1565181867 (paper).
VII.12 *Freedom and Choice in a Democracy, Volume II: The Difficult Passage to Freedom.* Robert Magliola and Richard Khuri, eds. ISBN 1565181859 (paper).
VII 13 *Cultural Identity, Pluralism and Globalization* (2 volumes). John P. Hogan, ed. ISBN 1565182170 (paper).
VII.14 *Democracy: In the Throes of Liberalism and Totalitarianism.* George F. McLean, Robert Magliola, William Fox, eds. ISBN 1565181956 (paper).
VII.15 *Democracy and Values in Global Times: With Nigeria as a Case Study.* George F. McLean, Robert Magliola, Joseph Abah, eds. ISBN 1565181956 (paper).
VII.16 *Civil Society and Social Reconstruction.* George F. McLean, ed. ISBN 1565180860 (paper).

VII.17 *Civil Society: Who Belongs?* William A.Barbieri, Robert Magliola, Rosemary Winslow, eds. ISBN 1565181972 (paper).

VII.18 *The Humanization of Social Life: Theory and Challenges.* Christopher Wheatley, Robert P. Badillo, Rose B. Calabretta, Robert Magliola, eds. ISBN 1565182006 (paper).

VII.19 *The Humanization of Social Life: Cultural Resources and Historical Responses.* Ronald S. Calinger, Robert P. Badillo, Rose B. Calabretta, Robert Magliola, eds. ISBN 1565182006 (paper).

VII.20 *Religious Inspiration for Public Life: Religion in Public Life, Volume I.* George F. McLean, John A. Kromkowski and Robert Magliola, eds. ISBN 1565182103 (paper).

VII.21 *Religion and Political Structures from Fundamentalism to Public Service: Religion in Public Life, Volume II.* John T. Ford, Robert A. Destro and Charles R. Dechert, eds. ISBN 1565182111 (paper).

VII.22 *Civil Society as Democratic Practice.* Antonio F. Perez, Semou Pathé Gueye, Yang Fenggang, eds. ISBN 1565182146 (paper).

VII.23 *Ecumenism and Nostra Aetate in the 21st Century.* George F. McLean and John P. Hogan, eds. ISBN 1565182197 (paper).

VII.24 *Multiple Paths to God: Nostra Aetate: 40 years Later.* John P. Hogan and George F. McLean, eds. ISBN 1565182200 (paper).

VII.25 *Globalization and Identity.* Andrew Blasko, Taras Dobko, Pham Van Duc and George Pattery, eds. ISBN 1565182200 (paper).

The International Society for Metaphysics

ISM.1. *Person and Nature.* George F. McLean and Hugo Meynell, eds. ISBN 0819170267 (paper); 0819170259 (cloth).

ISM.2. *Person and Society.* George F. McLean and Hugo Meynell, eds. ISBN 0819169250 (paper); 0819169242 (cloth).

ISM.3. *Person and God.* George F. McLean and Hugo Meynell, eds. ISBN 0819169382 (paper); 0819169374 (cloth).

ISM.4. *The Nature of Metaphysical Knowledge.* George F. McLean and Hugo Meynell, eds. ISBN 0819169277 (paper); 0819169269 (cloth).

ISM.5. *Philosophhical Challenges and Opportunities of Globalization.* Oliva Blanchette, Tomonobu Imamichi and George F. McLean, eds. ISBN 1565181298 (paper).

The series is published and distributed by: The Council for Research in Values and Philosophy, Cardinal Station, P.O.Box 261, Washington, D.C.20064, Tel./ Fax.202/319-6089; e-mail: cua-rvp@cua.edu (paper); website: http://www.crvp.org. All titles are available in paper except as noted. Prices: $17.50 (paper).